Palace and Politics in Prewar Japan

Studies of the East Asian Institute
Columbia University

Palace and Politics in Prewar Japan

David Anson Titus

1974

Columbia University Press

New York and London

This study, prepared under the Graduate Faculties of Columbia University, was selected by a committee of those faculties to receive one of the Clarke F. Ansley awards given annually by Columbia University Press.

Library of Congress Cataloging in Publication Data

Titus, David Anson, 1934–
    Palace and politics in prewar Japan.

    Bibliography: p.
    1. Japan—Emperors. 2. Japan. Kunaishō—History.
3. Japan—Constitutional history. 4. Japan—Politics.
and government—1868– I. Title.
JQ1641.T55   354′.52′0312   74-6109
ISBN 0-231-03622-1

For Anne B. and Jesse E. Titus

THE EAST ASIAN INSTITUTE OF COLUMBIA UNIVERSITY

The East Asian Institute of Columbia University was established in 1949 to prepare graduate students for careers dealing with East Asia, and to aid research and publication on East Asia during the modern period. The faculty of the Institute are grateful to the Ford Foundation and the Rockefeller Foundation for their financial assistance.

The Studies of the East Asian Institute were inaugurated in 1962 to bring to a wider public the results of significant new research on modern and contemporary East Asia.

CONTENTS

Acknowledgments ix
1. Introduction 1
2. Political Legitimacy and Palace Autonomy 13
3. The Palace Bureaucracy: Gatekeepers of the
   Imperial Will 51
4. The Offices and Officers of Palace Leadership 97
5. Kido Kōichi and the Matrix of Palace Politics 193
6. Palace and Politics in Prewar Japan: An
   Interpretation 311
   Bibliography 335
   Index 343
   Studies of the East Asian Institute 359

ACKNOWLEDGMENTS

RESEARCH FOR THIS STUDY was initiated in Japan from 1963 to 1965 under the generous support of the Foreign Area Fellowship Program. Through the kind introduction of the late Professor Koizumi Shinzō, former President of Keiō University and at that time tutor to the crown prince, I was given access to palace records and an opportunity to interview palace officials. Without his cooperation, and that of many officials of the Imperial Household Agency, this study would not have been possible. I am also grateful to Professor Wada Hideo, Professor Yoshida Yoshiaki, and their colleagues in the Department of Law at Meiji University, to Professor Maruyama Masao, and to Professor Satō Isao for their immeasurable assistance during my stay in Japan.

Portions of this study, fortunately, received the more than helpful criticisms of the University Seminar on Modern Japan at Columbia University and the Japan seminar at Harvard University. I am also indebted to Professor Fred I. Greenstein and my colleagues at Wesleyan University, to Professor Shumpei Okamoto of Temple University, and to Professor James L. Payne of Texas A & M for their comments and encouragement during the last eight years of research, writing and revising.

The final revision of this manuscript, completed in Japan during 1971–72, was made possible by a grant from the American Council of Learned Societies and by Wesleyan University's generous leave and sabbatical arrangements. Professors Oka Yoshitake, Iwanaga

Kenkichirō, Satō Seizaburō, and Itō Takashi of Tokyo University were most helpful not only in suggesting revisions but also in guiding my research for a projected study of political leadership and political change in modern Japanese politics.

Amy Heinrich, Cynthia Brodhead, and Joan McQuary provided invaluable editorial suggestions during the last stages of preparation for press.

I am also grateful to Michael Harwood and Mary Durant for their encouragement and for their assistance in style and clarity. Mrs. Cheryl Cuyler, Mrs. Lee Messina, Mrs. Mildred Carter, and Mrs. Janice Brown typed the many revisions that this manuscript has seen.

Finally, Professors James Morley and Herschel Webb of Columbia University have seen this study through from start to finish. Intellectual guidance was but part of their contribution. Errors of omission and commission, interpretation, and evaluation unfortunately remain—and remain, unfortunately, solely mine.

D.A.T.

Cromwell, Connecticut
October 1973

Palace and Politics in Prewar Japan

Studies of the East Asian Institute
Columbia University

CHAPTER ONE

INTRODUCTION

ORIGINALLY THIS WAS INTENDED to be a study of the imperial institution in Japan after World War II. For three reasons it became a study of the prewar imperial institution, going back to the theory of imperial prerogative evolved during the Restoration settlement of 1868–89. First, the internal structure of the palace today is very close to what it had been from 1885 to 1945, although the emperor's constitutional role has been drastically altered. Second, there is very little information in Japanese or English about the prewar palace, its leaders, and its concrete relation to politics, despite the theoretical centrality of the imperial institution in politics. Third, the modernization of Japan between 1868 and 1945 was centrally managed; the articulated referent for modernization—political as well as economic and social—was the imperial institution.

The 1947 *Constitution of Japan* produced profound changes in the formal relationship between emperor and government. According to the prewar constitution of 1889, the emperor had "combined in his being the supreme rights of rule" and was consequently endowed with an immense range of constitutional prerogatives in military command, civil administration, and legislation. In the 1947 constitution, however, the people were made sovereign and the emperor was divested of all prerogatives. His constitutional position is now defined as "symbol of the State and of the unity of the people." The Prime Minister is no longer appointed by the emperor; he is "designated from among the members of the Diet by a resolution of

1

the Diet." Cabinet ministers are no longer appointed by the emperor but by the Prime Minister. The Office of Lord Keeper of the Privy Seal, an adjunct palace office that had linked the emperor and the civil side of the prewar government, was abolished in 1945, as was the Office of Chief Aide-de-Camp, an adjunct palace office that had linked the emperor to the military command. Palace personnel were reduced in number from approximately six thousand to one thousand. Imperial lands, stocks and bonds, and other sources of financial autonomy were eliminated. In 1947 the imperial house became dependent on funds provided in an annual budget passed by the legislature. The prewar aristocracy, including most branch houses of the imperial family, was abolished. Managed by the Imperial Household Ministry, the prewar aristocracy had been the "bulwark" of the throne. The Imperial Household Ministry, which had enjoyed an autonomous position in relation to the prewar government, was replaced by the present Imperial Household Agency under the direction of the Prime Minister.

The internal organization of the palace, however, has remained all but unchanged. There is still a palace office charged with the conduct of Shinto rites, despite the legal "denationalization" of Shinto as a state religion. There are informal offices in the Imperial Household Agency which link the palace of today with the prewar aristocracy. There are a Poetry Bureau, a Board of Chamberlains, a Board of the Ceremonies—just as in prewar times. Although the formal relationship between emperor and government has been revised, therefore, many of the symbolic and actual roles played by the emperor may have survived, overtly or covertly. Without an understanding of the prewar palace those roles could not be identified, much less evaluated.

Second is the problem of information. The most I have found in a single work, for example, are lists of and partial descriptions for the men who held the four leading palace offices from 1885 to 1945: the Imperial Household Minister, the Grand Chamberlain, the Chief Aide-de-Camp, and the Lord Keeper of the Privy Seal. There is no systematic analysis of their roles, or of the institutional structure created to manage the emperor's relationship to politics and society: the Imperial Household Ministry. The lack of such information and analysis is not without reason, however. Only recently has it been possible to subject the prewar imperial institution to scholarly inquiry and objective analysis. The sanctity surrounding the prewar palace vanished in 1945; since that time documents and private papers have become increasingly available, making it feasible to analyze the role of the palace in prewar politics.

Postwar Japanese scholarship on the role of the imperial institution in prewar politics has tended, however, to divide into two categories: the macrosocietal and the micropolitical. In the macrosocietal category fall such scholars and writers as Maruyama Masao, Ishida Takeshi, Inoue Kiyoshi, Yokota Kisaburō, Miyazawa Toshiyoshi, Kamiyama Shigeo, Yamazaki Tanshō, and Yamakawa Hitoshi. Although there are vast differences in both approach and interpretation among them, they all attempt to relate the imperial institution to one or more aspects of the total Japanese environment: to values and ideals in Japanese society, to the social structure, to the total legal order, or to norms and patterns of Japanese behavior.

Marxist historians, for example, quarrel over the class structure of the prewar "emperor system" (tennōsei). The debate centers on the nature of the class base of "absolutism" (zettai shugi) and "absolute monarchy" (zettai ōsei); the effort is to develop a model of prewar Japanese society. The founder of the absolutism school in Japan, according to Professor Tōyama Shigeki, is Hattori Shisō:

> It was Mr. Hattori Shisō's achievement [in 1928] to define the political regime produced by the Meiji Restoration as "absolutism" and thus to locate it in the developmental stages of world history. . . . Absolutism, or rule by an absolute monarch, is that state power which, resting on an equilibrium of two contending class forces (the feudal nobility-landlord class and the bourgeoisie), carries out its policies by utilizing the opposition between the two while at the same time representing the interests of both. Absolutism is produced in the course of the transformation from a feudal to a capitalist system. . . . Constructing a state consolidated under centralized authority by means of a monarch's despotic and autocratic power, power that is protected both by an enormous standing army and by an entrenched bureaucracy, absolutism simultaneously undertakes the acceleration by force of primary accumulation, using its immense state power as a spur.[1]

1. Tōyama Shigeki, *Meiji Ishin Shi*, "Iwanami Zensho," vol. 128, 17th ed. (Tokyo: Iwanami Shoten, 1962), p. 23.

While they quite rightly point to the bureaucracy as the engine of prewar Japanese politics, scholars and writers who adopt the absolutism model go very little farther in their analysis of political institutions and behavior. They are content to argue whether Japanese absolutism was more "feudal" than "bourgeois," or the reverse. For example, Kamiyama Shigeo, perhaps the leading postwar exponent of the Hattori position and the feudal basis of Japanese absolutism, asserts the primacy of the bureaucracy in the political process. But the most one can find about the operations of the bureaucracy in his writings is:

> The exercise of the nation's powers covering all domestic and foreign policy was formally united under the imperial prerogative; in actuality, however, a flock of leaders in the bureaucratic structures and the factions at court which enveloped the emperor exercised [the emperor's prerogatives].[2]

Who were the bureaucratic leaders? What were the court factions that "enveloped the emperor"? How were bureaucratic leaders and court factions related?

The second category of Japanese scholarship, not near as voluminous as the macrosocietal, I have termed the micropolitical. Scholars and writers in this category focus on the emperor's individual role in politics, viewings events in relation to his "personal" actions. This approach points up contradictions in the emperor's behavior, shows his ineffectiveness, or asserts his individual responsibility for policy failures. Nezu Masashi, for example, argues that the emperor's actions during the Manchurian Incident and its aftermath in late 1931 and early 1932 were contradictory: the emperor condemned the Army's independent acts of aggression in Manchuria and at the same time sent formal "imperial words" of praise to that Army on October 18, 1931 and again at New Years in 1932.[3] Such apparent contradictions cannot be understood, however, without considering the emperor's opinions on policy, which he expressed to those "close to the throne," in relation to his institutional role,

2. Kamiyama Shigeo, *Tennō Sei ni kansuru Riron-teki Sho Mondai* (Tokyo: Ashi Shuppan Shin Sha, 1956), pp. 112–13.
3. Nezu Masashi, *Tennō Shōwa Ki*, 2 vols. (Tokyo: Shiseidō, 1961), vol. 1, "Dai Nippon Teikoku no Hōkai," pp. 110–14.

which was to legitimate policies and decisions produced by others for his ratification. The micropolitical approach tends to view the emperor as an autonomous individual in an institutional vacuum. The macrosocietal approach, in contrast, tends to see him in a social system without institutional content or empirically verified patterns of political behavior.

Third, the imperial institution was central to Japanese modernization. An effective national government was produced during the Restoration settlement of 1868–89. After the Restoration settlement the vast array of imperial prerogatives set down in the 1889 *Constitution of the Great Empire of Japan* gradually became institutionalized, so that by the 1920s Japanese politics was characterized by a high degree of confused competition among the institutions of imperial prerogative to monopolize the Imperial Will in politics—that is, to make or control national policy making. The Diet, for example, insisted on its supremacy in politics by asserting the supremacy of the emperor's prerogative of legislation. The Army, on the other hand, insisted on its right to make policy on the basis of the emperor's prerogative of supreme command. All other institutions of government were equally derived from imperial prerogative—and therefore equally justified in their policy-making demands. Paralleling the institutionalization of imperial prerogatives, moreover, political leadership passed from an oligarchy of autonomous Restoration leaders to coalitions of institutional elites who were creatures, not creators, of Japan's modern political institutions. Rapid and intense socioeconomic change accompanied the institutionalization of imperial prerogatives and political elites; by the 1930s, Japan was a formidable industrial and military power, her highly literate population enjoying universal adult male suffrage (1925) and being served by modern mass media.

All these changes—political, economic, and social—took place around a single, fixed referent: the imperial institution. As the pole star around which politics and society revolved, the imperial institution was looked to by most as the one fixed point in a vortex of change. How did it maintain its position in the face of such drastic changes? How could it survive the profound challenges of national defeat in 1945 and subsequent occupation by a foreign power? Only an examination of the theory and practice of palace politics and of the structure and leadership of the palace bureaucracy in prewar Japan could begin to answer the first question and to suggest answers to the second.

My concerns here are first with the theoretical position of the imperial institution in the governing process, second with the evolution of the palace as a formal structure and as personnel between 1885 and 1945, and third with the relation of the palace to the political process, primarily during the 1930s.

The theory of political legitimacy produced during the Restoration settlement of 1868–89 was based on the concept of imperial prerogative to be discussed in chapter 2. In that concept were fused modified religious myths and court practices from Japan's ancient past, shogunal powers from Japan's immediate past, and selected adaptations from Western constitutional monarchies. In theory, all political power derived from a "sacred and inviolable"[4] emperor who had "inherited from Our Ancestors" "the rights of sovereignty of the State."[5] If the imperial institution was to be the eternal fount of political authority, however, measures had to be taken to ensure that political failures would not reach the emperor and that the emperor's human frailties would not endanger the transcendental role of the throne in the Japanese polity. During the Restoration settlement, therefore, court and government were separated institutionally and each was given its own written constitution. Government officials were made responsible to the emperor for both policy making and policy implementation. The emperor was to ratify policies resolved upon by the officials who "advised and assisted" him. The emperor did not ratify policies as an individual monarch but as the representative of the Imperial Will—the bequeathed instructions of his ancestors "of a lineal succession unbroken for ages eternal."[6] "Imperial Will" was thus to serve as a major political fiction for legitimizing decisions of state while protecting the emperor from individual responsibility for the decisions he ratified.

In response to the theory of imperial prerogative and the institu-

---

4. *Constitution of the Great Empire of Japan,* Article 3.
5. Ibid., Preamble.
6. Ibid.

tional separation of court and government, a palace bureaucracy developed between 1868 and 1889 which was designed not only to preserve the imperial institution's transcendental authority in politics but also to manage that institution's role as symbol of all that was true, good, and beautiful in the Japanese polity. The creation and evolution of the palace bureaucracy are the subjects of chapter 3. Manipulating the transcendental Imperial Will in politics and managing the symbolic centrality of the imperial institution in Japanese society had originally been seen as complementary functions. As will be seen in chapter 4, however, this was so only when the court was under strong cohesive leadership and coordinated with equally strong and cohesive government leadership. Such leadership existed in both court and government from 1885 to 1912. But by the 1930s the court had become a mosaic of bureaucratic representatives who responded in a variety of ways to contradictory external and internal pressures. These pressures came mainly from the entrenched political institutions that had grown to maturity under the 1889 constitution.

Pluralism and competition in the institutions of government were reflected not only in the middle level of the palace bureaucracy but also in the palace leadership, the focus of discussion in chapter 4. Between 1885 and 1910 the four leading palace officers were either dutiful Court Nobles or Restoration leaders who belonged to the charmed circle of statesmen directing the course of Japan's modernization. But by the 1930s each of the four palace leaders was a distinguished bureaucrat drawn from a different component of the government bureaucracy—primarily the Foreign Ministry, Home Ministry, Navy, and Army. As both palace persons and careerist representatives of bureaucratic interests, these palace leaders were to see to it that what the emperor ratified was the correct, appropriate, or desirable "national consensus," despite competing demands from the multiple institutions of government. They were to protect the transcendence of the emperor as well as cope with the interests of their respective institutional constituencies. Under such countervailing pressures in the 1930s, negotiating the national consensus taxed to the utmost the political capabilities of the palace. No longer were palace leaders drawn from an ingroup of men who were creators, not creatures, of government institutions. No longer did they negotiate the imperial ratification of policies which were produced among themselves as Restoration comrades in arms and subject to personal, not institutional, grievances, competitions, and policy preferences.

Negotiating the national consensus for imperial ratification was not, however, the responsibility of the four leading palace officials alone. All or some of those who constitutionally or traditionally "advised and assisted" the emperor were involved: the four palace leaders, the Privy Councillors, the Ministers of State, the Chiefs of the High Command, the Elder and Senior Statesmen. Between 1885 and 1912 the advisers to the throne were a small group of like-minded men who shifted offices freely among themselves, most notably during the period from 1885 to 1901. Later, the number advising and assisting the emperor increased, as did the institutions they represented. In the 1930s the negotiation process leading to imperial ratification was complicated by the fact that partisan leaders initiated and implemented the policies which they themselves negotiated as national consensus. The outcome of the negotiation process was based on a balance of issue considerations, institutional loyalties, and personal ambitions—all involving institutionalized role perceptions on the part of the participants. By all criteria, however, the four palace leaders were to be the least involved in policy initiation and implementation, the most conscious of the national consensus, and the most experienced in the arts of Japanese domestic diplomacy. They and the retired statesmen were to be the negotiators par excellence; they were expected to discern the national consensus, regardless of their institutional experiences, and to be able to negotiate that consensus into effect.

Role behavior and the communication network linking court and government during the 1930s are the subjects of chapter 5. The focus of analysis is Marquis Kido Kōichi, whose patterns of association reveal the nature of prewar Japan's closed, or privatized, political process as well as the political roles required to sustain that process. Between 1930 and 1945 Kido held three different palace offices: Chief Secretary to the Lord Keeper of the Privy Seal, Director of Peerage Affairs, and Lord Keeper of the Privy Seal. Kido's behavior in each of these offices illustrates three roles that were basic to palace politics: the secretary, the bureaucrat, and the negotiator. The secretary was the functional equivalent of the feudal retainer; it was via the loyal secretary that a political decision maker received information that was both reliable and indispensable in judging the "trends of the times" on which he acted. The bureaucrat was an administrator whose role involved neutral or impartial administration. The negotiator was responsible for evaluating the "trends of the times" and forging the consensus on which policy and personnel decisions were based. Kido's associates in his three palace offices also illustrate other political roles essential to privatized decision making: the ratifier, who put the final seal of approval on political decisions; the policy advocate, who headed a faction within the government and whose partisan views and follower strength were key components of the "trends of the times"; and the instrument of pressure—a person or group who attempted to influence the political system "from below" or "from the outside"—including agitators, assassins, newsmen, interest groups, and political societies.

Chapter 6 concludes with a discussion of privatized decision making in prewar Japan that attempts (1) to contrast the Japanese bureaucratic policy process and its privatization of conflict with the democratic policy process and its socialization of conflict, (2) to illustrate the persistence of traditional patterns of decision making from Japan's immediate feudal past, and (3) to incorporate the role typology developed in chapter 5 in an intelligible model of political decision making. Political controversy in prewar Japan was not authoritatively resolved in an open public forum but in the corridors of bureaucratic institutions leading into the walled and moated imperial palace. Since decisions were to be presented to the public, not publicly resolved, basic political communication was maintained by secretaries to leading government and palace officials, negotiation took place verbally or "privately" among the principals involved, and the entire process was wrapped in secrecy—as best it could be. Such privatization of conflict in prewar Japan, which stands in contrast to the socialization of conflict characteristic of democracy in the United States, was made both possible and desirable given the theoretical and actual role of the palace in prewar Japanese politics.

This study is bound exclusively to the structure and operations of palace politics in Japan between 1868 and 1945. Since there have been no analytic descriptions of the workings of the palace, much less the relation between the palace and the political process, I consider such a focus justified. Although the concluding chapter suggests a model of prewar Japanese decision making that may ultimately prove useful for comparison with other political systems, the model is far from complete. The emphasis of this study is palace rather than government, and the model is distorted by the perspective taken.

A great deal more needs to be done on faction building, factional coalitions, and political roles in prewar Japanese politics before comparisons with other political systems and their development can be meaningfully made. Most critically needed in this respect is a study of the Japanese bureaucracy as it evolved under the theory and practice of imperial prerogative. Until very recently, Western and Japanese students of prewar Japanese politics have tended to ask why Japan was undemocratic and then to focus on the constitution, the legislature, political parties, voting, and democratic values as we know them. Although the question is certainly a proper one, the answers have been sought in the wrong *sumo* ring. It was the bureaucracy, initiating and implementing policy, that shaped the course of successful political modernization in Japan, however undemocratic. If British political development is any model of democratic development from a "traditional" society, moreover, one of the preconditions of democratic development in national politics is the creation of a strong central bureaucracy.[7] Of course, the creation of an effective national bureaucracy is no guarantee that democracy will follow, but without it "the people" have nothing to fight against— and nothing to control. Only in that society where the government did not govern and the land was "free" was there a different pattern of democratic development.[8]

---

7. This is certainly the import of G. R. Elton's analysis of Tudor bureaucracy under Thomas Cromwell in the 1530s in his *The Tudor Revolution in Government: Administrative Changes in the Reign of Henry VIII* (Cambridge: Cambridge University Press, 1953).

8. James Young has analyzed with great perception and humor the absence of national government in the United States during its foundling period in *The Washington Community, 1800–1828* (New York: Columbia University Press, 1966). Of course, the absence of government is no guarantee of democracy; nor is a frontier.

This is not, therefore, a comparative study. Nor is it a study of the decision-making process in terms of substantive issues, alternative courses of action, or reasons for ultimate policy decisions. These aspects of the political process are referred to only as illustrations of the institutional role of the palace, the structure and style of palace politics, and the political roles and behavior that linked palace and politics in prewar Japan.

Finally, I am not much concerned here either with the personalities of the Japanese emperors or with the prewar social forces, unleashed by Japan's modernization, which pressured the political system "from below"—mass movements, political parties, societies, pressure groups. Unlike the British monarch, or his portrait by British historians, "personality" had very little to do with the political functioning of the Japanese emperor. Those responsible for advising and assisting the emperor were responsible for making policies. This they did in view of the "trends of the times" outside the palace gates. As supreme ratifier in the Japanese state, the emperor was to put the seal of the Imperial Will on those policies. In doing so, he was to ensure as best he could that a national policy decision presented to him for ratification was truly a consensus among all concerned leaders on the best way to cope with the trends of the times. Whatever policy preferences the emperor might have had were known only to those close to the throne and of very limited effect. In the prewar decision-making process, therefore, the emperor was an institution, not an autonomous personality exercising an arbitrary individual will in politics.

If the personality and the policy preferences of the Japanese emperor were not very relevant to prewar politics, social forces certainly were. There are two reasons for giving them only the most tangential treatment here. First, this study simply had to be controlled in scope. Obviously not everything relevant to Japanese political development could be encompassed. Second, I do not think we have fully understood what these new social forces were pitted against politically. I hope that by analyzing the core institution in the prewar political process "from above," this study will aid our understanding of the forces "from below."

CHAPTER TWO

POLITICAL LEGITIMACY
AND
PALACE AUTONOMY

IN 1917 THE BIOGRAPHER of Tanaka Mitsuaki, Imperial Household
Minister from 1898 to 1909, described the imperial palace as "a
region of supreme scenic beauty, distant, far from the smoke of
human habitations, in the verdant hills, above the blue expanse of
sea . . . beyond the government, transcending, no one ever to invade
its sanctity."[1] But it was only after twenty years of groping experimentation, from the restoration of the emperor in 1868 to the promulgation of the *Constitution of the Great Empire of Japan* in 1889,
that such a transcendental position for the throne was agreed upon.
The new imperial institution was a creative fusion of three elements:
(1) practices, rituals, and an organization unique to the traditional
imperial institution on which nativist ideas about an idealized
ancient polity were based; (2) formal powers of rule previously held
by the shogun and "returned" to the emperor in 1867; and, finally,
(3) selected legal theories of constitutional monarchy prevalent in
continental Europe during the second half of the nineteenth century.

Although the pressures of Western thought and power made the
institutional and theoretical position of the restored emperor by no
means certain, historical precedents weighted the direction that the

1. Tomita Kōjirō, *Tanaka Seisan-haku* (Tokyo: Seisan Shoin, 1917), p. 293.

13

new government was to take. This was especially true of the political transcendence of the emperor. The position of the imperial institution during the preceding Tokugawa period (1603–1867) and earlier had been transcendental as well. From the twelfth century, political power had been exercised by a shogun, and only in times of political turmoil and warfare had the emperor and his court enjoyed any latitude of political maneuverability. The shogun had initially acquired his position by military power, and his de facto power was legitimized by the important fiction of imperial appointment. Successive shoguns of a ruling house, whether they ruled or were manipulated by persons in the shogunal house or government, were all appointed by the emperor. Each appointment, like that of the founding shogun, was a ritualistic ratification of a *fait accompli*. During the Tokugawa period the emperor and his court resided in the imperial palace in Kyoto, under the close control of the shogunal government headquartered in Edo—present-day Tokyo. The emperor was virtually a transcendental prisoner. He and his court, however, had performed unique religious rites in the Japanese polity from prehistoric times. These rites and the sociocultural status of the imperial institution had proved useful to all de facto rulers throughout the course of Japanese history. As a transcendental prisoner, therefore, the emperor lent legitimacy to the Tokugawa shogunate, and for all shoguns this was a valuable means toward stable government.

After a series of political failures, foreign and domestic, the shogun returned his mandate of rule to the emperor. The stage was thus set for the leaders of the Restoration to unite the traditional religious authority of the imperial institution with the powers previously held by the shogun. Those powers had largely involved military and police functions, as attested by the shogun's full title of "barbarian-subduing generalissimo." Such a unification was concretely symbolized when the emperor and court moved from Kyoto to Tokyo and took up residence in Edo castle, the fortress of the defunct shogunal government.

By 1889 the emperor's authority had been further enhanced. The Meiji Constitution, formally known as the *Constitution of the Great*

Empire of Japan, made Japan a constitutional monarchy in which the emperor was to exercise far-reaching prerogatives. Traditional religious rites were implicit in this constitution, which termed the emperor "sacred and inviolable." Shogunal powers recast as imperial prerogatives, as well as constitutional powers modeled most notably after the Prussian constitution, were explicit. In direct command of the armed forces both in peacetime administration and in wartime operations, the emperor appointed all generals of the Army and admirals of the Navy. He also appointed all Ministers of State, including the Prime Minister. He exercised the legislative power with the consent of the Imperial Diet, declared war, made peace, and concluded treaties. He had discretionary powers to issue ordinances in times of emergency.

Paradoxically, however, the court and the government were separated structurally and legally during the Restoration settlement. The court acquired its own autonomous bureaucracy, the Imperial Household Ministry. The imperial institution was also granted its own constitution, the Imperial House Law, concurrently with the enactment of the Meiji Constitution. Court affairs, furthermore, increasingly involved ritual practices or rites, and the public appearances of the emperor increasingly tended to be rigid, formalized affirmations of an imperial presence unique to Japan's sociopolitical order. Palace autonomy and the union of court and rites were paralleled by the union of government and rule. The emperor and court ritualized, the government decided and executed. This division of functions was also complementary: the emperor and court legitimized government decisions.

Far from being his personal decision-making powers, therefore, the emperor's prerogatives were the source of authority for rule by others—at first, by the statesmen who had engineered the Restoration and created the institutions of prewar Japanese government; later, by the leaders produced by the new institutions that grew to maturity under the constitution of 1889. In short, the imperial prerogatives laid down in the constitution became institutionalized in a government structure over which the emperor reigned but did not rule: the civil and military bureaucracies, the imperial legislature, and the courts. The emperor was once again a transcendental prisoner, but in a new and different political system: a constitutional monarchy based on imperial prerogative.

The separation of court and government, the union of court and rites, and the theory of imperial prerogative are the subjects of this chapter. These three elements constituted the theory of legitimacy on which Japanese government was based from 1889 to 1945, despite changes in Japanese society and shifting power configurations among the leaders and component structures of government.

THE SEPARATION OF COURT AND GOVERNMENT:
PALACE AUTONOMY

The "return to the kingly government of ancient times" (ōsei fukko), on the basis of which the emperor was restored physically to the center of the Japanese political order in 1868, had very little concrete content. "Direct imperial rule" (shinsei), a corollary slogan, was equally devoid of practical expression. It was the work of experimental nation-building efforts and political compromises during the Restoration settlement of 1868–89 that produced institutional and legal arrangements relating the emperor to the new political order.

Between 1868 and the creation of the cabinet system in 1885, Restoration governments were based on a union of court and palace affairs with government and state affairs under a literal interpretation of direct imperial rule. The first Restoration government of 1868 made no distinction between court and government.[2] The government organization established by the Instrument of Government (Seitaisho) of 21 April 1868 provided for an officer to manage court affairs. He was an official within a unified government and had concurrent governmental functions as well.[3]

2. Nezu Masashi, p. 38
3. Sōrifu, Kanchō Benran, 20 vols. (Tokyo: Ōkura Shō Insatsu, Kyoku, 1958), vol. 2, "Sōrifu II," pp. 3, 29. The Gregorian calendar was not officially adopted in Japan until January 1, 1873. Dates prior to this are listed according to the Japanese calendar without conversion and in the Japanese order: day, month, year.

But in early 1869 a "court affairs administrator" *(naibenji),*[4] later called a "court governor" *(naitei chiji),*[5] was created, only to be superseded by an "imperial household secretary" *(kunai kyō)* when the Imperial Household Ministry came into being on 8 July 1869.[6] All three of these 1869 functionaries were to devote themselves exclusively to court affairs. Although court affairs were no longer handled by an official who had other concurrent administrative duties, court administration remained an integral part of government. The Imperial Household Ministry, like other ministries created by the 1869 decree, was an administrative division of the Civil Government *(Dajōkan).*[7]

The heads of the ministries created in 1869 were not directly responsible for "advising and assisting" *(hohitsu)* the emperor, though they were to become so in 1889.[8] According to the 1871 reorganization of the ministries, for example, the privilege of assisting the throne directly was in theory limited to the Chancellor *(Dajō Daijin),* Minister of the Left *(Sa Daijin),* Minister of the Right *(U Daijin),* and the Councillors *(Sangi).*[9] The ministries, including the Imperial Household Ministry, were separate offices *(bunkan)* headed by secretaries.[10] The Imperial Household Secretary, however, was not included among those Secretaries of Ministries, Councillors, and Ministers constituting the inner circle of eighteen, called the "cabinet" *(naikaku),* who decided government policies.[11] By 1871 evidence thus emerges that court and government would eventually be institutionally separated. In 1869 the affairs of court had become the exclusive duty of one offical; two years later that official, the Im-

---

4. *Hōrei Zensho* (Tokyo: Ōkura Shō Insatsu Kyoku, 1869—), p. 143. Hereafter listed by title, year, and volume number when appropriate.

5. Sōrifu, *Kanchō Benran,* 2:26.

6. "Dajōkan Tasshi," no. 622, 8 July 1869, in *Hōrei Zensho,* 1869, pp. 249–64. This directive created the "eight ministry system" under a Chancellor, Minister of the Left, Minister of the Right, and Councillors. For the officers in this system, see Tōyama Shigeki and Adachi Yoshiko, *Kindai Nihon Seiji Shi Hikkei* (Tokyo: Iwanami Shoten, 1961), pp. 26–27.

7. *Hōrei Zensho,* 1869, pp. 249–64; Kyūtei Kishadan, *Kunai Chō* (Tokyo: Hōbun Sha, 1957), p. 8.

8. "Dai Nippon Teikoku Kempō," Article 55, in *Hōrei Zensho,* 1889, vol. 2, p. 6.

9. "Dajōkan Tasshi," no. 400, 10 August 1871, in *Hōrei Zensho,* 1871, p. 317.

10. Ibid.

11. Tanaka Sōgorō, *Kindai Nihon Kanryō Shi* (Tokyo: Tōyō Keizai Shimpō Sha Shuppan Bu, 1941), p. 99.

perial Household Secretary, was not asked to sit on the highest governing body, the informal cabinet of leading government officials.[12]

Paralleling the trend toward the structural separation of court and government between 1868 and 1871 was the displacement from central government offices of Court Nobles, the aristocrats who had accompanied the teenaged emperor from Kyoto to Tokyo. Between January and June 1868, forty-three of the 102 Conferees *(Sanyo)* appointed were Court Nobles, indicating that the initial Restoration government was in fact a fusion of court and government. Between June 1868 and August 1869, however, only three of the twenty-two appointments were Court Nobles, and none of the twenty-six Councillors appointed between August 1869 and December 1885 was a Court Noble.[13] Court Nobles did have a tenuous hold until 1885, however. The Chancellor, when that office was filled, was Court Noble Sanjō Sanetomi (1837-91) and the Ministers of the Right and Left were, with one exception, imperial princes or Court Nobles.[14] But the union of court and government was becoming a fiction, structurally and in terms of personnel, between 1868 and 1871.

The crumbling union between court and government did not go unchallenged, however. The theory and practice of direct imperial rule found a staunch proponent within the court in the person of Motoda Eifu (1818-91). At the recommendation of Ōkubo Toshimichi (1831-78), one of the leading oligarchs of the day, Motoda had entered the Imperial Household Ministry in 1871 as Imperial Reader to the emperor.[15] In September 1873 Motoda petitioned Minister of the Right Iwakura Tomomi to enlist the support of the government's ablest leaders for direct imperial rule. Motoda argued

12. The informal cabinet of 1871 is not to be confused with the formal cabinet system enacted in 1885. The "cabinets" of 1871-85, being collections of leading government officials, were of course the precursors of this system.

13. W. G. Beasley, "Councillors of Samurai Origin in the Early Meiji Government, 1868-1869," *Bulletin of the School of Oriental and African Studies, University of London* 20 (1957): 94.

14. Tōyama and Adachi, p. 26.

15. Kaigo Tokiomi, "Motoda Eifu," *Nippon Kyōiku Sentetsu Sōsho* (Tokyo: Bukyō Shoin, 1942), 19:2. Until his death in 1891 Motoda was a curtained influence at court. A dedicated Confucian, he exercised considerable influence over the political development of the Emperor Meiji as well as the content of public education in the new Japan's formative years.

that "at present the sovereign's wisdom is not yet extensive and his benevolence is not yet comprehensive."[16] Cultivating the emperor's virtue

> must be the responsibility of the ablest men in the country, and not left to second- and third-rate teachers as at present. The ablest men of the day have become Prime Minister [Chancellor], Ministers of the Left and Right, and Councillors, but these men rarely consult the Emperor on political matters.[17]

To this end, Motoda desired a union of court and government.

Motoda's ultimate test came with the creation of a group of court advisers, the *Jiho* (Advisers-in-Attendance), on August 29, 1877. According to Tsuda Shigemaro, biographer of *Jiho* Sasaki Takayuki, the office of *Jiho* "originated in a sincere intent to concentrate on cultivating the emperor's virtue." When Sasaki Takayuki joined the group in 1878 there were ten *Jiho*.[18] Both educators of the emperor and potential implementers of direct imperial rule, the *Jiho,* as court officers, came into competition with the Ministers and Councillors, collectively the government oligarchy.

Like Motoda, Sasaki Takayuki wished to have a powerful and capable political leader head the *Jiho,* given their "weighty office" of educating the emperor in political affairs.[19] He and the other *Jiho* agreed that they were simply not prepared for the task of remedying the emperor's deficiencies as Japan's central political figure. Sasaki also complained of the personnel surrounding the emperor at court: they had left everything as it was in Meiji's childhood. If the emperor refused advice on the most trifling of matters the palace people let him have his way. As far as politics was concerned, the emperor left everything to the "two Ministers" (presumably, the Chancellor and the Minister of the Left). Sasaki accused the Imperial Household Secretary, Tokudaiji Sanenori, of weakness—allowing too much power to the two Ministers and fearing the emperor's temper. Head Chamberlain Higashikuze Michitomi, Sasaki com-

---

16. Quoted by Donald H. Shively, "Motoda Eifu: Confucian Lecturer to the Meiji Emperor," in *Confucianism in Action,* ed. David S. Nivison and Arthur F. Wright (Stanford: Stanford University Press, 1959), p. 315.
17. Ibid; Shively paraphrases Motoda's argument.
18. Tsuda Shigemaro, *Meiji Seijō to Shin Takayuki* (Tokyo: Jishōkai, 1928), pp. 401, 403.
19. Ibid., "Preface" p. 3, and text p. 403.

plained, lacked drive and could do nothing to assist the emperor's virtue. Consequently, Sasaki and the other *Jiho* agreed to ask Ōkubo Toshimichi, possibly the most powerful member of the government at the time, to head the "Bureau of *Jiho*." Ōkubo agreed to turn over the Home Ministry to Itō Hirobumi, with Itō's consent, and then to take over the post of Imperial Household Secretary. But on the way to the palace on May 14, 1878, apparently to accept his new office, Ōkubo was struck down by assassins.[20] The *Jiho* once again found themselves powerless.

The aftermath of Okubo's assassination reveals the difficulty the *Jiho* faced in "advising" a politically apathetic emperor as well as the power struggle implicit in their role of "cultivating the emperor's virtue." The *Jiho* agreed among themselves that the leading assassin, Shimada Ichirō, spoke no small measure of truth when he argued that Japanese politics originated neither in the will of the emperor nor in the discussions of the people but in the autocratic decision making of a few officials. To meet such criticism from "public opinion," Sasaki urged that the emperor be made a more active political figure; it was their duty as *Jiho* to reproach the emperor soundly, without regard to their personal fortunes. When they appeared before the emperor, Senior *Jiho* Sasaki led the remonstration: if the emperor did not familiarize himself with foreign and domestic trends, the whole work of the Restoration would collapse. All of the *Jiho* spoke to the same effect.[21] Komeda Torao, *Jiho* of the third rank, was the most blunt: "If in the past [Your Majesty] had shown as much care for politics as he had passion for horsemanship, no such criticism from the public as 'politics by two or three Ministers' would have occurred."[22]

If "cultivating the emperor's virtue" meant making the emperor a direct participant in politics, it would also make the *Jiho* a formidable group should the emperor rule in fact. The implications of such an interpretation of direct imperial rule were not lost on the government. When the *Jiho* reported to the Councillors following

20. Ibid., pp. 403–07.
21. Ibid., pp. 408–10.
22. Ibid., p. 410.

Ōkubo's assassination, they urged that the emperor be present at meetings of the Councillors and Ministers as well as attend cabinet meetings daily, and that the *Jiho* themselves take part in such sessions.[23] Chancellor Sanjō Sanetomi replied that arrangements for the emperor's presence at such sessions would be made. The *Jiho,* however, would not be permitted to participate, since this would confuse the distinction between "internal" (court?) and "external" (government?). Councillor and Home Secretary Itō Hirobumi was much more explicit. It was the consensus of the cabinet, he said, that it would be improper for the *Jiho* to have knowledge of the confidential plans of the administration; in present-day administrative systems, imperial house *(teishitsu)* and cabinet *(naikaku)* ought to be separate. Since the Restoration, Itō continued, it had not been the practice for the Imperial Household Secretary to serve concurrently as Councillor in the government. Itō concluded that the *Jiho* were to concern themselves strictly with the emperor's education.[24] By clearly acknowledging the separation of court and government, Itō fended off an attempt by court officers to assume political power and thereby break the monopoly of power held by the government oligarchs in the cabinet.

The *Jiho* continued to be disgruntled after their bid for participatory power was denied. They complained that after their office was created in 1877 the Chamberlains had remained in charge of court ceremony and the Ministers and Councillors had retained control of political policy. As a result the *Jiho* were neither fish nor fowl, having almost no power to carry out their functions. Motoda and Sasaki finally presented the government with an ultimatum: either increase the powers of the *Jiho* or abolish the office. The government chose abolition.[25] Although Sasaki's biographer weakly claims that "they had absolutely no desire to violate the jurisdiction of the

23. Professor Shively is much more direct on the intentions of the *Jiho.* "Only four days after Ōkubo's death they [the *Jiho*] formally demanded that the Emperor be given the right to make political decisions and that the *jiho,* as his advisers, be permitted to participate in cabinet deliberations. The oligarchs—Iwakura and Itō, in particular—were indignant" (Shively, p. 313).

24. Tsuda Shigemaro, pp. 411–12.

25. Ibid., pp. 439–49.

Ministers and Councillors, to obstruct politics, or to confuse the distinction between court and government," the majority of government oligarchs clearly believed otherwise.[26]

The abolition of the *Jiho* as a court office on October 13, 1879 marked the end of direct imperial rule on the basis of a union between court and government. A thinly veiled power confrontation of unequal odds led ultimately to the enunciation of the converse principle: separation of court and government. The remaining question between 1879 and 1889 was what structural and legal form this separation should take.

Although Motoda, Sasaki, and the other *Jiho* failed in their efforts to integrate court and government under a politically active emperor, the separation of court and government did embody elements of compromise that benefited Confucian moralists such as Motoda. The concept of direct imperial rule was ambiguous in its implications, since the model Confucian emperor was more a paragon of virtues than a power wielder. By placing the palace—the imperial court and attendant imperial household bureaucracy—beyond the formal government, the oligarchs allowed Motoda and other court influences considerable freedom to make the emperor a supreme exemplar of political rectitude in the Confucian and Japanese image. But by restricting these court advocates of direct imperial rule to that function, the government oligarchs freed themselves from institutionalized court interference in the process of policy making and enforcement.[27] Only the cabinet remained as the emperor's direct advisory group in politics—and only the cabinet would rule directly.

Between the demise of the *Jiho* in 1879 and the enactment of the constitution in 1889, accusations of violating the distinction between court and government were leveled not at the court but at the government. Most frequently at the center of such controversy was government oligarch Itō Hirobumi, who had returned from his study of European constitutional systems on August 4, 1883. While there were those who feared that Itō, having studied in Germany, might

26. Ibid., p. 439.
27. The ambiguity of Motoda's power-morality theory of direct imperial rule resolved itself into both power and moral force: power to the *Jiho* on the basis of the emperor's moral force. Motoda "repeatedly urged the Emperor to exercise his Imperial right of personal decision, overriding the cabinet when necessary" (Shively, p. 304).

work for an autocratic monarchy on the Prussian model, many imperial household officials were apprehensive that he would so revise the institutions and practices of court that the emperor's "prerogatives" would be jeopardized. On March 17, 1884 Itō became director of the newly created Institutions Investigation Bureau *(Seido Torishirabe Kyoku)*, at the same time retaining his post as Councillor in the government.[28] The Institutions Investigation Bureau was charged with an inquiry into the institutions of both court and government and the drafting of an imperial house law and a national constitution. Four days later Itō became Imperial Household Secretary as well. Holding three major posts—in government, court, and Investigation Bureau, Itō fell under charges of "using the emperor." Opposition on this occasion originated not so much from the court as from out-of-power political leaders and from Itō's opponents within the government oligarchy.[29]

Chancellor Sanjō Sanetomi's cabinet, however, came to Itō's defense. To ensure that the palace structure would coincide with the new constitutional structure under consideration and at the same time preserve the distinction between court and government, Sanjō argued that a capable Councillor must serve concurrently in all three posts. Moreover, for constitutional government to be inaugurated successfully in Japan, the closest cooperation between court and government was required. But when Sanjō sent his endorsement of Itō's appointment as Imperial Household Secretary to the throne, the emperor withheld his approval. Motoda, who had remained at court as Grand Steward to the empress, was called in for advice. He replied in favor of Itō's appointment. Still the emperor hesitated. It appeared that influential leaders were supporting Itō's colleague and rival, Yamagata Aritomo, for the post. Only after Sanjō and the Minister of the Left, Prince Arisugawa, had formally petitioned the emperor on March 20 did the emperor sanction Itō's appointment.[30]

28. Shumpo Kōtsui Shōkai, *Itō Hirobumi Den,* 3 vols. (Tokyo: Shumpo Kōtsui Shōkai, 1940), 2:360-65, 371; Kyūtei Kishadan, p. 12. The Institutions Investigation Bureau succeeded the Rules and Regulations Investigation Bureau *(Naiki Torishirabe Kyoku)* created in December 1882 under Iwakura Tomomi. While Itō was abroad Iwakura died and the Rules and Regulations Investigation Bureau lapsed.

29. Shumpo Kōtsui Shōkai, 2:372-77; Sōrifu, *Kanchō Benran,* 2:27; Kyūtei Kishadan, p. 12.

30. Shumpo Kōtsui Shōkai, 2:374-77.

The emperor is reported to have questioned the wisdom of the appointment: "When one views [our] long history one sees that it is a mistake for those next to the throne to conduct politics."[31] Opposition to Itō's domination over court and government had reached such dimensions that the emperor was required to mediate the appointment of his own household manager. It may even have been that Itō's appointment went against the emperor's better judgment.

From his ascendant position in court and government, Itō instituted the cabinet system as a prior step to the enactment of a constitution. When the new system was inaugurated on December 22, 1885, the court was finally made explicitly autonomous. The Imperial Household Secretary was restyled Imperial Household Minister, and the Imperial Household Ministry was placed outside the formal government structure.[32] The Imperial Household Minister was now responsible directly and exclusively to the emperor for the management of court affairs. When the Imperial Household Ministry was reorganized in early 1886 it was done on the sole authority of incumbent Imperial Household Minister Itō, who exercised autonomous control over its organization,[33] directed the affairs of the imperial house, managed the aristocracy, and superintended the staff of the ministry. The period of Itō's tenure from March 1884 to September 1887 has been called the golden age of the Imperial Household Ministry. The ministry's jurisdiction expanded greatly under a minister "high in the emperor's confidence."[34]

While remaining as Imperial Household Minister, however, Itō became Japan's first Prime Minister, honoring the separation of court and government in the breach. As in 1884, Itō was once again attacked severely by government opponents. Publicly charging him

31. Kyūtei Kishadan, p. 12. My guess is that the quote is apocryphal, but given the emperor's political apathy, already noted, there may be considerable truth in his alleged desire to keep the court, and himself, out of politics.

32. "Dajōkan Tasshi," no. 69, December 22, 1885, in Hōrei Zensho, 1885, vol. 2, p. 1, 044; Sōrifu, Kanchō Benran, 2:3; Kyūtei Kishadan, p. 13. For an account of Itō's maneuvering to have the cabinet system adopted, especially his handling of former Councillor Kuroda Kiyotaka, see Shumpo Kōtsui Shōkai, 2:445–84.

33. "Kunai Shō Tasshi," no. 1, February 4, 1886, in Kampō (Tokyo: Naikaku Insatsu Kyoku), No. 776 (Friday, February 5, 1886).

34. Kyūtei Kishadan, p. 15.

with violating the distinction between court and government, the opposition made this issue part of a general attack on Itō and his policies. Itō modestly retorted that he had assumed both posts as the only qualified persons able to arrange palace affairs to accord with the constitutional form of government soon to be instituted. Without complete responsibility, Itō continued, he could not possibly carry out a comprehensive renovation. The current arrangement, furthermore, was only temporary. Itō accused the opposition of ignorance, deliberate scheming, or both. The opposition grew to such a crescendo, however, that he was forced to resign as Imperial Household Minister in September 1887, almost one year before the constitution and Imperial House Law were placed before the Privy Council for ratification.[35] Itō found himself hoisted with his own petard. The argument he had used against the *Jiho* in 1878 had been effectively turned against him. After 1887 no Prime Minister was again to hold the post of Imperial Household Minister concurrently. In fact, no ex-Prime Minister or future Prime Minister became Imperial Household Minister from 1887 to 1945.

Itō's resignation as Imperial Household Minister once again involved Motoda Eifu. When Itō submitted his resignation for the second time in July 1887, the emperor questioned Motoda on the propriety of Itō's concurrent posts.[36] Still clinging to his concept of direct imperial rule, Motoda answered that for one person to be both Prime Minister and Imperial Household Minister indicated that court and government were united. He knew of no reason why this was inadmissible from the standpoint of Japan's "national polity," the unalterable essence of Japan's governmental system. If, however, a person did hold both posts, Motoda continued, he must be a statesman of exceptional character, reputation, and discernment. Itō, though of ability and character, was not yet able to control "public sentiment" and, if left in charge of the court for any length of time, might cause difficulties for the imperial house. Motoda therefore

35. Shumpo Kōtsui Shōkai, 2:523–24, 547.
36. Ibid., pp. 524–25, 548–53. Itō first submitted his resignation in May 1887; the third submission was accepted. The emperor's refusal to accept the first two requests was in line with Confucian political etiquette: two refusals followed by reluctant acceptance of the third. This is a general rule of propriety often followed by biographers of political figures, if not by the figures themselves.

recommended that the emperor accept Itō's resignation without delay.[37]

Although Motoda's advice was not followed, his response to the throne indicates that a union between court and government might be achieved not on court but on government initiative. Separation of court and government for Motoda was merely an expedient should there be no sage-statesman to administer both concurrently. Such a position was entirely consonant with Motoda's concept of direct imperial rule. According to Confucian catechism, a true emperor ruled through exceptional ministers whom he guided by moral force. The presence of public opposition to a minister meant ipso facto that the minister was not a true statesman. Such public clamor might reach the emperor himself, embroiling him in political battle and thereby tarnishing the Imperial Virtue. Expediency, therefore, dictated even to Motoda that without statesmen to carry out the Imperial Will directly, separating court and government was the lesser of two evils.[38]

THE UNION OF COURT AND RITES

For Motoda, direct imperial rule meant both political power and moral transcendence for the imperial institution. If, however, the emperor were to have actual power—to be the central decision maker in the turbulent politics of modernization, how was his transcendental position to be maintained? According to Motoda, Japan's greatness was attributable to its imperial house, "transcending the entire world, being immutable, one line of all ages descendant of the gods."[39] It was the ethic of loyalty to this

37. Ibid., pp. 549–50.

38. In addition to assassinations and verbal assaults against government leaders for the evils attributed to the time, there were also direct accusations against the emperor himself. In 1877, for example, Kataoka Kenkichi blamed the emperor directly for the poverty of the people, for inequities in government, and for the lack of popular participation in politics. Kataoka was called down for insolence by a cabinet secretary who argued that the cabinet and the emperor were one (Inoue Kiyoshi, *Tennō Sei* [Tokyo: Tōkyō Daigaku Shuppan Kai, 1953], pp. 76–77). Direct exposure of the emperor in the light of political battle might have increased such attacks and deflated the moral authority of the throne, as Motoda feared.

39. Kaigo Tokiomi, p. 29.

transcendent imperial house, in Motoda's view, that constituted the basis of Japan's superior national polity.[40] But how could political involvement and transcendence coexist? How could loyalty be sustained to an institution that made political decisions, inevitably depriving some and benefiting others? As Motoda half-heartedly agreed, one solution was that arrived at by 1855: palace autonomy, the legal and structural separation of the court from the political process. Accepting the separation, the problems of giving meaning to the emperor's transcendence and then of transforming that meaning into political authority, into a theory of political legitimacy, remained.

The "return to the kingly government of ancient times" was supported and extended by a further restorationist slogan: "rites and rule are one" (*saisei itchi*).[41] A 1933 interpretation of this "ancient practice" posited that "to celebrate the gods is to rule the people."[42] Historically, ritual practices exclusive to the court had been central to the imperial institution's social and political role. The rites of court had formed the basis for the emperor's legitimizing function in politics throughout most of Japanese history. In the folk beliefs of the Japanese,

> blood descent from a god confers the unique power to communicate with the god. The Sun Goddess, Amaterasu Ōmikami, chief divinity of the Shinto pantheon, was the progenitrix of the imperial line. . . . Primitive Japanese as well as great numbers of their more recent descendants believed that ministrations to that most awesome personage were of potent efficacy in ordering the affairs of agriculture, warfare, and the governance of society.[43]

In its official structure, moreover, the court historically "symbolized more than the way it worked; it symbolized an elaborate conceptualization of timeless ethical precepts for ordering human society."[44] On the one hand, blood descent from the gods gave the emperor an exclusive power to communicate with those gods, and

40. Ibid., p. 35.
41. Ienaga Saburō et al., *Kindai Nihon Shisō Shi Kōza*, 8 vols. (Tokyo: Chikuma Shobō, 1959), 1:43.
42. Goseitoku Fukyū Kai, *Meiji-Taishō-Kinjō Santei Seitoku Roku*, ed. Watanabe Ikujirō (Tokyo: Handoku Kai, 1933), p. 9.
43. Herschel Webb, *The Japanese Imperial Institution in the Tokugawa Period* (New York: Columbia University Press, 1968), p. 13.
44. Ibid., p. 32.

such rites of communication were interpreted as effective means of ruling the country. On the other hand, the organization of the court for the performance of rites gave concrete expression to the ideal ethical polity.

Placing the emperor newly at the structural center of government in 1868 need not, of course, have changed the traditional relationship between dignified rites and efficient rule. Speaking of the thirteenth-century aristocrat-priest Jien, Herschel Webb notes that in Jien's theory, as well as in the traditional Chinese interpretation, "the sovereign's first function was something other than the administration of government"[45]: it was to legitimize rule through rites. And this function remained intact after the political revolution of 1868.[46]

The institutional form as well as the content that rites were to acquire in the new political order after 1868 were, however, determined in the same pragmatic fashion that led to the establishment of palace autonomy. The institutional experimentation that led to the separation of court and government also led to the union of court and rites.

Being based on the principle that rites and rule are one, the first Restoration government fused rites and rule as well as court and government.[47] Both a Civil Government and a Government of Rites (*Jingikan*) were revived on 17 November 1867.[48] With the creation of the Meiji government on 9 December 1867 (January 3, 1868), in accordance with the "great command to return to the kingly government of ancient times" (*ōsei fukko no daigōrei*), a Division of Rites (*Jingi Jimuka*) replaced the Government of Rites and became one of seven

45. Ibid., p. 165.

46. "One may point out that all new nations and post-revolutionary societies face the crucial problem of legitimacy. The old order has been abolished and with it the set of beliefs that justified its system of authority. Meiji Japan did not face this crisis; at the moment of change the imperial system had remained intact to give sanction to the new administration.

During the Tokugawa period and even before . . . , actual political power had not resided with the emperor. The legitimizing authority was always, however, implicitly or explicitly recognized as belonging to the imperial court" (Joseph Pittau, *Political Thought in Early Meiji Japan: 1868–1889* [Cambridge, Mass.: Harvard University Press, 1967], p. 10).

47. Kyūtei Kishadan, p. 9; Umeda Toshihiko, *Nihon Shūkyō Seido Shi* (Kyoto: Hyakkaen, 1962), p. 586.

48. "No. 7" of 17 November 1867, in *Hōrei Zensho*, 1867, pp. 3–4. The ideograph for "rites" in the slogan "rites and rule are one" and the ideographs for "rites" in "government of rites" are different. The former denotes rites in general, the latter denotes specifically Shinto rites. Both mean formal, ceremonial rituals.

divisions of the new Civil Government.[49] The initial dualism of Civil Government and Government of Rites was apparently eliminated by making the Government of Rites a division under the Civil Government. The leading persons in the Division of Rites did not, however, hold concurrent posts as Councillors or Junior Councillors in the deliberative chambers of the Civil Government.[50] After several administrative reorganizations in 1868 and 1869, the Government of Rites was once again restored and made separate from the Civil Government on 8 July 1869.[51] The duties of the Government of Rites in 1869 included the conduct of Shinto ceremonies and the preparation of ritual texts, the supervision of religion and prayers, and the management of shrines and tombs. In this year the Government of Rites was also given short-lived preeminence over the Civil Government. In theory both governments were under the direct rule of the emperor.[52]

That the performance of rites would eventually fall in large measure to the court is indicated by the fate of the Government of Rites after 1869. In 1871 it was demoted to Ministry of Rites (*Jingi Shō*) and placed under the Civil Government. On 14 March 1872 the Ministry of Rites was abolished[53] and reconstituted as the Ministry of Teachings (*Kyōbu Shō*). In that same year the Secretary of Education was also made Secretary of Teachings, concurrently managing the Ministry of Education (newly created in 1871) and the Ministry of Teachings. Finally, in 1877 the Ministry of Teachings was abolished in the aftermath of quarrels over the issue of separating church and state.[54]

Paralleling the demotion, transformation, and demise of the Government of Rites, the court acquired increased duties in the performance of rites. By imperial command on 14 September 1871, for example, it was ordered that rites to the imperial ancestors, to the

49. Tōyama and Adachi, pp. 1, 22.
50. Ibid., p. 1
51. "Dajōkan Tasshi," no. 622, 8 July 1869, in *Hōrei Zensho*, 1869, pp. 249–64; Umeda Toshihiko, p. 586.
52. *Hōrei Zensho*, 1869, p. 250; Umeda Toshihiko, p. 417. Inoue Kiyoshi, p. 63; Paul M. A. Linebarger, Ardath W. Burks, and Djang Chu, *Far Eastern Governments and Politics: China and Japan*, 2d ed., rev. (Princeton: D. Van Nostrand Company, 1956), p. 369.
53. "Dajōkan Tasshi," no. 398, 8 August 1871, in *Hōrei Zensho*, 1871, "Index," p. 24.
54. Tōyama and Adachi, pp. 2, 3.

spirits of past emperors, be transferred from the jurisdiction of the Ministry of Rites to that of the "inner shrine" (kashikodokoro) of the palace.[55] When the Ministry of Rites was abolished in 1872, matters pertaining to Shinto rites and scriptures came under an Office of the Ceremonies (Shikibu Ryō), which had been created within the Civil Government on 10 August 1871.[56] The Office of the Ceremonies was transferred to the Imperial Household Ministry in 1875, then back to the Civil Government at the end of that year, and finally returned permanently to the Imperial Household Ministry in 1877.[57]

The Office of the Ceremonies was originally created to conduct Shinto ceremonies in the palace and to superintend rites conducted at the national shrines, such as the Grand Shrine at Ise.[58] Its transfer to the Imperial Household Ministry meant that the court gained institutional control over rites at the palace as well as rites at the major national shrines. Management of local shrines and the priesthood, like other functions not transferred to the court, was turned over to the Bureau of Shrines and Temples in the Home Ministry.[59]

The evolution of the Board of the Ceremonies, as it was renamed after 1877, indicates that Shinto rites played an increasingly important role in the affairs of court. The 1886 reorganization of the Imperial Household Ministry made the Board one of seventeen divisions of the palace bureaucracy. Given charge of rites (saiten), ceremonies (gishiki), and court music, the board was headed by an official of imperial appointee (chokunin) rank, the second highest civil service category.[60] By the 1930s, however, the Chief of the Board of the Ceremonies had risen in rank to become one of the six court officials regularly given direct imperial appointment (shinnin), the highest civil service rating. His salary had also risen from 3,500–4,000 yen in 1886 to 5,800–6,200 yen in 1931.[61] By the 1930s the Chief of the

55. Umeda Toshihiko, p. 588.
56. Ibid., pp. 417, 588.
57. Hōrei Zensho, 1875, pp. 81, 439; ibid., 1877, pp. 208–09.
58. Umeda Toshihiko, p. 416.
59. Ibid., p. 415.
60. "Kunai Shō Tasshi," no. 1, February 4, 1886 (Kampō, February 5, 1886), in Hōrei Zensho, 1886, pp. 38–48.
61. "Kunai Shō Gōgai" of February 15, 1886, in Hōrei Zensho, 1886, p. 141; Shokuin Roku (Tokyo: Naikaku Insatsu Kyoku, 1931), pt. 2, p. 3. Hereafter referred to by title and date.

Board of the Ceremonies was equal in rank and salary to the Grand Chamberlain.[62]

The increased importance of the Board of the Ceremonies, as measured by the increased rank and salary of its chief relative to other leading court officials, was paralleled by the growth of the Division of Rituals. One of the chief sections of the Board of the Ceremonies by 1930, the Division of Rituals conducted "sacred rites" (*saiji*).[63] Whereas the Masters of the Ceremonies were responsible for such functions as court diplomacy involving both foreign and Japanese notables, the Masters of Ritual managed Shinto ceremonies. Of approximately 210 persons serving on the Board of the Ceremonies in 1931, 33 were employed in the Division of Rituals. Eight of those 33 held concurrent posts elsewhere in the Imperial Household Ministry, such as in the Imperial Poetry Bureau.[64] Like the Chief of the Board of Ceremonies, moreover, the Chief of Rituals increased in relative importance, as measured by rank and salary. His salary had more than doubled between 1886 (2,000–2,400 yen per annum) and 1931 (4,650–5,100 yen per annum).[65] By 1940 his rank was either imperial appointee or direct imperial appointee. Finally, the Division of Rituals was made independent of the Board of the Ceremonies in December 1939, when it became a full-fledged board and one of five basic divisions of the Imperial Household Ministry.[66] By 1943 the personnel involved in "Shinto ceremonies" (*saishi*) performed by the Board of Rituals had also increased to seventy-one, thirty-six of whom held concurrent posts in the palace bureaucracy.[67] The institutional growth of the Board of Rituals, the increased salary and rank of its chief, and the doubling of its personnel between 1930 and 1943 signify that the union of court and rites was fundamental to the role of the imperial institution in prewar Japan and even increased in importance after 1877.

62. The Grand Chamberlain was one of four palace leaders responsible for relating the emperor to politics and society from 1885 to 1945 (see chap. 4).

63. *Shokuin Roku,* 1931, pt. 1. p. 3; "Kōshitsu Rei," no. 7, October 7, 1921, in Naikaku Kiroku Ka, *Genkō Hōrei Shūran,* 2 vols. (Tokyo: Teikoku Chihō Gyōsei Gakkai, 1923), vol. 1, pt. 3, p. 6.

64. *Shokuin Roku,* 1931, pt. 3, pp. 10–11.

65. *Hōrei Zensho,* 1886, p. 142; *Shokuin Roku,* 1931, pt. 2, p. 4.

66. Naikaku Kiroku Ka, 1942, vol. 1, pt. 3, chap. 1, sec. 3, pp. 20–21.

67. Ibid.; *Kunai Shō Shokuin Roku* (Tokyo: Kunai Daijin Kambō, 1921–43), 1943, pp. 213–19.

Shinto rites had always been a major function of the emperor and his court; but to argue that rites had been a fundamental function of the imperial institution historically is not to explain the particular place of rites in modern Japan. The experimentation with Shinto institutions between 1868 and 1877 suggests that the Restoration leaders were as eclectic and pragmatic in adapting Japan's heritage as they were in adopting Western forms and ideas to buttress the new national government. After 1868 Shinto rites became an instrument for nationalizing public consciousness. No longer were the rites of court conducted in a secluded imperial palace for the knowledgeable members of a literate ruling elite. The Shinto reforms of the early Restoration years made court rites the property of the entire nation, linking those rites with local Shinto organizations in an attempt to mobilize national sentiment around the emperor.

The new organization and management of Shinto rites were intended to give the emperor a popular visibility that had never before existed. Inoue Kiyoshi, a Marxist historian markedly unsympathetic to the imperial institution, has described the intent and actions of Restoration leaders as follows:

None other than the gods were to be the final base of the emperor's, and his government's, authority. When people have been submerged too long and too continuously in lives of poverty they somehow come to yearn for something absolute to rely on. The Emperor System utilized this sentiment. And, while severely suppressing the Christian faith, which argued that all men are equal before God, the Emperor System enjoined the people to believe in gods who were the retainers of the Sun Goddess. To that end the emperor above all had to revere the gods himself. "Rites and rule are one" has its origins here. In terms of governmental organization as well, a Division of Rites was created in the first government system of January 1868; then, in July of 1869, the Government of Rites was placed above the Civil Government. Further, a shrine to the Eight Gods— the God of Creation and the others—was established in the Government of Rites and then transferred into the palace. (These gods were not derived from the ancient people's faith in nature but were conceived for the purpose of apotheosizing the ancestors of the imperial clan around the sixth and seventh centuries, when the imperial clan at last became chief of the clans. "God of Creation" means no more than something miraculous that gives birth to things.) On 3 January 1870 the Rite of the Beginning [Genshi Sai] was begun in order to celebrate the Gods of Heaven and

Earth, the Eight Gods, and the Imperial Spirit of emperors gone before. Preceding the Commencement of Government Affairs [*Seiji Hajime*] on 4 January [every year], this Rite was a national holiday until the end of the War.[68]

Inoue also states that fourteen shrines for imperial rites were established in 1868. Local shrines, hierarchically arranged and staffed by priest-officials, were created throughout Japan. Certain Shinto rites centering on the imperial line were also proclaimed national festivals. In 1871, for example, the Rite of Emperor Jimmu was made a state holiday, as was the legendary Jimmu's legendary enthronement, later to be called Empire Day (*Kigensetsu*), in 1872. As early as 1874 the practice of prostration before the emperor's photograph was begun.[69]

One need not accept Inoue's value judgments or his implications as to the effectiveness of such efforts to mobilize national consciousness in order to agree that the nationalization of Shinto was intended to secure popular loyalty to a transcendental emperor. The emperor and people were to be linked by national Shinto rites and a national organization for managing those rites that extended from the emperor and court into every village and hamlet.

Of course, not all those who advocated a transcendental emperor argued that Shinto rites be made the sole basis of the emperor's exemplary role in society. We have seen, for example, that Motoda Eifu's concept of direct imperial rule involved making the emperor a paragon of Confucian virtues. This also meant linking sovereign and subject in terms of filial piety, the absolute loyalty due a father from his sons. Making Shinto rites one function of an autonomous court interfered little with such Confucian concepts, however. Ethnocentric Shinto rites and universalist Confucian moral force would merely reinforce one another in sustaining the transcendental position of the imperial house. The compromise that separated court and government ultimately proved acceptable to both Confucianists and Shintoists. Confronting a rising storm of political ideas blowing in from the West, they received a sanctuary for their conservatism when ritual observances were delegated to an autonomous court.

68. Inoue Kiyoshi, pp. 63–64.
69. Ibid., pp. 64, 66, 67.

POLITICAL AUTHORITY AND
IMPERIAL PREROGATIVE

By the 1930s Shinto rites conducted by the emperor and court were thought by some to be the very core of Japan's national polity. The political implications of the union of court and rites, so strongly suggested by Professor Inoue, were confirmed by Sakamaki Yoshio, an official in the Imperial Household Ministry from 1918 to 1936, when he linked Shinto rites, popular loyalty, imperial authority, and state power with fearsome logic:

1. Man has a religious nature, which is to perceive the existence of gods above men and to resolve that all affairs should accord with the will of the gods.
2. The power of the gods is operative in the common existence of a people or nation.
3. Therefore, that which governs a people or nation is the will of the gods.
4. The incarnation of the will of the gods is the monarch.
5. The gods are eternal, therefore the monarch—not one generation but the imperial line—is also eternal.
6. Therefore, nation and imperial house are one and inseparable.
7. When strife occurs among groups or individuals, all search for the judgment of the gods.
8. Therefore, the judgment of the emperor, being the will of the gods, is obeyed.[70]

Elaborating, Sakamaki noted that "our nation has from ancient times believed in the Way of the Gods, been proud of ours being the land of the gods, duly respected rites to the nation's ancestral gods, and revered the Shinto shrines."[71] It is unquestionably the duty of all subjects to revere the ancestral gods. The Shinto shrines serve these deities; they are public places and those who serve there are public officials. Supreme management of Shinto rites is vested in the emperor, and his performance of rites is an example to all.[72] In taking the

70. Sakamaki Yoshio, *Kōshitsu Seido Gairon* (n.p., n.d.). A copy of this work was kindly lent me by a former Imperial Household Ministry official who said it was one of the few personal treasures he salvaged from the fires during the war. The *Gairon* was evidently the basis for Sakamaki's *Kōshitsu Seido Kōwa* (Tokyo: Iwanami Shoten, 1934), which is very similar in content.
71. Ibid., "Appendix," p. 2.
72. Ibid.

welfare of the nation as its primary principle, Shinto differs from other religions, which seek the salvation of all mankind. To pray to the gods is to pray for the welfare of the nation. Therefore, "these Shinto services have a deep and special quality, in fact and ideally, in that they are the divinely appointed work in the lifetime of the emperor himself."[73] Given the relation between rites and national welfare, "for our people to abandon reverence for the Gods of Heaven and Earth is completely impermissible."[74] The ultimate result of uniting Shinto rites with the court was to make the emperor a transcendental figure embodying the will of the gods in the Japanese polity—at least for those who accepted and believed in those rites.

Assuming a more practical and less muddled pattern of thinking on the part of those who engineered the Restoration settlement of 1868–89, how did the architects of the emperor's new role in the Japanese polity relate rites and rule, the imperial institution and political power?

Upon returning from Europe after his investigation of Western constitutional monarchies in 1883, Itō Hirobumi indicated that the focus of popular loyalty would also be made the focus of state power: the imperial institution. Having discussed his views on a constitution for Japan with Motoda Eifu, Itō reported to the throne on September 23, 1883 in order to allay the many fears about his intentions regarding such a constitution. In his discourse to the emperor, Itō declared that in Japan the emperor "of one line unbroken for ages eternal" exercised general control over all matters of state: "This is the national polity unparalleled throughout all nations."[75] As the person primarily responsible for creating the constitution, Itō therefore intended to legitimize government power by placing the emperor at the center of political authority. Since political power at this time had in fact gravitated to the government oligarchs, court rites would thus be made to serve government rule.

The relation of rites to rule eventually settled on was revealingly put by Itō in his explanation of the extensive imperial prerogatives granted by the draft *Constitution of the Great Empire of Japan,*

73. Ibid., p. 3.
74. Ibid.
75. Shumpo Kōtsui Shōkai, 2:365.

popularly known as the Meiji Constitution.[76] The draft was placed before the Privy Council, chaired not unnaturally by Itō himself, in June 1888. Itō argued:

> When we turn now to enacting a Constitution we must first seek the pivotal axis of the nation, firmly establishing what that axis shall be. Without such an axis the Government will lose its discipline and the State will eventually collapse when politics are entrusted to the reckless discussion of the people. . . . In Europe, not only have the people become proficient in constitutional government since it first took seed; there was also religion, and this constituted the axis, deeply infusing the popular mind. In this the people's hearts found unity. In our country, however, the power of the religions is feeble; not one can be deemed an axis of State. . . . In our country there is only the Imperial House that can become such an axis. With this point in mind I placed great value on the Throne's prerogatives and endeavored as far as possible not to restrict them in this draft Constitution.[77]

Itō thus saw in the imperial house a native Japanese emotional equivalent to Western religion. With Shinto rites firmly lodged in the court by 1877, the Meiji Constitution in effect grafted Western forms of monarchical prerogative onto the trunk of nationalized Shinto. Implicit in Itō's reasoning was the proposition that rite makes might: rites antecedent to prerogative would unify Japanese loyalty around a Western form of state power.

The Meiji Constitution was ratified by the Privy Council and proclaimed on February 11, 1889, the anniversary of the day when the Emperor Jimmu was alleged to have taken the throne almost 2,550 years before. In that document the emperor's moral authority was fused with political authority in the form of vast imperial preroga-

76. Our concern here is with the implications of the Restoration settlement for the imperial institution's role in politics and the emperor's personal relation to the political process, not the evolution of the Meiji Constitution. The theories and countertheories proposed up to 1889 have been admirably covered elsewhere: see Pittau, *Political Thought in Early Meiji Japan;* and George Akita, *Foundations of Constitutional Government in Modern Japan, 1868–1900* (Cambridge, Mass.: Harvard University Press, 1967). It is sufficient to note here that the Meiji Constitution, like palace autonomy and the nationalization of Shinto, was produced by experimentation and compromise—theoretical, institutional, and political. I have dwelt at length on the separation of court and government and the union of court and rites simply because these critical aspects of the imperial institution's modern political development have not been adequately dealt with.

77. Shimizu Noboru, *Teikoku Kempō Seitei Kaigi,* pp. 88–89, quoted in Maruyama Masao, *Nihon no Shisō,* 8th ed. (Tokyo: Iwanami Shinsho, 1964), pp. 29–30.

tives. The emperor was declared "sacred and inviolable" (Article 3), thereby making explicit his transcendent position based on rites. He "combined in his being the supreme rights of rule" (Article 4) and "exercised supreme command over the Army and Navy" (Article 11). From these two basic prerogatives flowed the many prerogatives of administration, welfare, legislation, and emergency that were reserved to him by the constitution.[78]

This immense range of imperial prerogatives was new to the role of the emperor. With one exception in the fourteenth century, not since the ninth century had the emperor claimed or been argued to possess even closely equivalent powers. In 1868, however, the emperor had inherited the shogun's traditional political powers, most notably those involving military command. These powers were recast as prerogatives similar to those held by authoritarian monarchs in the West. Other prerogatives, such as that of legislation, were derived solely from Western models. The emperor thus became the source of executive, legislative, and judicial powers, and all government acts were issued in his name.

To argue that this fusion of rite and prerogative was a violation of the separation of church and state, as several scholars in prewar Japan did, is somewhat misleading.[79] Historically, there was no single institution of church in pre-Restoration Japan to come in conflict with a single institution of state, in any way comparable to the struggles in Europe. Nor was there any philosophical issue of rendering unto Caesar that which is Caesar's and unto God that which is God's. Lacking both institutional and philosophical bases for a church-state controversy, there was consequently no basis for the principle of separation of church and state. The emperor's celebration of Shinto rites, moreover, resembled in many respects the performance of high rituals of state by Western monarchs. Much of the ceremony of the Western monarchies is of religious origin, and some of the rituals of state still carry religious significance. The Queen of England remains the formal head of the Church of Eng-

78. "Dai Nippon Teikoku Kempō", in Naikaku Kiroku Ka, 1942, vol. 1, pt. 1, chap. 1, sec. 1, pp. 7–18.
79. This argument was often advanced by the prewar Constitutional School of Japanese legal scholars led by Minobe Tatsukichi. See Miyazawa Toshiyoshi's review of Minobe's *Chikujō Kempō Seigi* in *Kokka Gakkai Zasshi* 42, no. 9 (September 1928), pp. 165–72.

land. The involvement of Western monarchs in such ceremonies and official positions has not generally been held to violate the distinction between church and state.

Shinto was something less than a religion, something more than formal ceremony. As it was developed and applied to Japan's national life after 1868, Shinto symbolized that the Japanese were Japanese, united in a national community that was peculiarly their own and somehow distinct from and superior to other national entities. The weakness of the Japanese religions, noted by Itō, meant that there was no institutional challenge of any major import to the nationalization of Shinto. And the absence of a religious challenge to Shinto may have produced a more intense sentimental adherence to nationalized Shinto than might otherwise have occurred.

Since the major figure in Shinto rites was the emperor, quasi-religious authority was given to state power by Itō and the framers of the constitution. In this respect, Sakuma Shōzan's apt slogan for Japan's modernizing aspirations, "Eastern ethics, Western techniques," may be applied with equal aptness to the government produced by the Restoration settlement. The basis of Japan's "immutable and peerless" national polity (*kokutai*) was the imperial institution, whose spiritual and ethical authority ultimately derived from Shinto rites implicit in the constitution's provision that the emperor was "sacred and inviolable."[80] The constitution was explicit in stipulating a Western form of mutable state structure (*seitai*): the

80. "National polity" (*kokutai*) was the subject of academic and political controversy in prewar Japan as well as in the immediate postwar period. There were at least three meanings, all of which were predicated on the existence of the imperial institution: (1) sovereignty residing in the imperial institution, (2) the existence of an imperial line from which authority flowed, and (3) the presence of an imperial institution symbolizing the spiritual unity of the Japanese state and people. None of these definitions was clearly distinct from the others and one or more could be combined or emphasized depending on what one wished to argue. Miyazawa Toshiyoshi, who inherited the mantle of leadership of the Constitutional School from Minobe Tatsukichi, has argued that imperial sovereignty, in the Western sense of being the final locus of decision-making power, was the most widely accepted definition in prewar Japan. But because the emperor's spiritual role, based on Shinto rites, was central to both sovereignty and ancestral authority, and because that role was the only consistent role played by the imperial institution historically, I have taken a position that tends to support definitions (2) and (3). This ambiguous position is consonant with the final and hopelessly ambiguous discussion of the national polity produced by the Japanese government in the 1930s. "National polity" was literally the national system, "state structure" (*seitai*) was literally the government system. In prewar Japan the imperial institution was central to both.

Japanese monarchy. To exaggerate, the existence of the imperial institution was to be eternal, the operation of the monarchy temporal. It is in this context that Itō's insistence on the centrality of the imperial institution to state power should be evaluated, not in the context of the separation of church and state.

Itō and the Meiji oligarchs thus hoped to make the imperial institution an impregnable stronghold of political legitimacy, the centripetal point around which statesmen would gather to govern. The theory of imperial prerogative was the basis for political leadership that looked to the imperial institution and not elsewhere for its justification. Religious and natural law, the "people," a social "class"—none had theoretical independence from the emperor and none became sources of distinctive doctrines that seriously challenged the theory of prerogative.[81] For example, Minobe Tatsukichi, perhaps prewar Japan's leading constitutional theorist, argued that Japan was an organic state under law. His rationalization of constitutional monarchy, widely accepted between 1913 and 1935, did not, however, attack the sovereign position of the emperor. He made the emperor the highest organ of state and attempted at most to make the Cabinet, appointed by the emperor, ultimately responsible to the lower house of the Imperial Diet—but on the basis of the emperor's legislative prerogative. Minobe in effect made the elected house of the Imperial Diet the central of several governmental institutions competing to declare the Imperial Will in politics during the 1920s and 1930s.[82]

81. See, for example, Robert A. Scalapino, *Democracy and the Party Movement in Prewar Japan: The Failure of the First Attempt* (Berkeley and Los Angeles: University of California Press, 1962); and Maruyama Masao, *Thought and Behaviour in Modern Japanese Politics,* ed. Ivan Morris (London: Oxford University Press, 1963).

82. Minobe is the subject of an outstanding study by Frank O. Miller, *Minobe Tatsukichi: Interpreter of Constitutionalism in Japan* (Berkeley and Los Angeles: University of California Press, 1965). Although Minobe was forced to resign from the House of Peers in 1935 for allegedly transgressing the sacred national polity, it is difficult to conceive of a Japanese more loyal to the imperial institution (ibid., pp. 165–253). At the end of the war Minobe resisted all revisions of the constitution that would demote the imperial institution or suggest popular sovereignty. He argued that the Japanese have unbounded faith in the imperial house, a faith unparalleled in any other nation. The war was the willful doing of the military, which was completely oblivious to the general will of the people. Only from loyalty to the emperor did the Japanese devote themselves to the war effort. Should Japan lose the imperial house as its central institution, there would be a ceaseless train of disturbances (Minobe Tatsukichi, "Minshu Shugi to Waga Gikai Seido," *Sekai* [January 1946]: 21–24).

If, however, the emperor's prerogatives were attributed to him personally or wielded by him in fact, how could he avoid censure when the government failed to solve a major political crisis? How could he wield prerogatives and yet be "inviolable"? In addition to palace autonomy and the union of court and rites, two measures were taken by the oligarchs. First the Ministers of State were to be individually responsible to the emperor for the government and its policies. Article 55 of the constitution made each Minister of State responsible for "advising and assisting" the emperor in the exercise of his prerogatives, and therefore the Ministers of State, not the emperor, were to be held accountable for governmental actions based on the emperor's prerogatives.[83]

Second, sovereignty in the constitution was placed in the imperial line, not in the emperor as an individual ruler. As Itō explained in his commentaries on the constitution:

The sovereign power of reigning over and of governing the State, is inherited by the Emperor from His Ancestors, and by Him bequeathed to His posterity. All the different legislative as well as executive powers of the State, by means of which He reigns over the country and governs the people, are united in this Most Exalted Personage, who thus holds in His hands, as it were, all the ramifying threads of the political life of the country, . . .[84]

Miyazawa Toshiyoshi, a leading constitutional theorist in postwar Japan, has termed the type of sovereignty that existed under the Meiji Constitution "oracle sovereignty."[85] The emperor was the transmitter, not the independent judge, of the Imperial Will. The traditional role of the emperor for "ages eternal" as medium between the Japanese people and the gods was therefore adopted as the basis of sovereignty in the Meiji Constitution.

Noting the vast difference that separated the Japanese emperor from Western divine-right monarchs, Maruyama Masao has argued that

83. "Dai Nippon Teikoku Kempō", in Naikaku Kiroku Ka, 1942, vol. 1, pt. 1, chap. 1, sec. l, pp. 7–18.

84. Itō Hirobumi, Commentaries on the Constitution of the Empire of Japan, trans. Itō Miyoji, 3d ed. (Chū-ō Daigaku, 1931), p. 7.

85. Miyazawa Toshiyoshi, Kempō, 4th ed., rev. (Tokyo: Yūhikaku, 1953), pp. 25, 157–58.

The amalgamation of spiritual authority with political power was regarded not as any new departure in the concept of sovereignty, but simply as a return to 'the ancient days of the Jimmu Foundation.' Though the Emperor was regarded as the embodiment of ultimate value, he was infinitely removed from the possibility of creating values out of nothing. His Majesty was heir to the Imperial line unbroken for ages eternal and he ruled by virtue of the final injunctions of his ancestors. The Imperial Constitution, granted to the people in 1889, was not regarded as having been created by the Emperor himself; rather it was a document that 'transmitted the immutable law according to which the land has been governed.'

Thus the Emperor too was saddled with a burden—in his case a tradition that derived from the infinitely remote past. It was only because his existence was inextricably involved with the ancestral tradition, in such a way that he and his Imperial Ancestors formed a single unit, that he was regarded as being the ultimate embodiment of internal values.[86]

The emperor's prerogatives were prerogatives of the imperial line, and the Meiji Constitution embodied the bequeathed instructions of the emperor's ancestors. His role as medium, through rites, between subjects and ancestors placed political authority beyond his immediate person and fused the past, present, and future in an unbroken continuum of eternal Right. This displacement into antiquity of political authority for present political rule was a deliberate and creative act of statesmanship by the drafters of the constitution. The Ministers of State were responsible to an emperor who in turn was responsible to his ancestors. Since the emperor was not even in theory a free agent in the process of ruling but acted only in accordance with bequeathed instructions, the Ministers of State were left potentially the sole free agents in governing the nation.

The enactment of the Imperial House Law (Kōshitsu Tempan) concurrently with the Meiji Constitution was the final stone in the foundation of the Meiji state. Explicitly recognizing the principle of palace autonomy, the Meiji Constitution reserved to the imperial house its self-governance. Itō's intent in the Imperial House Law, as indeed in the constitution, was to preserve the dignity of the throne "coeval with heaven and earth."[87] The Imperial House Law was not

86. Maruyama Masao, Thought and Behaviour, p. 20.
87. Shumpo Kōtsui Shōkai, 2:574; Constitution of the Great Empire of Japan, Article 74.

even to be discussed, much less altered, by the national legislature. In his commentaries Itō states that the Imperial House Law "will be regarded as the family law of the Imperial House. That these provisions are not expressed in the Constitution shows that no interference of the subject shall ever be tolerated regarding them."[88] Against allowing the Diet a participatory role in determining when a regency should be instituted, for example, Itō argued that if "the decision of a matter of great importance to the Imperial family is thus delegated to the will of the majority of the people there would be a tendency to bring about the degradation of the Imperial dignity."[89] To make the Imperial House Law as sacred and inviolable as the imperial institution itself, therefore, Itō first placed it beyond the reach of "the people" and their representatives in the Diet.

At the same time, Itō attempted to buttress the immutability of the Imperial House Law by the fiction that it merely set forth practices which had existed from time immemorial. The Imperial House Law was the ancestral law of the imperial line—provisions governing the imperial family that were a "clarification of bequeathed instructions" from the imperial forebears.[90] The Imperial House Law was not "enacted" but "clarified," not created but already extant. It was not to be amended even at the emperor's sole discretion;[91] amendment, if required, was to be made by the Imperial Family Council and the Privy Council.[92] The emperor was thus freed of personal responsibility even for his own house law. As with the constitution, Itō and the government oligarchs made every attempt to remove from the emperor any personal initiative for which he might subsequently be held accountable.

The Imperial House Law gave concrete expression to palace au-

88. Itō Hirobumi, p. 6.
89. Ibid., pp. 33–34.
90. Kōshitsu Tempan, in Naikaku Kiroku Ka, 1942, vol. 1, pt. 1, chap. 1., sec. 2, p. 21.
91. Shumpo Kōtsui Shōkai, 2:571–75.
92. Naikaku Kiroku Ka, 1942, vol. 1, pt. 1, chap. 1, sec. 2, p. 28. Created by the Imperial House Law of 1889, the Imperial Family Council as modified in 1907 was composed of all male members of the imperial family of majority age who were eligible to become Regent. The Lord Keeper of the Privy Seal, President of the Privy Council, Imperial Household Minister, Minister of Justice, and President of the Supreme Court participated without vote. In addition to amending powers, the Imperial Family Council and the Privy Council decided on modifications in the order of succession to the throne and on the creation of a regency. The Imperial Family Council also dealt with disciplinary matters involving members of the imperial family.

tonomy.[93] Its sixty-two articles dealt with succession, accession, and enthronement ceremonies, titles, regency, tutors and education, imperial family members, imperial house expenses, property litigation, the Imperial Family Council, amendment, and coming of age. As head of the imperial family, the emperor exercised supervision over that family (Article 35). He sanctioned the marriages of the family members (Article 41), appointed or approved tutors to their children (Article 37), approved travel abroad for family members (Article 43), sanctioned the summons or arrest of a family member (Article 51), and suspended or divested of rights a family member who humiliated or degraded the imperial house or was disobedient (Article 52). In the execution of all major duties the emperor was advised by the Imperial Family Council and the Privy Council.[94]

Strangely enough, however, the Imperial House Law was not promulgated with the Meiji Constitution on February 11, 1889. It is to be found neither in the *Kampō* (Official Gazette) for February 1889, in which the constitution appears, nor in the *Hōrei Zensho* (Complete Laws) for 1889 or 1890. When it was promulgated in later editions of the *Hōrei Zensho,* it was not countersigned by the Ministers of State, as was the usual practice with laws. Minobe Tatsukichi has surmised that the Imperial House Law was not promulgated in 1889 because its framers considered it as applying only to the internal affairs of the imperial house. Minobe claims that the drafters believed the Imperial House Law had no bearing on the political life of the people and did not concern regulations of the state. In support of his opinion, he cites Itō Hirobumi's commentaries on the Imperial House Law, in which Itō declares that "the Imperial House Law is something the Imperial House has itself enacted as its house law; it is not something, therefore, to be promulgated to [Japanese] subjects by public ceremony."[95] It would appear that Itō and those responsible for the Imperial House Law did not regard affairs of court as matters for either the government or the public: the affairs of court should remain a mystery to ensure greater transcendence for the imperial institution.

93. Sōrifu, *Kanchō Benran, 2:3.*
94. *Naikaku Kiroku Ka, 1942, vol. 1, pt. 1, chap. 1, sec. 2, pp. 21–28.*
95. Minobe Tatsukichi, *Kempō Kōwa,* 1st ed., rev. (Tokyo: Yūhikaku, 1918), p. 466.

Minobe took issue with Itō's interpretation of the "private" nature of the Imperial House Law while agreeing with him on the spiritual centrality of the imperial house. He argued that the Imperial House Law was in fact a fundamental law of the land because it established two rules of basic constitutional importance: provisions for succession to the throne and regulations for the creation of a regency. Far from concerning merely the private affairs of the imperial family, the Imperial House Law bore a critical relation to the state. As evidence, Minobe cited the 1907 decree that made revisions and supplements to the Imperial House Law subject to countersignature by the Ministers of State and also to promulgation.[96] The supplement to the Imperial House Law of February 21, 1907 was consequently countersigned by the Prime Minister and all Ministers of State. The only other prewar supplement or revision of the Imperial House Law—that of February 28, 1918—was similarly countersigned and promulgated.[97]

At the same time, Minobe argued that the Imperial House Law was of all state provisions the one "most based on national conditions peculiar to Japan." From the standpoint of Japan's "unique national polity," matters pertaining to the imperial house dare not be subject to participation by the people, and consequently the Diet's power to consent to laws did not reach imperial house affairs in any way whatever.[98] Even as outspoken a constitutionalist as Minobe Tatsukichi willingly acknowledged the principle of palace autonomy and its corollary: Japan's unique national polity centered on its imperial institution. Although Minobe may have disagreed with Itō on a host of issues regarding constitutional interpretation, the transcendental position of the throne as the center of Japanese life was not one of them.

By the 1930s the theoretical relationships between rites and rule and between the Imperial House Law and the Meiji Constitution had become blurred to a considerable extent. Some constitutional theorists, such as Uesugi Shinkichi, argued that the "emperor is in

96. Ibid.; Kōshiki Rei, "Chokurei" no. 6, January 31, 1907, Articles 4 and 5, in Hōrei Zensho, 1907, vol. 1.

97. Naikaku Kiroku Ka, 1942, vol. 1, pt. 1, chap. 1, sec. 2, pp. 31–33, 37–38.

98. Minobe Tatsukichi, Kempō Kōwa, p. 468.

fact the state"—stressing the principles of absolute Western monarchies adapted to Japan's unique national polity. Others, like Minobe, made the emperor the highest organ of a state under law—stressing the constitutional aspects of Western monarchy. Yet others, notably Kakehi Katsuhiko, posited the centrality of Shinto and Shinto rites in Japan's prewar constitutional order. At the root of the confusion was the issue of sovereignty—its location and the consequent distribution of powers among political entities such as the Diet. The Orthodox School of Uesugi and others clearly maintained that the emperor was sovereign. The Constitutional School, led by Minobe, argued that the emperor was sovereign "under law" and that the "supreme rights of rule" were invested in the state as a legal person. The Shinto School dissolved the issue of sovereignty in a murky fusion of rite and rule in the imperial line, placing it in the eternal "becoming" of the imperial line in history, a Japanese version of the Hegelian unfolding of cultural progress concretely expressed by Japan's imperial institution.[99]

Sakamaki Yoshio, the imperial household official whose tortured logic on the role of rites has already been noted, attempted to resolve the ambiguities that had arisen by integrating many aspects from many schools of interpretation. Following Minobe's argument that the imperial house was a public, not a private entity, Sakamaki asserted that since the imperial house had at its center the wielder of the supreme rights of rule in the state, "the state and the Imperial House are one and inseparable."[100] "The vitality of the Imperial House is nothing less than the prosperity of the State."[101] The

99. Miller, Minobe Tatsukichi, *Kempō Kōwa*, Suzuki Yasuzō, *Meiji Kempō to Shin Kempō* (Tokyo: Sekai Shoin, 1947), pp. 71 ff.; Kokuritsu Kokkai Toshokan, *Kempō Shiryō Tenji Kai Mokuroku* (Tokyo: 1957); Uesugi Shinkichi, *Kokutai Kempō oyobi Kensei*, 2d ed. (Tokyo: Yūhikaku, 1917). Kakehi Katsuhiko, *Dai Nippon Teikoku Kempō no Kompon Gi* (Tokyo: Iwanami Shoten, 1936). Among the plethora of schools of interpretation, the two most important were the Orthodox School (Uesugi Shinkichi) and the Constitutional School (Minobe Tatsukichi). The word in the Meiji Constitution that has frequently been translated as "sovereignty" is *tōchiken*, which literally means "supreme rights of rule" or "prerogatives of government," just as *tōsuiken* means "prerogatives of supreme command." The word used by Minobe for sovereignty, or sovereign power, is *shuken*, the word used for sovereignty in the present *Constitution of Japan*. It is likely that a terminological problem complicated the controversy over sovereignty and its relation to the "national polity" both in prewar Japan and in the immediate postwar period.
100. Sakamaki Yoshio, *Kōshitsu Seido Kōwa*, p. 10.
101. Ibid., p.9.

constituents of a monarchy, states Sakamaki, are a ruling monarch, a royal family from whom successors will come, and a general populace. It is the state's function, in accordance with these three constituents, to make the position of the monarch secure and tranquil, to make the monarch and the royal house "shine forth with increasing splendor," and to advance the people's welfare, tranquility, and national consciousness. In a constitutional monarchy like Japan, argued Sakamaki, the people assist the monarch in ruling, the monarch seeks the advice of public leaders and the Ministers of State, and the people participate in maintaining the public welfare. One aspect of the separation of court and government can be found in the division of functions among those who advise the emperor. On court affairs the Imperial Household Minister, the Imperial Family Council, and the Privy Council advise. The separation of court and government, however, is merely a division of functions: the emperor's court and government prerogatives both derive from his position as Chief of State. Consequently, the Imperial House Law is as much a constitution as the constitution itself. Although the distinction between court and government embodied in these two basic laws makes Japan's a dual legal system, Sakamaki argued, both are equally state laws deriving from the emperor's indivisible supreme right of rule.[102]

Separate but equal, the Imperial House Law and the constitution achieved reverential status by the 1930s as the oracular pronouncements of the apotheosized Meiji Emperor. As already noted, the Imperial House Law was supplemented only twice between 1889 and 1945; the effect was to make the imperial house a more public entity and to elevate the Imperial House Law to equal status with the constitution. The Meiji Constitution remained unchanged to the letter.

Made structurally and legally independent by 1889, the imperial house was placed in a transcendental but symbiotic relation to political power. The principle of palace autonomy was firmly united with the emperor's moral authority implied by the union of court and rites. The resultant moral transcendence was then made the

102. Ibid., pp. 13–22.

basis of political authority. These linkages evolved as the result of (1) compromises between the theories and aspirations of traditionalists, such as Motoda Eifu, and those of the modernizing oligarchs, such as Itō Hirobumi; (2) political conflict between the "in" oligarchs and the "out" leaders of "public opinion," conflicts which threatened to embroil the emperor as well as unseat the oligarchs; and (3) creative nation-building efforts by the Meiji oligarchs, who eclectically applied both native Japanese and imported Western theories of state power in seeking to place their political power on an unassailable foundation of legitimacy.

The implications of the theoretical and institutional arrangements arrived at by 1889 were twofold. First, the imperial institution was hopefully placed beyond the criticism of the "Japanese subject". As high priest, shogun, and constitutional monarch, the emperor was to be the transcendental institution of state power, "far from the smoke of human habitations, no one ever to invade its sanctity." This awesome distance was to provide the basis of popular loyalty and obedience to the state. Second, the emperor was not to be a free agent in an open political process. His personal will, which was fallible, was not identical with the Imperial Will, which was by definition the eternal will of the imperial ancestors. This in turn meant restricting the emperor's public role to formal rituals, such as Shinto rites and the formal sanctioning of government decisions. By removing the emperor from open and direct participation in the decision-making process, while issuing all government acts in the emperor's name, the oligarchs apparently hoped to ensure their own power to develop Japanese political institutions around a core of bureaucratic initiative supported by prerogative above and loyalty below.

Surrounded by walls and moats in the 275-acre castle that had formerly been the fortress of shogunal power, the emperor found his personal freedom of movement, as well as his personal will in politics, forfeited for shogunal powers recast in Western monarchical form. An indication of the price the emperor paid by becoming the sacrosanct center of Japanese politics is the decreased number of imperial outings from his Tokyo residence after 1890. Table 1 lists the number of imperial tours from 1868 to 1910, with a partial listing of the purposes

TABLE 1.   IMPERIAL TOURS, 1868–1910

Year	Total	Within Tokyo	Outside Tokyo	Purpose[a] G	M	R	S	I	P
1868	17	9	8						
1869	37	36	1						
1870	87	86	1	0	4	3	0	0	80
1871	112	111	1						
1872	42	38	4						
1873	105	101	4						
1874	80	77	3						
1875	100	97	3	50	9	1	1	0	39
1876	55	51	4						
1877	58	56	2						
1878	89	86	3						
1879	98	96	2						
1880	163	161	2	135	13	0	8	0	7
1881	127	118	9						
1882	96	91	5						
1883	95	91	4						
1884	81	75	6						
1885	57	55	2	29	9	0	9	1	9
1886	36	33	3						
1887	44	42	2						
1888	62	60	2						
1889	47	46	1						
1890	47	44	3	24	9	0	7	0	7
1891	21	17	4						
1892	21	19	2						
1893	20	18	2						
1894	18	14	4						
1895	9	8	1	1	4	1	2	0	1
1896	21	18	3						
1897	4	3	1						
1898	10	9	1						
1899	25	23	2						
1900	25	21	4	11	11	0	2	1	0
1901	8	7	1						
1902	16	15	1						
1903	14	11	3						
1904	12	12	0						
1905	12	10	2	4	3	2	2	0	1
1906	18	17	1						
1907	17	15	2						
1908	13	12	1						
1909	18	17	1						
1910	18	16	2	5	9	0	2	0	2

for which they were made. It is abundantly clear that the period of the Restoration settlement, from 1868 to 1889, was also the period of the emperor's greatest mobility. From 1871 to 1880 there were an average of 90.2 imperial tours a year; from 1881 to 1890 the average was 69.2 per year.

Once the new state was formed, however, the emperor was increasingly restricted to his palace. Between 1891 and 1900 there were but 17.4 imperial outings a year; from 1901 to 1910, only 14.6. And, as table 1 clearly shows, the emperor did not go to the government very often after 1890; the government came to him. The decrease in imperial visits to the government does not necessarily mean, of course, that the emperor's political influence, if there was any, decreased. It does mean that whatever influence he had over government leaders was exercised within the palace sanctuary. His personal will was restricted to those close to the throne: leaders of the palace bureaucracy and those of the government, civil and military, who were allowed access to his castled prerogatives. To exaggerate, the emperor's personal will ended at the palace gates where public scrutiny began. The keepers of the gates were the officials of the palace bureaucracy.

SOURCE FOR TABLE 1: Kunai Daijin Kambō Sōmuka, *Gyōkō Hyō* (Tokyo: 1933).

ᵃ The code under *Purpose*, based on places visited by the emperor, is as follows: G = government; M = military, including maneuvers and academies; R = religious institutions, such as shrines; S = social, including prefectural tours, attendance at cultural events, and visits to factories; I = international, such as banquets with royal visitors held outside the palace; P = personal, such as summer visits to the imperial villas.

CHAPTER THREE

THE PALACE BUREAUCRACY:
GATEKEEPERS OF THE IMPERIAL WILL

THE OLD SHOGUNAL FORTRESS was ideally suited to be the new imperial palace. With its spacious grounds, securely walled and moated, it gave physical meaning to palace autonomy and imperial transcendence. It also provided ample space to house the palace bureaucracy which managed the affairs of the imperial institution and isolated the emperor as a person from the public Imperial Will; by 1900 the number of palace officials had grown to approximately four thousand.

What was the structure and composition of the palace bureaucracy? What specifically did it manage and how? We may begin by attempting a schematization of the roles created for the emperor as a logical result of the theory of legitimacy and the institutional arrangements evolved by the Restoration settlement of 1868–89 (fig. 1). Although the imperial institution tended to be undifferentiated to its more dedicated adherents, the analysis of the separation of court and government in chapter 2 suggests that there were two fundamental imperial roles: Emperor-in-Court and Emperor-in-State. Both roles had two aspects: Emperor-in-Public and Emperor-in-Chambers. The Emperor-in-Public represented the Imperial Will in politics and society; the Emperor-in-Chambers was the emperor as a person who expressed his own views and ideas to those "close to the throne."

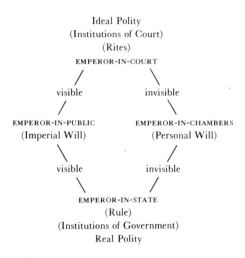

FIGURE 1.   IMPERIAL ROLES IN PREWAR JAPAN

The Emperor-in-Court. Bagehot informs us that the British
monarch in the late nineteenth century performed the "dignified"
function in government and that the monarchy's dignity derived from
its "mystery." The dignified mystery of the monarchy, however, was
directed not so much toward the "efficient" political leaders as
toward the general public. Its mystery served to make the monarchy
the focus of popular loyalty and identification, deflecting public attention away from the tough business of actually ruling the nation
and how that was accomplished. To exaggerate, the dignified
mystery of the monarchy served the purposes of efficient rule by
eliciting popular obedience to political decisions produced by an almost invisible political process.[1]

Mystery, by definition, meant that the actual workings of the
monarchy would be screened from popular scrutiny so that the
monarch would appear to be above the ordinary lot of men. In Japan
the need for such transcendence was apparently intensified by the vast
changes in Japanese society that were planned or anticipated by the
modernizing oligarchs after 1868. Fostering an almost religious at-

1. Walter Bagehot, *The English Constitution* (London: Kegan Paul, Trench, Trübner,
1904).

tachment to the imperial institution, Restoration leaders and their heirs attempted to make the Imperial Will a diffuse mystery around which all kinds of individuals and social groups could be mobilized.

The mystery of the Japanese imperial institution was, of course, already there to be adapted by the Restoration leaders. Throughout Japan's recorded history the emperor had been the most exalted figure in Japanese society. By virtue of his hereditary position, he had exercised an exclusive monopoly over certain religious rites that many considered basic to the well-being of the entire society. The court had also been the repository of ancient Japanese culture and its accretions from China. Indeed, from the twelfth century onward, rites and cultural practices were the only consistently autonomous functions performed by the imperial institution. Finally, the emperor and his court had been isolated from society at large and from the seat of de facto government for over 250 years when the Restoration occurred in 1868. The restored emperor was very much a transcendental mystery to the vast majorty of Japanese.

Given this background and the fact that the emperor had not ruled for centuries, the Japanese imperial institution had perhaps more potential than any other modern monarchy to become the symbol of the nation as a people, as distinct from the nation as a state. This distinction may very well have been the true basis for the separation of court and government and for the functional union of court and rites on the one hand and of government and rule on the other, as discussed in chapter 2. The new imperial institution, bringing its distinctive character to bear in the building of a new Japan, could be made to symbolize the unity and continuity of Japanese society as it underwent the disruptive effects of extensive modernization. Thus, when the emperor made a tour of the provinces, presided over an imperial poetry contest, or performed rites at one of the national Shinto shrines, he symbolized the unity of the Japanese people, their shared cultural heritage and skills, and their unique religious communality, of which he was chief priest. He was Emperor-in-Court acting as Emperor-in-Public, presumably reminding all Japanese that, by virtue of his majesty and mystery, they were a unique and united people.

The Emperor-in-Court also symbolized something new in his

public functions: the desirable course of Japan's modernization. The emperor and imperial family were among the first to don Western dress and to use the latest modes of transportation. The imperial house was first in line to invest in new manufacturing enterprises. Modern educational facilities received imperial support and the emperor distributed rewards to those who successfully introduced "Western techniques" into Japanese society. The emperor and his court were thus made to stand for the modernizing aspirations of the Japanese people as well.

The first duty of the palace bureaucracy was the management of the Emperor-in-Court as Emperor-in-Public. In this function the palace bureaucrats were gatekeepers of the Imperial Will in Japanese society, sealing off the emperor's personal will so that the Imperial Will might be made the focal point of unquestioning popular esteem and reverence. To do so, the palace bureaucracy was divided into two components: an outer side and an inner side. The outer side contained the bureaucratic machinery for maintaining the transcendental dignity of the emperor in society. It arranged formal appearances of the emperor and imperial family members, wrote and regulated publicity, managed the imperial estate and finances of the imperial house, and watched over its own bureaucratic concerns. The inner side managed the Emperor-in-Court as Emperor-in-Chambers. The officials of the inner side were chamberlains, valets, aides, tutors, ladies-in-waiting. They provided for the personal well-being and private education of the emperor and imperial family. As immediate companions and servants to the emperor, they were the innermost guardians of his privacy. They were consequently responsible for keeping the emperor's personal will and his human indiscretions from escaping into the public arena. The palace bureaucracy, both its outer and inner sides, was to see that the emperor as a person was made invisible. Only the emperor as a social paragon, as an ideal, was to be visible.

Finally, the imperial institution was to be the expression of all that was true, good, and beautiful in the Japanese polity. In its structure, therefore, the court was to be a model of the ideal polity, of the ideal social arrangements that ought to prevail in Japan. The second basic duty of the palace bureaucracy was to maintain itself as social paragon.

The Emperor-in-State. The emperor was also to be the transcendental source of state power. For centuries, of course, the emperor had been the source of political legitimacy. It was his theoretical and physical proximity to politics that was new. As Emperor-in-State the emperor was to express the Imperial Will in politics, and the Imperial Will was to be the referent for all acts of government. Just as the court was responsible to the Emperor-in-Court for maintaining the "ideal polity," the government was responsible to the Emperor-in-State for actuating the "real polity." Again, the emperor was not to be involved as a person but as an institution. The Emperor-in-State, as Emperor-in-Public, was to ratify decisions reached by responsible government leaders. As the final act in the prewar decision-making process, imperial ratification meant that a given policy was a legitimate decision of state, having been sanctioned by the Imperial Will. The Imperial Will in politics was not the emperor's personal will but the will of the "imperial line unbroken for ages eternal."

Far more than was the case with the emperor's personal will as Emperor-in-Court, it was imperative that the emperor's personal will as Emperor-in-State be hidden from public view. If the personal preferences of the emperor were publicly known on a sharply disputed issue prior to its resolution by the government, the emperor might well be charged with political partisanship and his individual role challenged. And if those preferences were widely credited as the source of a disastrous political policy, the imperial institution itself might be questioned, undermining the foundation of the state.

Because the mysterious dignity of the imperial institution was the basis of state power, however, the gatekeepers of the Imperial Will in politics were not only palace bureaucrats but virtually all political leaders of account: Ministers of State, generals and admirals of the Supreme Command, Privy Councillors, Elder Statesmen, and all others who by law or custom "advised and assisted" the emperor. But it was primarily the responsibility of four palace officials to manage the Emperor-in-State so that the palace remained the inviolable sanctuary of the emperor's personal will in politics. These four were the Imperial Household Minister, the Grand Chamberlain, the Chief Aide-de-Camp, and the Lord Keeper of the Privy Seal. To ensure the transcendental position of the throne in politics as well as in society, they were primarily concerned that the Emperor-in-State as Emperor-in-Public appear as the representative of the Imperial Will in politics, and therefore that the emperor's personal will be made invisible. The emperor was to be neither a political partisan nor a policy maker. He was to ratify decisions produced by government leaders with the Imperial Seal. With these considerations in mind, the four palace leaders cooperated with the government leaders of the day in arranging the public display and involvement of the Emperor-in-State.

In practice, of course, the distinction between Emperor-in-Court and Emperor-in-State, as well as that between Emperor-in-Chambers and Emperor-in-Public, proved ambiguous and very flexible, depending on the discretion of court and government leaders of the day, the nature of political pressures, and the state of public opinion. The Emperor-in-State and the Emperor-in-Court were one and the same person. And the gatekeepers between Emperor-in-Chambers and Emperor-in-Public for both these roles were the same palace officials. Ultimately it proved as difficult to preserve a fixed distinction between Emperor-in-Public and Emperor-in-Chambers as it was to maintain the distinction between Emperor-in-State and Emperor-in-Court. During the 1930s, for example, the emperor pursued his interest in marine biology within the palace sanctuary and collected specimens near the imperial villa at Hayama. Many found this activity beneath the sublime Japanese emperor. Was this avocation public or private? Public criticism of the emperor's pastime in the 1930s illustrates the prevailing state of public opinion as well as a major breach in the human fortifications around the Emperor-in-Chambers. At this time in Japan's modern history not even the emperor's private life was free from public scrutiny.

By way of contrast, there was little danger prior to 1910 that what the emperor said or did in chambers as Emperor-in-State or Emperor-in-Court would leak out indiscreetly to the public. Those who surrounded the emperor in the early half of Japan's modern history formed a tight knot of political leaders, the oligarchs, who may have disagreed among themselves over policies but not on the privileged status of remarks made by the Emperor-in-Chambers. There is no indication, for example, that the criticism of the emperor's passion for horsemanship made by the *Jiho* in 1878 reached the public or became a source of public criticism of the emperor at that time (see above, p. 20). Differences among the Meiji oligarchs, however great, were fought out person-to-person without visibly involving the Emperor-in-Chambers. The dearth of information about the Meiji emperor's personal views on politics and his personal policy preferences, if he had any, is a tribute to the cohesiveness of those close to the throne in preserving the privileged status of the Emperor-in-Chambers in both his roles as Emperor-in-State and Emperor-in-Court.

By the 1930s this knot of political leaders had been untied. Those close to the throne included institutional spokesmen, whose primary loyalties were to their respective institutions of imperial prerogative—Army, Navy, Home Ministry, Foreign Ministry. If the Emperor-in-Chambers favored one policy over another (personally or at the prompting of advisers), one of these institutional representatives would invariably be slighted. When the slighted representative conferred with his institutional cohorts, leaks to the outside often followed. Ominous remarks about "evil advisers" close to the throne might also filter through the injured institution and seep out to the press as well. The privileged nature of the emperor's remarks in chambers was thus destroyed by the encroachment of institutional pluralism into the very heart of the palace.

Our concern in this chapter is the institutional setting of palace politics: the structure and functions of the Imperial Household Ministry, which managed the day-to-day activities of the Emperor-in-Court and coordinated the routine affairs of the Emperor-in-State. We are concerned, therefore, with the palace bureaucracy, as structure and personnel, between 1885 and 1945. Chapter 4 describes the nature and function of palace leadership, which set the policies for managing the public Emperor-in-Court and coordinated the process of imperial ratification by the Emperor-in-State.

THE OFFICES AND PERSONNEL OF THE PALACE BUREAUCRACY

Many theorists and commentators have argued that the prewar Japanese state was a family writ large. Japanese subjects were not individual citizens but members of families which in turn were units of the national family headed by the imperial house. The emperor was the father of his people and all his subjects were bound to him by the absolute loyalty owed a father by his children.[2] If the prewar Japanese state was a family writ large, however, the imperial institution was a state writ small. The imperial institution had its own constitution, the Imperial House Law, and its own council, the Imperial Family Council, which jointly with the Privy Council advised the throne on that constitution. The Imperial Household Minister was responsible for advising and assisting the emperor in all matters of court, much as the Prime Minister and other Ministers of State were responsible in all matters of government. The Imperial Household Ministry housed in miniature all that in the large was encompassed by the government's bureaucracy: fiscal and property management, capital investment, foreign affairs, police functions, military operations, education, and welfare. The Imperial Household Ministry was thus a concrete symbol of modern bureaucratic government.

Not only did the Restoration settlement produce a separation of court and government and a unification of court and rites; it also resulted in a new administration for court affairs. The creation of modern bureaucratic structures in government was paralleled in court, especially during Itō Hirobumi's tenure as Imperial Household Secretary and Imperial Household Minister from 1884 to 1887. When he left the Imperial Household Ministry the bureaucratic structure for managing court affairs had been largely consolidated.

From the end of the Restoration settlement in 1889 to the end of 1945, when the prewar government ceased to operate as it had, only minor revisions were made in the functional domain and structure of the ministry. A list of its offices in 1945 indicates the wide range of functions under its jurisdiction (see table 2). The earliest date for each office, or its cognate predecessor, also indicates that the struc-

---

2. For example, see Maruyama Masao, *Thought and Behaviour,* pp. 36–37 and passim, for a critique, and Hibino Yukata, *Nippon Shindo Ron, or the National Ideals of the Japanese People* (Cambridge: Cambridge University Press, 1928), for a glorification of family-state ideals.

TABLE 2. OFFICES OF THE IMPERIAL HOUSEHOLD MINISTRY, 1945

Title of Office	Date Created
Minister's Secretariat	1908
Board of Chamberlains	1884
Board of the Ceremonies	1877
Office of Peerage Affairs	1877
Office of Imperial Mausolea	1878
Office of Archives	1883
Office of Court Physicians	1886
Office of Imperial Cuisine	1886
Office of the Privy Purse	1885
Office of Imperial Works	1885
Office of Imperial Stables	1886
General Affairs Bureau	1941
Bureau of Imperial Guards	1886
Board of Rituals	1939
Board of the Empress's Affairs	1869
Board of the Crown Prince's Affairs	1889
Board of the Empress Dowager's Affairs	1869
Imperial House Audit Bureau	1889
Imperial Poetry Bureau	1888
Imperial House Museum	1886
Shōsōin Curator's Office	1884
Bureau of Imperial Lands and Forests	1885
Peers School	1877
Peers School for Women	1885
Board of Prince Ri's Affairs	1911
Kyoto Office	1883
Office of Lord Keeper of the Privy Seal	1885
Office of Aides-de-Camp	1896

SOURCES: "Sho Sankō Hyō," handwritten document provided by the Imperial Household Agency; Sōrifu, *Kanchō Benran*, 2: 26–32; Matsushita Yoshio, *Meiji Gunsei Shi Ron*, 2 vols, (Tokyo: Yūhikaku, 1956), 2: 206.

NOTE: The English names of the offices have been taken mostly from prewar Japanese yearbooks and biographical dictionaries in English. Where I considered the name clumsy or ambiguous I took the liberty of changing it. The dates listed are as accurate as possible, given the frequent changes in office names from 1869 through 1945.

ture of the palace bureaucracy remained almost unchanged after 1889. Of the twenty-eight offices in 1945, only one was entirely new to the twentieth century: the Board of Prince Ri's Affairs created after the annexation of Korea in 1910. The Minister's Secretariat and the General Affairs Bureau, created in 1908 and 1941 respectively, were organizational refinements of two or three secretarial divisions of 1886–89. As noted in chapter 2, the Board of Rituals originated as a subdivision of the Board of the Ceremonies around 1880. Other offices, such as the Board of the Empress Dowager's Affairs, were created and abolished according to the composition of the imperial family at any given time. In addition, ad hoc offices were established and then terminated when their work was completed: palace construction bureaus, investigatory bodies, and the like.

One of the offices listed in table 2 was not formally included in the Imperial Household Ministry's organization chart: the Office of Aides-de-Camp. Organizationally, the Aides-de-Camp were considered members of the General Staff Office, and it was the military, not the palace bureaucracy, that initiated their appointments. But because the Aides were in fact regular attendants on the emperor and members of the imperial family, they were operationally very much a part of the palace bureaucracy, if not the Imperial Household Ministry strictly speaking. It also appears that an office for the Ladies-in-Waiting was never created as a formal part of the Imperial Household Ministry. Whether or not they were acknowledged as "officials" of the ministry, however, there were always Ladies-in-Waiting in the inner circle surrounding the Emperor-in-Chambers. Finally, there were a number of Court Advisers (*Kyūchū Komon*) and Imperial Household Ministry Consultants (*Kunai Shō Goyōgakari*) who advised the court on such matters as finances, diplomatic etiquette, Shinto ceremonies, and the distribution of honors. Some of them were extra court appointees while others served concurrently in formal court offices.

As the formal and informal offices of the Imperial Household Ministry reveal, management of the court was an extensive and many-faceted operation. A considerable bureaucracy was required to maintain the imperial institution as a state within a state. Table 3 lists at three-year intervals the total number of Imperial Household Ministry officials from 1924 to 1942, the numbers of persons in the two highest civil service categories of direct imperial appointee (*shinnin*) and imperial appointee (*chokunin*) for those years, and the number of officials in the Tokyo palace and in the provincial offices

TABLE 3. IMPERIAL HOUSEHOLD MINISTRY OFFICIALS, 1924–1942

Year[a]	Total	Direct Imperial Appointees[b]	Imperial Appointees[b]	Other	Tokyo	Provinces
1924	4,749	8	101	4,640	—	—
1927	4,581	7	109	4,465	—	—
1930	4,922	8	111	4,803	—	—
1933	4,899	8	115	4,776	—	—
1936	5,145	6	134	5,005	—	—
1939	5,342	6	140	5,196	3,161	2,181
1942	5,677	8	133	5,536	3,209	2,468

SOURCE: *Kunai Shō Shokuin Roku*, 1924–42. Although this source goes back to 1921, figures on total personnel and civil service allotments by rank are not listed until 1924.

a Three-year intervals have been selected because two of the annual *Kunai Shō Shokuin Roku*, those for 1926 and 1932, are missing from the Imperial Household Agency files and because there was neither a very great increase in officials over the twenty-year period nor much variation on a yearly basis.

b The number of direct imperial appointees from 1935 on includes both those officially of that rank and those treated as such. In 1942, for example, 6 of the 8 direct imperial appointees were officially of that rank. The same applies to those of imperial appointee rank: of the 133 imperial appointees in 1942, 75 were imperial appointees strictly speaking.

for years in which these figures were available. The personnel breakdown of the ministry's officials in 1943 was as follows:[3]

Direct imperial appointee or treated as such	9
Imperial appointee or treated as such	132
Executive appointee or treated as such	356
Official or treated as such	2,631
Attached staff	203
Staff	1,161
Employees	1,325
Total	5,817

With nine officials of direct imperial appointee rank in 1943, and from six to nine of that rank from the 1920s on, the Imperial Household Ministry ranked among the top bureaucratic structures in prewar Japan. Only the Foreign Ministry, whose minister and

3. *Kunai Shō Shokuin Roku*, 1943, p. 19.

ambassadors plenipotentiary were direct imperial appointees, and the armed forces, whose generals and admirals were also of that rank, outranked the Imperial Household Ministry in this respect. And only the Foreign Ministry outranked the Imperial Household Ministry in its ratio of direct imperial appointees to total personnel.

Only the Prime Minister and the Speakers of the two houses of the Imperial Diet, moreover, received higher official salaries than the Imperial Household Minister. In 1939, for example, the maximum official salaries (yen per annum) of the leading officials of the government and the court were:[4]

Government

Prime Minister	9,600 ¥
Speaker of the House of Peers	7,500
Speaker of the House of Representatives	7,500
Ministers of State	6,800
President of the Privy Council	6,600
Ambassadors Plenipotentiary	6,600
Admirals and generals	6,600
Vice Ministers of State	5,800

Court

Imperial Household Minister	6,800 ¥
Lord Keeper of the Privy Seal	6,800
Chief Aide-de-Camp	6,600
Grand Chamberlain	6,200

Finally, in the years from 1924 to 1943 there were approximately fifty officials at court who held concurrent posts in the government but were not carried on the Imperial Household Ministry's official roster. Of these, about twelve were direct imperial appointees in rank.

As measured by the ranks and salaries of its officials, therefore, the Imperial Household Ministry was a very powerful and prestigious bureaucratic organization. The transcendental dignity of the imperial institution, of course, made it necessary for the Imperial Household Ministry to be prestigious and dignified as well. Why the ministry should have been led by such high-ranking bureaucrats, however, is a question that cannot be answered merely in terms of status, as we shall see in the following chapters. Here we turn to the

4. *Shokuin Roku*, 1939, pt. 2, pp. 1–157.

institutional and personnel structure around the emperor for the routine management of the imperial dignity.

THE OUTER SIDE: BUREAUCRATIC OPERATIVES
OF THE EMPEROR-IN-COURT AS EMPEROR-IN-PUBLIC

Functionally, the Imperial Household Ministry had two sides: an "outer" side and an "inner" side.[5] The outer side comprised the modern bureaucratic aspects of court administration—arrangement of imperial tours, management of imperial lands and forests, accounting, records, public relations—and was located in provincial offices or in office buildings outside and around the inner palace, the Fukiage park, where the emperor resided. The inner side comprised those in regular attendance on the emperor and his immediate family: Chamberlains, Ladies-in-Waiting, Aides-de-Camp, tutors to the imperial family and so on. As "family" members of the court, these persons had access to the emperor and imperial family in the inner palace. As will become apparent, the line separating the outer and inner sides was not clear-cut or absolute; there was a constant flow of communication between the two. As a rule, however, the work of the outer side was office work, that of the inner side, attendance. The former were bureaucrats, the latter, imperial emissaries and elegant valets.

A glance at the 1945 offices listed in table 2 will reveal generally which of the offices were outer offices: the Minister's Secretariat, Office of Imperial Mausolea, Office of Archives, Office of the Privy Purse, Office of Imperial Works, General Affairs Bureau, etc. Approximately eighteen of the twenty-eight offices were clearly involved with court administration and estate management. The Minister's Secretariat, for example, was responsible for "secret" matters, the promotion, status, and retirement of ministry officials, pensions, correspondence, statistics, and reports for the *Official Gazette*, coordination of ministry offices and bureaus, investigations, the drafting of

5. Kyūtei Kishadan, pp. 3–4. Although this source applies the "outer" (*omote*) and "inner" (*oku*) distinction to the postwar court bureaucracy, it is equally valid, if not more so, for the prewar court administration.

papers, and matters not assigned to other offices. The General Affairs Bureau handled arrangements for imperial tours, public announcements and photographs, and miscellaneous work for other ministry offices. The Imperial Guards Bureau was responsible for palace security, escorting imperial processions and other police functions, sanitation, air defense, and fire-fighting. Reception of foreign dignitaries and protocol matters fell under the Foreign Affairs Section of the Board of the Ceremonies.[6] The outer side was thus responsible for the Emperor-in-Court acting as Emperor-in-Public, a charge they guarded jealously.

If the living emperor's public image, as well as that of the immediate imperial family, was the first duty of the outer side, the dignity of the imperial line—the imperial presence in the land from antiquity—was also in its charge. It was the responsibility of the Office of Imperial Mausolea to maintain the 734 tombs and shrines of past emperors and imperial family members that were located in twenty-seven of the forty-seven local divisions of Japan.[7] These were physical reminders to the people that theirs was a divine land which had existed from "time immemorial." Supporting the physical presence of the imperial line among the populace were the rites conducted by the Board of Rituals on national festival days. To emphasize the cultural centrality of the imperial line, the Imperial Household Ministry also managed the Shōsōin, repository of Japan's cultural treasures and court relics dating from the eighth century on. Ancient court music was preserved by the music division of the Board of the Ceremonies.[8]

The management of court finances. Nothing better illustrates the essentially administrative nature of the outer side, and, incidentally, the separation of court and government, than the management of court finances. Managing the financial operations of the palace was a major function of the outer side, and approximately half of the Ministry's total personnel were engaged in imperial estate and finance management.

6. "Kunai Shō Kansei," Article 10, *Kōshitsu Rei*, no. 7, October 7, 1921, as amended through 1941; in Naikaku Kiroku Ka, 1942, vol. 1, pt. 3, chap. 1. sec. 3, pp. 16, 17.

7. "Ryōbo Sū Ichiran Hyō," handwritten document provided by the Imperial Household Agency. In the 1930s Japan comprised forty-three prefectures, three municipalities, and one circuit.

8. Sōrifu, *Kanchō Benran*, 2:20–21; Kyūtei Kishadan, p. 50.

As part of their preparations to create a transcendental emperor during the Restoration settlement, the Meiji oligarchs strengthened the independent base of court organization by transferring vast amounts of state land to the imperial house and by placing the court's finances under sole jurisdiction of the palace bureaucracy. In 1882 Iwakura Tomomi pressed upon the cabinet a strongly worded argument in favor of imperial house properties which would serve as the "material foundation" of the constitution soon to be drafted and implemented. He argued that all state lands as well as railways and a number of industrial plants should be placed under autonomous control of the imperial house.[9] Imperial house property would give the imperial institution financial autonomy commensurate with its all-embracing political authority. The oligarchs were agreed that the creation of an autonomous source of income for the imperial house was an essential step to be taken before the constitution came into effect.[10] The legal and administrative separation of court and government was therefore to be bolstered by granting financial independence to the court.

The court's financial autonomy was consolidated during Itō Hirobumi's tenure as Imperial Household Minister from 1885 to 1887. First, lands and capital investments were turned over to the Imperial Household Ministry in such amounts that by 1915 the court was able to defray the major part of its expenses from income derived from its own independent sources. Second, budgets and accounts, not only for its own revenues from capital and lands but also for its allotment from the national treasury to meet court expenses, were completely under court (Imperial Household Ministry) control. The government had no formal jurisdiction over court finances except over increases in the national treasury allotment.

In 1885 a Bureau of Imperial Lands was created to administer the vast public lands transferred or to be transferred to the management of the Imperial Household Ministry. Between 1885 and 1890 the imperial estate increased from 54,717 acres to some 8.7 million acres. Article 45 of the Imperial House Law of 1889 also provided for hereditary imperial property; approximately 2.5 million of the 8.7

9. Kuroda Hisata, *Tennō Ke no Zaisan* (Tokyo: Sanichi Shinsho, 1966), pp. 22–24; Inoue Kiyoshi, pp. 88–89.

10. Kuroda Hisata, pp. 24, 26; Inoue Kiyoshi, p. 89.

million acres were consequently designated as hereditary, "forever" to belong to the imperial family.[11] Between 1890 and 1945, however, the imperial estate decreased considerably. Disparities between registered area and actual surveys, the sale of unnecessary lands and lands difficult to administer, and the return of lands, originally acquired for development purposes, to prefectural authorities largely accounted for the decrease. In 1895, for example, 3.3 million acres of imperial land in Hokkaido were returned to local administration. Lands in Yamanashi prefecture, apparently acquired for development, were largely returned to local prefectural administration by 1916. Surveys of imperial lands proved the registered area of imperial land to be as much as 18 percent greater than the actual area.[12] Even the hereditary lands were greatly reduced.

Consequently, the imperial estate in 1940 totaled 3,226,388 acres, not including "unnecessary lands" yet to be disposed of, of which 512,204 acres were hereditary imperial property. Forest lands constituted approximately 97 percent of the imperial estate, while palaces, villas, and imperial tombs accounted for 0.5 percent. The remainder was agricultural land. Imperial lands were held in forty of the forty-seven local divisions of Japan.[13] At least 1,300 of the Imperial Household Ministry's 5,400 registered officials were engaged in the management of the imperial lands and forests in 1940.[14] In addition to maintaining an imperial presence throughout the land, the Bureau of Imperial Lands and Forests also provided a substantial income to the court from 1897 on. In 1915 it is estimated that three million of the imperial house's total income of sixteen million yen derived from the Bureau of Imperial Lands.[15]

The period from 1885 to 1890, years of enormous expansion of the imperial estate, were also years of great increase in imperial capital investments, most notably in the field of banking. In 1884 Matsukata Masayoshi, leading government oligarch in the world of finance, urged that government stocks in the Bank of Japan and the Yokohama Specie Bank be turned over to the imperial house. The

11. Kuroda Hisata, pp. 26, 31–32, 37.
12. Ibid., pp. 108–09 passim, 46–48, 51–52.
13. Ibid., pp. 108–09, 111.
14. *Kunai Shō Shokuin Roku,* 1940.
15. Kuroda Hisata, pp. 132, 248–49, 100.

government subsequently transferred shares valued at five million yen in the former and one million yen in the latter to the Chief of the Privy Purse, Imperial Household Ministry, in February 1885. These stocks were to remain the nucleus of imperial house investments until 1947, when all imperial house properties were dissolved. Additional stocks were acquired between 1885 and 1890 in the Nippon Yūsen Kaisha (a shipping company), Japan Railways, Sapporo Sugar, Tokyo Hotel, and industrial railways in Hokkaido.[16] And although the imperial estate dwindled after 1890, imperial house investments in banking and industry continued to grow until 1945. Each venture in foreign expansion netted monies for the Privy Purse. In 1898 part of the indemnity garnered from the Sino-Japanese War, in the amount of twenty million yen, was granted to the imperial house by resolution of both houses of the Imperial Diet. This money was then invested by the court in government securities. The imperial house also invested in the Bank of Taiwan (1899), Taiwan Sugar (1901), the Bank of Korea (1909), the Chosen Industrial Bank (1918), the Manchurian Railway (1924–25), and banks belonging to private combines, such as the Sumitomo Bank.[17] Moreover, imperial house capital investments grew steadily in each of these enterprises as the result of stock increases and divisions. For example, the modest holding of 4,000 Manchurian Railway stocks in 1925 grew to 84,375 stocks by 1945.[18]

Profits from lands, forests, and capital investments were supplemented by sums allotted from the national treasury to meet the "imperial house expenditure" (kōshitsu hi). As early as 1869 the Civil Government had allotted a regular sum for court expenses, but the expenses of the imperial family and the salaries of Imperial Household Ministry personnel were paid by the Ministry of Finance. From 1886 onward, however, a lump sum to cover all court expenses was granted to the Imperial Household Ministry. Moreover, the Imperial Household Ministry was in no way accountable to the government for the use of the government allotment; the court was to have financial autonomy even with respect to

16. Ibid., pp. 27–29, 63–64.
17. Ibid., pp. 61–62, 66, 92–93.
18. Ibid., p. 93.

monies granted from the national treasury. From 1889 to 1909 the sum disbursed from the national treasury was fixed at 3 million yen. In 1909 the sum was increased to 4.5 million, where it remained until the end of World War II.[19]

The only accurate figures on imperial house finances from 1897 are this disbursement from the national treasury and the financial records of the Bureau of Imperial Lands and Forests. Imperial investments in public bonds and in both public and private enterprises were cloaked in secrecy, with only occasional figures available on certain investments.[20] Kuroda Hisata, however, estimates the annual income of the imperial house in 1916 as follows:[21]

National treasury	4,500,000 ¥
Bureau of Imperial Lands and Forests	3,000,000
Stocks	4,500,000
Public and other securities	4,000,000
Total	16,000,000 ¥

By 1916 at the latest it is clear that the imperial house financed the major portion of its operations from its own resources. From 1914 it even had its own bank, the Jūgo Ginkō. At the end of the war imperial capital (stocks, public securities, cash on hand) was valued by the Occupation authorities at 336,158,890 yen, yielding annual income of possibly as much as 20 million yen. Income derived from lands and forests plus sales of land in 1937 was approximately 8.7 million yen.[22] A very rough estimate of annual imperial house income around 1940 would thus be:[23]

National treasury	4,500,000 ¥
Bureau of Imperial Lands and Forests	9,000,000
Capital investments	15,000,000
Total	28,500,000 ¥

19. Ibid., pp. 12–13, 14, 36, 78.
20. Ibid., p. 72.
21. Ibid., p. 100. According to Japanese yearbooks, the average exchange rate of U.S. dollars to yen in 1916 was $50.50 to 100 ¥. The income of the imperial house was therefore over $8,000,000 per annum in 1916 U.S. dollars.
22. Ibid., pp. 120, 122, 249.
23. The biographers of Ishiwatari Sōtarō, the last Imperial Household Minister, claim that there had never been a complete estimate of imperial house properties until the Occupation authorities demanded such a valuation after the war. The value finally arrived at by Ishiwatari was 1.6 billion yen (Ishiwatari Sōtarō, [Tokyo: Ishiwatari Sōtarō Denki Hensan Kai, 1954],

All but autonomous in its financial resources, the imperial house was accountable only to itself for both revenues and expenditures. Only increases in the national treasury allotment required Diet approval, and by 1940 the national treasury allotment was a mere fifth of the total court income. The court audit, as well as its budget, was completely distinct from the government's audit and budget and exclusively under the control of the Imperial Household Ministry. Even the court's fiscal year (January–December) after 1891 was different from that of the government (April-March).[24]

The chief advisory body on court financial operations was the Imperial House Economic Council, created in 1891. According to the 1891 regulations governing the council, it was to be composed of specially appointed imperial house economic advisers, the Imperial Household Minister, the Vice Minister, the Chief of the Privy Purse, and the Chief of the Bureau of Imperial Lands. The emperor was to be present at council meetings, which decided on regulations governing the management of the hereditary estate, designation of hereditary properties, general provisions concerning the imperial estate, capital investments, the amount and use of the current account, budget increases and decreases in the imperial estate and in capital investments, and regulations governing the court audit. Three accounts were created for auditing purposes by the Imperial House Finance Law of March 1891: the imperial estate account, the capital account, and the current account. The Chief of the Bureau of Imperial Lands was responsible for the estate account, the Chief of the Privy Purse for the capital account, and division and bureau chiefs of the ministry for the current account.[25] Three accounts were retained after the revision of imperial house auditing procedures in 1912 as well: current, special, and capital. The special account after

p. 478). It is also claimed that the imperial house had originally acquired stocks to give the public confidence in this new form of economic activity: if the emperor invested, others would follow suit (ibid., p. 479). However accurate these claims—and both are subject to serious doubts—it remains that imperial property and investment contributed greatly to the political purposes of palace autonomy.

The exchange rate at the Yokohama Specie Bank in 1940 was U.S. $23.40 to 100 ¥. The annual income of the imperial house in 1940 was therefore around $6.7 million in 1940 U.S. dollars.

24. Kuroda Hisata, pp. 36, 37–38, 44.
25. Ibid., pp. 39–44.

1921 applied exclusively to the imperial estate and was the responsibility of the Chief of the Bureau of Imperial Lands and Forests. The Chief of the Privy Purse looked after both current and capital accounts and was responsible to the Imperial Household Minister for drafting the court budget. These accounts were investigated by the Imperial House Audit Bureau, which did not, however, examine the inner court and "secret" expenditures. Apparently, the budgeting and accounting practices of the court were considerably more flexible than those of the government.[26]

Imperial lands and forests, imperial house capital, and an all but untouchable government disbursement gave the court the wherewithal for legal and administrative autonomy. How these resources were employed, however, depended on who controlled the Imperial Household Ministry. With great wealth at its disposal, the palace bureaucracy could conceivably use court funds for political purposes. This would appear to be all the more likely if the Imperial Household Minister had political aspirations or owed obligations to government leaders, or if his tenure in office depended on cooperation with the government leadership of the day. Contributions to individual government leaders and politicians, and even to political parties, likewise depended on the nature of palace leadership. The secrecy that enshrouded the financial operations of the court is circumstantial evidence that court funds were not used strictly for court purposes. The very autonomy of the court, paradoxically, constituted a potential for political abuse. As will be shown in chapter 4, there is some evidence that this potential was indeed exploited, blurring in operation the distinction between court and government.

Managing the aristocracy. If in fact the imperial institution were to be an operating symbol of all that was true, good and beautiful in the Japanese polity, the Imperial Household Ministry logically would also manage the affairs of social status. This was concretely implemented by giving the Ministry control over the aristocracy.

After several unsuccessful attempts to settle on a system of ranks following the Restoration, a modern aristocracy finally came into being in 1884. The new aristocracy was to be open to ex-samurai

26. Ibid., pp. 80–83.

and commoners who had made outstanding contributions to the new Japanese polity as well as to ex-feudal lords and ex-Court Nobles. By 1878 the Councillors had agreed to create five ranks, and these were formalized in 1884 as follows: prince, marquis, count, viscount, and baron. Centering on the imperial house, the new aristocracy was to be the statused bulwark of the throne. On the day following the establishment of the aristocracy the emperor reported the investment of titles to the inner shrine (*kashikodokoro*), to the shrine of the imperial spirits (*kōreiden*), and to the shrine of the gods (*shinden*). The newly invested aristocrats then paid their respects to the inner shrine, dedicating themselves to the service of the imperial house.[27]

As early as 1877 a bureau within the Imperial Household Ministry had been established to manage the affairs of the aristocracy.[28] In 1884 the Ministry was given custody of the family registers of the aristocracy. Marriages and adoptions required its approval;[29] in 1886 the Ministry was charged with managing the hereditary property of the aristocracy as well.[30] After several changes in name and clarifications of jurisdiction, the Imperial Household Ministry office in charge of the aristocracy was finally styled the Office of Peerage Affairs (*Sōchitsu Ryō*). As such, it handled (1) matters regarding the aristocracy, the imperial family, princely families, and such families as the Korean royal house, including conferences of princes-of-the-blood and of princes as well as meetings of the Imperial Family Council; (2) supervision of personnel assigned to the imperial family, princes-of-the-blood, and princes; (3) announcements of conferrals of court rank and peerage titles; (4) regulations governing the Peers School and the Peers School for Women; and (5) preparation of the electoral list of counts, viscounts, and barons for the House of Peers.[31] The director of the Office of Peerage Affairs was either a direct imperial appointee or an imperial appointee.[32]

Itō Hirobumi, architect of the new peerage system of 1884, not

27. Shumpo Kōtsui Shōkai, 2:384–88; Inoue Kiyoshi, pp. 94–95.
28. "Kunai Shō Tasshi Kōka," no. 1, January 10, 1877; in *Hōrei Zensho,* 1877, p. 950; Kyūtei Kishadan, p. 11.
29. Shumpo Kōtsui Shōkai, 2:386.
30. *Hōrei Zensho,* 1886, vol. 1, pp. 178–81.
31. Naikaku Kiroku Ka, 1942, pt. 3, chap. 1, sec. 3, p. 16; *Shokuin Roku,* 1943, pt. 1, p. 60.
32. Naikaku Kiroku Ka, 1942, pt. 3, chap. 1, sec. 3, p. 19.

only managed the affairs of this new class as Imperial Household
Minister but was instrumental in clarifying the relationship of the
new aristocracy to the social order. First, the Peers School was to
train the sons of the aristocracy in service to the nation. Second, Itō
insisted that the new aristocracy reward achievement as well as
family heritage in its composition.[33]

One of Itō's first acts after becoming Imperial Household Secretary in March 1884 was to resolve the long-standing issue of jurisdiction over the Peers School. Created in 1887, the Peers School was
initially supported by contributions from the court and the "peers
club," the latter including the entire aristocracy at the time. After
considerable difficulty, Itō had the Peers School made a government
school under the management of the Imperial Household Ministry
on April 17, 1884. In so doing, Itō argued that the aristocracy
existed to support the social order and to preserve the prosperity of
the imperial house. For the aristocracy to operate merely for its own
group interest was "disloyal."[34] Reflecting the public service
orientation of the aristocracy as intended by Itō, the curriculum of
the Peers School emphasized military subjects and ethics as well as
the natural sciences and literature.[35] The new aristocrats were to
embody the cultural values of the new Japanese nation, combining in
their education both Eastern ethics and Western techniques. An emphasis on military subjects reinforced the role of the aristocracy as
bulwark of the throne and hence, of national defense. Almost invariably the headmaster was a prominent military figure; among
them were such famous war horses as General Nogi Kiten and
General Tani Kanjō. Except those given special exemption, princes-
of-the-blood all became military officers.[36] Moreover, the Peers
School gave concrete expression to the identification of the
aristocracy with imperial rites. Peers School holidays, for example,
included the anniversary of the death of Emperor Kōmei (1866), the
Rite of Emperor Jimmu, Empire Day, the emperor's birthday, and
Shinto festivals of the autumnal and vernal equinoxes, new rice, and

33. Shumpo Kōtsui Shōkai, 2:384.
34. Shumpo Kōtsui Shōkai, 2:378–80.
35. *Hōrei Zensho*, 1884, p. 12.
36. Goseitoku Fukyū Kai, p. 103.

harvest.[37] The destiny of the aristocracy as a public class was thus made institutionally coeval with the fortunes of the state and the imperial house.

In the formative years of the new aristocracy (1884–87), the aristocracy of merit increased from 33 to 80 families[38] By 1928 the total number of aristocratic families was 956, excluding princes-of-the-blood. As indicated in table 4, a bare majority of aristocratic families (487 of 956, or 50.8 percent) were of "miscellaneous" family origins. This category was mixed in composition and included highly statused hereditary priests, high-ranking feudal branch families, leading retainers of the greater feudal lords (including the shogun), and families of high status in pre-Restoration Japan—some of the old Osaka business families, for example—as well as those families whose titles were acquired solely as reward for service to the state and society.[39] In this latter category—the merit aristocracy—

TABLE 4. COMPOSITION OF THE JAPANESE ARISTOCRACY IN 1928, EXCLUDING MEMBERS OF THE IMPERIAL FAMILIES (PRINCES-OF-THE-BLOOD)

Title	Family Origins				
	Imperial House	Court Noble	Feudal Lord	Miscellaneous	Total
Prince	0	9	3	6	18
Marquis	5	10	16	9	40
Count	4	29	33	42	108
Viscount	0	85	220	74	379
Baron	0	43	12	356	411
Total	9	176	284	487	956

SOURCE: *Gendai Kazoku Fuyō* (Tokyo: Nihon Shiseki Kyōkai, 1929), p. 720.

37. *Hōrei Zensho,* 1884, p. 1, 298.
38. Inoue Kiyoshi, p. 96.
39. I am indebted to Herschel Webb for calling my attention to the diversity in the backgrounds of those aristocrats in the miscellaneous category. In overall composition, therefore, the pre-Restoration ascribed aristocracy outnumbered the post-Restoration merit aristocracy, even though the merit aristocracy dominated in the miscellaneous category.

were Itō Hirobumi and Yamagata Aritomo, both of whom were eventually created princes. Of low rank within the warrior class, both acquired their titles on the basis of merit alone. And like the titles of all prewar aristocrats, those granted to Itō and Yamagata were made hereditary.

The conferral of titles on "servants of the throne" conveyed fiscal reward as well as status. Around 1884, for example, those granted the title of count, such as Itō Hirobumi and Yamagata Aritomo, were each given lump sums of 35,000 yen. In 1887 each count was given 350 shares of stock, valued at 17,500 yen, in the Nippon Yūsen Kaisha.[40] Both the 1884 and the 1887 awards were disbursed from the emperor's Privy Purse. Since the Imperial Household Mininstry managed both the affairs of the aristocracy and an autonomous imperial estate, the financial resources of the imperial house were used to sustain not only the dignity of the imperial house but also that of its bulwark. The Imperial Household Ministry, therefore, was the bureaucratic means of fusing the hierarchy of social status with that of wealth, or at least of ensuring that social status and wealth were commensurate.

The aristocracy discharged its public service function in several ways. One of the major areas of service was the Imperial Household Ministry itself. Of the fifty-two men serving in the six leading palace offices between 1885 and 1945, forty-five were or became titled. There were nine princes (including one prince-of-the-blood), six marquis, ten counts, seven viscounts, and thirteen barons. All twelve men who served as Directors of Peerage Affairs were titled: two princes, five marquis, three viscounts, and only two barons, indicating that the aristocracy played a considerable role in defining its bulwark functions as well as in managing the affairs of the Imperial Household Ministry.

THE INNER SIDE: SANCTUARY
OF THE EMPEROR-IN-CHAMBERS

While some aristocrats held leading palace posts, others served in lesser roles, primarily on the inner side of the Imperial Household

40. Inoue Kiyoshi, p. 96.

Ministry as Chamberlains and Stewards. The inner side of the palace bureaucracy and certain positions, such as Master of the Ceremonies, on the outer side, constituted refuges for aristocrats consonant with their inherited dignity and status while not demanding from them the tough-minded abilities required outside the palace to achieve social and political success—abilities that in many cases had been possessed by those who first acquired titles. Among those who served a lifetime in the palace, for example, was no less a figure than the adopted son of Itō Hirobumi, Prince Itō Hirokuni (1870–1931). After graduating from the Peers School and studying briefly in Germany, Hirokuni entered the Imperial Household Ministry, where he remained for thirty-nine years. Eventually achieving the post of Grand Master of the Ceremonies (1926–29), he became known as the "lord of the great inner mountain."[41] If Itō Hirokuni is a classic instance of an aristocratic scion taking refuge in the Imperial Household Ministry, he was by no means the only one. In 1931, for example, we find the grandson of oligarch Yamagata Aritomo, Prince Yamagata Arimichi, among the Chamberlains and concurrently among the Masters of the Ceremonies.[42]

The Chamberlains. It was among the Chamberlains in particular that many an aristocrat found sanctuary. In 1942 the Imperial Household Ministry's regulations provided for a Grand Chamberlain, two Deputy Grand Chamberlains, and ten Chamberlains.[43] In 1943, however, there were twelve Chamberlains in addition to the Grand and Deputy Grand Chamberlains.[44] Of the fifteen, eight were titled or in line to succeed and at least three were younger brothers of titled aristocrats. In addition to their predominantly aristocratic background, the Chamberlains also found a measure of group cohesion in educational experience. Twelve of the fifteen Chamberlains in 1943 had graduated from prewar Japan's foremost university, Tokyo Imperial University.[45] Forming the inner ring around the em-

41. *Dai Jimmei Jiten,* ed. Shimonaka Yusaburō, 10 vols. (Tokyo: Heibon Sha, 1937–41), 1:261.
42. *Shokuin Roku,* 1931, pt. 3, p. 10.
43. Naikaku Kiroku Ka, 1942, vol. 1, pt. 3, chap. 1, sec. 3, p. 1.
44. *Kunai Shō Shokuin Roku,* 1943.
45. Data on the personal backgrounds and careers of the Chamberlains, as well as all other officials discussed hereafter, have been obtained from published rosters of officials, biographical dictionaries, biographies, diaries, interviews, and the Imperial Household Agency's personnel files.

peror and his immediate family, the Chamberlains, usually of high educational attainment and impeccable lineage, were elegant men-servants and imperial messengers—paragons of the Imperial Household Ministry's inner side.

In contrast to the bureaucrats of the outer side, whose duties were clearly outlined in the organic law of the Imperial Household Ministry, the Chamberlains had no prescribed duties other than to serve at the emperor's side. Even after the palace administration had become highly bureaucratized, the basic regulation governing the Imperial Household Ministry merely stated that the Board of Chamberlains "takes charge of matters at the side of the emperor."[46] A characteristic of the ministry's inner side, as demonstrated by the Chamberlains, was its lack of formal structure and officially stipulated duties. This was, of course, natural to offices that called for constant companionship with the emperor and imperial family. Irie Sukemasa, Chamberlain to the emperor since 1934 and formerly a viscount, has articulated by hyperbole what that companionship entailed:

> Outside there may be persons whom the emperor trusts deeply. Outside there may be persons whom the emperor respects. But those he considers just like the atmosphere, like the breezes, paying no heed that they are there—being just the same whether there or not—those are Chamberlains.[47]

Irie notes that the role of companion and messenger played by the Chamberlains might involve helping the emperor collect marine life specimens or going to Taiwan to express the emperor's condolences on such occasions as the great earthquake of 1934.[48]

Irie also recalls that considerable freedom prevailed at the side of the Emperor-in-Chambers. In 1935, for example, the Chamberlains kept a book of fines for improprieties in speech and the sums collected were used for a year-end party. Outside the palace such improprieties, claims Irie, would have been dealt with as disrespect, causing offenders to lose their positions or suffer other serious penalties. Even during the Pacific War, continues Irie, such freedom

46. Naikaku Kiroku Ka, 1942, vol. 1, pt. 3, chap. 1, sec. 3.
47. Irie Sukemasa, *Tennō-sama no Kanreki* (Tokyo: Asahi Shimbun Sha, 1962), p. 242.
48. Ibid., pp. 232–33, 238–39.

was protected in the palace. Yoshida Shigeru (1878–1967), a prewar Foreign Ministry bureaucrat and one of Japan's outstanding postwar leaders, was arrested during the war for mentioning the possibility of Japanese defeat. Yet "we" at the palace talked openly about the inevitability of defeat.[49] "At the emperor's side freedom of speech has been guarded at every turn; there is absolutely no more democratic a place than this."[50]

Such "freedom" at the emperor's side also meant the prankstering freedom that prevails among those of an intimate ingroup. Count Kanroji Osanaga, classmate of the Taishō Emperor (r. 1912–26) at the Peers School and a lifetime official of the Imperial Household Ministry's inner side, states that both the Meiji and Taishō Emperors were surrounded by a band of stalwarts fond of practical jokes. Kanroji's uncle, Kadenokōji Sugekoto (1860–1925), was one of them, claims Kanroji. When "Kade" was a page to the Meiji Emperor he, like the other pages, slept in the young emperor's room. On one occasion Kade, unable to sleep, decided to kick the bed in which the emperor was sleeping soundly. The emperor bolted out of bed—it was a time of earthquakes—and looked around him. Kade was of course very fast asleep by then. This same Kade, according to Kanroji again, was known to yank the sleeping Taishō Emperor's blankets off when his own had fallen off in the dead of the night. Kanroji also relates that when he himself and the Taishō Emperor were schoolboys together, they were taught to swim by being thrown willy-nilly into the water by a Colonel Tachibana.[51] Such pranks, according to Irie, continued as a regular part of inner court life in the Shōwa period (1926—) as well.[52] Even acknowledging the at-

49. Irie Sukemasa, *Jijū to Paipu* (Tokyo: Mainichi Shimbun Sha, 1957), pp. 97–98.

50. Irie Sukemasa, "Okajiki," *Matsudaira Tsuneo Tsuisō Roku*, ed. Tokyo PR Tsūshin Sha (Tokyo: Matsudaira Tsuneo-shi Tsuioku Kai, 1961), p. 83. Irie's essays on court life have all been written in the postwar period. Given the theoretical role played by the emperor in prewar Japan and the protective shell imposed by the palace bureaucracy, such anecdotes could not have been published then. With the postwar "democratization" of the imperial institution, however, Irie and other court persons have published essays, anecdotes, and memoirs about the inner court during the prewar period. Irie in particular has gained a reputation for being the emperor's foremost public relations man. Although his views may be exaggerated and one-sided in an effort to create a more humanistic image for the emperor and court, his essays capture at least some of the atmosphere and activity of court life in prewar Japan.

51. Kanroji Osanaga, *Sebiro no Tennō* (Tokyo: Tōzai Bummei Sha, 1957), pp. 42–43, 45.

52. Irie Sukemasa, "Okajiki."

tempts to "humanize" and "democratize" the emperor and court that are so readily apparent in these postwar accounts of prewar inner court life, there was clearly a very great gap between the rigid formality and cold sanctity surrounding the Emperor-in-Public and the freewheeling informality and intimate fraternity surrounding the Emperor-in-Chambers.

Also characteristic of the Chamberlains was the practice of holding concurrent posts in both the inner and outer sides of the Imperial Household Ministry. Of the fifteen Chamberlains in 1943, for example, one was concurrently Grand Steward to the Empress, one headed a section of the Office of Court Physicians, and three were on the tutorial board for the children of the imperial family. Not unnaturally, a Chamberlain headed each of the three sections of the Board of Chamberlains, the outer office through which communication between the inner court and outer ministry offices was channelled.[53] Since audiences granted to foreign dignitaries as well as visits of worship to the inner shrine were scheduled by the Board of the Ceremonies,[54] it is not surprising that three Chamberlains served concurrently as Masters of the Ceremonies. One Chamberlain also served concurrently as a secretary in the General Affairs Bureau,[55] an outer office concerned with imperial tours and public relations. The holding of concurrent posts was evidently deemed necessary because it was the Chamberlains who had primary responsibility for managing access to the Emperor-in-Chambers, as well as providing companionship to the emperor and members of the imperial family.

The primacy of the Chamberlains in maintaining the privacy of the imperial family by controlling access to the inner court, at least during the 1930s and 1940s, is also clear from the official duties of the Board of Chamberlains. Although the Imperial Household Ministry's organic law did not specify the functions of the board, the ministry's regulations governing divisions and sections did. The first section of the Board of Chamberlains, the Miscellaneous Section, handled (1) imperial lectures, (2) audiences at court, (3) court allowances and imperial gifts, (4) imperial family records, (5) cus-

---

53. *Kunai Shō Shokuin Roku,* 1943.
54. "Kunai Shō Bunka Kitei," in *Shokuin Roku,* 1943, pt. 1, p. 60.
55. *Kunai Shō Shokuin Roku,* 1943.

tody of the board's seal, and (6) matters not assigned to the other two sections. In coordination with the Office of Aides-de-Camp, that section also scheduled audiences for military personnel. The Inner Court Section of the board managed such matters as butlering. The third and last section, the Management Section, was in charge of accounts and possessions of the imperial family.[56] Thus the Board of Chamberlains managed the inner court and liaison between the Emperor-in-Chambers and the Emperor-in-Public.

The term of service for a Chamberlain was generally his lifetime. The fifteen Chamberlains in 1943 averaged nine years in office, ranging from three to twenty-nine years service. Six of the fifteen were still Chamberlains in 1962.[57] Obviously, the post of Chamberlain was not a rung on the ladder of advancement to higher office; it was a terminal appointment. It may be surmised that their seniority, as well as their aristocratic station and educational background, gave the Chamberlains considerable authority in dealing with the outer side bureaucrats, enhancing their ability to preserve the privacy of imperial family life from outside scrutiny.

The Ladies-in-Waiting and Aides-de-Camp. The Chamberlains did not, however, have a complete monopoly over the inner court circuit. There were two other groups who shared in the function of regular attendance: the Ladies-in-Waiting and the Aides-de-Camp. Until the early twentieth century the Ladies-in-Waiting had had quite a different function from others in regular attendance: to ensure that there would be an heir to the throne. In fact, a court lady of the second rank (*gon-tenji*), Yanagihara Naruko (1855–1943), was the mother of the Taishō Emperor. Meiji's empress had no offspring.[58] The Ladies-in-Waiting had been members of the inner court throughout the recorded history of Japan, and Kanroji Osanaga estimates that some three hundred of them accompanied the young emperor to Tokyo when he was restored as the center of the Japanese polity in 1868.[59]

Only when the present emperor became regent in November 1921,

56. "Kunai Shō Bunka Kitei," in *Shokuin Roku,* 1943, pt. 1, pp. 59–60.
57. *Kunai Shō Shokuin Roku,* 1943; Kunai Chō Chōkan Kambō Hisho Ka, *Kunai Chō Shokuin Roku* (Tokyo: 1962).
58. Kyūtei Kishadan, pp. 17, 151.
59. Kanroji Osanaga, p. 142.

however, was a successful reform of the Ladies' court life begun, and
it was not until 1926, when the present emperor began his reign,
that monogamy was established.[60] Until 1921, and especially in the
early Meiji period, the Ladies-in-Waiting were a power to be
reckoned with. Like the Chamberlains, they acted as intermediaries
between the emperor and the outside world. It is even rumored that
some leading Restoration figures were turned away by the Ladies
when they appeared for audience at the emperor's inner residence.
Such Restoration leaders as Sanjō Sanetomi, Iwakura Tomomi, and
Saigō Takamori were victims of their perversity.[61] In 1871 an attempt was evidently made to put a stop to the political maneuverings
of the Ladies by having prominent civilian and military officials appointed to court posts. Among the appointees were the future *Jiho*
Yoshii Tomozane and Komeda Torao, two "modernizers" devoted
to the reform of the imperial institution.[62] But even with major efforts at housecleaning, the traditions of life in the "back interior" of
the emperor's residence continued up to the end of the Taishō period.[63] Until the Shōwa period, the lives of the one hundred Ladies
and their attendants, isolated from the outside world, were replete
with jealousies, viciousness, and feuds.[64] Even such a life-long
member of the court's inner side as Kanroji Osanaga states that their
existence was "inhuman, inappropriate to the new times."[65] When
the present emperor married in 1924, the old system and practices of
court Ladies-in-Waiting were finally abolished. The "machines for
producing the emperor's heirs" were replaced by salaried women attendants.[66]

The attempted reform of such ancient court practices and institutions indicates the intent of the Meiji oligarchs to make the imperial
institution a modern structure around which popular loyalty could

60. Nezu Masashi, p. 39; Kyūtei Kishadan, p. 156.
61. Kyūtei Kishadan, pp. 152–53; Kanroji Osanaga, p. 143.
62. Tokutomi Iichirō, *Kōshaku Yamagata Aritomo Den,* 3 vols. (Tokyo: Yamagata Aritomo-kō Kinen Jigyō Kai, 1933), 2 : 288–89.
63. Kyūtei Kishadan, p. 149; Watanabe Ikujirō, *Meiji Tennō,* 2 vols. (Tokyo: Meiji
Tennō Shotoku Kai, 1958), 1 : 125–31.
64. Yanagihara Byakuren, "Yanagihara Ichii Tsubone no Kainin," *Bungei Shunjū*
(Tokushū), no. 10 (1956): 44; Kyūtei Kishadan, pp. 150–53.
65. Kanroji Osanaga, p. 142.
66. Nezu Masashi, p. 39; Kyūtei Kishadan, p. 145.

be mobilized in support of the "new Japan." The emperor was not
to be the captive of inner court anachronisms but a modern symbol
of old virtues, and the difficulties posed by as seemingly innocuous
an institution as the Ladies-in-Waiting were typical of the whole
range of problems confronting the politicians of modernization.

Quite a different component of the court's inner circle was the Office of Aides-de-Camp. Like the Chamberlains, the Aides-de-Camp
served as imperial messengers and regular attendants. Whereas the
Chamberlains in their capacity as messengers linked emperor and
government, however, the Aides as messengers linked emperor and
military. The Office of Aides was institutionally unique in the Imperial Household Ministry: provisions governing the organization
and duties of the Aides were established by Imperial Ordinance, not
by Imperial Household Ministry decree. Personnel assigned to the
palace as Aides were listed in the Army and Navy rosters as well as
in the official roster of the Imperial Household Ministry, indicating
that the Aides were less court officials than representatives of the
military at court.[67]

The organization of the Office of Aides-de-Camp in 1943 was established by Imperial Ordinance Number 319 of December 28,
1908, as amended in 1919 and 1920. That ordinance was
countersigned by the Prime Minister, Minister of the Army, and
Minister of the Navy—but not by the Imperial Household
Minister.[68] Its provisions reveal that control over the Aides rested only
minimally with the Imperial Household Ministry:

1. The Chief Aide shall be a General or Lieutenant General of the Army
   or an Admiral or Vice Admiral of the Navy, by direct imperial appointment [shimpo].
2. Aides shall be officers ranking from Army Captain or Navy Lieutenant

67. There had been Aides to the emperor from at least 1875. In 1873 a dispute occurred
over whether Aides should be officers of the Imperial Guard or of the armed forces. Yamagata
Aritomo's argument for Aides appointed from the military services won the day. As early as
1879 a Chief Aide-de-Camp was named directly. In 1885 General Katsura Tarō proposed the
creation of an Office of Aides-de-Camp after investigating European military organizations;
his proposals apparently were the basis for the establishment of the Office of Aides-de-Camp
which finally occurred in 1896 (Matsushita Yoshio, 2: 205–06; Tokutomi Iichirō, *Kōshaku
Yamagata*, 2: 288–92; Nezu Masashi, p. 115).
68. "Jijū Bukan Sei", in Kunai Shō, ed., *Genkō Kunai Shō Hōki Shū*, 2 vols. (Tokyo: Dai
Nippon Hōrei Shuppan Kabushiki Kaisha, 1927), with changes entered through 1938.

to Army Lieutenant General or Navy Vice Admiral; there shall be five from the Army and three from the Navy.

3. The functions of the Chief Aide and Aides are:
   a. ordinary services to the emperor
   b. reporting and replying to the throne on military matters
   c. conveying military orders and commands
   d. accompanying the emperor at military parades, maneuvers, tours, festivals, rites, banquets, audiences. The Chief Aide and Aides shall be dispatched to military exercises and military inspections.

4. The Chief Aide supervises the work of the Aides.

5. The Chief Aide and Aides are to be treated as members of the General Staff [Sambō].

6. When the Chief Aide and Aides are at court they shall observe the regulations of the Imperial Household Ministry.[69]

Only the last provision gave the Imperial Household Ministry any measure of control over the actions of the Aides.

The Office of Aides-de-Camp was thus an extra-court institution imposed on the very center of court life. In addition to the eight Aides there was also a staff of seven military officials attached to the office.[70] Furthermore, military Aides from the Army and the Navy were attached to every male of majority age in the imperial families. The regulations governing the duties of Aides to imperial family members were almost identical to those governing the Aides to the emperor. Like the ordinance creating the Office of Aides-de-Camp, these regulations were countersigned only by the Prime Minister, Army Minister, and Navy Minister.[71] As table 5 indicates, the total number of military appointees at court varied from twenty-eight to thirty-eight during the period from 1921 to 1943. Since there were only eight Aides to the emperor, they and their staff were only one of the military's windows into court life. Moreover, the majority of Aides to the emperor as well as Aides to imperial family members were Army officers. After 1931 the predominance of Army over

69. Ibid, paraphrased.
70. Ibid.
71. "Kōzoku-tsuki Rikugun Bukan Kansei," Imperial Ordinance no. 281, August 10, 1896, as amended in 1900, 1915, and 1932; "Kōzoku-tsuki Kaigun Bukan Kansei," Imperial Ordinance no. 3, October 14, 1897, as amended in 1899 and 1916 (ibid.). Interestingly, the rules for Aides to imperial family members were made by each of the two services separately and not by cosponsored Imperial Ordinance.

TABLE 5. AIDES TO THE EMPEROR AND IMPERIAL FAMILIES:
ALTERNATE YEARS, 1921–1943

Year	Total	Army	Navy	Office of Aides (Aides and Staff)			Imperial Family Aides		
				Total	Army	Navy	Total	Army	Navy
1921	38	24 (63%)	14 (37%)	15	10	5	23	14	9
1923	35	21 (60%)	14 (40%)	19	12	7	16	9	7
1925	33	20 (61%)	13 (39%)	18	11	7	15	9	6
1927	30	19 (63%)	11 (37%)	15	10	5	15	9	6
1929	28	17 (61%)	11 (39%)	14	9	5	14	8	6
1931	28	17 (61%)	11 (39%)	13	8	5	15	9	6
1933	30	20 (67%)	10 (33%)	13	8	5	17	12	5
1935	31	21 (68%)	10 (32%)	13	8	5	18	13	5
1937	31	21 (68%)	10 (32%)	13	8	5	18	13	5
1939	29	20 (69%)	9 (31%)	13	8	5	16	12	4
1941[a]	29	20 (69%)	9 (31%)	13	8	5	16	12	4
1943[a]	29	22 (76%)	7 (24%)	13	8	5	16	14	2

SOURCE: *Kunai Shō Shokuin Roku*, 1921–43. Aides attached to the Korean royal house have been excluded. It is interesting to note that the roster of officials for the government in toto (*Shokuin Roku*) does not list the Aides under the Imperial Household Ministry but under the Army and Navy. The Imperial Household Ministry's official roster (*Kunai Shō Shokuin Roku*) lists the Aides under "attached office" and under each of the imperial princes.

[a] In 1941 and 1943 one civilian was attached to the Office of Aides; he is excluded from the tabulation.

Navy at court was even more marked, especially among Aides to imperial family members.

That the initiative in appointing Aides to the emperor lay with the armed forces is strongly suggested by the fact that the Aides were members of their respective General Staffs. General Honjō Shigeru, Chief Aide-de-Camp from 1933 to 1936, has verified that during the 1930s the military proposed and the emperor and court disposed on appointments to the Office of Aides. In his diary entry of May 25, 1935 Honjō states that after considerable difficulty in arriving at its selection of the candidate to be its ranking Aide-de-Camp, the Navy finally proposed two candidates to the throne with clear preference indicated for the first nominee. The emperor, however, selected the second candidate, Rear Admiral Hirata Noboru. Honjō immediately notified the Navy of the emperor's decision. The Navy Minister told Honjō that it was almost without precedent for the emperor to select the second nominee. Admiral Fushimi Hiroyasu, Chief of the Navy General Staff, believed that the emperor had questioned the "integrity" of the Navy Minister, or that someone in the palace was engaging in disruptive activities. The Navy Minister, however, told Honjō that the matter was closed because the emperor had acted.[72]

If in fact this was an unprecedented case, it reveals that the military had more than the power to initiate the appointments of Aides-de-Camp: a recommendation by the military was closer to an order that, if not followed by the emperor and court, could create a difficult situation. The emperor did review candidates for the post of Aide and had some voice in the matter, as the above case indicates. General Yoshihashi Kaizō, Aide-de-Camp from December 1944 to November 1945, has stated that the emperor checked the qualifications of each Aide prior to his appointment. In addition to "ability," qualifications such as "honesty" and the capacity to perform liaison work reliably were required.[73] Although the appointment of Aides was subject to a measure of negotiation between the military and the court, however, the military had the upper hand.

Strengthening the independence of the Aides as palace personnel was the transient nature of their service at court. The Aides were not "permanent" servants of the palace, as were the Chamberlains, but served a tour of duty at the side of the emperor. Chief Aide Honjō Shigeru, for example, obtained permission from the emperor in 1934 to have Aides serve three-year tours to duty.[74] In 1943 the eight Aides, including the Chief Aide, had been in office an average of slightly over two years, ranging from nine months to three years eleven months (the Chief Aide, General Hasunuma Shigeru). Only the Chief Aide resembled anything like a permanent official close to the throne. By contrast, we have seen that the fifteen Chamberlains had been in office an average of nine years as of August 1943.

72. Honjō Shigeru, *Honjō Nikki* (Tokyo: Hara Shobō, 1967), p. 212.
73. Interview with General Yoshihashi Kaizō, March 24, 1965. At the time of the interview, General Yoshihashi was President of the Self-Defense Force Staff College.
74. Honjō Shigeru, p. 199.

Moreover, a tour of duty as Aide-de-Camp was usually followed by promotion in rank and advancement in the military hierarchy.[75] Of the forty-three Aides who served from December 1926, when the era name changed to Shōwa, to November 1945, when the Office of Aides-de-Camp was abolished, seven were in office when the office was abolished and ten were listed as having been transferred without any further notation. Of the remaining twenty-six, twelve were transferred to commands.[76] A tour of duty as Aide-de-Camp, therefore, was a stepping-stone to higher office within the military bureaucracy. To take an extreme example, General Anami Kore-chika became Army Minister under Prime Minister Suzuki Kantarō in April 1945; Anami had been an Aide-de-Camp from August 1929 to August 1933 during Suzuki's tenure as Grand Chamberlain.

Appointment to the post of Aide-de-Camp sometimes involved status as well as strictly military qualifications. In 1943, for example, at least one of the Aides was an aristocrat: Baron Lieutenant Colonel Yamagata Ariakira, a grandson of Prince Yama-gata Aritomo. A glance at the roster of forty-three Aides between 1926 and 1943 reveals a few more aristocrats. Viscount Machijiri Kazumoto, who eventually became a general, was an Aide from May 1930 to March 1935 and again from March 1937 to October 1937. A career Army officer, Machijiri was married to the eldest sister of Prince-of-the-Blood Kaya Tsunenori and was considered influential because of his marriage. Marquis Rear Admiral Daigo Tadashige, Aide from December 1938 to October 1941, was of Court Noble origin: his wife was the eldest daughter of Prince Mōri Motoaki. In addition to those of aristocratic background, there were also Aides related to officials who had been close to the throne. Hirata Noboru, a naval officer who served as Aide from 1935 to 1939, for example, was the son of former Lord Keeper of the Privy Seal Hirata Tōsuke.[77] Given the emphasis on military careers for aristocrats, however, the number of aristocratic Aides was not extraordinary. It is quite possible that more military officers of aristocratic origin

75. Yoshihashi interview; interview with Chamberlain Irie Sukemasa, 1964.
76. Photocopy of a document written by General Yoshihashi Kaizō on Imperial Household Agency stationery [1965].
77. Ibid.; Yoshihashi interview.

served tours of duty as Aides-de-Camp than did those of common origin. As Irie Sukemasa remarked, only "the best" were allowed to become Aides.[78]

In general, however, the Aides-de-Camp, who managed the inner court's liaison with the military commands, were very different from the Chamberlains, who managed access to the Emperor-in-Chambers and were primarily responsible for liaison between the inner court and civilian personnel, both court and government. The Aides were career military officers whose service at court was temporary. The Chamberlains were overwhelmingly civilian and their positions were all but permanent. A tour of duty as an Aide was in most cases a step up in the military, not the palace bureaucracy. There was virtually no upward mobility among the Chamberlains, at court or elsewhere. Although some Aides were of aristocratic origin, they were far less aristocratic than the Chamberlains. Finally, all the Aides were graduates of the service academies. Only two of the fifteen Chamberlains in 1943 were products of the academies.

INSTITUTIONAL PLURALISM AT COURT

The Office of Aides-de-Camp exemplifies the presence at court of institutional representatives from the "outside"—personnel from the numerous institutions of imperial prerogative beyond the palace gates. Since the emperor was the supreme commander of the armed forces, the General Staff officers of the Office Aides, who linked the emperor to the operational commands of the military establishment, could be fully justified on constitutional grounds. But the emperor also possessed extensive prerogatives in government administration, foreign affairs, and legislation. By the same logic that led to the presence of the military at court, one would expect that the other basic institutions of imperial prerogative—the government ministries and the Imperial Diet—would also be represented there.

By the 1930s the court was in fact a mosaic of such institutional representatives. This was especially true of palace bureaucrats in

78. Irie interview.

positions of responsibility. Moreover, the higher the position of a palace official, the more likely it was that he had had extensive bureaucratic experience outside the palace. As we shall see in the following chapter, for example, the four top palace officers after 1927 were invariably brought into the palace directly from high positions in the government and military bureaucracies.

But the "outside" institutional representation at court was selective. Not all institutions of imperial prerogative were represented, nor were they represented equally. Table 6 illustrates the nature of institutional representation at court by giving a statistical summary of the careers and backgrounds of eighty-three palace officials in responsible positions at court during 1943, from the top four palace officers down to and including the officials who managed the various sections of which the Imperial Household Ministry's boards, bureaus, and offices were composed. Ladies-in-Waiting and some thirty palace advisers have been excluded from the tabulation. Of the eighty-three persons included, fifty-seven were section chiefs or above, fifteen were Chamberlains, eight were Aides-de-Camp, and three were court physicians. Thirty-six of the eighty-three (43.4 percent) had had at least one year's experience in the civil bureaucracy prior to entering the Imperial Household Ministry. Twelve (14.5 percent) had come from the military establishment, and nine (10.8 percent) had some degree of other professional experience, such as teaching in private universities. Thus, 68.7 percent of the Imperial Household Ministry's leading officials in 1943 came from the "outside." Those whose careers were apparently confined exclusively to the palace numbered only twenty-six (31.3 percent).

The personnel mosaic at court was essentially made up of the civil, court, and military bureaucracies, these three clusters accounting for 89.2 percent of the leading palace officers in 1943. Most numerous were representatives from the civil bureaucracy (43.4 percent), who outnumbered their "outside" colleagues from the military bureaucracy by three to one. At least seven of the eleven ministries of the central civilian bureaucracy in 1940 were represented. One of those ministries, the Home Ministry, was the most strongly represented of all the outside institutions of imperial prerogative, civilian or military: 18.1 percent of the leading palace

TABLE 6.   CAREERS, EDUCATION, AND STATUS OF LEADING
IMPERIAL HOUSEHOLD MINISTRY OFFICIALS, 1943

(83 PERSONS)

	Number of persons	Percentage
CAREER BACKGROUND:		
Civil Bureaucracy	*36*	*43.4*
Home Ministry	15	18.1
Ministry of Agriculture and Commerce[a]	6	7.2
Finance Ministry	4	4.8
Foreign Ministry	3	3.6
Ministry of Justice	3	3.6
Ministry of Communications	3	3.6
Ministry of Education	2	2.4
Court Bureaucracy	*26*	*31.3*
Military Bureaucracy	*12*	*14.5*
Army	7	8.4
Navy	5	6.0
Other[b]	*9*	*10.8*
Business and banking	3	3.6
Medical	3	3.6
Education	3	3.6
Mass media	0	0
Total	83	100.0%
LEGISLATIVE EXPERIENCE:		
House of Peers	5	6.0
House of Representatives	0	0
None	78	94.0
Total	83	100.0%
COLLEGE EDUCATION:		
Tokyo Imperial University	49	59.0
Other state universities	15	18.1
Military academies	12	14.5
Private universities	4	4.8
None	3	3.6
Total	83	100.0%

TABLE 6.—*Continued*

STATUS:	Number of persons	Percentage
Titled or in line to succeed but not taxpayers	12	14.5
Titled taxpayers	13	15.7
Titled subtotal	25	30.1
Nontitled taxpayers	25	30.1
Taxpayer subtotal	38	45.8
Neither titled nor taxpayer	33	39.8
Total	83	100.1%

SOURCE: *Kunai Shō Shokuin Roku*, 1943, and terse data available in Japanese biographical dictionaries and palace files. Given the limited information available, the information presented in table 6 may not be very complete. It is highly likely, for example, that many more than 13 of the 25 aristocrats had tax obligations.

NOTE: 1943 has been chosen because one might expect that in the midst of Japan's greatest war military representation at the side of the emperor would be greater than at any other time. This was obviously not the case. From my perusal of personnel lists and official rosters after 1920, it would appear that 1943 was not unrepresentative of the personnel complexion of the Imperial Household Ministry after 1920, when the institutionalization of imperial prerogatives was largely completed.

ᵃ Includes the Ministry of Agriculture and Forestry and the Ministry of Commerce and Industry, which were created from the Ministry of Agriculture and Commerce in 1925.

ᵇ *Other* is not quite synonymous with "private sector," since private educational institutions were not entirely free from regulation by the Ministry of Education and certain business and banking activities were closely involved with the state bureaucracy.

officials in 1943 had served in the Home Ministry prior to entering the Imperial Household Ministry. Notably underrepresented was the Imperial Diet. None of the eighty-three officials had ever been elected to the House of Representatives. Only five were from the House of Peers, and those five, two princes and three marquis, served exclusively by right of hereditary title. None of the eighty-three ranking officials of the palace in 1943 had ever been elected by any kind of electorate to any kind of political office.

Finally, representatives from the "private sector" of Japanese society—mass media (0 percent), private education (3.6 percent), business and banking (3.6 percent), and other professions (3.6 percent)—were also underrepresented. The palace bureaucracy was first and foremost a mosaic of representatives of the bureaucratic institutions of imperial prerogative. Underlining the bureaucratic character of these palace officials was the fact that in 1943, 59.0 percent had graduated from prewar Japan's most prestigious state university, Tokyo Imperial University, while only 4.8 percent were graduates of private universities.

Since the imperial institution was the state writ small, it is not unnatural that offices resembling those of the state existed at court. But it does not necessarily follow that officials from the state bureaucracy should serve in the Imperial Household Ministry, however closely state and court offices resembled each other. In other words, an explanation is required for the relatively low percentage (31.3 percent) of purely court bureaucrats in the ministry and for the selective representation of outside institutions.

In the first place, the palace was the hub of the negotiation process in prewar Japanese politics. The theory of legitimacy set forth in the Meiji Constitution, if practiced, would make the imperial institution the ultimate locus of political resolution because it was at court that policies were to receive final ratification. To have representatives at court from the major political components involved in policy making might conceivably facilitate that process. The existence of the Office of Aides-de-Camp and the Board of Chamberlains attests to the interaction of the military and civil bureaucracies with the court. All of the Aides were career officers in the Army or Navy and four of the fifteen Chamberlains in 1943 had prior careers in the civil bureaucracy. It was the emperor's role as Emperor-in-State that made such offices and outside representation necessary.

The absence of officials with any experience in the elected House of Representatives and the small number and hereditary nature of those from the House of Peers suggests that at least by 1943 the legislature simply was not important to the process of political negotiation and ratification that centered on the Emperor-in-State. And the 1943 composition of the palace bureaucracy was not, in fact, atypical of the Imperial Household Ministry throughout the prewar period, especially after imperial prerogatives had become thoroughly institutionalized in the 1920s. As we shall see in the following chapter, for example, none of the four top palace officers from 1885 to 1945 had ever been elected to the House of Representatives. Even though the House of Representatives had acquired considerable power by 1920, it never managed to place its institutional representatives in positions of power at the side of the emperor.

The selectivity of institutional representation at court substantiates the profoundly bureaucratic nature of the political process in prewar Japan. Although a law, to be a law, required passage by the Imperial Diet, the role of law per se was very limited, and all laws required imperial sanction as well. Such vital decisions as declarations of war and appointments of Prime Ministers were always made by the responsible Ministers of State, military chiefs, and imperial advisers and then ratified at the palace, not in the Imperial Diet. To exaggerate, it was the imperial seal that ultimately made a government policy the legitimate policy of the state, not its passage by the Imperial Diet.

The imperial institution was intricately interwoven not only with the government but also with society at large. The arrangements for imperial tours by the Emperor-in-Court, for example, could best be made by officials familiar with local operations; hence the impressive number of ex-Home Ministry officials among the leading court officials. The same applies to management of imperial house properties scattered throughout Japan and the number of officials at court from the Ministry of Agriculture and Commerce. Finally, the imperial institution was the ideal polity writ small. In addition to the bureaucracy, representatives of status and wealth were prominent at court. At least 30.1 percent of the leading palace officials in 1943 were titled or in line to succeed, and at least 45.8 percent were wealthy enough to pay taxes. The Imperial Household Ministry was therefore an intricate mosaic of bureaucracy, aristocracy, and plutocracy—the elements in prewar Japanese society most highly valued as components of the "ideal."

But if these court officials symbolized the "ideal" structure of the prewar Japanese polity, they also operationalized that symbol both in government and in society. Guardians of the emperor's personal will, they were also responsible for translating the imperial symbol into the Imperial Will. By the 1930s the human mosaic at court no longer reflected a unified and stabilized agreement concerning the privileged status of the Emperor-in-Chambers. With the gradual disappearance of a unified elite in government after the turn of the century, the imperial institution itself lost its internal unity. By the 1930s struggles for supremacy among the institutions of imperial prerogative outside the palace had infected even the lower levels of the palace bureaucracy.

The following incident reveals the extent to which the walls around the Emperor-in-Chambers had been breached. In October 1931 a Major Endō Saburō called on his section chief in the General Staff Office, Colonel Imamura Hitoshi.[79] Had Colonel Imamura ever met Sekiya Teisaburō, the Vice Minister of the Imperial Household Ministry, Major Endō asked. Imamura replied that he had met Sekiya but once, and only formally. Endō then told Imamura that after he had returned from Europe with Sekiya's son he had been a regular visitor to the Sekiya house. Suddenly, continued Endō, Sekiya had called him to his official residence and asked him about the October Incident, a plot by young Army officers to overthrow the government in October 1931. Sekiya inquired if it were true that one objective of the plot was to "rectify" the Imperial Household Ministry. Since Sekiya had heard from the police that Endō's superior, Colonel Imamura, was investigating the matter, he asked Endō to make an appointment for him to see Imamura. Commenting, Sekiya said that he was not worried about the fate of the Imperial Household Ministry but was concerned over "causing a disturbance at the emperor's side." After delaying two or three days because Imamura was so "busy," Endō had finally come to Imamura with Sekiya's request.

In response, Imamura told Endō that he had heard that Sekiya was a practicing Christian, but that he would meet him after checking with the Military Affairs Bureau in the Army Ministry. This precaution was necessary, claimed Imamura, because to discuss

79. The following account is from Imamura Hitoshi, *Kōzoku to Kashikan* (Tokyo: Jiyū Ajia Sha, 1960), pp. 234–44. Although Major Endō is listed in the 1931 and 1932 *Shokuin Roku* as a member of the General Staff Office, Colonel Imamura is not. According to Imamura's account, he became Chief of the Strategy Section, General Staff Office, on August 1, 1931 but was transferred to the Shanghai front in February 1932. This would explain his absence from both official rosters, which are dated July (Imamura Hitoshi, pp. 192, 258).

the October Incident with "outsiders" required permission from the bureau, which had general jurisdiction over such incidents. The bureau consented to Imamura's meeting with Sekiya. Imamura then had Endō arrange a meeting with Sekiya for 8:30 p.m. at Sekiya's official residence, the time and place having been selected so that few would see them meeting.

When they met, Vice Minister Sekiya told Imamura that persons in the Metropolitan Police Office had told him that Colonel Imamura had tracked down the plan of the October Incident written by its organizers, and that, after divulging its contents only to the top Army leaders, the Chief of the Military Affairs Bureau, General Koiso Kuniaki, had burned the document. Sekiya said it had been discovered that the radicals had intended to discipline the Imperial Household Ministry thoroughly. Colonel Imamura was dismayed that there might be persons within the Army who had set such rumors flying and that the Metropolitan Police Office should have spied out the plan of the radicals. He then denied that the organizers were in any way disloyal, asserting to Sekiya that those of the twelve arrested whom he knew were loyal and far above the ordinary in integrity, however improper their methods.

But it was true, Imamura continued, that the plotters had intended to rectify the Imperial Household Ministry. He guessed that the Incident's organizers harked back to the early Meiji period, when the emperor was surrounded by talented men "of the people"; at present those at court were mostly aristocrats, and "persons truly able to render assistance to His Majesty are not to be found." Praising their "loyal hearts," Imamura then warned Sekiya that many officers of the Imperial Guards had been involved in the blood-sealed pact among the organizers. Knowing full well what transpired at the palace, Imamura stated, the officers of the Imperial Guards detested the officials of the Imperial Household Ministry.

Asked to give the reasons for this hatred, Imamura replied that according to what he had heard, the officers of the Imperial Guards felt that Imperial Household Ministry officials treated the emperor as "their emperor," separating him from the eyes and hearts of the people. With police and officials surrounding him every minute, the emperor was kept away from the people when outside the palace, as if he were "touring an enemy country or battleground." The officials

of the ministry, in other words, were impairing the closeness
between sovereign and subject that had prevailed in the Meiji period. Moreover, the members of the Imperial Guards were not the
sons of aristocrats as they had been in the Meiji period but came
from middle and lower class homes. Since the soldiers came largely
from farm villages, and the officers bore heartfelt affection for their
men, it was only natural that the officers should be sympathetic to
the banners of village relief being waved by Lieutenant Colonel Hashimoto Kingorō.[80] Specifying some of the concrete complaints he
had heard, and commenting on them, Imamura stated:

> When Their Majesties walk in the palace garden the Chamberlains al-
> ways go first along the itinerary. To the sentries of the Imperial Guards,
> who act as imperial escorts, they announce: "You're an eyesore. Go to the
> very back, move to a place where they won't catch sight of you." Even the
> more polite Chamberlains say: "Soon Their Majesties will be in sight.
> Please wait over there until they have passed." From what I hear the
> Chamberlains behave as if it were the era of the tsars of Russia, even in the
> palace.
>   I have a request to make of those close to the throne. Instead of this, I
> would like them to say: "Soon the emperor will pass here. Possibly he may
> have questions. Be close at hand along the route." As it is now, I am com-
> pelled to say that the Chamberlains are forcibly trying to separate His
> Majesty, who is the father, from the soldiers, who are the children. The
> soldiers are indignant. If the Imperial Household officials think the
> soldiers are such eyesores, why shouldn't every imperial escort be made up
> from only palace police? Why shouldn't the Imperial Guards be
> dropped?[81]

To which Sekiya replied: "That's probably because the sentiments
of the Board of Chamberlains are not clearly transmitted to the Imperial Guards units." Earlier in their conversation he had confessed
great concern and promised to look into the officers' complaints. He
cautioned Colonel Imamura, however, that "even within the
ministry my authority is weak; I just don't have the power to reform
this fundamentally." After talking with Sekiya for three hours,
Colonel Imamura left, much impressed with the sincerity of the Imperial Household Ministry's vice minister.

80. Hashimoto Kingorō (1890–1957), an active leader of the radical Cherry Blossom
Association composed largely of young Army officers, was involved in many of the coup attempts of the 1930s as well as military adventurism in China.
81. Imamura Hitoshi, pp. 242–43.

The above incident reveals the extent to which inner palace events had become sources of outer institutional complaints, however fatuous. Complaints of this sort, however, were verbalizations of the deeper institutional struggle to declare the Imperial Will in politics—that is, to determine state policy. In this instance, maltreatment of soldiers by imperial household officials while the emperor and empress were walking within the palace grounds became a rationalization for military plotting to "rectify" the Imperial Household Ministry. Such rectification usually meant assassination or attempted assassination of officials close to the throne, as events soon proved. The leadership of the Army not only declared its sympathy with the October plotters' motives but also screened the entire plot from public scrutiny, as well as the plotters from public prosecution, on the remarkable ground that the Incident was a strictly "military" matter to be disposed of by strictly "military" personnel. Events of the inner court, no matter how trifling, thus became rationalizations for action on the part of institutionalized political leaders—in this case the Army's—in their struggle for supremacy in the state.

Despite the institutionalization of palace autonomy, so carefully engineered during the Restoration settlement, and the sophisticated structure of the court for managing the Emperor-in-Public and Emperor-in-Chambers in both his state and court roles, the palace bureaucracy was obviously not very successful in preserving the emperor's privacy during the early 1930s. The *imperial institution*, however, remained all but unchallenged during the extensive changes in Japanese society and the pluralization of political power among the institutions of imperial prerogative, both of which forced the palace gates open to an extent that threatened the security of the Emperor-in-Chambers and the lives of "those close to the throne." The emperor's transcendental position was maintained in large measure by the tradition that supported the imperial institution as symbol of the nation as a people, not as a state, and the ability of palace leaders to cope with the trends of the times outside the palace gates.[82]

82. Negatively, thorough police and thought controls made the transcendental imperial institution virtually a taboo by the 1930s, at least as far as the general public was concerned.

CHAPTER FOUR

THE OFFICES AND OFFICERS OF
PALACE LEADERSHIP

THE INCREASING INVASION of the emperor's palace sanctuary was the result of institutional competition to declare the Imperial Will in politics and the palace leadership's response to that competition. To place palace leadership in its proper context, therefore, it is first necessary to describe two developments affecting political leadership outside the palace: the institutionalization of imperial prerogatives and the institutionalization of political elites. Both affected the nature of political leadership directly, while the politicization of society influenced the environment in which that leadership operated.[1]

The institutionalization of imperial prerogatives. By the 1930s the emperor's prerogatives had been completely institutionalized. The Imperial Diet exercised the emperor's legislative prerogative, in cooperation with or in opposition to the government leaders of the day. From 1890, when the first Diet was convoked, to 1900, when oligarch Itō Hirobumi attempted to fuse oligarchic and political party power, the elected House of Representatives was the institutional base for antioligarch forces: a composite of antimodernizers, political leaders excluded from the Cabinet by the oligarchs, landowning malcontents, and "liberals" espousing various forms of party government.

1. The generalizations that follow about the nature of prewar political leadership are tentative observations based on preliminary research for a projected study of Japanese political leadership and political change after 1868.

Between 1900 and 1918, however, the House of Representatives was led by strengthened political parties whose leaders for the most part had had both bureaucratic and electoral experience. During this period the House became strong enough to mount an effective challenge to "transcendental Cabinets"—Cabinets composed exclusively of civil and military bureaucrats and the bureaucratic protégés of the oligarchs.

The House of Representatives' bid for institutional supremacy after 1913, rationalized by Professor Minobe Tatsukichi's theory of the supremacy of the emperor's legislative prerogative, was a consequence of the institutionalization of but one of the emperor's prerogatives. The Home Ministry exercised the emperor's prerogatives in maintaining peace and order. The emperor's treaty-making prerogative was exercised by the Foreign Ministry. The military commands of the Army and Navy wielded the emperor's prerogative of supreme command, and the military ministries his prerogative of military administration.

Because all institutions were equally derived from imperial prerogatives, however, serious jurisdictional disputes developed among them. From at least 1914 the "prerogative of supreme command" was used by the military services to defend their institutional interests against the Imperial Diet. When the Diet refused to increase military appropriations, for example, the military accused the Diet of violating the prerogative of supreme command. But did a legislative proposal concerning the size of the military establishment involve the emperor's legislative prerogative or his military prerogative? The London Naval Treaty of 1930, as we shall see in this chapter, produced a sharp conflict between the Navy General Staff and the Cabinet. Did a treaty involving combatant ships fall under the emperor's prerogative of treaty making, exercised by the Foreign Ministry, or the prerogative of supreme command, exercised by the naval command? And who was to decide which institution of prerogative had jurisdiction? The Privy Council, which advised the emperor on constitutional issues? The Supreme War Council, which advised the emperor on basic military policies? Or the Cabinet, which was responsible for producing and managing unified national policies?

The institutions of prerogative were also fragmented into subinstitutions and factional groupings. For example, the legislative prerogative was exercised by the Imperial Diet, but the Diet was composed of two feuding houses: the appointive and aristocratic upper House of Peers and the elected lower House of Representatives. After 1903 the prerogative of supreme command was institutionalized in two separate and equal command structures: the Army General Staff and Navy General Staff. These subinstitutions were further fragmented into smaller structures, personal cliques, and opinion groups. The consequences of institutionalization, fragmentation, and factionalism were twofold. First, political leaders were able to maneuver and manipulate by playing one institution or component of imperial prerogative off against another: the Army command against the Navy command, the House of Peers against the House of Representatives, the Navy Ministry against the Navy General Staff, the Foreign Ministry against the Army Ministry. Second, if one institution of prerogative or any of its subinstitutions or groups wished to make or dominate policy, it had to form cross-institutional coalitions. The height of the House of Representatives' influence, for example, was reached between 1918 and 1931, when its leaders united with civilian bureaucrats—most notably those in the Home and Finance Ministries. The Control Faction of the Army was able to gain predominance in the government only after 1932, when it formed a coalition with segments of the Navy, renovationist bureaucrats in the civil ministries, and a number of sympathetic leaders in the Imperial Diet.

The institutionalization of political elites. Disputes among the plural institutions of prerogative, complicated by intrainstitutional competition, might not have endangered the palace sanctuary had it not been for a parallel trend in Japanese politics: the institutionalization of political elites. By the 1930s the institutions of imperial prerogative tended to be led by men who were products of those institutions. Leadership in the House of Representatives was frequently held by those with party seniority and the longest record of electoral success. The Army and Navy were led by generals and admirals who had risen to positions of leadership via standardized achievement routes exclusively within their respective services. If the Foreign Minister was not a career diplomat, which he often was, those in positions of leadership under him almost invariably were. The institutions of imperial prerogative were for the most part closed systems under parochial leadership. Under such conditions, political leaders more often than not equated the demands of their institution or subinstitution with the national interest, translating a parochial concern into the Imperial Will. Even when a minister was a "generalist" of lengthy and diverse political experience, he still had to cope with the careerist leaders of his ministry and their often narrow policy references. Thus, after the assassination of Prime Minister Hara Kei in 1921 and the death of oligarch Yamagata Aritomo in 1922,

> each of the governmental organs began to insist on its own power—the foreign ministry on its control over diplomacy, the ministry of justice on its control over the legal system, the army on its prerogative of supreme command, and the Privy Council and House of Peers on their unique positions—so much that political agreement became extremely difficult to maintain.[2]

Such jurisdictional disputes, especially between the military and civil institutions, infused the entire polity. Occasionally they bordered on the inane. The qōsutoppu incident of 1933 is an extreme example of rivalry between the Army and the Home Ministry—and of the consequences of institutionalized elites operating the plural institutions of imperial prerogative. In June 1933 a traffic policeman in Osaka tried to arrest a private first class who had twice crashed a traffic signal (go-stop). The private insisted that as a soldier he was not subject to orders from a policeman. A fight broke out and a crowd gathered. The military police (kempeitai) immediately took custody of the private. The incident then went from the local chief of police to the Governor of Osaka, then via the Home Ministry's Chief of the Police Bureau to the Home Minister himself. It went right to the top of the Army Ministry, via the Chief of Staff and Commander of the Army's Fourth Division, to which the private was attached. Home Minister Yamamoto Tatsuo argued firmly that Army vehicles must obey the law. Army Minister Araki Sadao and other Army leaders insisted that soldiers were the "emperor's soldiers." The Home Ministry's police

2. Ito Takashi, "Conflicts and Coalitions in Japan, 1930: Political Groups [and] the London Naval Disarmament Conference," in *The Study of Coalition Behavior: Theoretical Perspectives and Cases from Four Continents,* ed. Sven Groennings, E. W. Kelley, and Michael Leiserson (New York: Holt, Rinehart & Winston, 1970), p. 162. Ito's list could be longer and should include the House of Representatives as well.

authorities retorted that policemen, too, were the "emperor's policemen." The Chief of Staff of the Army's Fourth Division declared publicly that the incident involved acts that were "violent, injurious, and insulting to soldiers on active duty," "a grave incident involving the dignity of the imperial army." Even the emperor finally heard about the dispute. During Army exercises in October, the emperor asked Army Minister Araki what was going on. Mortified, Araki ordered the affair settled immediately. The Governor of Hyōgo Prefecture, who was not involved in the incident, was asked to mediate. In November he produced a compromise to which both sides subsequently agreed. Harmony was finally restored after some five months of feuding.[3]

In this example, the intensity of institutional loyalties caused a major dispute over the most minor of incidents, embroiling Japanese political leaders in a five-month conflict. The time involved in reaching compromises is but one measure of the intensity of institutional loyalties in prewar Japanese politics. Another is the viability of the compromises reached—whether in fact they settled the disputes. A third measure is the extent to which institutionalized elites were willing, or unwilling to condone and manipulate assassination to satisfy their demands. The intensity of such loyalties not only affected the efficiency and viability of Japanese decision making; it also made politics a very dangerous undertaking. During the 1930s, for example, the Army made demands, backed by threat and intimidation, that the entire population be mobilized for "national defense," and assassination became a means to that end.[4] Since all policies required imperial sanction, threat and intimidation reached into the palace itself, as we saw in the conclusion to chapter 3. And since the imperial institution was the sole referent for each political institution and its policymaking claims, it was not uncommon for political elites like those in the Army to grasp for any imperial token that would make their institution's claims to declare the Imperial Will more forceful or those of other institutions less so, again as illustrated in chapter 3.

3. Nezu Masashi, pp. 128–29.
4. For an analysis of the Army's invasion into all areas of politics in the name of national defense and the prerogative of supreme command, see James B. Crowley, *Japan's Quest for Autonomy: National Security and Foreign Policy, 1930–1938* (Princeton: Princeton University Press, 1966).

Institutionalization, Cabinet coalitions, and the palace. The institutionalization of imperial prerogatives and the institutionalization of elites profoundly affected the operations of the Japanese Cabinet, which was the central institution for translating political demands from the components of the "real polity" into national policies, and the operations of the palace, which was the central institution of political ratification for both policy decisions and personnel appointments at the apex of the Japanese political system.

The first effect was an increase in Cabinet instability. Prewar Japanese Cabinets were not noted for their stability, averaging only 1.4 years in length. But Cabinets between 1885 and 1921 lasted an average of 1.9 years, while the life of those between 1921 and 1945 averaged a mere 1.0 years. Instability was also reflected in the number of new Ministers of State produced annually. Between 1885 and 1921 there were 3.1 new ministers per year; from 1921 to 1945, 6.9.

Since some twenty men in both periods served as Minister of State four times or more, Japanese politics remained oligarchic as far as the Cabinet was concerned. But the nature of that oligarchy changed drastically. The second effect of plural institutionalization was to make the Cabinet a coalition of elites representing the competing institutions of prerogative rather than a coalition of autonomous individuals as it had been from 1885 to 1901, when the oligarchs held the major Cabinet posts.[5]

By the 1930s, therefore, Cabinet coalitions reflected the mix of institutional strengths at any given time. The Hamaguchi Cabinet of 1929, for example, emphasized that the House of Representatives was

---

5. Much has been made of the fact that the oligarchs who held most Cabinet posts most of the time between 1885 and 1901, and even after, were from the two domains of Satsuma and Chōshū. Cabinets between 1885 and 1901 were assailed as being monopolized by these two "domain cliques." But the oligarchs were leaders of the nation, not local clans. Although they may have favored as their political protégés those from their own domains, this was by no means always the case. Second, it would be more than difficult to demonstrate that their policies were directed only to the benefit of their local domains. They ruled as national figures, whose loyalties to their domains and to the specific institutions of government they had created were subsidiary to their abiding concern with Japan's national development. In this respect they were far more autonomous than their successors, whose institutional origins and loyalties often caused them to equate their institution's interests with the national interest, rather than vice versa. To exaggerate, a political leader in the 1930s tended to see his institution as the nation, not the nation as a whole composed of many legitimate parts of which his institution was but one.

the "most equal" of the institutions or subinstitutions of imperial prerogative at that time. Seven of the fourteen Cabinet ministers, including Prime Minister Hamaguchi, held seats in the House of Representatives, and one more had served in the House for four years prior to 1929. These eight ministers had been in the House an average of fourteen years. At the same time, however, the Army Minister was a career Army officer, the Navy Minister a career Navy officer, and the Foreign Minister a career diplomat. None of the three had had significant, if any, experience outside his own institution of prerogative. In addition, the Finance Minister had moved directly into Cabinet politics from a career in state banking. Both he and the Foreign Minister held seats in the House of Peers by imperial appointment. An ex-bureaucrat who had served in the House of Peers since 1916 and a career Army officer completed the institutional coalition on which the Hamaguchi Cabinet was based.

By way of contrast, General Tōjō's Cabinet, created less than two months before the outbreak of war with the United States, represented the triumph of the military. Seven of the fifteen Cabinet posts were held by career Army and Navy officers, and an eighth was held by a doctor whose career had been exclusively in Army medical schools and hospitals. None of Tōjō's Cabinet Ministers had even served in the House of Representatives and only one, a career Finance Ministry bureaucrat, held a seat in the House of Peers when the Cabinet was formed. Again, however, the Cabinet was a coalition of institutionalized elites. The Foreign Minister was a career diplomat. The Minister of Justice had spent his entire career in the Justice Ministry. The Minister of Commerce and Industry and the Minister of Agriculture and Forestry were exclusive products of those ministries and their predecessor, the Ministry of Agriculture and Commerce.

Tōjō's Cabinet was thus a coalition of the bureaucratic institutions of prerogative with the military bureaucracy being the "most equal." But even under total mobilization for war Tōjō had to cope with the Imperial Diet. Thus in the "Tōjō election" of 1942 two of his ministers were elected to the House of Representatives. Later, three were appointed to the House of Peers. Throughout his tenure as Prime Minister, from 1941 to mid-1944, Tōjō was obliged to appear before the House of Representatives and defend his policies. One

Diet member even suggested publicly that Tōjō was becoming a "dictator."[6] However weakly, the Imperial Diet continued to function as the institution of the imperial prerogative of legislation.

Because Cabinets were unstable coalitions of institutionalized elites reflecting the mix of institutional strengths at any given moment, policy making at the national level was a tortured and time-consuming process that more often than not produced incoherent and inconsistent policies, or policies that simply could not be implemented. The elites could and did break apart the delicate coalitions on which Cabinets were based by insisting on their respective institutional demands. As early as 1912, for example, the Army brought down Saionji Kimmochi's second Cabinet when Saionji refused to accommodate the Army's demand for two new divisions.[7] Although the Army may well have been the greatest offender, given the increasing intensity with which it insisted on its parochial demands, other institutions of imperial prerogative were guilty of similar behavior at various times and with varying degrees of success: the House of Representatives, the Privy Council, House of Peers, Navy General Staff, and coalitions of civil bureaucrats. For example, Kiyoura Keigo's "bureaucratic" Cabinet of 1924 collapsed very shortly after its inauguration when the House of Representatives "flatly refused to cooperate with the Cabinet."[8]

The problem was not only to find a coalition appropriate to the times in terms of institutional mix. It was also one of finding Prime Ministers and Ministers of State, each of whom commanded the respect of more than one institution of imperial prerogative and would be willing to cooperate in forging a united policy which the institutions of prerogative would implement, willingly or unwillingly. This meant finding leaders with cross-institutional connections, political views that were representative of more than one institution's parochial demands, sophisticated abilities in the arts of compromise and coalition building, and, given the frequent assassinations of Prime Ministers and other leading officials after 1930, a great deal of courage. The institutionalization of elites made such statesmen scarce.

6. Maruyama Masao, *Thought and Behaviour*, p. 17.
7. Hugh Borton, *Japan's Modern Century* (New York: Ronald Press, 1955), p. 250.
8. Ibid., p. 307.

The institutionalization of prerogatives made it difficult for such statesmen to forge a coherent policy, or to carry out a policy once it was agreed upon.

Since the emperor appointed the Prime Minister and Ministers of State, the palace was deeply involved in the process of forming Cabinet coalitions. All Cabinets after 1921 reflected a balance of the institutions of prerogative and their representatives in accordance with the estimated strengths of those institutions and their leaders. Estimating the strengths of institutions and leaders and discovering appropriate coalitions was the responsibility of those who advised the throne on political appointments: the Elder Statesmen (the remaining oligarchs after 1901), the Senior Retainers (ex-Prime Ministers), and palace officers, most notably the Lord Keeper of the Privy Seal. These advisers, who in effect exercised the emperor's prerogative of Cabinet appointments, were the "generalists" in Japanese politics. For the most part they had had extensive political experience in more than one institution of imperial prerogative and were the most skilled among Japanese political leaders in the arts of coalition building and the politics of consensus. Cabinets therefore reflected coalitions of institutionalized elites according to what palace advisers believed desirable for "coping with the trends of the time"—which may have meant their own policy and personnel preferences rather than a dispassionate and objective evaluation of institutional and leadership strengths. Whether palace advisers were partisan consensus makers or objective consensus takers, they held primary responsibility for negotiating Cabinet coalitions into existence. More than any other single prerogative, therefore, it was the emperor's prerogative of appointment that brought the palace into the political process.

The palace officers responsible for coordinating and facilitating the palace advisory machinery, as well as for gatekeeping policies in the face of institutional pressures to declare the Imperial Will, were the Imperial Household Minister, the Grand Chamberlain, the Chief Aide-de-Camp, and the Lord Keeper of the Privy Seal. The Imperial Household Minister, as head manager of the palace bureaucracy, was primarily responsible for maintaining palace autonomy and the transcendental position of the Emperor-in-Court. The Grand Chamberlain was the emperor's chief messenger in attendance; his role was far more ambiguous than that of the other three palace leaders, as we shall see in this chapter. The Chief Aide-de-Camp was the emperor's key military adviser in the palace and his chief liaison with the operational commands of the Army and Navy. The Lord Keeper of the Privy Seal was the emperor's principal palace adviser on political affairs, excluding matters clearly under the jurisdiction of the military commands. Unlike the Imperial Household Minister and the Grand Chamberlain, who were strictly court officers and responsible primarily for the Emperor-in-Court, the Chief Aide and the Privy Seal were adjunct palace officers primarily responsible for the Emperor-in-State in his military and governmental capacities respectively. Behind all four palace leaders were the curtained advisers to the throne—the Elder Statesmen and Senior Retainers who held primary responsibility for advising the Emperor-in-State, via the Privy Seal, on who should be appointed to make and manage national policies.

These four palace officers also managed the process of imperial ratification of political policies in cooperation with the government leaders of the day, both civil and military. Imperial ratification, as the final act in an essentially closed and bureaucratic political process, was to endow decisions of state with dignified mystery. Conducted within the walled and moated imperial palace, imperial ratification was an "invisible" process designed to keep the entire prewar system of decision making invisible. Only the decision was to be public, not the process itself.

The assertions that have just been made about the political process outside the palace and the relation of the palace to that process are substantiated at least in part by the following discussion of the Imperial Household Minister, Grand Chamberlain, Chief Aide-de-Camp, and Lord Keeper of the Privy Seal as officers and offices of palace leadership from 1885 to 1945. All four officers were members or partners of the oligarchy as it evolved from a group of autonomous political leaders to an unstable collection of institutionalized elites. Beginning with a description of the evolution of palace leadership from 1885 to 1945, this chapter deals in considerable detail with the duties, personalities, and behavior of each of the four palace officers. It concludes with a comparative portrait of these leaders and an analysis of the role of the palace as it evolved over time, with an emphasis on the 1930s.

THE EVOLUTION OF PALACE LEADERSHIP:
A PRELIMINARY PERIODIZATION AND ANALYSIS

We may begin our discussion of the four most important palace officers by dividing the evolution of palace leadership into a sequence of stages. The starting point is 1885, the year in which the cabinet system was adopted and the first Lord Keeper of the Privy Seal appointed. By 1885 oligarchic power had been consolidated both in government and in court. The structure and offices of the palace bureaucracy had also been largely consolidated. The only office of court leadership not in existence by 1885 was that of Chief Aide-de-Camp; although there had been Aides-de-Camp at court from at least 1875, the formal creation of the Office of Aides-de-Camp did not occur until 1896.

The evolution of palace leadership after 1885 may be divided into five stages: (1) oligarchic control (1885–1912); (2) transition to leadership by career bureaucrats from the institutions of imperial prerogative outside the palace (1912–21); (3) bureaucratic leadership at the emperor's side by the constitutional monarchists (1921–36); (4) replacement of the constitutional monarchists by the traditionalists (1936–40); and (5) bureaucratic leadership by the traditionalists (1940–45). These periods may also be viewed as subdivisions of imperial reigns. The last two-thirds of the Meiji period (1885–1912) was a time of oligarchic unity at the palace. The Taishō period (1912–26) was a one of transition, and the prewar and wartime part of the current Shōwa period (1926–45) a period of balanced institutional representation at court led first by the constitutional monarchists and then by the traditionalists. Both periodizations, however rough, reveal a continuous response on the part of palace leadership to the changing circumstances of politics outside the palace gates.

Table 7 lists the names and years of appointment of all persons holding the four leading palace offices between 1885 and 1945. In contrast to the Taishō and Shōwa periods, the Meiji period witnessed a high degree of tranquility at the emperor's side. From the end of 1885 through 1912 there were only nine changes in the personnel of the four offices. If we calculate changes in office against cumulative years, the average tenure for each palace officer was 10.7 years. Until late 1912, when Prince Katsura Tarō became Privy Seal and concur-

TABLE 7. PERSONS HOLDING THE FOUR LEADING PALACE OFFICES AND THEIR YEARS OF APPOINTMENT, 1885–1945

Year Appointed	Position			
	Household Minister	Grand Chamberlain	Chief Aide	Privy Seal
1885	Itō Hirobumi			Sanjō Sanetomi
1886				
1887	Hijikata Hisamoto			
1888				
1889				
1890				
1891		Tokudaiji Sanenori		Tokudaiji Sanenori
1892				
1893				
1894				
1895				
1896			Okazawa Kuwashi	
1897				
1898	Tanaka Mitsuaki			
1899				
1900				
1901				
1902				
1903				
1904				
1905				
1906				
1907				
1908			Nakamura Satoru	

1909	Iwakura Tomosada			
1910	Watanabe Chiaki			
1911				Katsura Tarō
1912		Hatano Takanao		Fushimi Sadanaru
1913	Hatano Takanao	Katsura Tarō		Ōyama Iwao
1914		Takatsukasa Hiromichi		
1915				
1916			Uchiyama Kojirō	
1917				Matsukata Masayoshi
1918		Ōgimachi Sanemasa		
1919				
1920	Nakamura Yūjirō			
1921	Makino Nobuaki			
1922		Tokugawa Sadataka	Nara Takeji	Hirata Tōsuke
1923				
1924				Hamao Arata
1925	Ichiki Kitokurō			Makino Nobuaki
1926				
1927		Chinda Sutemi		
1928				
1929		Suzuki Kantarō		
1930				
1931				
1932				
1933	Yuasa Kurahei		Honjō Shigeru	
1934				
1935				Saitō Makoto
1936	Matsudaira Tsuneo	Hyakutake Saburō	Usami Okiie	Ichiki Kitokurō

TABLE 7.—*Continued*

Year	Position			
1937				Yuasa Kurahei
1938				
1939		Hata Shunroku Hasunuma Shigeru		
1940			Kido Kōichi	
1941				
1942				
1943				
1944	Fujita Hisanori			
1945	Ishiwatari Sōtarō			

SOURCE: IHMD; *Shokuin Roku*; Ijiri Tsunekichi, *Rekidai Kenkan Roku* (Tokyo: Chōyōkai, 1925); and Tōyama and Adachi.

NOTE: Itō Hirobumi had headed the Imperial Household Ministry since 1871. In 1936 Ichiki Kitokurō was appointed Privy Seal for one day as a procedural step to have the murdered Saitō replaced. The list of Chief Aides is as accurate as possible, given the lack of information on this office available from the Imperial Household Agency before 1926.

rently Grand Chamberlain, leadership at the palace like that in the government was firmly in the hands of the oligarchs, who either held Cabinet offices (1885–1901) or exercised control indirectly as Elder Statesmen and via protégés in the Cabinet (1901–12). Palace leaders were securely under the oligarchs in terms of both status and allegiance throughout the Meiji period, despite the fact that, with the one exception of Itō Hirobumi from Chōshū, they were either Court Nobles or restorationist samurai from other than Chōshū or Satsuma, the two domains that had spearheaded the Restoration. That a Court Noble, Prince Tokudaiji Sanenori, was able to serve concurrently as both Grand Chamberlain and Privy Seal for over twenty years, from 1891 to 1912, attests to the solidity of the Restoration settlement as far as palace leadership was concerned.

The first ten years of the Taishō period, from 1912 to 1921, were, however, years of transition and confusion in the nature of palace leadership. This is indicated by the high rate of turnover in the leading palace offices (a change in one of the four officers every 3.4 years) and the diversity in origins and status of those holding leading palace posts during that period. A political protégé of oligarch Yamagata Aritomo (Katsura Tarō), oligarchs as Elder Statesmen (Ōyama Iwao and Matsukata Masayoshi), a prince-of-the-blood (Fushimi Sadanaru), former Court Nobles (Ōgimachi Sanemasa and Takatsukasa Hiromichi), successful civil bureaucrats (Watanabe Chiaki and Hatano Takanao), and creatures of the military bureaucracy (Uchiyama Kojirō and Nakamura Yūjirō) all found their way into the four leading palace offices. There seems to be no pattern in their appointments—no effort, for example, to balance institutional forces at the side of the emperor—although Yamagata and his allies apparently dominated at court. Judged by the marked increase in personnel changes and the diversity of palace leadership between 1912 and 1921, the oligarchic unity surrounding the throne up to 1912 was clearly lost. Those close to the throne were no longer exclusively the band of Restoration "stalwarts" praised by Kanroji Osanaga.[9]

With the appointment of Count Makino Nobuaki as Imperial Household Minister in February 1921, palace leadership entered a new era. The leaders who dominated the palace from Makino's ap-

9. See above, p. 77.

pointment until 1936 were constitutional monarchists—proponents of Minobe Tatsukichi's theory of constitutional monarchy or a more conservative variant—led outside the palace by Prince Saionji Kimmochi and inside the palace by, most notably, Count Makino, Baron Ichiki Kitokurō, and Admiral Suzuki Kantarō. After the death of Prince Matsukata Masayoshi in 1924, moreover, the powers previously held collectively by the Elder Statesmen devolved solely on Prince Saionji as the "last of the Elder Statesmen." From 1921 to 1936, therefore, palace leadership was primarily in the hands of a small group of partisan bureaucrats under Prince Saionji's tutelage who were the products of Japan's new bureaucratic and educational system. With one exception they were political leaders brought into the palace from successful careers "on the outside." A measure of stability at the side of the emperor was also restored by this likeminded group of palace officers. Between 1921 and 1936 a change in one of the four palace officers occurred on an average of once every five years.

The young officers' unsuccessful but bloody coup of February 26, 1936, followed by the only complete shift in palace leaders during the entire period from 1885 to 1945, marks the start of the last phase in the evolution of palace leadership. The new palace group emerging during the 1930s, the traditionalists, achieved preeminence in court councils with the appointment of Marquis Kido Kōichi as Privy Seal in 1940 and the death of Prince Saionji that same year. Led by Prince Konoe Fumimaro outside the palace and by Marquis Kido inside, the traditionalists disavowed the partisan stance of the constitutional monarchists. In effect, they restored the "neutrality" of the throne in politics by recommending personnel and policies "appropriate to the new times." As such, the traditionalists were concerned more with national unity than with substantive policies, more with discovering and having the emperor ratify a true "national consensus" than with pursuing a specific set of domestic or foreign policies.

The constitutional monarchists persisted in their policy and personnel preferences until the assassinations and threats of assassination from 1930 to 1936 forced them to desist. One reason why the traditionalists, Kido Kōichi in particular, took a "neutral" stance was precisely to preserve the transcendental position of the emperor: to persist in recommending to the throne "liberal" domestic policies and "pro-Anglo–American" foreign policies was to invite assassination not only of government leaders but also of the leading palace officers, thereby jeopardizing the emperor and the imperial institution.

The traditionalists, like the constitutional monarchists at court, were all creatures of Japan's modern bureaucracy. They also maintained the same balance of institutional forces at the emperor's side that had been established by the constitutional monarchists. Whereas the constitutional monarchists had manipulated this institutional balance as best they could to realize their partisan purposes, however, the traditionalists used it to ensure the accuracy of the "national consensus" on which they based their recommendations to the throne. Since the traditionalists were "neutral," moreover, they could allow new policies and men to lead the nation in accordance with the "trends of the times" revealed by the national consensus, regardless of the direction of those trends. Thus Privy Seal Kido, as the emperor's chief adviser from 1940 to 1945, could preside over both the commencement of war against the United States in 1941 and the surrender of Japan in August 1945. In short, he was able to recommend the appointment of a Prime Minister who would be able to lead the nation into war "in accord with the times" in 1941 and one who would be able to surrender the nation "in accord with the times" in 1945, before the nation was obliterated. That meant General Tōjō in 1941 and retired Admiral Suzuki Kantarō in 1945.

Finally, as in 1912–21, the rise of the traditionalists was marked by great instability in the four palace offices, chiefly as a result of the February 26 Incident of 1936. Between 1936 and 1940 a change in one of the four officers occurred every 2.3 years. With Kido's appointment as Privy Seal in 1940 and the Japanese government under the near hegemony of the military, stability was once again restored at the side of the emperor.

Accepting this summary statement about the evolution of palace leadership from 1885 to 1945 for the moment, what general characteristics did all four palace leaders have in common throughout that period? First, to point out what palace leaders were not, it is most conspicuous that none had ever held elective public office (excluding those elected to the House of Peers from among their aristocratic peer group). Second, only five of the thirty-seven men (13.5 percent) who held the top four positions at court from 1885 to 1945 could possibly be identified as career court figures: Tokudaiji Sanenori, Iwakura Tomosada, Takatsukasa Hiromichi, Tokugawa Sadataka, and Ōgimachi Sanemasa. All of the others were brought into positions of leadership at the emperor's side from successful careers outside the imperial household. After 1927 not a single appointment was made from among career court bureaucrats, although some of those appointed served for a time in the palace prior to assuming one of the four top positions.

Table 8 presents career data on the thirty-seven men who held one or more of the top four offices at court from 1885 to 1945. Quite obviously, palace leadership was composed predominantly of members of the House of Peers with considerable bureaucratic experience and achievement: 59.5 percent were at one time or other members of the House of Peers, 45.9 percent Privy Councillors, 37.8 percent Ministers of State, and 27.0 percent Supreme War Councillors. Since the number of times a person held high official position is also indicative of his political success or importance, column 5 has been included in table 8. Most revealing in this respect is the fact that the fourteen who had served as Ministers of State served thirty-seven times in that capacity, suggesting a high degree of political success and competence prior to entering the palace. That the thirty-seven palace leaders should have among them six Prime Ministers, serving in that capacity twelve times, is also a measure of the high political achievement of the group in general.

Table 8 (columns 3 and 4) also reveals that appointment to one of the four leading palace offices generally terminated the given person's official public career. Of the 126 times the thirty-seven palace leaders served in high government office, 104 times (82.5 percent) occurred prior to or concurrent with holding top palace office; only 22 times (17.5 percent) occurred after leaving palace office. Since the average age of the palace leaders upon assuming office was 61.7 years, there was, of course, not much time left for future political aspirations. In fact, thirteen of the thirty-seven (35.1 percent) died within two years of leaving office.

The career backgrounds of the palace leaders also suggest that the

TABLE 8. HIGH GOVERNMENT OFFICES OF THE FOUR LEADING
PALACE OFFICIALS, 1885–1945

(37 PERSONS)

Position (1)	Number[a] of Persons (2)	Number of Times in Position		
		Before or Concurrent with Palace Office (3)	After Palace Office (4)	Total Number of Times (5)
Prime Minister	6 (16.2%)	7	5	12 (9.5%)
Minister of State	14 (37.8%)	36	1	37 (29.4%)
President of the Privy Council	4 (10.8%)	2	5	7 (5.6%)
Privy Councillor	17 (45.9%)	14	6	20 (15.9%)
Supreme War Councillor	10 (27.0%)	8	3	11 (8.7%)
Top military posts[b]	8 (21.6%)	11	1	12 (9.5%)
House of Peers[c]	22 (59.5%)	22	1	23 (18.3%)
Ambassadors	3 (8.1%)	4	0	4 (3.2%)
House of Representatives	0 (0%)	0	0	0 (0%)
Total	—	104	22	126 (100%)

SOURCES: Miwa Kai and Philip B. Yampolsky, *Political Chronology of Japan, 1885–1957*
(New York: East Asian Institute of Columbia University, 1957); Tōyama and Adachi;
Gikai Seido Shichijū Nen Shi (*Kizokuin-Sangiin Giin Meikan*), ed. Shūgiin-Sangiin (Tokyo:
Ōkura Shō Insatsu Kyoku, 1960); biographical dictionaries in Japanese and English.
   [a] Since almost all of the 37 palace officers served in more than one important government position, the totals for column 2 add up to more than 37 and 100 percent.
   [b] For the purposes of tabulation, "top military posts" were limited to the following:
Chief of the Army General Staff, Chief of the Navy General Staff, Chief of the Military
Affairs Bureau (Army Ministry), Inspector General of Military Education, and Chief
of the Naval Affairs Bureau (Navy Ministry).
   [c] Only one person, Baron General Nakamura Yūjirō, was elected or appointed to
the House of Peers twice. Of the 23 times the 37 leading palace officers served in the
House of Peers, 9 were by imperial appointment, 10 by right of title, and 4 by election
(among counts, viscounts, and barons).

palace leadership was even more a mosaic of the valued institutional
forces in prewar Japanese political society than was the second
echelon of palace officialdom described in chapter 3. In terms of
achievement, it was a far more prestigious group of military and civilian leaders; fully twenty-eight of the thirty-seven (75.7 percent)

held at one time or another one or more of the highest military or civilian offices, excluding ambassadorships and memberships in the House of Peers.

Palace leaders were also of high status. Of the thirty-seven, at least thirty (81.1 percent) achieved or inherited titles. Of these thirty, one was a prince-of-the-blood, eight were princes, one a marquis, eight counts, four viscounts, and eight barons. In proportion to the total aristocracy (table 4), palace leaders were drawn more often from the upper than from the lower artistocracy in terms of titles ultimately achieved. Palace leaders were also drawn more from the merit than the hereditary aristocracy: twenty-six of the thirty acquired their titles as rewards for service to the state. Top palace office was not generally a refuge for the scions of aristocrats.

Palace leaders were, however, linked by family ties not only among themselves but also with political and social leaders outside the palace. In the Meiji period, Prince Tokudaiji Sanenori epitomized the intricate web of family that connected Japan's sociopolitical elites by marriage and adoption. One of Tokudaiji's younger brothers was Prince Saionji Kimmochi (1849–1940), who was closely aligned with Itō Hirobumi's side of the oligarchy.[10] The political opponent of Yamagata Aritomo's willful protégé, Katsura Tarō, Saionji alternated as Prime Minister with Katsura between 1901 and 1912. As mentioned previously, Saionji became the leading spirit of the constitutional monarchists at court and leading adviser to the throne after the last of the oligarchs, Matsukata Masayoshi, died in 1924. Another of Tokudaiji's brothers was Baron Sumitomo Kichizaemon (1864–1926), a leading figure in one of prewar Japan's four leading industrial and financial combines. Tokudaiji's eldest daughter married Prince Takatsukasa Hiromichi (1855–1918), Grand Chamberlain from 1912 to 1918. Tokudaiji's second daughter married a marquis scion of the feudal domain of Akita; his third, a Mitsui of the Mitsui combine; his fourth, a viscount scion of another feudal domain; and his fifth, a prince of the Satsuma domain. One of Tokudaiji's sons became a consultant (goyōgakari) to the Household

10. Saionji served in three of Itō's four Cabinets and Matsukata Masayoshi's second Cabinet; he never served under Yamagata or other uncompromising advocates of "transcendental Cabinets."

Ministry, another a Chamberlain, and the third a director of Mitsubishi Heavy Industries. Tokudaiji was thus related directly to top
court and government leaders, scions of the old feudal domains, and
leaders in three of the four major industrial-financial complexes in
prewar Japan.

Japan's last Privy Seal (1940–45), Marquis Kido Kōichi (b. 1889),
was almost equally well connected. His wife was the fifth daughter of
General Count Kodama Gentarō (1852–1916), Army Minister from
1900 to 1902. Kido's sister, Yaeko, married Kodama's fourth son,
Kodama Tsuneo, an Army officer and one-time director of Manchuria
Airlines. Among Kido's brothers-in-law were Kodama Hideo
(1876–1947), Minister of Overseas Affairs from 1934 to 1936 and
subsequently three times Minister of State; Kodama Kyūichi, a Home
Ministry bureaucrat; Kodama Kunio and Kodama Sadao, both
business executives, and Kodama Tomoo, one time commander of the
Japanese Army in Taiwan, who was married to the third daughter of
Baron General Nakamura Yūjirō, Household Minister from 1920 to
1921 and a protégé of Yamagata Aritomo. Kido's younger brother,
Wada Koroku, was a famous aeronautical engineer. Kido's eldest
daughter, Takiko, married the eldest son of General Abe Nobuyuki,
Prime Minister in 1939–40.

The family relationships of Prince Tokudaiji and Marquis Kido
illustrate the iron law of family that linked Japan's sociopolitical elites
throughout the prewar period. Family connections served to unite
merit and ascribed status as well as to link the components of Japanese
society laterally across the top. But much too much behavioral cau-
sality has been attributed to family connections in Japan. Family only
opened up opportunities; it did not ensure success. On the contrary,
the great use of marriage and adoption may have even assured the in-
fusion of talent and ability into leading social and political roles.

The four leading officials at court, in summary, had generally
achieved high bureaucratic positions outside the palace prior to becoming palace leaders, were representatives of the military and
government bureaucracy as well as the interlocking merit and ascribed
aristocracy, and terminated successful public careers "at the side of
the emperor." Why the palace required such capable public leaders
from the outside is answered in part by the theory of legitimacy, which

made the imperial institution the center of political authority. If in fact that theory were operative, all acts of government would require ratification by the Imperial Will. And if the Imperial Will were to have authoritative meaning, ratification would require a high degree of political skill at court—to ensure that the emperor ratified a generally agreed upon policy (a consensus) or that he ratified a partisan policy promoted by palace leaders in alliance with policy advocates in the government proper. That bureaucrats from the top strata of Japanese political society held or controlled the four leading palace offices from 1885 to 1945 is prima facie evidence that such a theory was indeed operative and that government leaders held to the theory of imperial prerogative with tenacity.

THE IMPERIAL HOUSEHOLD MINISTER:
CHIEF MANAGER OF THE EMPEROR-IN-COURT

If you were to ask me I'd say that it's by having the Minister and Vice Minister brought in from the outside that the Imperial Household Ministry gets its *raison d'etre* as an "Imperial Household Ministry in line with the times" in the first place. To cover its tracks, as it were, with persons from within the ministry—since neither a Kido nor a Hirohata are in fact outside people—and not to bring in people from the outside would be tantamount to letting the Imperial Household Ministry dig its own grave. If that know-nothing bunch [in the ministry] alone had their own way, wouldn't they ultimately deprive themselves of their own *raison d'etre*?

Prince Saionji Kimmochi[11]

The policy of selecting the Imperial Household Minister from outside the "know-nothing" career officials at court was consistently pursued from 1885 to 1945. All twelve of the Household Ministers between 1885 and 1945, and indeed many of the Vice Ministers, achieved some measure of success in the government bureaucracy prior to entering the palace. Although only one Prime Minister was among their number, six (50 percent) had been Ministers of State, seven (58.3 percent) had been or became Privy Councillors (including

11. As quoted by Baron Harada Kumao, Prince Saionji's political secretary, in 1932 (Harada Kumao, *Saionji-kō to Seikyoku,* 9 vols. [Tokyo: Iwanami Shoten, 1950–56], 2 : 397).

two Presidents), one (8.3 percent) had served in one of the leading
military positions, and six (50 percent) received imperial appointments to the House of Peers at one time or another. Only two (16.7
percent)—the last two Household Ministers—were not titled; only
one (8.3 percent), Iwakura Tomosada, was anything approaching a
court figure, and he had served for nine years as Privy Councillor
before his appointment as Household Minister in 1909.

If approximately twenty years in a given institution is arbitrarily
selected as sufficient for defining "career," the number of Imperial
Household Ministers whose careers were in the Home Ministry numbered three (25 percent), in the Foreign Ministry two (16.7 percent),
and in the Army, the Finance Ministry, the Justice Ministry, and the
court bureaucracy one each (8.3 percent). I have classified the
remaining three Household Ministers (25 percent) as Restoration bureaucrats, since these Household Ministers had served in a variety of
positions in a bureaucracy and political system that was of their own
creation prior to becoming Household Ministers; they do not fit any
fixed career category.

More revealing, however, is the correlation between career background and length of tenure in office as Household Minister:

Restoration bureaucrats	23 years
Home Ministry bureaucrats	15 years
Foreign Ministry bureaucrats	13 years
Justice Ministry bureaucrats	6 years
Army officers	1 year
Finance Ministry bureaucrats	1 year
Court bureaucrats	1 year
Total	60 years

Throughout the sixty-year period between 1885 and 1945 career
Army officers held the ministership but one year, indicating that the
normal practice was for civilian bureaucrats to occupy that post, especially those from the Home and Foreign Ministries after 1921.

In general, an Imperial Household Minister terminated a successful public career in that office. There were notable exceptions,
however. Itō Hirobumi became Prime Minister three times and
President of the Privy Council twice after he resigned as Household
Minister in 1887. Ichiki Kitokurō became President of the Privy

Council in 1934 after having served as Household Minister for eight years. Makino Nobuaki became Privy Seal in 1925 after four years as Household Minister; Yuasa Kurahei also became Privy Seal after serving as Household Minister. Averaging five years in office, however, the Household Ministers held office independent of Cabinet changes, except in 1936 when assassinations caused changes in both court and Cabinet, and were thus "above politics" throughout the prewar period. The average age on assuming office, moreover, was 58.3 years; ranging in ages from 44 to 67, the Household Ministers were quite young. As a group they were not venerables given their office as reward for services rendered but competent bureaucrats expected to end their public careers "at the side of the emperor."

Perhaps an examination of the prescribed duties of the Imperial Household Minister's office will reveal, at least in part, why Prince Saionji would insist on extra-court bureaucrats to administer the court bureaucracy. The 1886 reorganization of the Imperial Household Ministry merely stated that the Household Minister was to decide upon all matters regarding the affairs of the imperial house, to supervise the palace staff and staffs to the imperial family and family members, and to manage the aristocracy. The 1886 act was signed by the Household Minister alone.[12] As early as 1889, however, the organic law of the Imperial Household Ministry was revised to specify the jurisdiction of the Household Minister in greater detail. In addition to the duties set forth in 1886, the Household Minister was empowered to issue directives to subjects of the realm regarding imperial house matters such as palace ceremonies, festivals, and imperial tours. He was also empowered in this respect to issue directives to the Superintendent General of Metropolitan Police (Tokyo), the Governors of the Prefectures, and other government officials.[13] As chief manager of the public role of the Emperor-in-Court, therefore, the Household Minister was directly involved with the government, especially the Home Ministry, which had jurisdiction over prefectural Governors as well as over the ordinary police establishment. Palace autonomy did not mean the isolation of the court from the government but rather a symbiotic relation between the two in which initiative in

12. "Kunaishō Tasshi," no. 1, February 4, 1886.
13. *Shokuin Roku,* 1894, vol. 1, pt. 2, p. 13.

arranging the public display of the Emperor-in-Court rested with the Household Ministry, while the actual arrangements required government cooperation.

The Household Ministry's reorganization of 1907 further acknowledged the entanglement of court and government that actually occurred in the exercise of the ministry's duties.[14] Significantly, the 1907 act was countersigned by the Prime Minister and Home Minister as well as by the Household Minister.[15] A paraphrase of the fifteen articles concerning the Household Minister reveals the problems of relating court and government that had emerged between 1886 and 1907:

1. The Imperial Household Minister shall be a direct imperial appointee [*shinnin*] and shall be responsible for "advising and assisting" [*hohitsu*] the throne on all matters regarding the imperial house.
2. He supervises the personnel of the ministry and concurrently has jurisdiction over the aristocracy.
3. When it is necessary to abolish, revise or enact Imperial House Ordinances [*Kōshitsu Rei*], the Household Minister prepares appropriate drafts for presentation to the throne. If the draft concerns the work of other Ministers of State, the Household Minister shall report the draft jointly with the Prime Minister or with the Prime Minister and concerned Ministers of State.
4. The Household Minister may prescribe regulations necessary to enforce Imperial House Ordinances and carry out his other duties. If such regulations concern the functions or responsibilities of other Ministers of State they shall be passed upon by the Prime Minister and concerned Ministers of State.
5. The Household Minister may promulgate ordinances on matters under his jurisdiction.
6. He may issue orders and directives to the Superintendent General of Metropolitan Police and to local officials regarding matters under his jurisdiction.
7. In accordance with imperial command, he may dispense relief, awards, and grants.
8. He reports to the throne promotions and retirements of Household Ministry executive appointees [*sōnin*], as well as officials treated as imperial appointees [*chokunin*] and executive appointees. He decides

14. Although there was one more ministry reorganization prior to the end of the Pacific War, the 1907 reorganization was in fact the last major revision regarding the duties of the Household Minister. The last prewar reorganization took place in 1921.
15. Naikaku Kiroku Ka, 1920, vol. 1, pt. 3, pp. 6–8.

on promotions and retirements of official appointees [*hannin*], those treated as official appointees, and other lower ranking officials.

9. He reports to the throne investitures in rank of Household Ministry personnel and members of the aristocracy. He reports conferrals of decorations to the throne through the Prime Minister.

10. With imperial sanction the Household Minister may create advisers and special officers to the ministry regarding matters under his jurisdiction.

11. When in ill health or otherwise indisposed the Household Minister may appoint the Vice Minister to perform the duties of Minister temporarily. But in this capacity the Vice Minister shall not go beyond public promulgations in accordance with the Imperial House Law and countersigning in accordance with the Public Forms Ordinance [*Kōshiki Rei*].

12. The Household Minister may delegate part of his duties to the Vice Minister and the bureau and section chiefs.

13. He may not obstruct the proceedings of the audit.

14. He may establish, regulate, and abolish divisions or sections within the secretariat and other bureaus and divisions under his jurisdiction.

15. He may establish posts of imperial appointee, executive appointee, and official appointee and stipulate their duties; posts of executive appointee and above require imperial sanction.[16]

No later than 1907, therefore, the fact of interaction between court and government was officially acknowledged regarding (1) drafts of Imperial House Ordinances, (2) regulations established to carry out those ordinances, (3) police and local officials, predominantly those under the Home Ministry, and (4) conferrals of decorations, which were handled through the Bureau of Decorations in the Prime Minister's Office.

The Imperial Household Minister in 1907 was Count Tanaka Mitsuaki (1843–1939), the second of two loyalists from the domain of Tosa to head the household bureaucracy between 1887 and 1909. Tosa had been one of the four major domains in the politics of Restoration, but its role had been one primarily of negotiation and mediation between the two most active restorationist domains of Chōshū and Satsuma. Both Tanaka and his predecessor as Household Minister, Count Hijikata Hisamoto (1833–1918), had played negotiator roles in forging the Chōshū-Satsuma alliance on which the 1868

16. *Shokuin Roku,* 1910, pt. 2, sec. 1, p. 61.

Restoration was engineered.[17] After the Restoration, more importantly, Tanaka continued his role as negotiator *within* the oligarchy, the oligarchy being primarily from Chōshū and Satsuma. He has been credited, for example, with acting as midwife for Itō Hirobumi's third Cabinet in January 1898.[18] After Tanaka became Household Minister in February of that same year, he remained a middleman to the oligarchy; that Tanaka "acted as a safety valve in the political world while in office as Imperial Household Minister is an absolutely inescapable fact."[19]

Tanaka was the last true Restoration loyalist, or participant in the politics of Restoration, to head the household bureaucracy. But he was a loyalist of a particular stamp.[20] He did not seek to challenge the Chōshū-Satsuma oligarchs from within by building a court constituency, as his fellow clansman, Sasaki Takayuki, apparently did as a *Jiho* in 1877–79. Nor did he attempt to challenge them from without by building an antioligarch political party, as did another Tosa clansman, Itagaki Taisuke. Tanaka appeared content to be a member of the charmed Restoration ingroup surrounding the throne and to negotiate among and on behalf of the oligarchs.

Since the government was in fact dominated by leaders from Chōshū and Satsuma well into the twentieth century, it was also logical to have the Household Minister appointed from a domain other than those two: such a selection would give the Imperial Household Ministry at least the semblance of detachment from alleged factional strife in the government while allowing the oligarchs influence at court as well, depending on the person selected as Household Minister. As late as 1921 Count Makino Nobuaki told

---

17. Tomita Kōjirō, p. 292; Sawamoto Kenzō, ed., *Hakushaku Tanaka Seisan* (Tokyo: Tanaka-haku Denki Kankō Kai, 1929), pp. 161–83; *Hijikata-haku,* 2d.ed. (Tokyo: Tōyō Insatsu Kyoku, 1914), pp. 240–49. On Tosa's role in the Restoration see Marius B. Jansen, *Sakamoto Ryōma and the Meiji Restoration* (Princeton: Princeton University Press, 1961).

18. Tomita Kōjirō, pp. 298–301; Sawamoto Kenzō, pp. 426–28.

19. Sawamoto Kenzō, p. 430.

20. The variety of Army, police, and court offices held by Tanaka between 1868 and 1909 reveals the difficulty in categorizing the "career background" of all the Restoration leaders. Tanaka achieved the rank of major general in the Army and was at one time the Superintendent General of Metropolitan Police. He also served as Chief Cabinet Secretary, a post that this predecessor, Hijikata Hisamoto, had also held. Tanaka entered the palace as a court adviser in 1891 and served as Vice Minister of the Household Ministry from 1895 to 1897.

Privy Seal Prince Matsukata Masayoshi that in selecting a successor to Household Minister General Nakamura Yūjirō:

> We should select as successor to the Imperial Household Minister someone suitable from among persons other than those of Satsuma or Chōshū origins. The times have changed. To give the people the impression that Satsuma and Chōshū have always monopolized power even in the palace is simply wrong.[21]

As second-ranking members of the Restoration ingroup, both Tanaka and his predecessor were ideal candidates for leading the court bureaucracy: they possessed Restoration status and were committed as negotiator-mediators to the new government evolved by the oligarchs.

Tanaka's actions as Household Minister (1898–1909) indicate that the Household Minister's interaction with the government, as suggested by the 1907 description of the Household Minister's duties, occurred largely in his capacity as chief manager of the Emperor-in-Court. In that capacity Tanaka defended the formal autonomy of the court with ferocious tenacity, down to the most trifling matters of ceremony. He had resigned as Vice Minister of the Household Ministry in 1897 over a dispute with the government concerning who was to announce the death of the empress dowager, the Imperial Household Minister or the Prime Minister. The emperor's view was solicited and the Privy Council's advice asked. Tanaka's insistence that the announcement be made in the name of the Imperial Household Minister was upheld but at the expense of Prime Minister Matsukata's friendship, and Tanaka resigned over the difficulties caused.[22]

After becoming Household Minister in 1898 Tanaka continued to defend the formal parity of court and government with equal stubbornness. On one occasion Prime Minister Katsura Tarō asked Tanaka to come to the Prime Minister's residence for a discussion. Tanaka refused:

> I'm not under the Prime Minister; the Imperial Household Minister is in an independent position outside the Cabinet. Other than His Majesty I am to be under no one's orders. Of course, I have the greatest respect for

---

21. Shimozono Sakichi, *Makino Nobuaki-haku* (Tokyo: Jimbunkaku, 1940), p. 186. Ironically, Nakamura's successor was Makino, who was himself from Satsuma.
22. Sawamoto Kenzō, pp. 422–24.

Prince Katsura as an individual. . . . I refused because if Prince Katsura had some matter to take up with me he should come here. For me to go on summons would be unacceptable in view of my office.[23]

Katsura then called back and said he would come see Tanaka if Tanaka were inconvenienced. Once he received this ritualistic acknowledgment of his "office" from the Prime Minister, Tanaka replied that he would go see the Prime Minister and immediately ordered a carriage.[24] How Tanaka served as political mediator among government leaders and participated in policy at this time is not the issue here; his behavior in both instances cited above showed extraordinary sensitivity to the symbolic separation of court and government and to the formalistic role of office in palace politics.

Preservation of parity also involved the preservation of the court's financial autonomy from government encroachment. In 1902, for example, Tanaka refused to give imperial lumber to the Home Ministry free of charge for the reconstruction of the Grand Shrine at Ise. Tanaka argued that since the court and the government had separate budgets, and since the government already had a budget allocation for rebuilding the shrine, the Home Ministry should pay the Imperial Household Ministry a suitable price. To keep the distinction between court and government free of confusion, he continued, there must be no government inroads on imperial house property. The Cabinet reconsidered the matter and the Home Ministry subsequently bought the lumber.[25] Household Minister Tanaka was in no sense the servant of the government, and he perceived his office as granting him great freedom of action against the government and its leaders on court matters, as he defined them.

If Tanaka kept the government at bay, he also acted firmly with both the court and the emperor. Just after Tanaka had become Household Minister in February 1898, Prince-of-the-Blood Komatsu requested a Buddhist funeral for the late Prince-of-the-Blood Yamashina, as Prince Yamashina had requested in his will. With the support of the Privy Council Tanaka refused the request on the grounds that a member of the imperial house held a position above

23. Tomita Kōjirō, p. 477.
24. Ibid., pp. 477–78.
25. Ibid., pp. 310–11.

all religions; the funeral service had to be one appropriate to the status and position of the imperial family.[26]

Tanaka also had a considerable reputation for going against the emperor's wishes and for doing precisely what he believed his office demanded. Tanaka's biographer, Tomita Kōjirō, states that hardly anyone dared counter the emperor to his face, not even the Elder Statesmen, Grand Chamberlain, or Privy Seal. Tanaka, however, would argue with the emperor "as a comrade."[27] On one occasion the emperor is reported to have flared out at Tanaka's stubborn resistance: "Aren't you a Major General? You're breaking military discipline if you don't listen to the order of your supreme commander." Tanaka retorted: "I'm sorry, I wasn't speaking in my capacity as Major General. I must beg your indulgence on this matter from my position as Imperial Household Minister."[28]

In 1904 General Yamagata Aritomo was dispatched to the front to review the Russo-Japanese War situation. For this purpose he requested that Tanaka obtain two of the emperor's horses. The emperor, claims Tomita, had very little he could truly call his own other than his beloved horses. When Tanaka approached the emperor with Yamagata's request, the emperor flatly refused. After unsuccessful attempts to obtain the emperor's permission, Tanaka finally handed over two of the emperor's horses to Yamagata without a word to the emperor. Overjoyed, Yamagata immediately audienced with the emperor and thanked him for his generosity.[29] Tanaka viewed his relationship with the emperor as one of sole responsibility for advising and assisting the throne on court and household affairs, but "to obey imperial directives to the letter, without offering the slightest admonition, cannot be called fulfilling the responsibility of advice and assistance, to my way of thinking."[30] In this instance "admonition" took the form of disobedience.

Commenting on Tanaka's position as Imperial Household Minister, Tomita argues that a courageous person of Tanaka's integrity was needed to maintain the separation of court and

26. Ibid., pp. 308–09.
27. Ibid., pp. 484–85.
28. Ibid., p. 483.
29. Ibid., pp. 484–87.
30. Ibid., p. 479.

government in the face of clique politicians anxious to achieve their ambitions.[31] Tanaka evidently demonstrated such courage not only toward the government but also toward the court and the emperor as well. It would appear that for Tanaka the emperor was a fellow Restoration "stalwart," a comrade in arms who could be rebuked both from the standpoint of Tanaka's perception of "office" and from the spirit of competitive comradeship that prevailed among the oligarchy.

As recognized in the 1907 organic law of the Imperial Household Ministry, palace autonomy obviously did not mean isolation for the emperor as Emperor-in-Court. Imperial house funds were used to emphasize the role of the emperor as social paragon, as symbol of socially desirable styles, activties, and goals. To encourage education, for example, an imperial gift of 50,000 yen was granted to Fukuzawa Yukichi in 1900. In 1908 Waseda University received 30,000 yen from the Imperial Household Ministry.[32] Since the emperor was "the father and mother of his people," the "standard of public morals," and the "fundamental basis of institutions and culture," such uses of privy monies were amply rationalized.[33]

But the emperor was also the "fount of politics."[34] The vast sums available to the Household Minister had political uses as well. In 1892, for example, the Imperial Diet refused to pass the government's naval shipbuilding budget. At the request of the Cabinet, which sought to overcome Diet opposition by imperial rescript, the emperor called a meeting of the Prime Minister, Privy Councillors, and the Speakers of both houses of the Diet. An imperial rescript was subsequently issued to the effect that for the next six years 300,000 yen per year would be allocated from the court fund for naval shipbuilding.[35] This sum was one tenth the annual allotment to the court from the national treasury. Quite clearly, the oligarchs in government and the leaders at court cooperated in a political maneuver to maintain the supremacy of oligarchic decision making.

31. Ibid., pp. 306–07.
32. Ibid., pp. 329–30.
33. Sawamoto Kenzō, p. 441.
34. Ibid.
35. Kuroda Hisata, pp. 75–77.

This action also demonstrated the "sacrifices" that the emperor was willing to make for "patriotic" goals. But privy monies were also used for political manipulation that had no such patriotic rationalization. Hara Kei, for example, recorded a conversation with oligarch Inoue Kaoru on December 4, 1901, in which Inoue stated that the Imperial Household Ministry had on at least one occasion given oligarch Yamagata Aritomo court funds. When Hara spoke with Prince Saionji two days later, Saionji told him that Yamagata had at one time received the enormous sum of 980,000 yen from the Household Ministry. Hara confessed amazement: it was difficult to believe that such a sum was needed merely to establish a Cabinet, as Yamagata's request to the throne had stipulated. Despite Yamagata's reputation for integrity, Hara was firmly convinced that Yamagata had used this and other sums from the court to bribe members of the House of Representatives. In 1901 Prime Minister Katsura Tarō asked Household Minister Tanaka for a similar "contribution." Although he had given funds from the privy purse to a number of oligarchs up to that point, Tanaka refused Katsura's request, evidently because Katsura was not an oligarch. Hara speculated that Katsura, like Yamagata, intended to use such court funds, had they been made available, to entice members of the House of Representatives to go along with Cabinet policies.[36] Apparently Yamagata continued to tap court funds later as well by having his protégés appointed Household Minister from 1909 to 1921.[37]

There exists, therefore, some evidence to support Inoue Kiyoshi's claim that "this extensive imperial house property did play the political and military role that Iwakura [Tomomi] had hoped."[38] Household Minister Tanaka was in fact an agent of the oligarchs brought into the palace from the "outside" to enhance cooperation between court and government in managing the Emperor-in-State. As indicated by Tanaka's refusal to give Katsura court monies and other uncooperative acts already noted, Tanaka cooperated only with the oligarchs (Elder Statesmen), not with their protégés or other

36. *Hara Kei Nikki,* 9 vols. (Tokyo: Tōkyō Kengen Sha, 1950), 2: 454–56.
37. Fukumoto Kunio, *Kanryō* (Tokyo: Kōbundō, 1959), p. 66.
38. Inoue Kiyoshi, p. 94. Unfortunately, I have been unable to find any further evidence of such political uses and abuses of court funds. It is difficult to believe that they were not greater than I have found and that they did not continue.

lesser political leaders.[39] The available evidence suggests that Tanaka willingly coordinated the Imperial Will in politics with the policies of the oligarchs, while maintaining the formal separation of court and government. Tanaka's actions as Household Minister reveal the significance of Saionji's caveat that Household Ministers be "brought in from the outside": a Household Ministry "in line with the times" was one that cooperated with the dominant political forces at any given moment in managing the Emperor-in-State, while maintaining the autonomy of the Emperor-in-Court. The "dominant political forces"—in Tanaka's time a handful of Cabinet oligarchs or oligarchs acting as Elder Statesmen—had chief responsibility for political decision making, for defining the official Imperial Will in politics. The Household Ministry cooperated with the government in this process. With regard to the Emperor-in-Court, however, the palace bureaucracy held the initiative, and the government cooperated with the Household Minister in maintaining the autonomous image of the public Emperor-in-Court.

Between 1909, when Tanaka resigned, and 1921, when Count Makino Nobuaki became Household Minister, there were four Household Ministers. One was predominantly a palace official (Iwakura Tomosada), one a Home Ministry bureaucrat (Watanabe Chiaki), one a Justice Ministry official (Hatano Takanao), and one a career Army officer (Nakamura Yūjirō). The average term of office between 1885 and 1945 was five years. The average between 1885 and 1909, however, was eight years, while that between 1909 and 1921 was but three years. Both the frequency of changes and the variety of career backgrounds brought to the office of Household Minister between 1909 and 1921 suggest that this was a period of transition for the court bureaucracy as it adjusted to the loss of Restoration leaders. In contrast to the tranquility that had prevailed at the side of the emperor during the period 1885 to 1909, the period 1909 to 1921 was one of confusion as the leadership at court struggled to get in line with the new times.

From 1921 to 1945, however, the Imperial Household Ministers, with the possible exception of Ishiwatari Sōtarō, were drawn from a

39. Katsura was Yamagata's leading protégé (Tetsuo Najita, *Hara Kei in the Politics of Compromise, 1905–1915* [Cambridge, Mass.: Harvard University Press, 1967], p. 81).

group of civilian bureaucrats whom I have called the constitutional monarchists. Most important, perhaps, was Ichiki Kitokurō, Household Minister from 1925 to 1933. Although Ichiki had been a career bureaucrat in the Home Ministry and served as Education Minister in 1914–15, Home Minister in 1915–16, and Privy Councillor from 1917, his importance did not derive from such national visibility. In 1894 Ichiki had become professor of law at Tokyo Imperial University while remaining an official in the Home Ministry. In that same year Ichiki's most celebrated pupil, Minobe Tatsukichi, entered the university. It was from Ichiki that Minobe was to acquire the basic ideas of his "organ theory" (*kikan setsu*) of constitutional monarchy, a theory that gained primacy in Japanese constitutional thought during the 1920s and which was also accepted by a number of Japan's leading bureaucrats.[40] Ichiki's very presence in the palace as chief manager of the Emperor-in-Court suggests the acceptance of his theory, or of Minobe's more liberal variant, by the court leadership during the 1920s and early 1930s.

Ichiki argued that the "supreme right of rule" over which the emperor exercised general supervision was lodged in the state as a legal person. The state exercised its supreme right of rule through "organs" (*kikan*), the highest of which exercised general control. When a monarch was the highest organ of state but governed with the cooperation of other organs, such as a legislature, he was a constitutional monarch. For these reasons, Ichiki concluded, Japan under the Meiji Constitution was a constitutional monarchy. The emperor as highest organ of state was, however, under very little restriction: he could at any time divest another organ of state of its power. The Imperial Diet, according to Ichiki, could not assert its powers over Ministers of State, since ministers were responsible individually to the emperor. While placing the emperor under law, as embodied in the constitution, Ichiki allowed no government organ to check the emperor.[41]

In Minobe's hands, however, Ichiki's organ theory was greatly liberalized. While maintaining that the emperor was the highest organ of state, Minobe insisted that the emperor was bound by the

40. *Nihon Jimbutsu Shi Taikei*, 7 vols., 3d ed. (Tokyo: Asakura Shoten, 1963), 7 : 270.
41. Ibid., pp. 271–73.

constitution; were he to act arbitrarily, the emperor would be violating Japan's long history as well as the constitution. Moreover, Minobe made the Imperial Diet in effect the highest organ of state under the emperor. Minobe's theory was ultimately an attack on the independence of the bureaucratic institutions of prerogative and on "transcendental Cabinets." If pushed to its logical conclusion, his theory justified the creation of Cabinets responsible to the elected House of Representatives, while still preserving the sanctity of the emperor as sovereign under law. Minobe never asserted the democratic principle of popular sovereignty, but his theory might have led to democratic government.

The orthodoxy of Minobe's theory, as far as the palace leaders and their allies were concerned, is indicated by the fact that he received an imperial appointment to the House of Peers in June 1932. By this time, however, the worldwide depression and rightwing movements in Japan had brought on a reaction that ultimately forced Minobe to resign that post. His theory was condemned in 1935 as contrary to the ideals of Japan's national polity—ironically, with the support of rightists and ultraconservatives in the very institution he had so strongly supported: the Imperial Diet. More significantly, Ichiki was dislodged less than a year later from the presidency of the Privy Council, an office he had taken in May 1934. The attack on Minobe became the vehicle for bringing about Ichiki's downfall, since Ichiki was allegedly responsible for "the importation of the hateful doctrines."[42] By extension, it also became an attack on court leaders and the emperor's close advisers, ultimately encouraging the outbreak of assassinations and attempted assassinations that peaked on February 26, 1936. Miller's analysis of the Minobe incident of 1935 shows most dramatically that the condemnation of Minobe's theory was the catalyst for a massive attack on the constitutional monarchists in government and court by renovationist and militarist bureaucrats in the government.[43]

Despite the eclipse of the constititional monarchists following Minobe's ouster and the assassination and attempted assassination of

42. Miller, p. 218.
43. Ibid., pp. 196–253.

the emperor's close advisers in February 1936, the constitutional monarchists never lost control of the Household Minister's office. The Household Minister from 1936 to 1945 was Matsudaira Tsuneo, a career diplomat who had been ambassador to the United States (1925–28) and England (1929–35). He was, like most palace leaders of the 1920s and early 1930s, pro-Anglo–American and a circumspect moderate in domestic politics. The forces of extremism never quite managed to capture the Emperor-in-Court "from the inside," however much they manipulated the imperial symbol outside the palace gates. The court remained, in Irie Sukemasa's exaggerated terms, a place "where freedom of speech has been guarded at every turn": Irie could still claim that there was "no more democratic a place than this".

THE GRAND CHAMBERLAIN:
CHIEF MESSENGER IN ATTENDANCE

Well, I became Grand Chamberlain. How best go about the job? Even on that score I had no idea, but I did hear various things from the Board of Chamberlains, learned about His Majesty's daily routine, was helped out by Kawai Yahachi, the Deputy Grand Chamberlain, . . .

Suzuki Kantarō[44]

Even more than the duties of the Chamberlains, those of the Grand Chamberlain were ill-defined. After the Imperial Household Ministry was reorganized in 1886, the 1871 office of Grand Chamberlain[45] was given two vague and flexible functions: (1) to render assistance at the emperor's side, and (2) to supervise the Chamberlains and Stewards.[46] Between 1886 and 1945 there was no further specification of the Grand Chamberlain's duties, in marked contrast to the considerably detailed regulations to which the Imperial Household Minister was subjected after 1886. When an outsider took up that post, as Admiral Suzuki Kantarō did in 1929, he could either unearth the precedents

44. Suzuki Kantarō, *Suzuki Kantarō Jiden,* ed. Suzuki Hajime (Tokyo: Ōgikukai, 1949), p. 270.
45. "Dajōkan Tasshi," no. 400, 10 August 1871, in *Hōrei Zensho,* 1871.
46. "Kunai Shō Tasshi," no. 1, February 5, 1886, in *Hōrei Zensho,* 1886.

applying to his new office—or make them himself. Such vagueness was disconcerting to a career military officer like Admiral Suzuki, but it allowed an incumbent considerable latitude to interpret the meaning of rendering "attendance at the emperor's side." For example, Chamberlain Irie Sukemasa writes of Admiral Suzuki's tenure as Grand Chamberlain from 1929 to 1936, "Since Makino and Saitō as Privy Seals did not come to their offices but once a week or once a month, *it was natural that the Grand Chamberlain should come to handle part of the Privy Seal's work*."[47] In terms of jurisdiction and behavior the Grand Chamberlain, at least by 1929, played a highly flexible role in the politics of relating emperor and government, despite the fact that he was in charge of the "inner side" of the court and presumably a purely court figure.

The career backgrounds of the personnel appointed Grand Chamberlain between 1885 and 1945 were quite different from those of the Household Ministers. There were ten Grand Chamberlains during the sixty-year period: only two (20 percent) had been Ministers of State and only one (10 percent) had been Prime Minister. The two Ministers of State (Hatano Takanao and Katsura Tarō) and the Prime Minister (Katsura Tarō), moreover, held the post of Grand Chamberlain a total of less than six months, indicating the irregularity of such appointments. Two (Katsura Tarō and Suzuki Kantarō) did become Prime Minister after serving as Grand Chamberlain, but once again this was not the norm. In contrast to the Household Ministers, the Grand Chamberlains were frequently drawn from the court and the military. Whereas the Household Ministers numbered only one military (8.3 percent) and one court figure (8.3 percent), the Grand Chamberlains numbered four (40 percent) who had served in high military posts, five (50 percent) whose careers had been largely military, and three (30 percent) career court figures. Only three Grand Chamberlains (30 percent) had served at one time or another on the Privy Council; seven Household Ministers (58.3 percent) had done so.

A striking pattern emerges over time in the career backgrounds of the Grand Chamberlains between 1885 and 1945, a pattern that reflects the bureaucratization of palace leadership from the outside.

---

47. Irie Sukemasa, *Jijū to Paipu*, p. 99. My emphasis.

In the years 1885 to 1929 the Grand Chamberlains were drawn almost exclusively from the court; from 1929 to 1945 they were exclusively retired admirals of the Navy. Calculating career background (twenty years or more) against length of service as Grand Chamberlain, the following institutional emphases emerge:

Court	36 years
Navy	17 years
Army[48]	5 years
Foreign Ministry	2 years
Total	60 years

Additionally, it was a rare coincidence for the Grand Chamberlain and the Household Minister to be drawn from the same institutional constituency between 1885 and 1945. Only in 1909 did this occur, when both were drawn from the court bureaucracy. This fact suggests that there was a carefully contrived balance of institutional representatives at the side of the emperor, not merely a mosaic of status, especially after 1929.

Like the Household Ministers, however, the Grand Chamberlains after 1927 generally terminated successful public careers on the "outside" by serving at court. The average age of the Grand Chamberlains on assuming office was 61.1 years, ranging from 46 to 71. The average term of office was six years. It is important to note, however, that the Grand Chamberlain throughout the Meiji period was one person, Prince Tokudaiji Sanenori.[49] The very length of his service, from 1871 to 1912, suggests the high degree of tranquility at the emperor's side if not in the outside political arena. Tokudaiji was the only palace official, moreover, to have held three of the four leading palace offices: he was concurrently Imperial Household

48. The Army official was Takatsukasa Hiromichi (1855–1918), Grand Chamberlain from 1912 to 1918. Although Takatsukasa achieved the rank of major general he was basically a court person of Court Noble lineage. In 1896 he was Aide-de-Camp to the crown prince (*Shokuin Roku*, 1896, p. 138). In such cases it is obviously difficult to separate court from extra-court careers.

49. Ijiri Tsunekichi lists four persons as Grand Chamberlain during the period 1871–84, with Tokudaiji becoming Grand Chamberlain in 1884 (Ijiri Tsunekichi, *Rekidai Kenkan Roku* [Tokyo: Chōyō Kai, 1925]). The Imperial Household Agency, however, has Tokudaiji listed as Grand Chamberlain from 1871 to 1912 and lists him as serving concurrently as Imperial Household Secretary from 1871 to 1884. Without being able to account for the discrepancy between the Ijiri and Agency records, I have accepted the Agency roster as official.

Secretary from 1871 to 1884 and concurrently Privy Seal from 1891 to 1912.

Despite his length of service at court, Prince Tokudaiji has enjoyed singular obscurity. There is no biography of this venerable figure;[50] most biographical dictionaries refer to him simply as "Emperor Meiji's Grand Chamberlain." He has also been referred to as "a classic court official" who, in constantly attending the Emperor Meiji, "was so humble and diligent that no one ever saw him stand in a fully upright position."[51] Apparently Tokudaiji was a perfectly resistance-free conduit between the emperor and the oligarchs. He was the emperor's messenger on all important matters of state, such as Cabinet formations and questions of foreign policy, but was never credited with offering his own views, advising the throne or the oligarchs, or blocking access to the throne.[52] In 1878, he was accused by *Jiho* Sasaki, as we saw in chapter 2, of catering to the emperor's every whim and of being weak. The meager references to him that appear in the biographies of the Meiji oligarchs credit him with no other function than a punctilious execution of liaison between the emperor and the oligarchs.

Even as hostile a critic of Meiji "absolutism" as Inoue Kiyoshi indicates that Tokudaiji was merely a faithful servant to the emperor. In 1881 Prince Saionji Kimmochi, one of Tokudaiji's younger brothers, became president of the *Tōyō Jiyū Shimbun,* a liberal newspaper which numbered Nakae Chōmin among its outspoken critics of the oligarchs. Sanjō Sanetomi, Iwakura Tomomi, and Tokudaiji—all three Court Noble restorationists—attempted to dissuade Saionji from the venture, but to no avail. Finally the oligarchs took the problem to the emperor. "The emperor, too, was greatly alarmed and ordered Tokudaiji to have his younger brother quit the newspaper." But Saionji held firm until a "clear" imperial command was issued against his participation.[53] In the absence of

50. There is no listing, for example, in Takanishi Kōshi's bibliography of Meiji biographies, *Shiseki Kaidai (Denki Hen)* (Tokyo: Meiji Shoin, 1935).

51. Watanabe Ikujirō, *Meiji Tennō to Hohitsu no Hitobito* (Tokyo: Chigura Shobō, 1938), p. 125.

52. Inada Masatsugu, "Taiheiyō Sensō Boppatsu to Tennō Genrō oyobi Jūshin no Chii," Nihon Gaikō Gakkai, ed., *Taiheiyō Sensō Genin Ron* (Tokyo: Shimbun Gekkan Sha, 1953), p. 31. Inoue Kiyoshi, p. 116.

53. Inoue Kiyoshi, pp. 79–80, 116.

evidence to the contrary, Tokudaiji appears to have been merely a liaison between emperor and oligarchs and a faithful executor of oligarchic wills, and not extremely effective at the latter. He was evidently an opinionless member of the Restoration ingroup, which fought over policies on a person-to-person, face-to-face basis but stood united on the privileged position of the Emperor-in-Chambers.

Once Tokudaiji left his posts as Grand Chamberlain and Privy Seal in 1912, however, there was instability at the side of the emperor. Between 1912 and 1921 there were no less than four Grand Chamberlains, or one every 2.3 years. The average term of office being six years between 1885 and 1945, the period 1912 to 1921, as for the Household Ministers, was the most unstable in the history of the Grand Chamberlain's office. It was in these years that court leadership was in effect transferred from men of the court to bureaucrats from the outside in all four leading palace offices.

The confusion involved in the transition is well illustrated by General Prince Katsura Tarō's brief tenure as Grand Chamberlain and Privy Seal from August 13 to December 21, 1912. The precedent for holding both posts concurrently had, of course, been set by Katsura's predecessor, Tokudaiji Sanenori. But there was a vast difference between a life-long civil-military official and protégé of oligarch Yamagata Aritomo, who was twice Prime Minister before entering the court, and a life-long court personage, who knew no other than palace life. Public response to Katsura's appointment as Privy Seal and Grand Chamberlain was immediate and sharply critical: the previous Privy Seals had been the "flower of the court aristocracy," while Katsura was of "rustic" origins and thereby an affront to court office. A "tidal wave" of rumor and gossip engulfed Katsura and he became the focal point of public censure, controversy and slander:[54]

> The public believed that Katsura's entrance into the Imperial Household, as chamberlain and keeper of the imperial seal, was a plot of the Yamagata faction to dominate the Imperial Household and establish control over the new Emperor.[55]

54. Tokutomi Iichirō, *Kōshaku Katsura Tarō Den,* 2 vols. (Tokyo: Ko-Katsura Kōshaku Kinen Jigyō Kai, 1917), 2:596–97.
55. Tetsuo Najita, p. 93.

Even as astute a political leader as Hara Kei, Home Minister at the time of Katsura's appointment, concurred in this widely held view. Hara wrote in his diary on the day of Katsura's appointment:

> Katsura Tarō was appointed Grand Chamberlain and concurrently Lord Keeper of the Privy Seal. I had been unclear about the meaning of what he had said yesterday regarding court and government, but his conversation became understandable as the result of this appointment: it was evident that he had taken part in a scheme, a plot of the Yamagata faction to garner the Privy Council along with the court wholly into its hands.[56]

Despite these perceptions, quite the opposite reason appears to have motivated Yamagata to engineer Katsura's entrance into an office of court leadership. Yamagata and other members of his group were fearful that Katsura, though Yamagata's leading protégé, would take an independent course from the Yamagata main line and found a political party to counter the predominant influence of the Seiyūkai in the Diet. The Seiyūkai president was Saionji Kimmochi and Hara Kei was Saionji's chief lieutenant. Between 1901 and 1912 Saionji had alternated with Katsura as Prime Minister. Both Saionji and Yamagata agreed, for different reasons, to "retire" Katsura into the palace, thus bringing Katsura's active political career to an end. Yamagata hoped by this measure to obtain his goal of "transcendental Cabinets" composed of officials above party and not responsible to the Diet; Saionji, who was Prime Minister at the time, hoped to rid himself of his and Hara Kei's political rival. Katsura, the victim of collaboration between patron and rival, was evidently quite unhappy about his "imprisonment" in the palace.[57]

But Katsura did not stay imprisoned for long. After some four months as Privy Seal-Grand Chamberlain, he emerged to become Prime Minister for the third time on the very day, December 21, 1912, that he resigned his palace offices. His exit from the palace was accompanied by a public outcry of equal vehemence to that when he was appointed:

> [It] was being said generally of Katsura: He had entered the Imperial Household in August 1912 to establish the control of Yamagata's faction

---

56. *Hara Kei Nikki,* ed. Hara Keiichirō, (Tokyo: Fukumura Shuppan Kabushiki Kaisha, 1965), 3:245.

57. Tetsuo Najita, pp. 92–95. Tokutomi Iichirō, *Kōshaku Katsura Tarō Den,* pp. 593–96. *Hara Kei Nikki* (1965), 3:245.

there; on the basis of his influence in the Imperial Household, he had destroyed the Second Saionji Cabinet and then had issued an imperial rescript to himself to become prime minister for the third time.[58]

Katsura's reemergence into active politics, from palace leader to Prime Minister, was "deeply resented by the public."[59] If the distinction between court and government was violated by Katsura's entrance into court office it was more than equally violated by his exit. Not since Itō Hirobumi's first Cabinet in 1885 had there been such a public clamor over manipulating the throne for political purposes.

Although a court personage was eventually selected to replace Katsura as Grand Chamberlain and an imperial prince appointed as Privy Seal, there was some question as to when the successors would be selected. Hara Kei was deeply suspicious of Katsura: on December 18, 1912 Saionji told Hara that Katsura had said he intended to appoint no successor as Privy Seal for the moment. In his diary Hara comments, ". . . maybe there was no person for this [post], and maybe he [Katsura] would keep it open as a place for him to take refuge in again later."[60] Here, at least in Hara's mind, was direct manipulation of palace office by political partisans for political purposes.

More important, however, is the *institutionalized* nature of the conflict over Katsura's appointment and subsequent actions. On the theoretical level, it was a conflict between the concepts of "party" versus "transcendental" cabinets. On the institutional level it was a conflict over the composition of the Japanese executive between the Imperial Diet, specifically the House of Representatives, and the bureaucracy, specifically the ministries, operating on the principle of executive imperial prerogatives. On the personal level it was a conflict between oligarch Yamagata and his protégés on the one side and Saionji and his protégés on the other, specifically protégé Katsura versus protégé Hara. Both the theoretical and the personal aspects masked the profoundly institutional nature of the conflict. It is in this context that Dietman Ozaki Yukio's famous denunciation of

58. Tetsuo Najita, p. 116.
59. Ibid., p. 117.
60. *Hara Kei Nikki* (1965), 3 : p. 274.

Katsura's use of the emperor in politics on February 5, 1913 ought to be evaluated:

> They [Katsura and the oligarchs] always mouth "loyalty" and "patriotism" but what they are actually doing is to hide themselves behind the Throne, and shoot at their political enemies from their secure ambush. [*Applause.*] The Throne is their rampart. Rescripts are their missiles.[61]

Ozaki pitted Diet against bureaucracy and attacked the assumption of the bureaucracy that it rightfully monopolized the Imperial Will.

The uncertainties introduced into Japanese politics as a result of the emerging institutional competition underlying Katsura's appointment are obtusely suggested by Hara on August 14, 1912: "Katsura's appointment had been proposed by Yamagata; they might have satisfied their ambitions by this, *but the future of bureaucratic politics when it comes to this cannot possibly be long.*"[62] If a leading practitioner of "bureaucratic politics" had to assume court office in order to protect his and his faction's power from the institutional challenge of Diet politicians, then he and his faction, according to Hara, revealed their actual weakness. They had to take "refuge" in the palace. Conversely, palace leadership ought not to be in the hands of active political partisans but in the hands of neutral negotiators who were able to keep faction out of the palace:

> I heard from Saionji the truth about Grand Chamberlain Tokudaiji's resignation. Although the domain cliques had coveted that office, trying any number of schemes up to that time, Tokudaiji had dedicated himself and been sincere in his service to the throne.[63]

According to Hara, therefore, Tokudaiji as Privy Seal and Grand Chamberlain was the ideal type for the post: neutral, above faction, and "sincere." As we have seen, Tokudaiji was a master of liaison to the point of obscurity.

Hara's actions while Katsura was Privy Seal and Grand Chamberlain, however, reveal that Hara *expected* Katsura to act as a nonpartisan negotiator, despite the longstanding competition between the two over political power. Throughout Katsura's brief tenure in

---

61. Speech by Ozaki Yukio, House of Representatives, as published in *The Japan Mail,* February 15, 1913, pp. 197–98; cited in Scalapino, p. 194.
62. *Hara Kei Nikki* (1965), 3:245. My emphasis.
63. Ibid.

high palace office Hara attempted to enlist his efforts as mediator between the Saionji Cabinet and the Army to prevent a direct confrontation between the two which might bring about Saionji's resignation. On August 18, 1912 "Katsura made it clear that from now on he would not participate in politics"[64] but it was Hara himself who attempted to reinvolve him. On November 16, for example, Hara met with Katsura to discuss the Army's demand for two new divisions and to enlist Katsura's efforts as a negotiator. At first Katsura declined, arguing that in his present office he could not speak on such issues. But Hara pressed him, and he finally agreed to arbitrate on the Cabinet's behalf. Although Hara doubted that Katsura would be sincere in his efforts,[65] he clearly believed that the office of Privy Seal-Grand Chamberlain was no bar to participation as a negotiator in the political process. On the contrary, Hara expected the Privy Seal-Grand Chamberlain to act as an arbitrator, especially when it came to the survival of a Cabinet, regardless of the political preferences of the individual holding the offices.

Within the court Katsura also "tutored" the new Taishō Emperor and coordinated court and government functions. His biographer implies that one of Katsura's main functions, like that of the *Jiho* in the 1870s, was to cultivate the imperial virtue:

> Although the office of Privy Seal, a completely noble and pure office administering the imperial seal in service to the throne, was no more than a court office serving the throne in attendance, there was, in regard to the present Emperor [Taishō], a certain necessity for someone with qualifications as a master teacher in politics to be Privy Seal.[66]

Like the young Meiji Emperor in the 1870s, the new Taishō Emperor in 1912 had to be brought in line with the times—his "virtue" made responsive to the dominant political forces of the day. Katsura was particularly concerned with devising a regular series of lectures to the emperor on basic political information and current events: essentials of the constitution, "the reason why Japan's national polity was unsurpassed in the world," other political systems of the world, ideal emperors of antiquity, Japanese military preparedness

64. Ibid., p. 247.
65. Ibid., p. 262.
66. Tokutomi Iichirō, *Kōshaku Katsura Tarō Den*, 2:595.

and that of the Western nations. Military lectures were to be given by the chiefs and deputy chiefs of the armed services' General Staffs.[67] In his coordinating duties Katsura had considerable contact with the Home Minister, Hara Kei, in regard to imperial outings and imperial amnesties for political prisoners.[68] The Privy Seal-Grand Chamberlain was therefore a key figure in controlling the political information reaching the emperor as well as a liaison-coordinator of court functions that involved government cooperation.

After Katsura's brief and stormy period in high court offices, no one was ever again to be Grand Chamberlain and Privy Seal concurrently. Nor was any ex-Prime Minister ever to be appointed Grand Chamberlain. Between 1912 and 1927 there were but three Grand Chamberlains: two were of Court Noble origin and one was related to the shogunal house of Tokugawa. All three were predominantly court figures, although one achieved the rank of major general (Takatsukasa Hiromichi) and another served as Governor of Saitama Prefecture (Ōgimachi Sanemasa). The period between 1912 and 1927 thus represents a return to the tradition that the Grand Chamberlain was to be a neutral figure from the flower of the ascribed aristocracy. Since the Privy Seals from 1914 and 1922 were aged but powerful Elder Statesmen and the Household Ministers from 1910 on were competent bureaucrats from the outside, it would appear that there was no need for powerful men in the office of Grand Chamberlain.

In 1927, however, Chinda Sutemi, an aged career diplomat who had been educated in the United States, was made Grand Chamberlain in a final break with the precedent of neutral and aristocratic Grand Chamberlains. His successor as Grand Chamberlain in 1929, Admiral Suzuki Kantarō, was appointed directly from the post of Chief of the Navy General Staff. From 1929 to 1945 the post of Grand Chamberlain was occupied exclusively by Navy admirals.

Not only does the appointment of Suzuki reveal the bureaucratization of the Grand Chamberlain's office from the outside; it also reveals the efforts of partisan palace advisers, the constitutional monarchists, to balance the institutional influence of the Army at the

67. Ibid., pp. 602–03.
68. *Hara Kei Nikki* (1965), 3:259.

emperor's side. The Chief Aide and a majority of Aides had always been ranking Army officers whom the Army had nominated. By 1929, moreover, the Army had mounted its claim to be the leading institution of prerogative and thereby entitled to declare the Imperial Will in both domestic and international affairs. With a Navy admiral at the emperor's side, the palace leaders could pit the institutional interests of the Navy against those of the Army without frontally violating the prerogative of supreme command. And since the palace leaders had sole responsibility for appointing the Grand Chamberlain, as they did not in the case of the Chief Aide and Aides, they could choose a Navy officer "in line with the times"— and their partisan purposes—who would be useful in controlling the military, including the Navy itself. Finally, because the office of Grand Chamberlain was quite possibly the most ambiguous and flexible of the four palace offices, its incumbent had considerable discretion in the performance of his vague duties—on his own initiative or at the behest of partisan colleagues.

The appointment of Admiral Suzuki and his subsequent actions as Grand Chamberlain from 1929 to 1936 illustrate these assertions. Although Suzuki's successors were also admirals, there is no indication that they became involved in politics as palace partisans, as did Suzuki. Since the palace partisanship of the constitutional monarchists was drastically curtailed after the assassinations of February 26, 1936, the Grand Chamberlains who succeeded Suzuki were far more neutral figures. Unity in government was also restored in some measure after 1936 by the Army and its allies in the bureaucracy and Imperial Diet. It might be well, then, to conclude our discussion of the Grand Chamberlain with Admiral Suzuki and his relation to palace involvement in politics.

When Grand Chamberlain Chinda Sutemi died in office, the Imperial Household Minister, Ichiki Kitokurō, personally pressed Suzuki into the post of Grand Chamberlain, despite the Navy's reluctance to part with Suzuki and Suzuki's own hesitations. Ichiki had consulted with his palace colleague and fellow constitutional monarchist, Privy Seal Makino Nobuaki, and the emperor himself prior to pressuring Suzuki to accept. The reasons why the palace selected Suzuki, as given in Suzuki's biography, were: (1) the Chief

Aides had always been Army generals, (2) there were no "suitable" candidates in the civil bureaucracy, and (3) the only other Navy prospect was from Satsuma and would not be acceptable because Privy Seal Makino was also from Satsuma.[69] More important, however, was the congeniality of Suzuki's views with those of the two constitutional monarchists, Household Minister Ichiki and Privy Seal Makino, who managed the palace under Prince Saionji's direction.[70] It is claimed, for example, that Suzuki "detested" politics and that he believed military men should stand completely clear of political activity. He is also alleged to have believed that by the late 1920s military officers were clearly violating the Emperor Meiji's "Instructions to Soldiers and Sailors," which forbade military intervention in politics.[71] Despite being a career Navy officer, Suzuki apparently supported Minobe's theory of constitutional monarchy.[72] In terms of his institutional constituency and political views, therefore, Suzuki was ideally suited to the partisan purposes of the constitutional monarchists in their struggle against the militarists and renovationists.

That Suzuki served the interests of the constitutional monarchists is well illustrated by his alleged involvement in the fall of the Tanaka Cabinet in 1929 and his clear involvement in the London Naval Treaty controversy of 1930.

69. *Suzuki Kantarō Den* (Tokyo: Suzuki Kantarō Denki Hensan Iinkai, 1960), pp. 101–02. It is interesting to note that Suzuki's wife had served as a companion to the emperor when he was age three to fourteen (1904–15). Suzuki was therefore linked to the palace long before he became a candidate for Grand Chamberlain (Kanroji Osanaga, p. 28).

70. A career bureaucrat in the Home Ministry, Ichiki was regarded as a protégé of Yamagata Aritomo (Roger F. Hackett, *Yamagata Aritomo in the Rise of Modern Japan, 1838–1922* [Cambridge, Mass.: Harvard University Press, 1971], p. 268). As we have seen, however, Ichiki was the originator of the Minobe theory of constitutional monarchy. He was also accused by conservative household officials of "disrespectful acts" toward the imperial house and the late Taishō Emperor and was intensely disliked by court conservatives, the Army, and right-wing groups who considered his views on constitutional monarchy to be the source of his disrespect. Public rumor had it that Ichiki did not even know the Japanese national anthem (Nezu Masashi, p. 136).

Makino was a cosmopolitan bureaucrat whose career had been largely diplomatic. Foreign Minister in Admiral Yamamoto Gombei's first Cabinet (1913–14), Makino had served in both Saionji Cabinets, first as Minister of Education (1906–08) and then as Minister of Agriculture and Commerce (1911–12). As Privy Seal, Makino was also the subject of wild rumors, such as having flirted with the empress in the palace forests, which were evidently believed by right-wing societies (ibid., p. 137). Makino was sixty-three when he became Privy Seal in 1925.

71. Suzuki Takeshi, *Shūsenji Saishō Suzuki Kantarō-ō: Jūsan Kaiki ni Omou* (Tokyo: Jimbutsu Jidai Sha, 1960), pp. 20–22.

72. Nakase Jūichi, *Kindai ni okeru Tennō Kan* (Tokyo: Sanichi Shobō, 1963), p. 27.

Tanaka Giichi's Cabinet resigned in July 1929. The cause of his fall was his disposition of the Chang Tso-lin affair. Chang Tso-lin, Warlord of Manchuria, had been killed by Japanese Army officers and their conspirators in June 1928. The Army, in which Prime Minister Tanaka had spent his entire career before turning politician, and the political party of which he was president, the Seiyūkai, wished to hide the facts by passing off the murder as the work of Nationalist Chinese soldiers. Prince Saionji, his colleagues in the palace, and the leaders of the other main political party, the Minseitō, were aware that the facts were widely known abroad and could not, nor should not, be so clumsily buried. They therefore argued for full disclosure of the truth and for strict action against the Japanese officers involved—courts-martial. While the Army and its allies insisted that admission of the facts and strict punishment would tarnish the Army and the emperor, Saionji and his compatriots argued that international trust in Japan would be seriously undermined if Japan were unwilling or unable to maintain her own house in order, and that this would be an even more serious affront to the emperor.

Shortly after Chang's murder, Prime Minister Tanaka reported to the emperor that the plotters were evidently Japanese officers stationed in Manchuria. If that were the case, Tanaka continued, strict measures would be taken. Tanaka also told the Privy Seal and Prince Saionji the same thing in the strictest confidence.[73] Subsequent investigation by the Army itself verified beyond a doubt that Japanese Army officers were responsible.[74] In the face of Army and Seiyūkai pressure to hide the affair as much as possible and to deal lightly with the officers involved, Tanaka finally reported to the throne in May 1929—almost a year after Chang's murder and five months after Suzuki's appointment as Grand Chamberlain—that the plotters were not Japanese but that because the murder took place in an area under Japanese guard the responsible officers would be disciplined "administratively"—transferred to different posts. The em-

73. Suzuki Hajime, ed., *Suzuki Kantarō Jiden* (Tokyo: Jiji Tsūshin Sha, 1968), p. 254. Okada Keisuke, *Okada Keisuke Kaikoroku* (Tokyo: Mainichi Shimbun Sha, 1950), p. 37. Harada Kumao, 1 : 1.
74. Okada Keisuke, p. 37.

peror pointedly remarked that this report was in flat contradiction to what Tanaka had originally reported.

According to the recollections of Admiral Okada Keisuke, Navy Minister in Tanaka's Cabinet, the emperor told Tanaka when he attempted to explain the contradiction: "There is no need for an explanation." Tanaka then returned to meet his Cabinet Ministers. They urged that Tanaka attempt to arrange another audience and explain why the government had made its final disposition of the Chang Tso-lin affair in the way it did. But when Tanaka went to see Grand Chamberlain Suzuki to arrange the audience, claims Okada, Suzuki said: "I shall pass your request on, but I fear that it might be to no avail." Having lost the emperor's confidence, Tanaka decided to resign.[75] Prince Saionji's secretary, Harada Kumao, gives a slightly different account. After the emperor had scolded Tanaka for contradicting himself, Harada relates, the emperor retired into the inner palace and told Grand Chamberlain Suzuki, "I simply don't understand what Prime Minister Tanaka says. I don't want to hear him out again." Harada then claims that "since the Grand Chamberlain was new to his post and not yet used to it," Suzuki told Tanaka exactly what the emperor had said.[76]

Neither Okada nor Harada were present when the alleged conversations took place and their records are obviously hearsay. Suzuki's biographers claim that he played no part in Tanaka's resignation:

> [Tanaka's resignation] . . . had no relation whatever to the work of the Grand Chamberlain. The matter was between the Army and the government. Matters involving the military fell under the jurisdiction of the Chief Aide-de-Camp; if it were a matter involving politics, the Lord Keeper of the Privy Seal would have been responsible for rendering advice and assistance in attendance. However, it was publicly bruited about that Grand Chamberlain Suzuki had gotten involved and that for this reason the Cabinet may have fallen.[77]

In his autobiography Suzuki also claims that he was in no way involved:

> Then, since the Army Minister made a report to the throne that was

75. Ibid., pp. 40, 41.
76. Harada Kumao, 1:11.
77. *Suzuki Kantarō Den*, p. 107.

completely different from what the Prime Minister had previously reported to the throne, the Emperor pointedly inquired about the discrepancy between the two reports when Prime Minister Tanaka audienced. That is what Mr. Tanaka told me [just] after he withdrew in humble respect from the presence of the Emperor. Although [Mr. Tanaka] also said he was going to resign, I, as Grand Chamberlain, could make no reply whatever to this. As far as the Prime Minister's report to the Throne is concerned, the Grand Chamberlain [Suzuki himself, that is] was not, of course, in attendance. I haven't the slightest notion about the nature of the conversation between His Majesty and the Prime Minister. The Prime Minister merely told me in confidence of his resolve [to resign].

This is the cause for the resignation of the Tanaka Cabinet. Later I heard the following about the state of affairs at the time:

> Various contentions seethed in the Cabinet. There were even some who held that it would not do for the Prime Minister to decide at his own discretion that the Cabinet should resign: they wanted to report on the situation to the Throne once again and dispose of the matter without resigning. Mr. Tanaka refused, saying that his will had been broken and that he simply couldn't do it.

That was probably what did it. Two or three Cabinet ministers came to see the Grand Chamberlain [Suzuki] and I think said something to the effect that it would be a good thing if I were to be a go-between—that is, use my good offices between His Majesty and the Prime Minister. I remember having refused, telling them:

> For me that would be improper. The [office of] Grand Chamberlain is not that kind of position. The Grand Chamberlain [Suzuki] merely heard what the Prime Minister volunteered to let out and left it at that; [the Grand Chamberlain] is unable to do anything more than that.[78]

But if Suzuki was not actively involved in bringing the Tanaka Cabinet down, he did very little to help the Prime Minister stay in office. Although it was quite proper for him to refuse to mediate on behalf of the Cabinet, since that was the role of the Privy Seal, the net result was to assist Prince Saionji, his palace partisans, and opposition leaders in the House of Representatives in ousting Tanaka. One of Saionji's principal allies was Privy Seal Makino, who was allegedly maneuvering "behind the scenes" against Tanaka because he, like Saionji, was opposed to "military diplomacy" in China.[79] It would

---

78. Suzuki Hajime, pp. 254–55. Note that Suzuki's account states that the Army Minister, not Tanaka, made the contradictory report.
79. Nezu Masashi, p. 99.

also appear that the emperor himself, who had been sharply critical of Tanaka's "contradictory" actions, was one of Saionji's major allies.

As a result, Grand Chamberlain Suzuki was accused of partisan activities at the emperor's side. Suzuki's biographers claim that they have no idea where the "facts" "got twisted," giving rise to "groundless misunderstandings."[80] But there are at least three basic factors that combined to create such "misunderstandings": (1) the ambiguity of the Grand Chamberlain's role in law and practice, (2) the "privatized" nature of Japanese decision making, and (3) the intensity of competition among the institutions of imperial prerogative and their coalitions of institutionalized elites to declare the Imperial Will in politics.

I noted at the outset of this discussion of the Grand Chamberlain that his office, as defined by Imperial Household Ministry regulations, was perhaps the most ambiguous of the four leading palace offices. In practice, moreover, that office between 1891 and 1912 was held concurrently by the Privy Seal. Since the Privy Seal was the emperor's chief political adviser in the palace, this role was inevitably merged with that of the Grand Chamberlain during those years. We have also seen that Chamberlain Irie considered it "natural" that the Grand Chamberlain in the 1930s should have acted as Privy Seal when the Privy Seal was not at the palace. Moreover, if the Grand Chamberlain was a powerful representative from one of the governmental institutions of prerogative, rather than a neutral and discreet court bureaucrat from the high aristocracy, he would very probably be viewed as a "political partisan" by government leaders and the public at large. This was certainly true of Katsura Tarō in 1912, and it was equally true of Suzuki Kantarō from 1929 to 1936. It is highly revealing, for example, that Grand Chamberlain Suzuki was asked by some of Tanaka's Cabinet Ministers to act as "go-between" for the emperor and the Prime Minister in order to save the Cabinet; in the eyes of political actors outside the palace, the Grand Chamberlain was a potential political negotiator, despite Suzuki's proper disclaimer that the office of Grand Chamberlain was "not that kind of position." Finally, the

80. *Suzuki Kantarō Den,* p. 108.

Grand Chamberlain scheduled audiences for the Prime Minister and Ministers of State. If, for whatever reason, a Prime Minister or Minister of State was unable to report to the throne, or his report was delayed, the Grand Chamberlain could be, and occasionally was, accused of "blocking access to the throne."

Since there was no record of what the Grand Chamberlain actually said or what he thought and did in the course of arranging audiences, such accusations could not be refuted or substantiated. Even if Suzuki disclaimed, as he certainly did, any partisanship in scheduling audiences, he could be accused of disingenuousness by those who considered themselves injured. Given the verbal and closed nature of the prewar decision-making process, as the disposition of the Chang Tso-lin affair illustrates, it is no wonder that the "facts" "got twisted" and that leading court and government officials were subject to "misunderstandings." More important than the ambiguity of the Grand Chamberlain's office, therefore, was the nature of the decision-making process itself. Privatized decision making on issues of the gravest national import—such as Cabinet formations, Cabinet resignations, and basic foreign and domestic policy directions— characterized the Japanese political process throughout the prewar period. Since there were no public transcripts of these exchanges and since the entire process was kept from public scrutiny, there was no way to verify the actions of the men involved. Only the decisions were known; how, why, and even by whom decisions were made were therefore matters of endless speculation. As a result, charges and countercharges, rumor mongering, uncertainty, and "misunder-standings" infused the entire political process. The confusion was exacerbated in the 1920s and 1930s by the dedicated efforts of Japan's extensive and energetic mass media industry in unearthing and pub-licizing any and all political rumors. Had there been records, had those records been public, had voting for public officials been a critical part of the political process, had open discussions and voting in the legislature been a decisive factor in shaping political decisions, rumor might have played only a Drew Pearson role in politics. But such a public or "socialized" process of decision making was neither prac-ticed nor considered desirable in prewar Japan. Ultimately all deci-sions, both ideally and in practice, were to be made by the "emperor's advisers" communicating verbally among themselves and issuing their decisions in the name of the emperor from the presumably secure sanctuary of the imperial palace.

Privatized decision making and the flexibility of leading palace offices were consistent features of Japanese politics throughout the entire prewar period. Consequently, Japanese politics had always been marked by rumor, uncertainty, and "misunderstandings." Along with the politicization of society,[81] however, the institutionalization of imperial prerogatives and political elites added new dimensions to these traditional by-products of Japanese politics during the late 1920s and early 1930s, producing an intensity and extensiveness of rumor mongering and a degree of uncertainty in basic policy directions that challenged the effectiveness of Japan's traditional system of privatized decision making.

The Chang Tso-lin affair, for example, profoundly affected the disposition of institutions competing to declare the Imperial Will. If the Japanese officers who had plotted and executed Chang's murder were court-martialed and severely punished, both the Army's China ambitions and its institutional right to declare the Imperial Will in an increasingly wide arena would have been seriously jeopardized. The institutional strength of the Army in politics was ultimately demonstrated by the fact that Prince Saionji's views did not prevail, but it took the Army a year of pressure and behind-the-scenes maneuvering to achieve its purposes. And Tanaka's Cabinet collapsed as a result. Grand Chamberlain Suzuki was inevitably involved in the rumor mongering and back-stage maneuverings because he scheduled audiences for the Prime Minister. Regardless of the "facts," Suzuki was held at least partially responsible for Tanaka's fall by Tanaka's political party, the Seiyūkai. One of the institutions of prerogative, or its components, had been adversely affected by a decision reached verbally in the closed corridors of the imperial palace.

During and after the 1920s the institutions of prerogative and their

---

81. The expansion of mass media after the 1870s, the emergence of mass demonstrations and popular movements after 1905, the proliferation of right-wing societies after 1918, and the enfranchisement of all adult males in 1925 are some of the prominent indications of such politicization.

elites increasingly "twisted" the "facts" to serve their partisan and parochial interests. As the institutional competition for political power widened and intensified, so did the rumor mongering. Allegations of violating one or another prerogative, of interfering in a given institution's alleged decision-making domain, of scheming behind the scenes, of engaging in political activities improper to one's office, were used to vault one institution and its allies into political power against a multiplicity of competing institutions and their allies. Goverment by rumor occurred precisely because of the intensely privatized nature of decision making; such rumor mongering and its attendant uncertainties in policy directions were vastly intensified when the parochial elites of the plural institutions of prerogative replaced the autonomous individuals of Restoration leadership at the top of Japanese political society. Institutional rather than "personal" resources were brought to bear in the struggle for political power, yet the system for resolving conflicts remained based on verbal decisions and face-to-face relations centered on the imperial palace.

If Grand Chamberlain Suzuki's alleged involvement in the collapse of Tanaka Giichi's Cabinet illustrates palace partisanship in politics on the one hand, therefore, it also illustrates the nature and effect of privatized decision making in an environment of institutionalized prerogatives and parochial elites. But the partisan activities of Prince Saionji and his constitutional monarchist allies in the palace—the "palace group" as they have been called by one Japanese political scientist[82]—and the problems of privatized decision making in this period are much more clearly illustrated by the London Naval Treaty controversy of 1930.

Whereas the Chang Tso-lin affair basically involved only the Army, the Prime Minister and his Cabinet, and Prince Saionji and his allies, the London Naval Treaty brought to bear a complicated set of institutional forces: the Navy Ministry, which administered the naval establishment; the Navy General Staff, which commanded the Navy's operating forces; the Foreign Ministry, which managed the prerogative of treaty making; the Prime Minister and his Cabinet, who were responsible for setting overall national policies; the Su-

82. Matsushita Keiichi, *Sengo Minshushugi no Tenbō* (Tokyo: Nihon Hyōron Sha, 1965), p. 219.

preme War Council, which advised the emperor on basic military policies; and the Privy Council, which advised the emperor on treaty ratification. Behind each stage in policy formation, negotiation, and ratification in which these institutions were involved was the firm hand of Prince Saionji who, at eighty years of age, was determined to see the London Naval Treaty through to a successful conclusion.

As in the Chang Tso-lin affair, the necessity for Japan to act responsibly in international affairs was uppermost in Prince Saionji's mind. At the outset of the negotiations in London, which began formally in January 1930, the Navy hard-liners had publicly taken a "70 percent or bust" stand: Japan had to have a minimum tonnage ratio of 70 percent with the American fleet in all categories of auxiliary combatant ships, from heavy cruisers to submarines. Saionji was severely critical of this position. If Japan were completely unwilling to compromise, the London Conference would fail and the responsibility for its failure would rest securely with Japan. Saionji therefore argued that Japan should lead the conference to a successful conclusion, increasing Japan's international stature and impressing the Great Powers that Japan intended peace. In alliance with Great Britain and the United States, continued Saionji, Japan could share in wielding "the baton of command." By insisting on a 70 percent ratio Japan would "throw away its grip on the handle" and "join the ranks of France and Italy." Saionji concluded that there was nothing to Japan's interest in parting company with Great Britain and the United States: in fact, closer ties between Japan and these two Great Powers were desirable.[83]

Given Saionji's pro-Anglo–American stance, what resources did he have to implement his views? First, Prime Minister Hamaguchi and his Cabinet were overwhelmingly of Saionji's opinion. As president of the Minseitō in the House of Representatives, the Prime Minister had a strong base of support. Second, Japan's chief delegate to the conference was ex-Prime Minister Wakatsuki Reijirō, a pro-Saionji bureaucrat with whom the Prime Minister had been very closely associated. Wakatsuki was responsible for signing the American

83. Harada Kumao, 1:17–18. It should be noted that Saionji, like all Japanese leaders of the modern period, was deeply concerned with Japan's international prestige and national strength. He differed drastically from the militarists and other right-wing leaders on how that prestige and strength were to be established, maintained, and used.

compromise proposal of March 1930, which ultimately led to the successful conclusion of the London Naval Treaty.[84] Third, Saionji had powerful support within the Navy itself, most notably from Admirals Okada Keisuke and Saitō Makoto. As a Supreme War Councillor, Okada was in a position to check those "Navy Elders" who opposed any compromise on the 70 percent ratio. Prince Saionji had urged Okada to act as the treaty's "matchmaker." Okada pursued that role by helping to control his hard-line colleagues in the Navy General Staff and the Supreme War Council from March to October, when Japan finally ratified the compromise treaty.[85] Admiral Saitō, at that time Governor General of Korea, was strongly in favor of the treaty and in complete accord with Prince Saionji. Although he was unable to stay in Tokyo to keep pressure on his hotheaded colleagues in the Navy, Saitō lent public support to the treaty by, for example, issuing a statement to the newspapers praising the results of the conference and criticizing the actions of the Navy General Staff as "most disagreeable."[86] Fourth, the Foreign Ministry was led by Baron Shidehara Kijūrō, a long-time opponent of "military diplomacy" in China and a strong pro-treaty partisan. Shidehara met with Admiral Okada at least once and urged Okada to help bring the treaty to a successful conclusion. Fifth, Prince Saionji had Prince Konoe Fumimaro in the House of Peers to do his bidding in that component of imperial prerogative.[87]

Finally, Saionji had his supporters at the side of the emperor: Privy Seal Makino, Household Minister Ichiki, and Grand Chamberlain Suzuki. Throughout the treaty controversy Saionji was in constant touch with all three, usually through his tireless secretary, Harada Kumao. In March 1930, for example, Saionji told Harada: "It is extremely important at this juncture that the Imperial Household Minister and Grand Chamberlain, along with the Lord Keeper of the Privy Seal, give us their complete understanding on this matter."[88] After the American proposal had been approved by the Japanese government in April, the problem of Privy Council ra-

84. Ibid., p. 19. *Suzuki Kantarō Den,* p. 110.
85. Okada Keisuke, pp. 44–55. Harada Kumao, 1:67.
86. Harada Kumao, 1:49–50.
87. Ibid., pp. 26, 21–22.
88. Ibid., p. 28.

tification arose. At that time Saionji told his secretary: "The Privy Council problem will ultimately come out all right if those at the side of the Emperor, like the Lord Keeper of the Privy Seal and the Grand Chamberlain, hold fast."[89]

And hold fast they did. Grand Chamberlain Suzuki was very much involved in keeping Admiral Katō Kanji, Suzuki's successor as Chief of the Navy General Staff, in line, although the exact nature of Suzuki's involvement is a matter of controversy and speculation. Suzuki heard from the Chief Aide-de-Camp, for example, that Katō had requested an audience for April 1. Prime Minister Hamaguchi had also requested an audience, via Grand Chamberlain Suzuki, for that same day to obtain imperial sanction for the government's approval of the American compromise. Suzuki suspected trouble: Katō probably wished an audience in order to denounce the government's position on the treaty. Suzuki therefore called Katō to his official residence. Did Katō intend a contrary report to the throne? When Katō replied that he did, Suzuki told him that this would cause His Majesty great difficulty: Katō should give careful consideration to the consequences of putting the emperor in a strait between the Prime Minister, who was responsible for politics, and the Chief of Staff, who was responsible for supreme command. As a result of his talk with Suzuki, Katō agreed to withdraw his April 1 report to the throne:

> The matter was most simple. As a friend, and as a senior in the Navy, Suzuki employed honest counsel so that no fault would lie with Katō and so that no trouble would be caused His Majesty. Katō, too, understood the good will of his senior and withdrew his report to the throne of April 1. Therefore, there should have been nothing that would become an issue, but. . . . [90]

According to his own recollection, Suzuki called Katō down sharply, telling him in effect that the size of the naval establishment was no business of the Navy General Staff, which was in charge of operations, not administration. As Chief of the Navy General Staff, Katō must go along with the Prime Minister and the Cabinet on which the Navy Minister sat.[91]

89. Ibid., p. 52.
90. *Suzuki Kantarō Den*, pp. 112–13.
91. Suzuki Hajime, pp. 256–57.

This account by Suzuki and his biographers, however, is but one of at least three differing accounts of the same event. Admiral Okada states in his memoirs that Katō came to see him on April 1. Saying that his request for an audience on that day had apparently been blocked by someone close to the throne, Katō told Okada to find out from Grand Chamberlain Suzuki what had happened. Okada saw Suzuki immediately and was greatly relieved to hear that Suzuki had not blocked Katō's report. Since the emperor's schedule had already been filled for that day, Suzuki informed Okada, it would have been very difficult to arrange an audience for Katō.[92] Suzuki also told Harada Kumao that he had not blocked Katō's report. Pointing out that reports by the Chiefs of Staff had no relation to the Grand Chamberlain, Suzuki argued that such reports fell under the jurisdiction of the Chief Aide-de-Camp. Since the emperor simply had no time that day, said Suzuki, Katō's report had to follow that by the Prime Minister.[93]

Suzuki's action on April 2, the day after he had allegedly counseled Katō to withdraw his report to the throne, is also the subject of conflicting accounts. On April 2 Katō made a grudgingly conciliatory report to the throne, telling the emperor that the Navy would make do with the treaty, though this would be difficult.[94] A newspaper later alleged that Grand Chamberlain Suzuki was in attendance during Katō's report, in place of the Chief Aide whose duty it was to attend such reports by officers of the Supreme Command. Harada categorically denies this, but Suzuki's biographers are equally categorical in claiming, on the contrary, that Suzuki was in attendance, taking the "completely unprecedented" action of replacing the Chief Aide.[95]

Whatever the facts, Suzuki's behavior was subject to the same kind of "misunderstandings" that arose regarding his alleged involvement in Tanaka Giichi's resignation less than a year earlier. He became the target of censure by antitreaty forces in the government and the public at large as they mobilized to defeat the treaty's

92. Okada Keisuke, pp. 55–56.
93. Harada Kumao, 1 : 48.
94. *Suzuki Kantarō Den,* p. 114.
95. Harada Kumao, 1 : 105; *Suzuki Kantarō Den,* p. 114.

ratification in the Privy Council.[96] In June, for example, a reporter came to see Harada with the following story. The Chief Secretary to the Privy Council had said that the Chief Aide had told him that the Grand Chamberlain and Privy Seal had prevented the Chief of the Navy General Staff from reporting his criticisms of the treaty to the throne. In so doing, they had bypassed the Chief Aide, and therefore the Chief Aide had submitted his resignation. The reporter then told Harada that the Chief Secretary to the Privy Council had concluded that the Privy Seal, Grand Chamberlain, and Household Minister should "accept responsibility" for this state of affairs by resigning their offices.[97] Thus an alleged event on April 1 was relayed to Harada in June by a newspaper reporter who heard about it from a treaty opponent who in turn heard about it from the Chief Aide who, as the responsible official at the emperor's side regarding military reports, was allegedly abused by his fellow palace officers.

An inevitable product of prewar Japan's privatized decision-making process, hearsay issuing from the palace inundated the public with uncertainties as institutionalized actors and their allies manipulated unverifiable rumors to serve their preferences on issues of basic importance to the direction of Japan's foreign and domestic policies. And given the oligarchic disunity in government, the palace officers were bound to be partisan, whether they were active or inactive, since they managed the imperial sanction of policies on which there was no effective consensus in the government.

Though distorted and contradictory, the evidence does sustain the conclusion that Grand Chamberlain Suzuki was actively involved as a palace partisan in seeing the treaty through to a successful conclusion:

> In this situation it was inevitable that Grand Chamberlain Suzuki, too, having been the previous Chief of the Navy General Staff and being one of the leading officials at the emperor's side in the palace, would not be allowed to stand aloof, looking on indifferently.[98]

The inherent flexibility of the Grand Chamberlain's role allowed

96. *Suzuki Kantarō Den,* p. 113. Harada Kumao, 1:48.
97. Harada Kumao, 1:104–05.
98. *Suzuki Kantarō Den,* p. 111.

Suzuki considerable latitude to use his office as he saw fit. And because he was Katō's predecessor as Chief of the Navy General Staff he could talk with Katō "as a friend, and as a senior in the Navy"— possibly without violating his official role as Grand Chamberlain in his own mind but certainly not serving as a neutral liaison between government and court in the minds of those adversely affected.

More remarkable is the argument that, as one of the "leading officials at the emperor's side in the palace," Suzuki *could not* remain aloof. As we have seen, the traditional role of the Grand Chamberlain was precisely such aloofness. The consequence of institutional fragmentation in the government and of bringing a powerful bureaucrat from that institutional world into the palace as Grand Chamberlain, however, was that the office of Grand Chamberlain became something quite different from the courtly office it had been in Tokudaiji Sanenori's day. The Grand Chamberlain was no longer a frictionless conduit between a transcendental court and a united oligarchy in government. He was one of three leading palace officers serving the partisan purposes of the constitutional monarchists as they attempted to achieve their policy preferences by controlling the palace and manipulating it against the forces of extremism in an environment of unstable government coalitions of institutionalized elites.

The fourth palace leader was not a constitutional monarchist. But the actions of the Chief Aide-de-Camp in the 1930s involved partisanship nonetheless—a partisanship that more often than not contradicted the efforts of the constitutional monarchists who were his palace colleagues.

THE CHIEF AIDE-DE-CAMP:
CHIEF MILITARY ADVISER IN ATTENDANCE

One other personal adviser, if he can be called so, on the Emperor's staff was the chief aide-de-camp (*jijū bukanchō*). Certainly he was the least helpful member, for he seems to have functioned as the eyes and ears of the General Staff rather than as the Emperor's trusted aide. . . . The chief aide-de-camp was at this time [1931] functioning as a General Staff informant in the Palace rather than as a discreet and devoted assistant to the Emperor in his difficult task of coordination.

Yale Candee Maxon[99]

The unique position of the Office of Aides-de-Camp among the offices of court has been described in chapter 3. The post of Chief Aide-de-Camp was explicitly recognized in a revision of Army regulations on October 10, 1879, although a set of regulations applying exclusively to the Office of Aides did not materialize until April 1, 1896. Aides had acted as messengers between the emperor and the organs of military command as early as 1875,[100] however, and prior to the formal creation of the Office of Aides in 1896, Aides had been acknowledged members of the General Staff. In 1893, for example, the wartime Imperial Headquarters included six Imperial Aides as well as both service ministers and the Chief of the High Command.[101] The Aides were the military equivalent of the Chamberlains, and the Chief Aide functioned as the liaison between the emperor and the military leadership, much as the Grand Chamberlain did between the emperor and the civilian leadership. More importantly, the Chief Aide was the military equivalent of the Privy Seal. He advised and assisted the emperor on military affairs in regular attendance, much as the Privy Seal did on civil affairs. Both emissary and adviser functions were implicit in the 1896 regulations discussed in chapter 3: the Chief Aide—and even the Aides—reported and *replied* to the throne.

Between April 1896 and November 1945, when the Office of Aides was abolished, there were but eight Chief Aides, or one every 6.3 years. Measured by personnel changes, therefore, the office of Chief Aide was the most stable of the four leading court offices: there was a new Household Minister every 5 years, a new Grand Chamberlain every 6 years and a new Privy Seal every 4.6 years. For three of the four court offices, the Meiji period witnessed the highest degree of personnel stability, but for the Chief Aide, the greatest stability occurred between 1913 and 1933. There were two Chief

99. Yale Candee Maxon, *Control of Japanese Foreign Policy: A Study of Civil-Military Rivalry, 1930–1945* (Berkeley and Los Angeles: University of California Press, 1957), p. 54.

100. Matsushita Yoshio, pp. 205–06.

101. Inaba Masao, "Nihon no Sensō Shidō: Sono Kikō to Jissai (1)," *Kokubō* 10 no. 7 (March 1962): 79.

Aides from April 1896 to November 1913 (9 years average), two from November 1913 to April 1933 (9.5 years average), and four between April 1933 and November 1945 (3.3 years average). The greatest instability at the emperor's side in military affairs thus came in the period when the military, particularly the Army, made its bid for institutional hegemony over government decision making. As the Army's demands on the government increased in scope and intensity, it became increasingly difficult to find a Chief Aide satisfactory to both the Army and the court, and this evidently produced frequent changes. Only when Japan settled down to mobilizing for total war under military leadership after 1939 did the office of Chief Aide restabilize.

Until the 1930s the Chief Aide, invariably an Army general, was notable mostly for his lack of visibility in the politics and operations of the military bureaucracy. The first Chief Aide, General Viscount Okazawa Kiyoshi (1834–1908), was from the restorationist domain of Chōshu. Prior to his appointment he had served as Vice Minister of the Army and concurrently Chief of the Military Affairs Bureau (1891–92). He had also been a member of the staff at Imperial Headquarters during the Sino-Japanese War of 1894–95. Okazawa's successor, however, was General Baron Nakamura Satoru (1854–1925), a famed swordsman of very little importance in the military bureaucracy. Having served as Aide to the crown prince in 1895 and as Aide to the emperor in 1896, Nakamura was appointed Chief Aide in 1908 without any experience in major Army positions. When he resigned as Chief Aide in 1913, Nakamura was appointed to the Supreme War Council. Composed of military venerables, the Supreme War Council was the military's equivalent of the largely civilian Privy Council. Nakamura's successor, General Uchiyama Kojirō (1859–?), also held no Army posts of significance; like Nakamura he had served previously as an Aide-de-Camp.

With the appointment of Nara Takeji as Chief Aide in 1922, the first of the Army's "China hands" came to the palace. In addition to having served as Director of the Military Affairs Bureau, the first to have held one of the major Army offices since Okazawa, Nara had commanded the Japanese garrison in China. Including Nara, four of the five Chief Aides from 1922 to 1945 had seen service in China:

Honjō Shigeru, Chief Aide from 1933 to 1936, had been commander of the Kwantung Army when the Manchurian Incident broke out in 1931; Hata Shunroku, Chief Aide briefly in 1939, had been commander of the Shanghai forces in 1938, and Hasunuma Shigeru, Chief Aide from 1939 to 1945, had at least some experience in China. Only Usami Okiie, Chief Aide from 1936 to 1939, apparently had no experience in the China theater. Since the Army's demands for policy control were inextricably interwoven with military actions on the Chinese mainland, it is noteworthy that Army officers with China experience served as Chief Aides for twenty of the twenty-three years from 1922 to 1945.

Like other palace leaders, the Chief Aides, with one exception, were all ending their active bureaucratic careers. The average age upon appointment was 56, ranging from 51 to 62, and the average age on leaving office was 62.1, ranging from 54 to 74. Only one achieved high military office after serving as Chief Aide: Hata Shunroku became Army Minister in 1939 directly after a brief tour of duty as Chief Aide. Until the 1930s, therefore, the Chief Aides were largely drawn from the second level of the Army bureaucracy; almost all terminated their active military careers as Chief Aides to the emperor. In contrast to the position of Aide-de-Camp, the office of Chief Aide was not a stepping-stone to higher military office, with the one exception of Hata Shunroku. Two Chief Aides in the 1930s did, however, become Privy Councillors. That Nara Takeji in 1937 and Honjō Shigeru in 1940 should have received such appointments is evidence of the weight that the Army as an institution carried in the councils of state in the late 1930s.

Although the Army held the initiative in appointing the Chief Aide, it would be misleading to label the Chief Aide as the "spy" of the General Staff in the palace throughout the prewar period. In the first place, the Chief Aides from 1896 to 1922 were neither major figures nor focal points of conflict resolution. When Hara Kei, as Saionji's Home Minister in 1912, attempted to negotiate the Army's demand for two new divisions, for example, he went to Privy Seal Katsura Tarō, not to Chief Aide Nakamura Satoru. Hara's diary records no contact with the Chief Aide nor does it mention any actions taken by the Chief Aide in connection with the dispute. It would appear that the Chief Aide was a loyal servant of the Meiji oligarchy until 1913 and a neutral figure until approximately 1928.

Second, leadership over the military was not yet in the hands of generals and admirals who were entirely the products of the military's rigidly institutionalized channels of recruitment, education, and career advancement—channels that were so all-encompassing and exclusive that a general or admiral tended to equate his institution's particular interests with the general national interest (Imperial Will).[102] The first Chief Aide to have graduated from the Military Academy, for example, was Uchiyama Kojirō, Chief Aide from 1913 to 1922. Thereafter every Chief Aide was a Military Academy graduate, and most were graduates of the Military Staff College as well. Finally, the Army's involvement in China did not reach the point of no return until 1928–31, beginning with the murder of Manchurian warlord Chang Tso-lin in June 1928 and made irrevocable by the Manchurian Incident in September 1931.[103] Only when the institutionalization of military leadership combined with an irrevocable commitment in China did the office of Chief Aide become a vehicle for Army activism in the palace.

The tenure of General Honjō Shigeru as Chief Aide from 1933 to 1936 is the most extreme example of institutionalized Army representation at the side of the emperor.[104] Honjō was one of five generals produced by the ninth class of the Military Academy, which was graduated in 1897. His fellow generals were Araki Sadao, a leading spirit in the Army's Imperial Way Faction; Mazaki Jinzaburō, also a leader of the Imperial Way Faction and deeply implicated in the coup of February 26, 1936; Matsui Iwane, commander in China during the rape of Nanking in 1937 and hanged as a war criminal after the war; and Abe Nobuyuki.[105] Two of the five

102. On the exclusiveness of Army education and its effects on Army leadership see Alvin D. Coox, "Year of the Tiger," *Orient/West* 9, no. 4 (July–August 1964): 34–71; and Maruyama Masao, *Thought and Behaviour,* pp. 13–15.

103. On the Army's role in Manchuria see Sadako N. Ogata, *Defiance in Manchuria: The Making of Japanese Foreign Policy, 1931–1932* (Berkeley and Los Angeles: University of California Press, 1964).

104. Honjō's diary, cited earlier, is to my knowledge the only primary source to have been published on the activities of any Chief Aide-de-Camp. Nor have I discovered biographies or autobiographies of any of the Chief Aides. My discussion of that office and its personnel is therefore at best fragmentary.

105. Honjō Shigeru, p. i.

were prominent Army politicians. Araki and Abe both served as Cabinet Ministers and Abe became Prime Minister in 1939 for a brief period. Three of the five—Honjō, Mazaki, and Matsui—had seen extensive service in China. As noted above, General Honjō had been commander of the Kwantung Army when the Manchurian Incident broke in September 1931. Honjō's appointment as Chief Aide in 1933, therefore, brought into that palace office military prominence, institutionalized career, and China experience. To this was added his association with the allegedly extremist Army group, the Imperial Way Faction.

As Chief Aide, Honjō played four interrelated roles: (1) adviser to the emperor; (2) defender of the institutional integrity of the military, primarily that of the Army, at the emperor's side; (3) liaison between the emperor and the military; and (4) consultant and confidant to the other three palace leaders.[106] The vagueness of "reporting and replying to the throne on military matters" allowed the Chief Aide considerable discretion in the performance of these functions. The role of adviser to the emperor in Honjō's case involved replying to rhetorical questions by the emperor as much as it did the rendering of advice. On April 18, 1933, twelve days after he had been appointed Chief Aide, Honjō was summoned by the emperor and asked whether a direct imperial command should not be issued to the Kwantung Army to halt its advance in the Jehol area of Manchuria. Honjō guessed that the emperor was pointing out by such a question that it would be a breach of faith for Japan to continue advancing while declaring to the foreign powers that Japan would not advance into China's interior. Fearing that this kind of imperial command would lead to undesirable consequences, he advised the emperor to wait. Honjō then retired from the emperor's presence

---

106. Unfortunately, the particulars of Honjō's appointment are not known. Nezu Masashi argues that his appointment was a personal reward by the emperor for service in Manchuria (Nezu Masashi, p. 116). There is as little evidence to support this view as there is for the contrary proposition that by being in the palace Honjō would be "neutralized" as a politically active military leader. The biographers of Suzuki Kantarō argue that Honjō became Chief Aide at the recommendation of General Araki Sadao, who was Army Minister when Honjō was appointed; subsequently, Honjō allegedly reported everything that went on in the palace to Araki (*Suzuki Kantarō Den*, p. 120). Nezu supports the "reward" theory of appointment, Suzuki's biographers the "spy" interpretation. Both require modification, although the latter is apparently more accurate. Honjō was forced to resign in 1936 because of complications caused by his son-in-law's participation in the February 26 coup.

and went to see the Deputy Chief of the Army General Staff, General Mazaki Jinzaburō. Honjō told Mazaki that what Mazaki and others had reported to the throne conflicted with the actual situation in China. As a result, the General Staff issued an order to the army in the field to pull back.[107] In this instance the Chief Aide advised the emperor to wait, which the emperor did, and then saw to it that the conditions provoking the emperor's rhetorical question were relieved.

On January 26, 1934 the emperor told Honjō that according to the newspapers the Army and Navy Ministers had stated to the Diet that there was nothing wrong in military men discussing and studying politics. Commenting, the emperor stated that even research might lead to evil influences if it went too far. That afternoon, in response to imperial summons, Honjō apprised the emperor of the meaning of the ministers' remarks. First, he argued, officers must know about politics at the national and local levels in order for them to command reservists and veterans as well as their own troops effectively. Without such knowledge, officers would be unable to possess the deep sympathy for their men that is required for leadership: communication problems would develop between officers and men. Second, under present conditions, when the strength of the nation must be increased and concentrated on preparedness for war, domestic politics must be shaped toward this end. Those loyal to national defense should petition through proper channels, such as the Army Ministry, for the remedy of political defects in this regard. Senior officers must know about politics for morale purposes and for unity in their views on national defense. Finally, although officers ought not to be diffident about politics, they must not participate in politics directly; direct political action was prohibited by military regulations. In response to Honjō's rationalization of the military's political attitudes, the emperor remarked that such an interpretation lay on the side of moderation and was acceptable.[108] Honjō's "advice" to the throne in this instance reveals an attempt by the Chief Aide to mollify the emperor while defending the integrity of the

107. Honjō Shigeru, p. 159.
108. Ibid., pp. 182–83.

military's political views. His remarks also show the degree of politicization that had taken place within the Army and his sympathy with it.

Honjō again defended the Army's political interests to the emperor on February 8, but with less success. The emperor told Honjō that the military's interest in agrarian problems and sympathy with rural distress should go only so far; the farmers also had their pleasures and the aristocracy their pains. The emperor pointedly remarked that the Taishō Emperor's illness was provoked by the cares and restraints of being emperor. At this veiled rebuke, Honjō was apparently contrite, "unable to restrain his emotion and awe."[109]

On occasion the Chief Aide and the emperor collided directly. At one point the emperor told Honjō point blank of the Army's obstruction between emperor and Cabinet during the Manchurian Incident. Honjō felt compelled to remonstrate with the emperor and replied in effect that no such thing could ever happen.[110] More important, however, was the emperor's constant conflict with his Chief Aide over Minobe's theory of constitutional monarchy. As often as the emperor explained the theory and castigated the Army's opposition to it, Honjō justified the Army's stance: the Army believed the emperor to be god manifest; to make the emperor a person would be troublesome for "troop education and supreme command."[111] When the emperor told the ranking naval Aide-de-Camp, Idemitsu Mambei, that the military was contradicting imperial wishes regarding Minobe's theory, Idemitsu replied that the emperor should "transcend" such debates.[112] Throughout the controversy over Minobe's theory, which raged in the Diet and elsewhere from March into October 1935, "advice" to the emperor from the Chief Aide as well as the ranking naval Aide amounted to staunch defense of the military's position and outright contradiction of the emperor's views.[113] Honjō's actions during the Minobe affair illustrate how much the office of Chief Aide-de-Camp had been transformed into a

109. Ibid., p. 185.
110. Ibid., p. 207.
111. Ibid., p. 204.
112. Ibid., p. 211.
113. Ibid., pp. 203–31.

channel for institutional representation at the emperor's side and a vehicle for countering opinions at the palace contrary to those of the military, including those of the emperor himself.

Honjō also used his office as military adviser to the throne to protect as best he could the interests and integrity of the Army in the aftermath of the February 26 Incident of 1936, a coup attempt by young officers which brought into question the capacity or willingness of the senior Army officers to control their younger colleagues. On March 6, 1936, shortly after the coup had been brought under control, the emperor asked Honjō whether he should not dissolve the regiments that had spawned the "insurgent officers and men." Honjō replied that the matter was now under investigation by those in positions of responsibility and pointed out to the emperor that to dissolve the "dishonorable" regiments would be a great reprimand to the entire military establishment. Not surprisingly, "those in responsible positions" subsequently decided not to abolish the concerned regiments. Because the regimental colors had been bestowed by the emperor, however, the Office of Aides-de-Camp thought it improper merely to present such a decision to him without first asking his view. Consequently, the Army Ministry, the Inspectorate of Military Education, and the Army General Staff reconsidered and decided to ascertain the emperor's views on the issue of dissolution.

The burden of negotiating a solution satisfactory to both Army and emperor now lay squarely on Chief Aide Honjō. On March 14 the Section Chief for Military Affairs went back and forth between the Aides' Office and the Army Ministry; he emphasized that if by any chance the emperor should press for dissolution of the tainted regiments the Army authorities would be in serious straits. Having reported this to the emperor and heard his views, Honjō asked the Director of the Military Affairs Bureau, General Imai Kiyoshi, to come to Honjō's office: it was the emperor's wish to permit the retention of the tainted regiments. On March 17 the Army Minister and Army Chief of Staff met with the emperor at the palace. They reported, over their joint signatures, that: (1) the coup was an unprecedented disgrace and a blot on the bright record of the Imperial Army, in particular of the regiments concerned; (2) although dissolving the four regiments involved was deemed unavoidable in view of regimental and officers' rules of conduct, those who planned and participated in the insurgency were but a small fraction of these regiments; and (3) the tainted regiments wished to redeem themselves. The emperor replied: "Then all is well. Guard aginst the future." After severely reprimanding their regiments, two of the four commanders came to visit the Chief Aide on March 20, expressing their gratitude and asking that their appreciation be reported to the throne.[114]

While the dissolution issue was pending, Honjō was also set to work on what the emperor was to say formally to the Army Minister when he proffered his apologies for the insurrection. The interaction among palace officials in arriving at the public Imperial Will in politics as well as the Chief Aide's efforts on behalf of his institutional constituency are both illustrated by the reprimand process. In late February the Office of Aides began to investigate the substance of a suitable reprimand, the procedures involved, and the locus of responsibility for the incident. Honjō asked the Privy Council President and former Imperial Household Minister, Ichiki Kitokurō, about procedures for the reprimand. Ichiki replied that on relatively routine matters it had been customary since the time of Meiji to relay the emperor's words precisely as he had stated them; on matters of grave import, however, the emperor's statement was to be "advised and assisted" on by the Privy Seal. Honjō agreed that consultation with the Privy Seal was required and the Office of Aides proceeded accordingly.[115]

The Army Minister apologized informally on February 29 and formally on March 3. But because a new Privy Seal had not yet been appointed to replace Privy Seal Saitō Makoto, one of the key senior leaders assassinated in the February 26 coup, the emperor did not reply to the Army Minister. Honjō urged the necessity of a prompt imperial response. When he was summoned by the emperor on March 4, Honjō was told that if the reprimand were too strong the Privy Seal would once again be menaced by radical rightists. Yet some disciplinary action had to be taken, the emperor implied, be-

114. Ibid., pp. 290–91.
115. Ibid., pp. 291–92.

cause for him personally the murder of his most trusted senior statesmen and military officers caused the greatest anguish. Moreover, such behavior went against the constitution, violated the Emperor Meiji's Instructions (to soldiers and sailors), and stained the national polity. On March 5 Honjō was again summoned by the emperor, who was concerned whether his words, given through the ordinary channels, would have any effect at all on officers who seemed so willing to defy the constitution.

The Office of Aides finally prepared a suitable reprimand and on March 8, after the New Privy Seal, Yuasa Kurahei, had agreed to and signed it, Honjō obtained the emperor's sanction. The reprimand was severe: the Army had frequently and repeatedly staged ominous incidents, finally giving rise to the recent disaster which utterly contradicted the Instructions to Soldiers and Sailors, tarnished the history of Japan, and caused insufferable anxiety. The military was ordered to clean house thoroughly and to guard against such a disgrace occurring again.[116]

But Honjō's labors were not at an end. One hour after the emperor had apparently sanctioned the text he summoned Honjō once again: the text did not include the phrase "stained the national polity." What was the Army's interpretation of the national polity, given its insistence on "clarification of the national polity"? Honjō replied that Japan's national polity "lay in an emperor of one line unbroken for ages eternal who ruled the state in obedience to the bequeathed instructions of the imperial ancestors and the imperial founder." But, Honjō continued, the fearsome incident of late "cannot . . . in any way be said to have stained the national polity."[117] Despite the emperor's pointed questions, the phrase "stained the national polity" was left out of the official reprimand. Honjō had once again succeeded in compromising the severity of action contemplated against his institutional constituency.

On March 10 the new Army Minister, General Terauchi Hisaichi, was summoned to the palace specifically to receive the formal imperial reprimand. Terauchi was ordered by the emperor to make the intent of the reprimand thoroughly known to subordinate

116. Ibid., p. 292.
117. Ibid., pp. 292–93.

personnel in the Army. To avoid future misunderstanding, Honjō gave the Army Minister a copy of the emperor's words. At four o'clock that afternoon the emperor summoned Honjō and asked him how the Army Minister planned to transmit the reprimand to the Army. Honjō relayed the emperor's question to the Army Minister, who took it under consideration immediately.[118] The responsible authorities of the Army, with the participation of Aide-de-Camp Sakai, met on March 19 and decided that (1) for the emperor to issue such an imperial rescript of reprimand to the entire Army was without precedent; (2) a rescript with such words as "tarnished the history of our country," when the conduct in question was that of a small segment of the Army, would leave a stain on the Army that would be difficult to remove; (3) a rescript of reprimand should only be given after all other efforts had failed, and the Army's leaders had not yet taken all alternative measures; therefore, (4) there should be no imperial rescript at this time.

Having received this decision from his responsible subordinates, the Army Minister asked Honjō the following day about distributing the emperor's reprimand to Army personnel. The Office of Aides consulted the Imperial Household Ministry secretaries and the Privy Seal's Office on the nature of imperial rescripts and declarations; the Army Minister was then advised that the intent of the imperial reprimand should be written into the Army Minister's instructions to the Army but that it would be advisable to avoid distributing copies of the reprimand to the Army. Copies could, however, be given to high-ranking officers, including division commanders.[119] The emperor's reprimand to the Army Minister in chambers was therefore not transformed into a public imperial declaration to the entire Army.

Throughout his tenure as Chief Aide Honjō reconciled the conflicting demands of Army and emperor, including those of the emperor's "advisers," as much in favor of the Army as possible. What was "possible" depended on (1) the emperor's stance and to whom that stance was known, (2) the intransigence of the Army, (3) the precedents and procedures available to rationalize given courses of

118. Ibid., p. 293.
119. Ibid., pp. 293–94.

action, and (4) the views of other palace leaders who shared in the process of conflict reconciliation. The emperor's stance in politics was conditioned by his civilian advisers, especially palace leaders and others, such as Prince Saionji, who held to Minobe's theory of constitutional monarchy or sympathized with it. The sharpness of the conflict between Chief Aide Honjō and the emperor over the Minobe theory indicates how partisan the emperor's stance was. Honjō was therefore restrained by the emperor to the extent that the emperor's actions and views had to be taken into account by the Chief Aide in discharging his function of advice and assistance.

The intransigence of Honjō's institutional constituency was apparently the most important factor in Honjō's actions; he felt constrained to "remonstrate" with the emperor when basic Army interests were threatened. While "remonstration" for Household Minister Tanaka Mitsuaki in the early twentieth century was largely based on his personal role conception and his person-to-person relations with the oligarchs and their protégés, Chief Aide Honjō's remonstration in the 1930s was based primarily on institutional considerations. It is important to repeat that the Chief Aide was an Army officer on active duty; both Honjō and his predecessor, Nara Takeji, for example, went into the Reserves after they resigned as Chief Aides. The fact that the Chief Aides were active-duty officers appointed on Army initiative reinforced their loyalty to the Army.

Also quite obvious in Honjō's behavior was a great concern for procedure and precedent. Honjō was meticulous in consulting the Privy Seal, the President of the Privy Council, and household officials whenever formal action was to be taken by the emperor, as indicated by his actions in the aftermath of the February 26 Incident. Precedent was useful in mitigating the emperor's actions against the Army in that critical period; a formal reprimand to the Army, for example, would have been "without precedent." But procedures and precedents worked two ways. Precedent had to be sought for actions on the part of the Chief Aide, as well as the emperor, and the observance of procedures quite obviously allowed palace leaders some influence over the behavior of the Chief Aide. Once he became one of the four leading palace officers, Honjō was surrounded by a different set of procedures and precedents from those in the Army, and a different set of colleagues.

Among his palace colleagues, the one with the greatest influence on Honjō appears to have been Grand Chamberlain Suzuki Kantarō. It was Suzuki who initially informed Honjō of the norms of conduct regarding the throne for both civilian and military leaders. This he did by discussing improprieties in the behavior of Prime Minister Tanaka Giichi in 1929 and, on instructions from the emperor, the contradictory actions of the Chief of the Navy General Staff during the London Naval Treaty controversy of 1930.[120] Although Chief Aide Honjō and those in the Office of Aides were the sole formal liaisons between the palace and the military commands, Honjō was careful to keep himself informed of the Privy Seal's views. On one occasion, for example, he ascertained the Privy Seal's opinion, via Grand Chamberlain Suzuki, on the revision of reporting procedures for the Navy General Staff.[121]

The Household Minister was also involved on occasion. When in January 1934 a request came from Prince-of-the-Blood Asaka for an imperial review of the Palace Guards (*Konoe Shidan*), Honjō busied himself with precedents for such a review and obtained the "understanding" of the Household Ministry as well as the Board of Chamberlains.[122] The Household Minister and Chief Aide also worked together when the Army objected to the emperor's reviewing Japanese troops with the emperor of Manchuria during the latter's visit to Japan. The Household Minister insisted that courtesies to a visiting head of state fell under his jurisdiction, not the Army's. Through Honjō, however, a compromise was reached whereby special courtesies were to be rendered by the Army to the Japanese emperor. The issue took two weeks to settle.[123]

Honjō also kept palace leaders informed, at least sporadically, of Army criticisms of those "at the emperor's side" or "close to the throne." Around September 1935, for example, Honjō told

---

120. Ibid., pp. 160–62. Suzuki thus continued his partisan activities on behalf of the constitutional monarchists. In the instances cited above he was used in an attempt to bring the Chief Aide into line with palace policy during 1933.
121. Ibid., pp. 163–67.
122. Ibid., pp. 179–80.
123. Ibid., pp. 201–03.

Household Minister Yuasa Kurahei that a segment of the Army was angry over the "weak" advice given the emperor by the Senior Retainers, including the emperor's palace advisers. Yuasa told Honjō that he, as Household Minister, was never asked political questions by the emperor, although some felt that the Household Minister should speak his mind on political issues. Grand Chamberlain Suzuki added that the emperor never asks the Privy Seal questions about military affairs. Honjō believed, however, that the Privy Seal might properly be consulted on the distinctions between civil and military matters.[124]

Honjō did, it appears, act as a colleague among fellow palace leaders in coordinating the emperor's role as Emperor-in-State. It is much too simple to classify even as extreme an example as Chief Aide Honjō as a military "spy" at the emperor's side. Although he tenaciously defended the policies and interests of the military, especially the Army, Honjō was meticulous in observing palace customs, procedures, and precedents. He kept the emperor and palace leaders informed of opinion within the Army. If he behaved as the representative of his institutional constituency at the emperor's side, he also demonstrated an awareness of his role as a palace person, as one of those involved in the coordination of the Imperial Will in politics. His actions reveal the complexity of pressures on him as military adviser and liaison to the throne, pressures that derived from his dual capacity as institutional representative and palace negotiator. As such, he was both the voice of military demands at the side of the emperor and the instrument of palace communication and negotiation with the military.

Having an active-duty status within the Army, having served a lifetime in that constituency, and having in fact been given his palace office by that constituency, the Chief Aide was, however, a very different palace officer from his palace colleagues. He was especially set apart from his civilian counterpart who advised the emperor on "politics": the Lord Keeper of the Privy Seal.

124. Ibid., pp. 224–25.

THE LORD KEEPER OF THE PRIVY SEAL:
CHIEF POLITICAL ADVISER IN ATTENDANCE

Because Count Makino also felt deep concern over his incapacity in office, [his infirmities] being such that it was completely impossible for him to take part even in court events at the year's end and the year's beginning, Prince Saionji, Prime Minister Okada, Household Minister Yuasa, Grand Chamberlain Suzuki, and others came to an agreement among themselves and finally brought about [Makino's resignation as Privy Seal]. Former Prime Minister Viscount Saitō was made his successor by direct imperial appointment because his character and career were considered most fit for discharging the heavy responsibilities of rendering advice and assistance in regular attendance on the Emperor, given that the viscount was already one of the Senior Retainers. Although some gave heed to his connections with the present Cabinet, since the viscount had been involved as midwife of the Okada Cabinet, in fact there was absolutely no political significance in this.

Tōkyō Asahi Shimbun[125]

However accurate as a picture of political reality, these comments on the appointment of the new Privy Seal in 1935 reflect idealized perceptions about the right man to be Privy Seal and the proper nature of his role. A Senior Retainer (ex-Prime Minister), Viscount Saitō was most "fit" to render advice and assistance to the throne, which he would have done indirectly in any case as one of those consulted by Prince Saionji when a Cabinet collapsed during the 1930s. There was "no political significance"—undue political partisanship or unhealthy political connections—in the fact that he had been "midwife" to the Okada Cabinet in July 1934, despite Viscount Saitō's pro-Saionji stance in politics and his long association with Okada in the Navy. As we shall see, the Privy Seal had always acted as liaison and negotiator between the throne and the political world outside the palace gates. That Saitō had midwifed the Okada Cabinet prior to his appointment as Privy Seal was evidence that he

125. December 27, 1935, as quoted in *Shishaku Saitō Makoto Den,* 3 vols. (Tokyo: Zaidan Hōjin Saitō Shishaku Kinen Kai, 1941), 3:646.

was in fact able to perform one of the Privy Seal's most important functions: political broker to the throne on Cabinet formations.

As indicated by the appointment of Senior Retainer Saitō in 1935, the Privy Seals generally were expected to be accomplished statesmen, and in fact they were the most prestigious of the palace leaders in career and status. Of the thirteen Privy Seals between 1885 and 1945, four (30.8 percent) had been Prime Ministers; nine (69.2 percent) had served as Ministers of State; seven (53.8 percent), including two presidents, had been Privy Councillors; and all but one (92.3 percent) were at one time members of the House of Peers. Two (15.4 percent) were Elder Statesmen. The only imperial prince among all four leading palace officers from 1885 to 1945, Fushimi Sadanaru, served as Privy Seal. All the Privy Seals were titled; among them they included one prince-of-the-blood (7.7 percent), five princes (38.5 percent), one marquis (7.7 percent), two counts (15.4 percent), two viscounts (15.4 percent), and two barons (15.4 percent). Averaging sixty-five years of age upon assuming office, ranging from forty-eight to eighty-two, the Privy Seals were also on the average the most senior members of the palace leadership. The average term of office was 4.6 years, although two Privy Seals served but one day in office, thus distorting the average downward. The Privy Seal, like all palace leaders, was expected to "serve a lifetime at the side of the emperor" once appointed to leading court office. And most of them did; eight of the thirteen died within two years of retirement.

Althouth many Privy Seals did not serve twenty years in any one given institutional constituency prior to appointment, their major career backgrounds were: restorationist, three (23.1 percent); Home Ministry, three (23.1 percent); Army, two (15.4 percent); and court, Education Ministry, Foreign Ministry, Navy, and Agriculture and Commerce Ministry, one each (7.7 percent). Calculating career background against length of service, however, it is apparent that court, restoration, and Foreign Ministry officials held the post of Privy Seal 75 percent of the time between 1885 and 1945:[126]

---

126. Four of the thirteen Privy Seals served less than six months: Hamao Arata (Education Ministry), Katsura Tarō (Army), Saitō Makoto (Navy), and Ichiki Kitokurō (Home Ministry).

Court	20 years
Restorationist	14 years
Foreign Ministry	11 years
Home Ministry	7 years
Agriculture and	
Commerce Ministry	6 years
Army	2 years
Total	60 years

That only three military officers should have received appointments, excluding Elder Statesman General Ōyama Iwao, and that they served a total of but two years indicates that the office of Privy Seal was very much a civilian post. The military officers who did hold the post, moreover, were senior officers who had either served as Prime Minister (two) or were members of the imperial house (one).

The only time a court person served as Privy Seal was from 1891 to 1912, when Prince Tokudaiji Sanenori served concurrently as Grand Chamberlain and Privy Seal. Like the other offices of court leadership, therefore, the office of Privy Seal also underwent bureaucratization from the outside once the oligarchic solidarity of the Meiji period ended. The official duties of the Privy Seal, the initial conception of his role in 1885—as revealed by the appointment and actions of the first Privy Seal, Prince Sanjō Sanetomi—and the actions of subsequent Privy Seals reveal the flexibility of that most important of court offices as it responded to changing times throughout the period 1885–1945.

As was the case with the Grand Chamberlain, the duties of the Lord Keeper of the Privy Seal were briefly defined and the jurisdiction of his office diffuse. The office of Privy Seal was created within the palace in December 1885. The Privy Seal was to (1) take custody of the Imperial Seal and the Great Seal of State, (2) render advice and assistance in attendance on the emperor, and (3) preside over the proceedings of the Court Advisers (*Kyūchū Komonkan*).[127] The ef-

---

127. "Dajōkan Tasshi," no. 68, December 22, 1885, in *Hōrei Zensho*, 1885, 2:1,043. Palace advisers, originally fifteen in number, were appointed for meritorius service and were to advise the throne on ceremonies stipulated in household regulations (ibid.). By 1907 the fifteen Court Advisers, as well as the Imperial Household Ministry Consultants (*Kunai Shō Goyōgakari*), fell under the Imperial Household Minister's office. In 1943, however, there were three special "consultants" (*goyōgakari*) to the Privy Seal: one a Privy Councillor, one an Imperial Household Ministry Councillor (*Sanjikan*) and the third a Bureau of Legislation Councillor (Prime Minister's Office) (*Shokuin Roku*, July 1943, pt. 2, pp. 14–15).

fective regulation governing the Privy Seal's office from 1907 until 1942 added that the Privy Seal was to take charge of imperial edicts, imperial rescripts, and matters regarding palace documents, while deleting the provision on presiding over the meetings of Court Advisers. In addition to two secretaries of executive appointee rank, the Privy Seal was assigned a Chief Secretary of imperial appointee rank to assist him in his duties.[128] Of the four leading palace officers only the Household Minister and the Privy Seal were empowered to "advise and assist" (*hohitsu*) the emperor, as were the Ministers of State; the Chief Aide, however, was permitted to "report and reply to" the throne, which allowed him similar influence, and the generality of "rendering attendance at the emperor's side" allowed the Grand Chamberlain influence as well. But except for precedents and the "trends of the time," the Privy Seal, unlike the Household Minister, was under no restriction regarding advice and assistance.

If the Privy Seal's was a distinctive office for assisting the emperor by rendering advice on both national affairs and imperial household matters, the manner in which the function of advice and assistance was fulfilled varied considerably throughout the period from 1885 to 1945. We have seen, for example, that from 1891 to 1912 Privy Seal-Grand Chamberlain Tokudaiji was a frictionless conduit between emperor and oligarchs. The first Privy Seal, Prince Sanjō Sanetomi (1837-91), was, however, an active member of the oligarchy. His role as Japan's first Privy Seal has been the subject of considerable speculation and controversy. One opinion is that the office of Privy Seal was created especially for Sanjō as a place for him to retire in dignity. According to this interpretation, Itō Hirobumi wished to find a place for Sanjō commensurate with the post of Chancellor, a post from which Sanjō would be forced to resign when the cabinet system was inaugurated in 1885.[129] Sanjō has also been characterized as a weak member of the oligarchy.[130] Even while Sanjō was Privy Seal, moreover, he was attacked for fawning ser-

---

128. "Kōshitsu Rei," no. 4, November 1, 1907, as amended in 1910, 1914, and 1917, in Naikaku Kiroku Ka, 1942, vol. 1, pt. 3, chap. 1, sec. 3, p. 20.
129. Inada Masatsugu, p. 35; Inoue Kiyoshi, p. 103.
130. Tsuji Kiyoaki, *Nihon Kanryō Sei no Kenkyū* (Tokyo: Kōbundō, 1952), p. 70.

vilely on the Itō Cabinet.[131] Thus the office of Privy Seal may have been created as a device for kicking the ineffectual Sanjō upstairs.

Inoue Kiyoshi disagrees with such an ad hoc interpretation of oligarchic intent behind the creation of the Privy Seal's office. He argues that the office of Privy Seal, which he believes should have been a government rather than a court office, was deliberately placed under the emperor and outside the government to ensure that the emperor could be used to rescue the government oligarchs in time of need, as in confrontations with the Imperial Diet. As such, the office of Privy Seal was intended to be the ultimate stronghold of the "emperor system's bureaucratic-military despotism."[132]

It is not necessary to subscribe to Inoue's theory of despotism to agree with him that the office of Privy Seal was intended to be pivotal in the politics of oligarchic decision making. Sanjō's experiences as a Restoration leader made him a valuable member of the oligarchy and ideally suited to serve oligarchic unity as Privy Seal. Prior to the creation of the cabinet system and the office of Privy Seal in 1885, Sanjō had been instrumental in coordinating personnel and policy. Throughout the process leading to the inauguration of the cabinet system, for example, he had worked closely with Itō in reaching and re-reaching compromises. At no point, according to Itō's biographer, was Sanjō anything but fair and impartial in his attitudes toward this major revision of government structure, a revision that would deprive him of his office as Chancellor. If oligarch Itō was the leader and initiator of policy, oligarch Sanjō was the key policy negotiator. As harmonizer of oligarchic wills, moreover, Sanjō did not hesitate to offer suggestions to Itō that did not always conform with Itō's views.[133] A high Court Noble outside the Satsuma-Chōshū group of leaders, Sanjō was also the chief link between Itō and the emperor. As an oligarch, Sanjō was a member of the government elite; as a Court Noble he had access to the emperor and was familiar with the ways and customs of court. Sanjō was therefore ideally suited to render "advice and

131. Shumpo Kōtsui Shōkai, 2:519.
132. Inoue Kiyoshi, pp. 102–03.
133. Shumpo Kōtsui Shōkai, 2:441–84.

assistance" at the emperor's side as negotiator, not initiator, within the oligarchy.

After he became Privy Seal, Sanjō continued to be an invaluable member of the oligarchy as it weathered the drafting of the Meiji Constitution between 1885 and 1889 and the opening of the first Imperial Diet in 1890. When in 1889, for example, no agreement could be reached among the oligarchs on a successor to Kuroda Kiyotaka as Prime Minister, Sanjō became Prime Minister *pro tempore*. For two months, from October 25 to December 24, 1889, Sanjō served as both Prime Minister and Privy Seal while engaged in negotiations that ultimately led to the formation of a Cabinet under Yamagata Aritomo.[134] Rather than "weakness" Sanjō demonstrated great skills as a negotiator, making his office of Privy Seal that of "Prime Minister in reserve."

Sanjō also stood staunchly behind the Prime Minister, believing it to be his duty as Privy Seal to do so until the Prime Minister himself had decided to resign. In the spring of 1887 Prime Minister Itō Hirobumi was attacked for blurring the distinction between court and government as well as for failing to revise the unequal treaties between Japan and the Western powers. Despite the possible tarnish on his career that his support of Itō might have caused, Sanjō refused to give in to "public opinion." Sanjō stood aloof, insisting that any question of resignation had to be delayed until Kuroda Kiyotaka had returned from abroad and all the oligarchs could assemble to reach agreement on a course of action.[135] Given Sanjō's career both before and during his tenure of office as Privy Seal, it might even be argued that he was one of the crucial figures in negotiating the Restoration settlement to a successful conclusion. It is tempting to speculate that the innocuous Tokudaiji was able to serve as both Privy Seal and Grand Chamberlain from 1891 to 1912 because Sanjō, as Privy Seal, had been so successful in consolidating oligarchic unity around the Meiji Emperor: a skilled negotiator was no longer required as Privy Seal after Sanjō's death in 1891.

There were but two Privy Seals from December 1885 to July

134. Ibid., pp. 698–705, 1,007.
135. Ibid., pp. 519–20.

1912, the terms of Sanjō and Tokudaiji averaging 13.3 years. As in the case of the Household Minister and the Grand Chamberlain, however, the end of the Meiji era was also the end of personnel stability in the Privy Seal's office. From August 1912, when ex-Prime Minister Katsura became both Privy Seal and Grand Chamberlain, to March 1925, when Makino Nobuaki was appointed Privy Seal, there were six Privy Seals, or one every 2.1 years. An ex-Prime Minister, a prince-of-the-blood, two Elder Statesmen, and two ex-Ministers of State, in that order, held the post of Privy Seal, illustrating the transition from restorationist to bureaucratic leadership at the palace.

The transition was one of trial and error, posing considerable difficulties both in government and in court. The difficulties involved in Katsura Tarō's entrance into and exit from the office of Privy Seal in 1912 have already been described. Katsura's successor, Prince-of-the-Blood Fushimi Sadanaru, caused problems of the reverse order. Rather than an active faction politician like Katsura, Fushimi was an imperial prince. His appointment was interpreted as rendering the office of Privy Seal impotent precisely because of his status.

When the issue of Household Minister Watanabe Chiaki's resignation arose in early 1914, for example, the Privy Council had to affirm Privy Seal Fushimi's powers, as an imperial prince, to countersign the resignation, giving rise to fears at the time that the office of Privy Seal might "stagnate." Consequently, the Elder Statesmen, affirming the need for a "full-time" Privy Seal, decided that one of their number, General Ōyama Iwao, should replace Fushimi.[136] Implicit in their action was the proposition that an imperial prince had to be "above politics," yet the Privy Seal's office involved political action—including even such details as the countersigning of ministerial appointments and resignations. And these acts, however formal, were potentially partisan. If an imperial prince were Privy Seal, his acts would ipso facto affect the impartiality of the imperial family—and the emperor. A Privy Seal had to act discreetly. By virtue of his station, Prince Fushimi could not act discreetly, and it is

---

136. *Gensui Kōshaku Ōyama Iwao* (Tokyo: Ōyama Gensui Den Kankō Kai, 1935), pp. 823–24.

significant that he was the only imperial prince to serve in any leading court office from 1885 to 1945.[137]

From 1915 to 1922 the office of Privy Seal was occupied by two aged Elder Statesmen, Ōyama Iwao and Matsukata Masayoshi. Their appointments suggest that the office of Privy Seal, in the tradition of Sanjō Sanetomi, belonged to experienced and influential statesmen who had no further ambitions in government and were thus ideally suited to act as impartial but effective negotiators in the political process. Since the Elder Statesmen advised the throne on major national policies as well as on the appointment of the Prime Minister, moreover, having one of their number as Privy Seal made this process of advice simpler and solidified the concept that such basic advice to the throne was the prerogative of the Elder Statesmen.

Count Hirata Tōsuke was appointed to succeed Prince Matsukata Masayoshi in 1922. Hirata was a protégé of Yamagata Aritomo. Next to Yamagata, apparently, Hirata was best known to Matsukata, and it was at Matsukata's recommendation that Hirata, at the age of seventy-three, was made Privy Seal.[138]

Hirata was not a complete stranger to the ways of court. In 1919 he had been appointed Imperial Household Ministry Consultant to assist the Imperial House Economic Council in the adjustment of imperial house properties. That council had traditionally included many of Japan's leading statesmen; Itō Hirobumi, Yamagata Aritomo, and Matsukata Masayoshi, for example, had at one time or another advised on court finances as members of the council. When the Elder Statesmen became few in number and aged, younger scholars and officials were appointed Consultants to assist in the council's work. As Consultant, Hirata investigated the finances of foreign royal houses, heard the views of men in the world of finance, and consulted with court officials.[139]

---

137. We have seen that one of the objections to Katsura was his "rustic" origins, and this may have been important in the selection of Prince Fushimi to replace Katsura. After Fushimi, however, no person of even Court Noble origin was to be Privy Seal. If "status" was one of the criteria in selecting the Privy Seal, it quickly gave way to "ability," as proven by the successful bureaucratic careers of all those who served as Privy Seals from 1915 on.

138. *Hakushaku Hirata Tōsuke Den* (Tokyo: Hirata-haku Denki Hensan Jimusho, 1927), p. 167.

139. Ibid., pp. 164–65.

The various posts for advising the court on one matter or another were devices for recruiting government leaders into the court, on the one hand, and for keeping leaders available to reenter the government after they had resigned or been forced to resign from their government posts, on the other. Under pressure over the treaty revision issue, for example, Inoue Kaoru had resigned as Foreign Minister in 1887 only to be appointed Court Adviser; he emerged from the palace less than a year later as Minister of Agriculture and Commerce.[140] Leading court officials also retired into palace advisory posts. Tanaka Mitsuaki, for example, became an Imperial House Economic Adviser after he retired as Household Minister in 1909, as did ex-Household Minister Ichiki Kitokurō when he was forced to resign as President of the Privy Council in 1936. The palace, with its multiplicity of advisory posts, thus served as a sanctuary for Japan's leading statesmen and bureaucrats. For Hirata, however, advising at court was evidently a device for acquainting the protégé of an Elder Statesman with the ways of court in preparation for high court office.

The fundamental role of the Privy Seal as political negotiator was continued by Hirata. Shortly after he had become Privy Seal in September 1922, dissension between the government and the Privy Council arose over the Sino-Japanese postal treaty. The issue was basically a procedural one, involving the timing of the Privy Council's advice on treaty ratification. The task of mediation fell to Hirata as Privy Seal. The Imperial Diet took up the issue in December 1922, causing further complications by subjecting the treaty to public criticism, and the issue required five months to settle. Throughout those five months Hirata was guided in his task of mediation by two negative principles: (1) not to leave future complications after the treaty had been ratified, and (2) not to "wound the face" (injure the pride) of either the government or the Privy Council.[141] If in Sanjō's case the role of Privy Seal was to negotiate among the powerful men of the oligarchy, Hirata's role was to mediate among institutions, in this instance the Cabinet and the

140. Shumpo Kōtsui Shōkai, 2:553.
141. *Hakushaku Hirata Tōsuke Den*, pp. 168–69.

Privy Council. Hirata was less concerned with personal reputations than with the prestige and status of institutions in conflict.

During Hirata's tenure as Privy Seal there were no less than three Cabinet changes. When Prime Minister Katō Tomosaburō died in office on August 25, 1923, the Regent "put the question" concerning a successor to the Elder Statesmen.[142] Saionji went to the imperial villa at Hayama to respond to the throne. There he met Privy Seal Hirata and told him that he had consulted with Matsukata Masayoshi, the only other remaining Elder Statesman, and that they wished to recommend Yamamoto Gombei as Katō's successor. Asked his opinion, Hirata replied that whomever the Elder Statesmen recommended, he deemed appropriate. The imperial command to form a Cabinet fell to Yamamoto on August 28, 1923.[143] In contrast to his role as institutional mediator in the postal treaty controversy, Privy Seal Hirata's role in Cabinet formations was evidently one of liaison between the throne and the elder Statesmen, although they solicited his view.[144]

From 1885 to 1945 the selection of the Prime Minister was a carefully preserved imperial prerogative. Because it was an imperial prerogative, however, the appointment of the Prime Minister was to be advised upon by various political leaders via the Privy Seal. During their active political leadership in the Cabinet from 1885 to 1901, the oligarchs usually agreed to have one of their number serve as Prime Minister. In 1892, for example, four oligarchs—Kuroda Kiyotaka, Yamagata Aritomo, Inoue Kaoru, and Itō Hirobumi—gathered to select a successor to Prime Minister Matsukata Masayoshi.[145] As a result, Itō succeeded Matsukata and Inoue became Itō's Home Minister. After 1901, however, the oligarchs retired from positions of direct leadership in the Cabinet, preferring to work behind the imperial screen. As the Council of Elder Statesmen (*Genrō Kaigi*), they "occupied a supreme position in Japanese politics up to the 1920's."[146] Under these circumstances the

---

142. The present emperor became Regent for his father in 1921.

143. *Hakushaku Hirata Tōsuke Den*, pp. 169–70.

144. Unfortunately, Hirata's biographer does not treat Hirata's role in the succeeding cabinet changes.

145. Chitoshi Yanaga, *Japan since Perry* (New York: McGraw-Hill Book Company, 1949), p. 219.

146. Scalapino, p. 150.

imperial prerogative of appointment was in fact exercised by the Elder Statesmen; the Privy Seal was primarily a liaison between them and the throne in this function.

In 1924 Prince Matsukata Masayoshi died, leaving Prince Saionji as the last Elder Statesman. Since palace leadership was almost exclusively in the hands of Prince Saionji's partisans, a measure of stability was restored in the Privy Seal's office. Between 1925 and 1936 there were but two Privy Seals, or one every 5.5 years, and both were constitutional monarchists. In 1932, however, Prince Saionji, who was over eighty, began to make provisions for an advisory system after his death. He therefore asked Kido Kōichi, the Chief Secretary to the Privy Seal, to examine and revise procedures for replying to the throne on appointing Prime Ministers. Kido subsequently drafted a plan whereby the Senior Retainers would meet to advise the throne when a Prime Minister resigned. The conference was to be composed of ex-Prime Ministers (Senior Retainers), the President of the Privy Council, the Privy Seal, and the Speakers of both houses of the Imperial Diet. Household Minister Ichiki Kitokurō, however, deleted the two Speakers from the proposed conference.[147] This conference, as modified by Ichiki, met with Saionji in the palace in July 1934 to assist him in selecting a successor to Prime Minister Saitō Makoto.[148] As a consultant in this process, the Privy Seal gained an increased voice in exercising the imperial prerogative of appointment.

From 1936, when Privy Seal Saitō Makoto was assassinated, to November 1945, when the office of Privy Seal was abolished, there were two Privy Seals, averaging five years in office. Neither were of Senior Retainer status, yet it was during this time that the Privy Seal acquired primary responsibility for recommending new Prime Ministers to the throne.[149] Yuasa Kurahei, Privy Seal from 1936 to 1940, had been a career Home Ministry official whose highest posts before becoming Privy Seal were Civil Governor of Korea (1925–27) and Imperial Household Minister (1933–36). His successor, Mar-

---

147. *Okada Keisuke* (Tokyo: Okada Taishō Kiroku Hensan Kai, 1956), pp. 233–34; Nezu Masashi, p. 131.
148. Harada Kumao, 3 : 347–48.
149. Inada Masatsugu, p. 93. Inada places the date of the Privy Seal's primacy in recommending Prime Ministers precisely at May 1937.

quis Kido Kōichi, had served in two Cabinets between 1937 and 1939 prior to his appointment as Privy Seal in 1940. With Prince Saionji's death in 1940, Privy Seal Kido became solely responsible for replying to the throne on basic policy directions and Cabinet changes.

The importance of the Privy Seal's office thus varied according to the composition of the forces competing to declare the Imperial Will and the nature of the emperor's senior advisers. The flexibility of the office, along with that of the other leading palace offices, allowed the Privy Seal and his palace colleagues considerable maneuverability to cope with any political situation. The Privy Seal, however, was the most important palace officer in relating emperor to politics throughout the period 1885 to 1945. As initially conceived by the oligarchs and as developed by the first Privy Seal from 1885 to 1891, the office of Privy Seal was to be the chief link between court and government. It is not surprising, therefore, that throughout the entire prewar period the Privy Seals as a group were the most highly statused in terms of titles, the most accomplished in terms of prior government careers, and on average the most senior of the four leading palace officers.

THE NATURE AND ROLE OF PALACE LEADERSHIP
IN PREWAR JAPANESE POLITICS

Table 9 summarizes data on each of the four leading palace officers from 1885 to 1945 and demonstrates once again the primacy of the Privy Seals in palace politics. In contrast to the diversity and stature of the Privy Seals, and indeed the Household Ministers and Grand Chamberlains, the Chief Aides were representatives of only one institutional constituency, the Army, achieved no titles higher than viscount, and on the average were the most junior of the four palace leaders. As table 9 also reveals, the Chief Aide's was the only office that remained strictly autonomous; no Chief Aide ever held any other position of palace leadership. There was considerable interchange among all the other offices: some officials held two posts concurrently; others transferred from one palace office to another. And Chief Aides

TABLE 9. A COMPARATIVE PORTRAIT OF THE FOUR LEADING PALACE
OFFICIALS BY OFFICES, 1885–1945

	Household Ministers (12 = 100%)	Grand Chamberlains (10 = 100%)	Chief Aides (8 = 100%)	Privy Seals (13 = 100%)
Average age on taking office	58.3	61.1	56	65
Range of ages	44–67	46–71	51–62	48–82
Average years in office	5	6	6.3	4.6
High offices held:				
Prime Minister	1 (8.3%)	2 (20%)	0	4 (30.8%)
Minister of State	6 (50%)	2 (20%)	1 (12.5%)	9 (69.2%)
Privy Council President	2 (16.7%)	1 (10%)	0	2 (15.4%)
Privy Councillor	7 (58.3%)	3 (30%)	2 (25%)	7 (53.8%)
Top military office	1 (8.3%)	2 (20%)	3 (37.5%)	3 (23.1%)
Supreme War Councillor	0	4 (40%)	4 (50%)	2 (15.4%)
Ambassador	2 (16.7%)	1 (10%)	0	1 (7.7%)
House of Peers	10 (83.3%)	6 (60%)	0	12 (92.3%)
One or more of the other top four palace offices	4 (33.3%)	3 (30%)	0	5 (38.5%)
Prior career against years in court office:				
Restorationist	23	0	0	14
Army	1	5	49	2
Navy	0	17	0	0
Foreign Ministry	13	2	0	11
Home Ministry	15	0	0	7
Justice Ministry	6	0	0	0
Finance Ministry	1	0	0	0
Agriculture and Commerce Ministry	0	0	0	6
Court	1	36	0	20
Titles eventually achieved:				
Prince	2 (16.7%)	3 (30%)	0	6 (46.2%)
Marquis	0	0	0	1 (7.7%)
Count	4 (33.3%)	3 (30%)	0	2 (15.4%)
Viscount	1 (8.3%)	1 (10%)	1 (12.5%)	2 (15.4%)
Baron	3 (25%)	1 (10%)	4 (50%)	2 (15.4%)
None	2 (16.7%)	2 (20%)	3 (37.5%)	0

simply did not move in the same circles as did other palace leaders, even if those others had also been career military officers. General Nakamura Yūjirō received two imperial appointments to the House of Peers prior to becoming Imperial Household Minister in 1920. No Chief Aides were appointed to the House of Peers. General Katsura Tarō had been Prime Minister twice before he became Privy Seal-Grand Chamberlain in 1912. Admiral Saitō Makoto had also been Prime Minister before his appointment as Privy Seal (1935). Admiral Suzuki Kantarō became President of the Privy Council (1944) and Prime Minister (1945) after having served as Grand Chamberlain. No Chief Aide, however, served at any time as Prime Minister or as President of the Privy Council. Unlike the Chief Aides, therefore, those military officers who held other leading palace offices were "generalists" and "negotiators," not dedicated institutional spokesmen. Like their civilian colleagues, they were part of the elaborate network that linked Japan's political leaders laterally across the top of the plural institutions of government after imperial prerogatives had been institutionalized. The Chief Aides, however, conceived of themselves as career Army officers who had no relation to politics except when the Army's interests were involved or when their role as court officials compelled collaboration with the other palace leaders.

The bureaucratization of the four leading palace offices over time and the nature of the evolved institutional balances at the emperor's side are illustrated in table 10. The periodization is by reigns, which, as I pointed out earlier, corresponds roughly with the major stages in the evolution of palace leadership. During the Meiji period court persons were the major component of palace leadership for the only time in the history of palace politics from 1885 to 1945. That Restoration leaders were the second component is evidence that court leadership was under the control of the oligarchs, bringing tranquility at the side of the emperor throughout the Meiji period. From 1912 to 1926, however, tranquility at the side of the emperor was lost. The diversity of career backgrounds brought to high palace office during that period indicates no firm pattern of oligarchic control or of balanced institutional representation at court.

After 1926, however, a fairly definite pattern of bureaucratic representation at the emperor's side emerged. Four bureaucratic in-

TABLE 10. BUREAUCRATIZATION AT THE SIDE OF THE EMPEROR: CAREERS PRIOR TO COURT OFFICE AGAINST YEARS IN COURT OFFICE

	Household Minister	Grand Chamberlain	Chief Aide	Privy Seal	Total
Meiji Period (1885–1912):					
Restorationist	23	0	0	6	29
Army	0	0	16	0	16
Navy	0	0	0	0	0
Foreign Ministry	0	0	0	0	0
Home Ministry	3	0	0	0	3
Justice Ministry	0	0	0	0	0
Finance Ministry	0	0	0	0	0
Agriculture and Commerce Ministry	0	0	0	0	0
Court	1	27	0	20	48
Taishō Period (1912—1926):					
Restorationist	0	0	0	8	8
Army	1	5	14	2	22
Navy	0	0	0	0	0
Foreign Ministry	4	0	0	2	6
Home Ministry	3	0	0	3	6
Justice Ministry	6	0	0	0	6
Finance Ministry	0	0	0	0	0
Agriculture and Commerce Ministry	0	0	0	0	0
Court	0	9	0	0	9
Shōwa Period (1926—1945):					
Restorationist	0	0	0	0	0
Army	0	0	19	0	19
Navy	0	17	0	0	17
Foreign Ministry	9	2	0	9	20
Home Ministry	9	0	0	4	13
Justice Ministry	0	0	0	0	0
Finance Ministry	1	0	0	0	1
Agriculture and Commerce Ministry	0	0	0	6	6
Court	0	0	0	0	0

NOTE: Because only those who served in office six months or more are listed, 5 of the 37 persons who held one or more of the four top palace offices are excluded from the tabulation: Privy Seal-Grand Chamberlain Katsura Tarō (Army), Privy Seal Hamao Arata (Education Ministry), Privy Seal Saitō Makoto (Navy), Privy Seal Ichiki Kitokurō (Home Ministry), and Chief Aide Hata Shunroku (Army).

stitutions of imperial prerogative were represented, and in fairly close balance: the Army, Navy, Home Ministry, and Foreign Ministry. These four, plus the Finance Ministry, were the major components of the prewar policy-making process. Why the Finance Ministry had only one of its representatives at the emperor's side, and for only one year in the entire period 1885 to 1945, is a matter for speculation. As noted in chapter 3, the court was financially autonomous and had no relation to the Ministry of Finance. More importantly, perhaps, the major issues facing Japan in terms of national defense, domestic controls, and foreign policy were managed primarily by the Army, Navy, Home Ministry, and Foreign Ministry. The Army and Navy exercised the emperor's prerogatives of supreme command and military administration. By the 1930s they received the lion's share of the national budget in order to carry out a rather extensive conception of "national defense." The Home Ministry controlled local government, shrines and temples, and the regular police force. With the Ministry of Education, the Home Ministry was involved in maintaining orthodox thought in Japanese society—but the Home Ministry had the instruments of force to maintain that orthodoxy. The Foreign Ministry exercised the emperor's prerogatives in diplomacy and was the primary source of information about the "trends of the times" internationally. These four bureaucratic structures dealt with the main substantive issues of domestic and foreign policy and were therefore of key importance to the palace in its negotiation and ratification roles.

During the 1930s the inner Cabinet was composed of the Prime Minister, Army Minister, Navy Minister, Foreign Minister, Home Minister, and Finance Minister, on whom all had budgetary demands. The inner Cabinet was most important in making and maintaining national policies until the Liaison Conference system was adopted in 1937.[150] When Prime Minister Saitō Makoto resigned in July 1934, for example, he attempted to ensure the continuity of his policies in the succeeding Cabinet by having his Army,

---

150. Liaison Conferences combined part of the inner Cabinet with the leaders of the General Staffs in an effort to produce unity between High Command and Cabinet policies. For a description of the Liaison Conference, see Ike Nobutaka, *Japan's Decision for War: Records of the 1941 Policy Conferences* (Stanford: Stanford University Press, 1967), pp. xv–xvi.

Navy, and Foreign Ministers carried over and his Minister of Agriculture and Forestry made Home Minister.[151] It appears to be no accident, therefore, that the main components of bureaucratic politics in government were represented at court on an almost one to one basis. And this balance of key institutional forces at the emperor's side remained intact from the late 1920s until the end of 1945.

Despite the institutionalization of imperial prerogatives and political elites outside the palace gates and the accompanying institutional balances at the emperor's side that had occurred by 1929, the palace remained the sole referent for all government decisions and the central institution through which the Imperial Will was declared in politics. Selection of the Prime Minister from 1885 to 1945, for example, was up to "the palace." This meant those who advised the throne at any given time: the oligarchs, Elder Statesmen, Senior Retainers, Privy Seal. These advisers reached their decisions on the basis of their personnel and policy preferences and the "trends of the times," as they evaluated them in consultation with other political leaders.

By the late 1920s Prince Saionji was the emperor's key adviser as to who was best able to form a Cabinet that could and would "control the situation" outside the palace gates. Prince Saionji's nomination was based on his policy preferences, whom he deemed most able to realize those preferences, and what was possible, both in terms of policies and personnel, given the state of institutional competition to declare the Imperial Will at any given moment. As we saw in the resignation of Tanaka Giichi in 1929 and the 1930 London Naval Treaty controversy, Saionji had strong preferences in domestic and international politics. He favored "party" Cabinets when possible—which meant appointing as Prime Minister the leader of a major political party in the House of Representatives, not Cabinets composed entirely of party men or Cabinets elected by the House of Representatives. More importantly, he was guided in his nomination by his strong views on foreign policy: the necessity of controlling the Japanese Army in China, and the desirability of maintaining Anglo-American amity. Tanaka Giichi, as a retired

151. *Okada Keisuke*, p. 231.

Army general respected by that institution of imperial prerogative and as president of the leading political party in the House of Representatives, appeared to be an ideal nomination as Prime Minister in 1927. Saionji evidently believed that Tanaka, having support in two major institutions of imperial prerogative, would be able to deal effectively with Army adventurism in Manchuria and northern China. The Chang Tso-lin affair proved that Tanaka was unable to do so, and Saionji and his allies in the government and in the palace forced Tanaka to resign.

Saionji nominated as Tanaka's successor Hamaguchi Osachi, president of the other leading political party in the House of Representatives. As we saw earlier, Hamaguchi proved willing and able to do Saionji's bidding during the London Naval Treaty controversy of 1930. Although Saionji was successful in obtaining his treaty, however, he lost his Prime Minister: within a month after imperial sanction of the treaty, Hamaguchi was critically wounded by an assassin. After a brief caretaker government in 1931 under Wakatsuki Reijirō, Saionji nominated Inukai Tsuyoshi to form a Cabinet. An aged party politician who had served in the House of Representatives continuously since 1890, Inukai had succeeded Tanaka Giichi as president of the Seiyūkai in 1929. But within six months of taking office, Inukai was assassinated.

Unable to persist in his party Cabinet policy, Saionji turned to the Navy. Between the assassination of Inukai in 1932 and the coup attempt of February 26, 1936, Saionji selected two senior naval officers as Prime Ministers: Admiral Saitō Makoto and Admiral Okada Keisuke. As already discussed, both were open supporters of Saionji's position on the London Naval Treaty and involved in controlling antitreaty forces within the Navy. As moderates, however, both were out of line with the trends of the times as far as militarists and right-wing leaders were concerned. Okada narrowly escaped assassination on February 26, 1936; Saitō, who had become Privy Seal in late 1935, did not.

With this attack on moderate government leaders and the emperor's palace officials, Saionji's partisan activities became all but futile. In early 1937, for example, he recommended as Prime Minister a retired general of the Army, Ugaki Kazunari, since he was aware of the "unlikelihood of the Army being satisfied with anything less than a cabinet headed by a general."[152] Ugaki had cooperated in reducing the size of the standing army during the 1920s. The Army therefore deemed him inappropriate and prevented him from forming a Cabinet by the simple device of refusing to nominate an Army Minister.[153]

Through his power to advise the throne on the appointment of the Prime Minister and on basic political issues, Saionji had managed to brake the forces of extremism from 1921 to 1936, but with decreasing effectiveness after 1930. He had also managed to keep constitutional monarchists dominant among the emperor's advisers during that period. The only leading palace office that eluded Saionji, as we have seen, was the office of Chief Aide-de-Camp. Ironically, it was during the domination of the constitutional monarchists at court that Japanese fascism became the dominant force in government. Professor Maruyama Masao divides the evolution of Japanese fascism into three periods: preparation (1919–31), maturation (1931–36), and consummation (1936–45). The union of militarist and renovationist political leaders with rightist societies, which occurred during the preparation period, produced the rash of assassinations, attempted coups, terrorist activities, and public agitation during the maturation period that ultimately vaulted the military into the center of political power.[154] While the palace became the main institution of political moderation, therefore, Japanese society and the government proper moved in the opposite direction—toward militarism, virulent ethnocentrism, and bureaucratic fascism.

Under such pressures from the "outside," an "Imperial Household Ministry in line with the times", which Prince Saionji so strongly insisted upon, could no longer be one led by himself and his "pro-Anglo-American," "liberal," "pro-party" partisans. To be "in line with the times" after 1930 meant following the lead of the renovationists and militarists in the institutions of imperial prerogative.

152. Robert J. C. Butow, *Tojo and the Coming of the War* (Princeton: Princeton University Press, 1961), p. 88.
153. Ibid., pp. 88–90.
154. Maruyama Masao, *Thought and Behaviour*, pp. 26–34.

The constitutional monarchists in court finally gave way to the traditionalists, just as the moderates in government were forced into the background by the renovationists and militarists. The traditionalists were concerned above all with the preservation of imperial transcendence, so seriously threatened by the terrorist activities of 1930–36. This meant having the Emperor-in-State ratify as accurate a consensus of national opinion as possible, regardless of where that consensus led the nation. It also meant that the emperor would not be permitted to persist in open support of constitutional monarchist policies, at least to the extent that his palace advisers would once again be threatened by assassins.[155] As managers of the Emperor-in-Court and coordinators of the public Emperor-in-State, therefore, the traditionalists in the palace presided over the consummation of Japanese fascism by moving away from the constitutional monarchist position toward a "neutral" evaluation of the "trends of the times" as the basis for advising the throne.

One of the most prominent handmaidens of bureaucratic fascism in government was Prince Konoe Fumimaro. Viewed as "a renovationist [*kakushin-teki*] politician bringing harmony to the oppositions among the military factions, bureaucrats, and political parties after the Manchurian Incident [1931]," Konoe was a hereditary member of the House of Peers, becoming its Vice President in 1931 and its President in 1933.[156] He held no other posts in government prior to becoming Prime Minister in 1937. During his three Cabinets between 1937 and 1941, Konoe presided over events and decisions of such magnitude as the commencement of the war in China (1937), the National General Mobilization Bill (1938), the Axis alliance (1940), and the inauguration of the Imperial Rule

155. Assassination plots continued to be directed against certain palace leaders and advisers after 1936, but they were quickly discovered and suppressed. That they were quickly put down, in contrast to the 1930–36 period, suggests that assassination of the emperor's palace advisers was no longer needed in order for the militarists and renovationists in government to have their way (see Butow, *Tojo*, pp. 128–29).

156. *Dai Jimmei Jiten*, 2:587. It is claimed that from the time when he went to the 1919 Paris Peace Conference, Konoe was held in great "affection" by Prince Saionji (ibid). During the 1930 London Naval Treaty controversy, Konoe was able to do Saionji's bidding by stifling antitreaty movements in the House of Peers (Harada Kumao, 1:21–22). But Konoe's chief political role was not so much that of policy advocate, either pro-Saionji or promilitarist, as it was that of political matchmaker or negotiator. Apparently he moved with the "trends of the times" rather than attempting to control those trends.

Assistance Association (1940), of which he became president.[157] In October 1941 General Tōjō Hideki replaced Konoe as Prime Minister. Tōjō was prepared to lead the nation in the event of war with the United States. Despite his role in preparing the road for such a war, Konoe, apparently, was not.[158]

The leading traditionalist at court was Marquis Kido Kōichi, one of Konoe's closest associates. With Kido's appointment as Privy Seal in June 1940 the traditionalists replaced the constitutional monarchists as the emperor's chief palace advisers. Since some constitutional monarchists, most notably Household Minister Matsudaira Tsuneo, remained at the emperor's side, Kido's appointment was neither a sudden transition nor a decisive break with the past. Nor, as we shall see in the next chapter, was Kido an advocate of renovationist or militarist policies. Rather, as chief manager of the Emperor-in-State from 1940 to 1945, Kido restored the emperor's "traditional" role as ratifier of personnel and policies "in line with the times." Kido was able to perform this role because, as the emperor's chief adviser after Prince Saionji's death in 1940, he took the consensus that led to his recommending candidates for Prime Minister to the emperor; he also took the consensus regarding national and international trends at any given moment, on the basis of which he rendered advice to the throne on political policies.

Despite the vast social, economic, and political changes that occurred during the course of Japanese modernization, the palace remained the key mechanism through which the Imperial Will was declared in politics from 1885 through 1945. It was able to remain so because Saionji's caveat that the Imperial Household Minister must come from "the outside" to keep the ministry "in line with the times" was applied with equal rigor to all four palace leaders. The high bureaucratic achievement of those serving in the four key palace offices, the reflection in their career backgrounds of the changing political forces outside the palace gates, and the flexibility inherent in those four offices attest to the critical role played by palace

157. Konoe's three cabinets were June 1937–January 1939, July 1940–July 1941, and July–October 1941. For discussions of Konoe's role in the 1930s and early 1940s, see Borton, pp. 347–69, and Butow, *Tojo*, pp. 77–315.
158. Butow, *Tojo*, p.314.

leadership in managing the Emperor-in-State so that the Imperial Will would be responsive to the "trends of the times"—not only during the "enlightened" modernization of the Meiji period but also during the periods of institutional pluralism and of bureaucratic fascism that followed. The key palace officer in maintaining the centrality of the palace in politics during the period of bureaucratic fascism was Japan's last Privy Seal, Marquis Kido Kōichi.

CHAPTER FIVE

KIDO KŌICHI AND THE MATRIX OF PALACE POLITICS

OUR DISCUSSION THUS FAR has dealt with the theory of legitimacy on which the prewar Japanese state rested, the court structure for managing palace autonomy, and the nature of palace leadership from 1885 to 1945. The purpose of this chapter is to examine the network of association and communication that linked court and government during the 1930s and early 1940s. It was during this period that Cabinets led by moderate bureaucrats and party leaders gave way to Cabinets led by renovationists in the civil and military bureaucracies and in the Imperial Diet, especially the House of Peers. And it was during this period that court leadership passed from the hands of the constitutional monarchists into the hands of the traditionalists.

The subject of our analysis is Kido Kōichi. Kido is especially suitable for study because he has left an extensive diary of his political associations and activities during the two periods he was in the palace: 1930 to 1937 and 1940 to 1945.[1] More an appointment book than a political commentary or record of substantive decisions, Kido's diary allows a comprehensive statistical reconstruction of the

---

1. Kido Kōichi, *Kido Kōichi Nikki*, 2 vols. (Tokyo: Tōkyō Daigaku Shuppan Kai, 1966). This record of 1,257 pages is supplemented by a volume of related documents and Kido's postwar comments on the diary: Kido Nikki Kenyū Kai, *Kido Kōichi Kankei Monjo* (Tokyo: Tōkyō Daigaku Shuppan Kai, 1966).

patterns of association that linked court and government in the case
of one of the court's most important political personages.

Kido's associations and behavior will be examined in 1932, 1936,
and 1941. These three years have been chosen for two reasons. First,
all three were years of crisis as bureaucratic fascism matured and
consolidated in government. On May 15, 1932 the last prewar party
Prime Minister was assassinated. The Shanghai crisis and the
formation of the puppet state of Manchukuo contributed to making
1932 an important year in Japanese foreign policy. In 1936 the most
extensive coup attempt since Saigō Takamori's 1877 revolt was
mounted against "evil advisers" close to the throne. As in 1932, a
new Cabinet came into being as the result of violence. Also in 1936
the Anti-Comintern Pact was concluded with Nazi Germany. In
1941 two Cabinets were formed and war was declared against the
United States. In all three years the palace was deeply involved in
Cabinet formations and foreign policy decisions.

Second, Kido held different palace posts in each of these three
years. His associations and behavior in each office reveal three different roles he played in the operation of palace politics: the
"secretary," the "bureaucrat," and the "negotiator." As Chief
Secretary to the Privy Seal in 1932, Kido acted as a political liaison
and information broker. His chief associate was another "secretary,"
Baron Harada Kumao. Harada was Prince Saionji's "public"
secretary and was also a member of Kido's ingroup—a small knot of
aristocrats who collectively facilitated Kido's information-gathering
role. Both his role as liaison and his efforts to gather information as
a "secretary" were primarily for the benefit of his superior, Privy
Seal Makino Nobuaki. As Privy Seal, Makino was one of the key
"negotiators" in the prewar political process: he was one of those
experienced statesmen responsible for making recommendations to
the throne on political appointments and basic national policies.

As Director of Peerage Affairs in 1936, Kido was a "bureaucrat"—a public official responsible for the day-to-day
management of a specific official jurisdiction. Although Kido was
concurrently Chief Secretary to the Privy Seal until June 13, 1936,

his associations and behavior throughout that year illustrate with sufficient clarity the role of the bureaucrat in palace politics. A bureaucrat might use his office to build a political faction and advocate policies, since policy initiatives emerged from within the bureaucracy. Most prewar bureaucrats, however, were circumspect administrators content to play a neutral role in politics. This was apparently the case with Kido. His chief associates in 1936 were fellow bureaucrats in the palace who had official duties that involved Kido's official duties. His diary gives no evidence that he used his office to build a political constituency at court to press his palace colleagues on policy matters, or that he used his office to consolidate a policy-advocating coalition of government and court leaders.

In 1941 Kido was a "negotiator." As Lord Keeper of the Privy Seal he was responsible to the emperor for negotiating Cabinet formations as well as advising on policies emanating from the institutions of imperial prerogative. Like Sanjō Sanetomi, Japan's first Privy Seal, Kido was the key negotiator in presenting unified government policy to the emperor for ratification. In that capacity, Kido's primary associates were the emperor, the Ministers of State, and the other three leading palace officers.

Kido's behavior changed markedly in terms of his patterns of association in each of the three years, showing a remarkable sensitivity to the political roles he was called upon to play. An examination of his associates reveals not only that others performed similar roles in both court and government but that there were other roles essential to the successful operation of Japan's privatized political system: the "ratifier," the "policy advocate," and the "instrument of pressure." The behavior of Kido and his associates was understandable, if not predictable or productive of "good" policies, given the institutional role of the palace as the center of the ratification process in prewar Japanese politics. Our discussion will conclude with a critique of Maruyama Masao's typology of political personality in prewar Japan in order to demonstrate the primacy of the bureaucracy in the political process and the effectiveness in that process of the political roles revealed by Kido and his associates.

KIDO'S APPOINTMENT AS CHIEF SECRETARY
TO THE PRIVY SEAL

Kido Kōichi was appointed Lord Keeper of the Privy Seal on June 1, 1940. Not only was he the last Privy Seal (the office was abolished on November 24, 1945); he was also the only Privy Seal to have served previously as Chief Secretary to the Privy Seal. Kido became Chief Secretary on October 28, 1930, after some fifteen years in the Ministry of Agriculture and Commerce and the Ministry of Commerce and Industry. Like other prominent leaders in the palace bureaucracy, he was brought in from "the outside." For the Chief Secretary previous governmental experience and wide associations were apparently desirable, just as they were for the Privy Seal himself.

The manner in which Kido was brought into the palace illustrates the high degree of informality that prevailed in the top echelons of Japan's prewar polity. On Sunday, August 17, 1930, Kido found himself at the golf course with Prince Konoe Fumimaro and Nagaike Chōji, a director of the Bank of Japan. While resting during the match, Konoe mentioned casually that he would like Kido to become Chief Secretary.[2] Kido replied that he had no positive desire to be Chief Secretary but would not decline if the circumstances were favorable. He would leave everything to Konoe.[3] Kido had begun to wonder what Konoe had in mind when he did not hear from him for well over a month. Then, on the evening of September 29, Konoe called: Privy Seal Makino Nobuaki wished to see Kido at nine o'clock the following morning.[4] Accordingly, Kido visited Makino at the Privy Seal's official residence on September 30. Since Kido had tentatively agreed with Konoe to become Chief Secretary, he assented when Makino asked him. Following his interview with Privy Seal Makino, Kido went to meet Imperial Household Minister Ichiki Kitokurō. Ichiki expressed his hope that Kido would accept the post of Chief Secretary and also asked him to serve concurrently as Counselor

2. The incumbent Chief Secretary, Viscount Okabe Nagakage, had met Kido on July 23 and talked about accepting election to the House of Peers; he subsequently resigned as Chief Secretary (Kido Nikki Kenyū Kai, p. 98).
3. Kido Kōichi, 1:33; Kido Nikki Kenyū Kai, p. 98.
4. Kido Kōichi, 1:38.

(*Sanjikan*) to the Imperial Household Ministry. Kido replied that he had no objection.[5]

Commenting many years later on his appointment, the "turning point in my destiny," Kido said that at the time he was somewhat worried about working on a person-to-person basis with Makino, since Makino was over seventy years old.[6] When he met Makino for the first time on September 30, however, he was greatly impressed and instantly made up his mind to accept. There was no "old man's stubbornness" in Makino; on the contrary, he was a man of "liberal" views, and Kido thought he would be able to learn from him. Kido was not, however, as enthusiastic about Imperial Household Minister Ichiki, who seemed more withdrawn than Makino. Summing up his impressions of the two men who were to be his superiors, Kido observed: "The Imperial Household Minister was, from a look at him, a person of the wise bureaucrat type, but I felt that the Privy Seal had more charm as a person."[7] Neither in this later commentary nor in the diary at the time of his appointment are there any queries or statements about the nature of the office Kido was to assume. He was concerned solely with the personalities he would be working with, not the official duties of the Chief Secretary to the Privy Seal. His interviews with both Makino and Ichiki were not "job interviews" as commonly understood in the West. Obviously, no examination was required.

On October 27 Kido had lunch at the Tokyo Club with Konoe, as he had done frequently in the past, and learned that his transfer to the Imperial Household Ministry would be approved by the Cabinet meeting of October 28. Kido arranged his affairs at the Ministry of Commerce and Industry accordingly: was this to be the final day in a fifteen-year period of his life? Around noon on October 28 Kinoshita Michio of the Imperial Household Ministry telephoned. Kido's presence at the ministry was desired at 1:30 p.m. When Kido arrived at the ministry he received his appointment from the Imperial Household Minister: "Appointed Chief Secretary to the Lord Keeper of the Privy Seal and concurrently Counselor to the Imperial

---

5. Ibid.
6. Kido Nikki Kenyū Kai, p. 98.
7. Ibid., p. 99.

Household Ministry."[8] Accompanied by a ministry official, Kido then made his round of greetings to the Privy Seal's Office, the Board of Chamberlains, and the administrative bureaus and divisions of the ministry. That afternoon and during the next few days he paid his respects to Prince Chichibu, one of the emperor's three brothers, and to other royal houses. He then made his farewells to officials in the Ministry of Commerce and Industry.[9]

In addition to the informality with which Kido was initially proposed as Chief Secretary, several other aspects of his appointment are worthy of note. Kido had been recommended to the post by both Prince Konoe and Viscount Okabe.[10] Both were aristocrats and friends of long standing. Okabe was not only Kido's predecessor in office; he was also a graduate of the Peers School, as was Kido. Although five years Kido's senior at the Peers School, Okabe had worked with Kido since graduation to form the Cherry Blossom Fraternity (Sakura Yūkai), a golfing club.[11] Okabe was also a charter member of the Eleven Club (Jūichikai), formed the eleventh day of the eleventh month in the eleventh year of the reign of Emperor Taishō (1922). Composed of a number of aristocrats, it was intended to be something approaching a literary society. As the years passed, most of the club members became members of the House of Peers. Some became Vice Ministers of State; some, like Kido and Okabe, even became Ministers. Accordingly, the Eleven Club became a forum for the discussion of current political issues, meeting regularly at Kido's home.[12] Konoe Fumimaro was evidently a member of the club but attended only infrequently. Thus the springboard for Kido's appointment was an aristocratic ingroup closely involved in clubs, golfing, and the House of Peers.

Another aspect of Kido's appointment is the official ritual of approval by persons in official positions whom Kido did not know socially or officially. Kido looked over and was looked over by both the Privy Seal and the Imperial Household Minister. His appointment was passed upon by the Cabinet. Formal appointment

8. Kido Kōichi, 1:42.
9. Ibid., pp. 42–43.
10. Kido Nikki Kenkyū Kai, p. 96.
11. Ibid., p. 98.
12. Ibid., p. 97.

was made by the Imperial Household Minister. Thus, constituted officials disposed formally of an appointment proposed informally by a casual social grouping. Such recruitment procedures were apparently standard for the leading palace offices, with the possible exception of the Chief Aide-de-Camp. Also noteworthy is the fact that the Privy Seal's office was, at least in this instance, under the joint jurisdiction of the Privy Seal and the Imperial Household Minister. The Imperial Household Minister interviewed the candidate for Chief Secretary to the Privy Seal and made the formal appointment. Though the Privy Seal's Office was an adjunct palace office, its affairs were apparently as much under the Imperial Household Minister as under the direct supervision of the Privy Seal.

The procedures involved in Kido's appointment indicate that a person neither sought directly nor campaigned for a leading palace position. In Kido's case, everything was "left to Konoe," who initiated Kido's candidacy and arranged his official interviews. This pattern of non–office-seeking was standard for palace personnel. Initiative, advocation, and approval all lay beyond the candidate's direct control, although he could presumably veto his own nomination.

Finally, Kido's appointment illustrates an emphasis on personal as opposed to official concerns by the candidate. As already mentioned, Kido was far more concerned about his personal relations with his future official superiors than about the duties of his future office. Possibly Kido knew what the job entailed as the result of close association with his predecessor in office, Viscount Okabe. The fact remains, however, that Kido agreed informally to accept the office and "kept his promise" to Konoe after judging the Privy Seal's personality, not the duties of the office or his technical qualifications for it.[13]

THE SECRETARY

When Kido became Chief Secretary to the Privy Seal in 1930, he brought to that position a network of sociopolitical associations, such

13. Kido did, however, express some reservations about his previous status: he had not been an important official in the Ministry of Commerce and Industry (Kido Nikki Kenkyū Kai, pp. 98–99).

as the Eleven Club, that would prove useful in discharging his secretarial duties. It was these associations, plus new official connections, that made Kido one of the liaisons between court and government and one of the information sources for palace leaders.

Table 11 classifies Kido's associations throughout 1932 according

TABLE 11. KIDO KŌICHI'S ASSOCIATIONS IN 1932: FREQUENCY AND MODE OF COMMUNICATION

Mode of Communication[d]	Total[a] (1)		Ten or More[b] (2)		Nine or Less[c] (3)	
	No.	%	No.	%	No.	%
OFFICIAL						
Office	78	7.6	31	6.2	47	8.9
Official residence	27	2.6	15	3.0	12	2.3
Official conference	11	1.1	5	1.0	6	1.1
Imperial lecture	14	1.4	0	0	14	2.7
Kido's reports	8	0.8	7	1.4	1	0.2
Reports to Kido	16	1.6	11	2.2	5	0.9
Official subtotal	154	15.0%	69	13.8%	85	16.1%
INFORMAL						
Home	144	14.0	79	15.8	65	12.3
Informal meeting	75	7.3	40	8.0	35	6.6
Meals	314	30.6	185	37.0	129	24.5
Banquets	55	5.4	9	1.8	46	8.7
Eleven Club	71	6.9	51	10.2	20	3.8
Sixth Day Club	12	1.2	0	0	12	2.3
Mist Club	2	0.2	0	0	2	0.4
Tuesday Luncheon Club	4	0.4	1	0.2	3	0.6
Golf	140	13.6	46	9.2	94	17.8
Social and miscellaneous	56	5.5	20	4.0	36	6.8
Informal subtotal	873	85.0%	431	86.2%	442	83.9%
Total	1,027	100%	500	100%	527	100%

SOURCE: Kido Kōichi, 1: 126–210.

[a] Based on a total of 1,027 meetings with 297 persons Kido records having met in 1932. Average: 3.5 meetings per person.

[b] Based on 500 meetings (48.7% of the total) with the 18 persons Kido met 10 times or more. Average: 27.8 meetings per person.

ᶜ Based on 527 meetings (51.3% of the total) with the 279 persons Kido met 9 times or less. Average: 1.9 meetings per person.

ᵈ The categories devised under *Mode of Communication* are mutually exclusive. For example, meetings tabulated under *Official conference* are not listed under *Office*, even though such meetings took place in official places. *Official conference* designates meetings with two or more people at an office to discuss official matters. If such a meeting took place at X's office, X would be tabulated under *Office* and all others present would be tabulated under *Official conference*. The same applies to *Informal meeting* and *Home*. If Kido met Okabe and Konoe at Harada's home, for example, Okabe and Konoe would be tabulated under *Informal meeting* and Harada under *Home*. *Social and miscellaneous* refers to weddings, trips, funerals, parties, social calls. *Kido's reports* and *Reports to Kido* refer almost exclusively to telephone conversations. *Imperial lecture* refers to Kido's contact with persons giving formal presentations to the throne. Although the emperor was obviously present, I have not included him in the statistics as having met with Kido because the emperor and Kido merely listened to the presentation, apparently without exchanging words. *Golf* has been listed separately because of the importance of this pastime to Kido. An avid golfer, Kido often recorded his matches and scores more meticulously than the subject, much less the content, of his political meetings. *Banquets* refers to formal social and state dinners attended by Kido. They have been listed under the informal category because most were social affairs and Kido recorded nothing of official importance at any of these ceremonial functions. Obviously, the basic division of "official" and "informal" that I have employed is somewhat arbitrary. The subdivisions within the categories do reveal, however, the specific kinds of sociopolitical activities in which Kido was absorbed.

NOTE: There are several opportunities for error and distortion in compiling such statistics. First, there are several persons with the same surnames whom Kido records only by surname and with no other identification, such as title or official position. There are several Kodamas, for example, some of whom were Kido's relatives and some not. It was not always clear, even using the index of persons at the end of vol. 2, which one was being referred to. Second, Kido does not mention all the people he met. For example, he frequently mentions attending a "Tuesday Luncheon Club," but without naming those whom he met there. This applies to official meetings of Imperial Household Counselors as well.

Despite technical problems in using Kido's diary in this manner, the diary provides thorough data amenable to statistical reconstruction of Kido's network of association. Since it is more an appointment book than a record of policy making or ex post facto reflections on events, Kido's diary can be used to demonstrate the nature of palace office and the matrix of communication and association supporting palace politics without relying on the author's value judgments about events, policies, and decisions. Harada Kumao's dictated record and Honjō Shigeru's diary, covering all or part of the period recorded by Kido, are selective accounts in which the authors exercised their judgments and prejudices regarding issues and personnel; both are to some extent revised accounts, not on-the-spot records. Although both are extremely valuable, they do not lend themselves to the same kind of objective analysis possible with the Kido diary.

Kido's wife and daughters, doctors and dentists, and various tutors—calligraphers, etc.—who came to Kido's home for various lessons are excluded from the tabulations in table 11. Such associations were neither numerous nor relevant to Kido's role.

to frequency and mode of communication. Kido recorded having met a total of 297 persons (column 1). Of these 297, he met 18 ten times or more (column 2) and 279 nine times or less (column 3). Meetings in all three frequency groups are divided into two basic categories, "official" and "informal," each of which is subdivided according to where or how the meetings took place. Mode of communication is thus defined by place or circumstances of meeting. The purposes of classifying Kido's association in this fashion are to analyze his political role as a secretary in terms of frequency of association and mode of communication in 1932 and to make comparisons later on with his role as a bureaucrat in 1936 and as a negotiator in 1941.

The most conspicious aspect of Kido's associations in 1932, immediately apparent in table 11, is the great predominance of informal over official modes of communication, regardless of frequency of association: 85 percent of Kido's meetings were informal, only 15 percent official. Variation according to frequency (columns 2 and 3) was a mere 2.3 percent, although there was a tendency for frequency of association to be related positively to informal modes of communication. This is especially true for Kido's meetings at meals: 37.0 percent of Kido's meetings with those he met ten times or more occurred at meals, while only 24.5 percent with those he met nine times or less took place in that setting.

When Privy Seal Makino interviewed Kido in 1930 he told him that as Chief Secretary he would have a great deal of free time. Did this mean that Kido was able to transform this legally undefined and apparently undemanding office into a vehicle for socializing with his aristocratic cronies on government pay and "company time"? Or does the role of the secretary in Japanese politics reveal why informal should dominate official modes of communication? Why does Kido note that 1930 was a turning point in his career, that after 1930 he was swamped in political activity?

A second aspect of Kido's associations in 1932 is the presence of a key group of persons frequently met. Eighteen persons met Kido ten times or more during that year. Those eighteen met him an average of 27.8 times each, whereas those who met him nine times or less averaged a mere 1.9 meetings (table 11). Moreover, there was considerable variation between the two frequency groups in modes of communication. Kido's meetings at meals, homes, and the Eleven Club account for 63.0 percent (315 meetings) of all his associations with the eighteen persons in the ten or more group but only 40.6 percent (214 meetings) of his associations with those he met nine times or less. Conversely, those meetings involving almost purely social and recreational activities—golf, banquets, social and miscellaneous—account for 33.4 percent (176 meetings) of Kido's total meetings with those in the nine or less group but only 15.0 percent (75 meetings) of those in the ten or more group. It might be well, therefore, to begin our analysis of Kido's activities and role in 1932 by determining who the eighteen persons were, what their social and political positions were, and what their dominant modes of communication with Kido were (table 12). These eighteen may be grouped into distinct type clusters: titled aristocrats (eleven), political contacts in the institutions of imperial prerogative (four), members of Kido's family (two), and golfing cronies (one). The two members of Kido's family, his brother Wada Koroku and eldest son Takazumi, held no political positions and were outside the network of Kido's aristocratic associations. Their meetings with Kido involved social and family activities of no significance to Kido's political office or role. Katō Kyōhei was a prominent business leader whose meetings with Kido all involved golfing. Like Kido's brother and son, Katō had no demonstrable relation to Kido's political activities. The remaining fifteen persons, however, formed the core of Kido's secretarial network—one of the associational matrices that linked court and government, the emperor and his palace officials with the leaders of political power and status outside the palace gates.

As revealed in table 12, eleven titled aristocrats were the center of Kido's associations in 1932, accounting for 82 percent of Kido's five hundred meetings with the eighteen persons he met ten times or more. Who were these aristocrats and what roles did they play in the accomplishment of Kido's secretarial functions?

Ten of the eleven aristocrats were currently in the House of Peers, as was Kido himself. All ten, again like Kido, had inherited their titles; they were all members of the new hereditary aristocracy that had matured under the Meiji constitutional order. None had been

TABLE 12.   PERSONS IN CONTACT WITH KIDO KŌICHI TEN OR
MORE TIMES, 1932
(18 PERSONS)

Person	Position	Number of Meetings	Dominant Mode of Communication	
			Mode	Number
BARON Harada Kumao	Sec'y to Prince Saionji Kimmochi; Member, House of Peers	135	Meals	53 (39.3%)
VISCOUNT Okabe Nagakage	Member, House of Peers; Kido's predecessor as Chief Sec'y to Privy Seal	67	Meals	28 (41.8%)
PRINCE Konoe Fumimaro	Member, House of Peers	57	Meals	29 (50.9%)
COUNT Makino Nobuaki	Lord Keeper of the Privy Seal	41	Official residence	15 (36.6%)
COUNT Sakai Tadamasa	Member, House of Peers	24	Meals	15 (62.5%)
COUNT Kuroki Sanji	Member, House of Peers	24	Eleven Club or Golf	Each (Each 8 33.3%)
Wada Koroku	Kido's brother	18	Social	6 (33.3%)
Katō Kyōhei	Director, Mitsubishi Trading Co., Ltd., etc.	16	Golf	12 (75.0%)
BARON Takagi Yoshihiro	Member, House of Peers	15	Meals	13 (86.7%)
MARQUIS Inoue Saburō	Member, House of Peers	13	Meals	6 (46.2%)
Suzuki Teiichi	Lt. Col., Military Affairs Bureau	13	Meals	9 (69.2%)
VISCOUNT Oda Nobutsune	Member, House of Peers	13	Eleven Club	8 (61.5%)
Inukai Takeru	Member, House of Representatives; son of incumbent Prime Minister Inukai Tsuyoshi and a secretary to him	12	Informal meetings	4 (33.3%)
MARQUIS Sasaki Yukitada	Member, House of Peers	11	Eleven Club	8 (72.7%)

TABLE 12—*Continued*

Persons	Position	Number of Meetings	Dominant Mode of Communication	
			Mode	Number
Tani Masayuki	Chief, Asia Bureau of the Foreign Ministry	11	Meals	9 (81.8%)
Fujinuma Shōhei	Chief, Metropolitan Police	10	Meals	6 (60.0%)
VISCOUNT Uramatsu Tomoaki (Tomomitsu)	Member, House of Peers	10	Eleven Club	9 (90.0%)
Kido Takazumi	Kido's eldest son	10	Golf *or* Social	Each (Each 5 50.0%)
Total		500		

imperially appointed to the House and none had earned his title as the result of individual contributions to state and society. The springboard of Kido's political activity in 1932, therefore, was a group of hereditary aristocrats in the House of Peers.[14]

Eight of the ten Peers were also members of the Eleven Club, Kido's ingroup within the aristocracy. These eight accounted for 68.2 percent of all Kido's meetings with those he met ten times or more, thus forming the core of Kido's associates in 1932. Including Kido, there were fourteen members of the club in 1932.[15] Ranging in

14. Marquis Kido served in the House of Peers from 1917 to 1945 by right of hereditary title. The political importance of the House of Peers and its hereditary aristocrats in the maturation and consummation of Japan's bureaucratic fascism is suggested by Kido's political career and by that of one of his closest political associates, Prince Konoe Fumimaro. Having held no positions of leadership outside the House of Peers, Konoe was the first aristocrat of Court Noble origins to serve as Prime Minister since Prince Saionji in 1911–12. Konoe served as Prime Minister three times between 1937 and 1941. Marquis Kido was the first purely hereditary Peer to serve as Privy Seal since Prince-of-the-Blood Fushimi Sadanaru in 1913–14.

15. The fourteen members were: Marquis Kido Kōichi, Baron Harada Kumao, Viscount Okabe Nagakage, Prince Konoe Fumimaro, Count Sakai Tadamasa, Count Kuroki Sanji, Viscount Oda Nobutsune, Marquis Sasaki Yukitada, Viscount Uramatsu Tomoaki (Tomomitsu), Viscount Sōma Taketane, Marquis Matsudaira Yasumasa, Marquis Hirohata Tadataka, Count Arima Yoriyasu, and Count Yanagisawa Yasutsugu.

age from thirty-nine to forty-eight, all fourteen had inherited their titles. Most had graduated from Kyōto Imperial University; the remainder were graduates of Tōkyō Imperial University. These two universities were the elite institutions of higher education in prewar Japan. In short, the Eleven Club was a group of approximately the same age, social station, educational background, and base of political operations. It was the inner ring of Kido's concentric rings of aristocratic association that reached ultimately into the palace, to Kido's direct superior, Privy Seal Count Makino Nobuaki. Count Makino was the only aristocrat Kido met ten times or more who was not a member of the House of Peers at that time. And he was the only aristocrat in the ten-or-more frequency group who achieved his highest title as the result of merit.

But since only eight of the thirteen Eleven Club members met Kido ten times or more in 1932 and the frequency of Kido's association with these eight varied from 10 to 135 meetings, something other than mere ingroup fraternizing would appear to be involved. The central person in Kido's 1932 network of associations was Baron Harada Kumao, a member of the Eleven Club who was also Prince Saionji's political secretary.[16] Kido's meetings with Harada were twice as numerous as those with any other person Kido met during 1932 and comprised 13 percent of his total meetings in that year. Harada's association with Kido, as with the other members of the Eleven Club, was of long standing. For example, when Harada was appointed Secretary to the Prime Minister in June 1924 (a post he held for two years), Kido, Viscount Okabe, and Prince Konoe

---

16. Saionji's private or personal secretary was Nakagawa Kojūrō. Consequently, Harada had been referred to as Saionji's "public" secretary (Harada Kumao, 1 : ii). Born in 1885, Harada was of Kido's age group and, like Kido, a descendant of the merit aristocracy created during the Meiji period. A graduate of Kyōto Imperial University, as was Kido, Harada served with the Bank of Japan (1916–22) and traveled in Europe and America under the auspices of the Imperial Household Ministry (1922–24). In 1926 he became a member of the Sumitomo Company, one of the four great financial and industrial combines in prewar Japan. That same year he became Prince Saionji's public secretary. In 1931 he was elected by his fellow aristocrats to serve in the House of Peers. Like Kido, therefore, Harada is an example of the agglutination of status, political position, and business connection that characterized the prewar aristocracy. Harada died on February 26, 1946, ten years to the day, ironically, after the coup which did so much to destroy Saionji's influence in politics (Ibid., "Bekkan," p. 389; Shūgiin-Sangiin, *Gikai Seido Shichijū Nen Shi* [*Kizokuin-Sangiin Giin Meikan*], "Danshoku Giin" section, p. 78).

were all involved.[17] In addition to being aristocratic associates, however, Kido and Harada were more importantly connected by virtue of their secretarial roles. Because Saionji was the highest political adviser in the Japanese state from 1924 to 1940, Harada, as his political secretary, had almost carte blanche access to all civil and military leaders. His position was one of an unofficial post to a semiofficial person, the last Elder Statesman.[18] Kido's position as Chief Secretary to the Privy Seal was that of an official post to an official person. The two secretaries were the key liaisons in the official process that commenced when the "imperial question" (*gokamon*) was put. When a Cabinet resigned, the emperor would ask the Privy Seal about appointing a new Prime Minister. The Privy Seal would then reply that the Elder Statesman—Prince Saionji—should receive the "imperial question," meaning that the Privy Seal would ascertain Saionji's views as to a suitable successor. In this fashion, the process of consultation, negotiation, resolution, and reply to the throne would be set in motion. Kido and Harada, in their secretarial roles, were brought together as liaisons in this critical process of responding to the throne when a "political change" (*seihen*) occurred—that is, when a Cabinet resigned.

One simple indicator that Harada and Kido were brought together primarily by virtue of their political roles is the very frequency with which the two met: 135 times throughout 1932. That the frequency of association was not merely ingroup socializing is further substantiated by contrasting the number of meetings between the two before and after Kido became Chief Secretary. During the first six months of 1930 Kido and Harada met only four times—at the "usual" Monday lunches at the Tokyo Club with fellow aristocrats such as Konoe and Okabe.[19] After Kido was appointed Chief Secretary on October 28, 1930, he saw Harada 10 times in the

17. Harada Kumao, 1 : vi; "Bekkan," p. 390.
18. Harada was not officially appointed by the government or court to be Saionji's secretary. Although Saionji had been imperially designated as Elder Statesman, this involved no official ceremony of appointment or allocation of specific government facilities for his use. Almost all of Saionji's duties after 1930 were performed at his villa in Okitsu, where he maintained touch with the "trends of the times" through his political secretary, visitors, and occasional correspondence. Only infrequently did he go to Tokyo to consult with the emperor and top government leaders.
19. Kido Kōichi, 1 : 3–22.

remaining two months of 1930, or 7.5 times more frequently than in the first six months of 1930.[20] Despite possible errors of omission in Kido's diary, the frequency gap is sufficiently great to indicate that communication between the two was a function of their respective political roles and not of their long-standing social acquaintance.

In performing their duties, the two secretaries communicated with one another on an almost exclusively informal basis. Although Harada was the most frequent visitor to Kido's office (a meager nine times), at least 86 percent of their meetings were informal. They met fifty-three times at meals (39.3 percent), forty-seven times at each other's homes (34.8 percent), nine times at informal meetings (6.7 percent), and seven times at Eleven Club sessions (5.2 percent). If their first role was to act as liaison between the Elder Statesman and the Privy Seal, bearing messages back and forth during political crises, they were also sources of information and advice to their respective superiors. Both were in constant and regular communication during 1932 as they kept track of the "trends of the times" in the institutions of imperial prerogative. The information gathered by the two was placed at the disposal of their superiors, both of whom were key advisers to the emperor: the Elder Statesman in times of political crisis and the Privy Seal both in times of crisis and on a regular basis.

Harada was therefore the pivot of Kido's information-gathering efforts as well as his key liaison counterpart outside the palace gates. The way in which information was gathered explains in large measure why the mode of communication between the two secretaries was so overwhelmingly informal. Harada regularly held breakfast meetings at his home which brought together members of the aristocratic ingroup and leading government officials. He also arranged informal meals to which were invited members of the aristocratic ingroup and select public officials, depending on the information desired. In fact, one of the key roles played by most of Kido's aristocratic friends, including Harada, was to provide the setting for Kido's information-gathering efforts, most notably with the four persons in government whom Kido met ten times or more:

20. Ibid., pp. 43–54.

Suzuki Teiichi, Inukai Takeru, Tani Masayuki, and Fujinuma Shōhei. These four were bureau-chief level officers in four different institutions of imperial prerogative: the Army, the House of Representatives, the Foreign Ministry, and the Home Ministry respectively.

On January 25, for example, Kido had breakfast at Harada's home. Present were the Minister to China, Shigemitsu Mamoru; the Chief of the Asia Bureau in the Foreign Ministry, Tani Masayuki; the Director of the Naval Affairs Bureau in the Navy Ministry, Toyoda Teijirō; Ōya Atsushi of Sumitomo Chemical; Marquis Inoue Saburō; Viscount Okabe; and Baron Takagi Yoshihiro. They "exchanged views on the China problem."[21] There were thus five aristocrats, three of whom were Eleven Club members, and four "outside" persons present. Since the issue under discussion was China, the Minister to China and the Chief of the Asia Bureau were present. The gathering of information took place in the informal setting of aristocratic association. Again, on March 29, Kido had breakfast at Harada's. Lieutenant Colonel Suzuki Teiichi of the Military Affairs Bureau and two others from the "outside" were brought in to have breakfast with Prince Konoe, Baron Kuroda Nagatoshi, and Baron Iwakura Michitomo. They discussed "problems of the times."[22]

Others of Kido's aristocratic colleagues also held such meetings at their homes. Marquis Inoue Saburō[23] gave a dinner at his home for Lieutenant Colonel Suzuki (again) and Colonel Obata Toshirō, along with Kido and Okabe, on February 19. Colonel Obata gave his views on trends within the military since the October Incident

21. Ibid., p. 131.
22. Ibid., p. 152.
23. Marquis Inoue Saburō (1887–1959) served in the House of Peers from 1929 to 1946. Although a member of Prince Konoe's Tuesday Society (*Kayōkai*) in the House of Peers, Inoue was not a member of Kido's Eleven Club. Unlike Konoe, Kido, and the other members of the Eleven Club, Inoue was a graduate of the Army Academy and a career Army officer.

Inoue founded a "breakfast club" in the early 1930s which "brought together the leading members of the bureaucracy and the army, and . . . paved the way for close collaboration between them. It was in this organization that the members of the Nagata faction of the army, the newly risen bureaucrats, and the House of Peers politicians established intimate contacts and started planning together to put their ideas into effect" (Yanaga, p. 520). Like Prince Konoe, Marquis Inoue apparently acted as an aristocratic political broker to the renovationist and militarist bureaucrats in their drive for political domination.

(1931), and this was followed by an "open exchange of views."
From this discussion Kido ascertained in great detail the three main
currents of thought in the military, the links between military cliques
and right-wing civilians, and the measures desired by military
leaders to placate extremists. They also discussed who would or
would not be supported by the Army as Prime Minister in the event
of a Cabinet resignation.[24] This meeting was followed up by a lunch
on March 1 at Prince Konoe's home, attended by Marquis Inoue,
Lieutenant Colonel Suzuki, and Kido. Suzuki commented critically
on Colonel Obata's previous remarks and described the situation in
the military since they last met at Marquis Inoue's.[25] In these two
instances, the "state of affairs" within the military was discussed.
Kido's contact with the "outside" military world was primarily
Lieutenant Colonel Suzuki, the only military official outside his
aristocratic set whom Kido met ten or more times in 1932.

The Eleven Club was the central group around which Kido
constructed an information-gathering and -sharing network that
embraced leading figures from the outside worlds of government, the
military, finance, and business. Of the eighteen persons Kido met ten
or more times, five were from these outside worlds. Katō Kyōhei, director of the Mitsubishi Trading Company and other Mitsubishi
concerns, was one of Kido's golf cronies and, as already noted, was
not a key outside contact. As we have just seen, however, Lieutenant
Colonel Suzuki was Kido's primary contact with the military world.
Inukai Takeru, secretary to his father the Prime Minister until mid-
May and a member of the House of Representatives, was Kido's main
contact with the Prime Minister's office and the political parties.
Tani Masayuki, Chief of the Asia Bureau, was Kido's leading
contact with the diplomatic world. The fifth outside person was
Fujinuma Shōhei, Chief of the Tokyo Metropolitan Police; it was
through him that Kido kept informed about right-wing activities and
other matters under the jurisdiction of the Home Ministry that affected palace security. Kido met these last four persons a total of
forty-six times, 10.1 percent of the meetings he had with the
politically relevant persons he met ten times or more in 1932. Only

24. Kido Kōichi, 1:140–41.
25. Ibid., p. 144.

three of the forty-six meetings, however, took place at offices; most were at meals. The style of association common to Kido's aristocratic ingroup was therefore extended to embrace public officials outside the palace bureaucracy, the institution of imperial prerogative to which Kido belonged. These contacts were acquired "in the line of duty"—as part of Kido's job as Chief Secretary to the Privy Seal. Informal association was an efficient and effective means for Secretary Kido to acquire information from the outside world.

Suzuki, Inukai, Tani, and Fujinuma were the outside contacts most often consulted by Kido in his secretarial role between court and government, but they were by no means the only ones. Kido's informal techniques of information gathering embraced many persons at the minister and bureau-chief levels of the government and military bureaucracies, director-level leaders in industry and finance, scholars, elected Representatives, reporters, and members of various social and political societies. He also met members of the imperial family, including the emperor. There can be no question that Kido had a wealth of varying information at his disposal, that this information was quite accurate, and that it covered every important sector of the Japanese polity. The leaders and representatives from all walks of Japanese life who clustered around Kido and his aristocratic group were absorbed into an intricate web that could be and was used to fulfill meaningful and purposeful political functions.

Kido's group of aristocrats also kept each other constantly informed of one another's activities. Each member of the group had access to persons and sources of information that overlapped and others that were exclusive. Konoe, for example, apparently had more contacts in the military than did Kido or Harada. Harada definitely had more contact with top civilian leaders than did Kido. From such differentiated sources they were able to pool and share information. This is especially true of Harada, who kept Kido continuously informed of his meetings with Prince Saionji and with Ministers of State. Depending on the problem under consideration and the personal relationships involved, these outside contacts could be brought together at homes, restaurants, and clubs.

Although Kido's chief aristocratic associates were members of the Eleven Club, the Eleven Club was but one of many organizations allowing Kido to gather and share information and to discuss public policies. For example, the Sixth Day Club (*Muikakai*), a more extensive organization than the Eleven Club, evidently centered on a group of business and finance leaders. On its executive committee were Baron Itō Bunkichi and Miyagawa Hyakutarō, both prominent businessmen.[26] Members of the Sixth Day Club gathered together with government and military persons to discuss political matters affecting the economy. General Mutō Nobuyoshi and Prince Konoe were both members.[27] In its membership, therefore, it was an overlapping group, including both aristocratic ingroup and public officials. Other clubs, such as the Cherry Blossom Fraternity, were devoted exclusively to social activities.

These are but three of the more frequently mentioned clubs of which Kido was a member. His clubs ranged from informal eating clubs to formal current events associations, from the strictly social to the political. These clubs had varying memberships but always included one or more from Kido's aristocratic ingroup. The combination of differentiated and overlapping memberships in the aggregate encompassed representatives of every major opinion- and decision-making institution in Japanese society. Kido's clubs and organizations were valuable forums for regularized information gathering and sharing, supplementing ad hoc contacts with his aristocratic ingroup and public officials.

How did this lateral liaison and information-gathering process reach vertically into the top palace echelons? As pointed out earlier, Kido's position as Chief Secretary involved him in the Privy Seal–Kido–Harada–Prince Saionji relay, a relay that sometimes saw direct communication between Privy Seal Makino and Prince Saionji, bypassing both secretaries, or that involved but one of the secretaries, Kido or Harada. Significantly, only one of the eighteen persons Kido met ten times or more in 1932 was a palace official: Kido's direct superior, Privy Seal Makino Nobuaki. Makino's mode of communication with Kido was almost exclusively "official," in marked contrast to Kido's mode of communication with the others in the ten or more frequency group. Of the forty-one times Kido met

26. Ibid., pp. 138, 146–47.
27. Ibid., pp. 179, 205.

with Makino, one was at an official banquet in the presence of the emperor and one was on a tour. Even these two meetings may be classified as "official," The remaining thirty-nine meetings between them took place at Makino's official residence, the Privy Seal's office, official conferences, or they involved reports. As with Kido's other associations, the communication between the two was almost exclusively verbal. Kido records hardly any documentary transactions between them. Vertical and lateral communication was therefore similar; both relied on direct verbal contact.

The communication between Kido and Makino is well illustrated during the Shanghai crisis of early 1932. Hostilities begun in Manchuria during 1931 eventually spread to the Shanghai area in January 1932.[28] The issue facing the government was whether, in view of the tense international situation there, to send reinforcements to Shanghai. The issue facing the Privy Seal and palace leadership was whether to involve the emperor or to activate extraordinary councils, such as a conference of the Elder Statesman and Senior Retainers, in order to bring the military under control.

On February 4 Kido went to his office at 10:30 a.m., his usual time for appearing at the palace. At noon he had lunch with Harada and Konoe at the Tokyo Club and they discussed the Shanghai incident. Harada told them that he had met with Finance Minister Takahashi Korekiyo. According to Harada, the Finance Minister was gravely concerned that positive military action in Shanghai would jeopardize international confidence in Japan and suggested that the emperor "speak to the military"—that is, caution the military to desist. Harada then related that he had asked Prince Saionji's views on this: Saionji had told Harada to consult the Privy Seal and dispose of the matter accordingly. Kido and Harada then returned to the palace and met with Privy Seal Makino.[29] The Privy Seal said that this sort of thing had come up in the past: whether it should be taken to the emperor was up to the Prime Minister. Shortly after 4 p.m. Kido returned home.[30]

On February 5 the Privy Seal audienced with the emperor from

28. Sadako N. Ogata, pp. 142–45.
29. Konoe probably accompanied them.
30. Kido Kōichi, 1 : 135.

9:30 to 9:45 a.m. Following this the Chief of the Navy General Staff, Prince-of-the-Blood Fushimi, and Deputy Chief of the Army General Staff, General Mazaki, audienced with the emperor.[31] Makino then sent Kido to ask Harada if Harada had ascertained the Prime Minister's views on the emperor's "speaking to the military." Kido went to see Harada at 11 a.m. According to Harada, the Prime Minister was concerned about the international repercussions that positive military measures in Shanghai would have. The Prime Minister's plan was first to caution the Army Deputy Chief of Staff and in particular the Ministers of the Army and the Navy. The Prime Minister, Harada continued, would then speak with both Chiefs of Staff and, following that, report to the emperor on the measures taken. In a note to this conversation with Harada, Kido remarked that Finance Minister Takahashi was strongly opposed to sending reinforcements to Shanghai. Repercussions in New York financial circles were serious and it was almost impossible to obtain foreign credit.[32]

From February 5 to February 21 Kido was involved in frantic rounds of informal discussions with leading members of the government and the military, leaders in finance and industry, and scholars, as well as in club meetings and meals with his aristocratic ingroup. He was in constant contact with the Privy Seal not only as his official liaison but also as informant and confidant. On February 17, for example, Kido had a long conversation with Privy Seal Makino during which *Makino* informed Kido of the contents of the Foreign Minister's and the Deputy Army Chief's reports to the throne. Makino also told Kido that the emperor was very concerned about the attitude of the League of Nations.[33] Makino, therefore, kept Kido informed of what transpired in the emperor's audience chamber while Kido kept Makino informed of what Kido had heard on the outside. Information sharing as well as information gathering and reporting was thus part of Kido's relationship with his superior.

Kido and Makino also discussed what measures should be taken to

31. Kido merely notes these audiences by military leaders. Evidently these were reports to the emperor requiring no comments on the emperor's part. Passive acceptance of reports from the military chiefs was apparently a routine matter at the palace.
32. Kido Kōichi, 1 : 135–36.
33. Ibid., p. 139.

bring the Shanghai Incident under control. In the same conversation on the seventeenth, Makino told Kido that there were opinions to the effect that a conference of the Elder Statesman and Senior Retainers would be necessary should the incident become a major crisis. There were also views to the contrary, said Makino: given the nature of the times such a conference would be anachronistic and not in accord with popular sentiment. Makino then asked Kido his opinion on holding such a conference. Kido believed that just to call a group of elderly men together without any concrete idea in mind—to hold a mere "festivity"—would give rise to popular ill will. He did believe, however, that such a conference would be meaningful if it were called to discuss plans for national unity *after* the Cabinet had, on its own responsibility, decided on a policy that would truly "revolutionize the times." Kido doubted that the Cabinet had reached this stage and thus questioned the wisdom of holding a conference of the Elder Statesman and Senior Retainers.[34] The relationship between the Chief Secretary and his Privy Seal went beyond one of liaison and mutual reporting. It was also one of mutual consultation, at the initiative of the Privy Seal, on issues of great national import that might ultimately involve the emperor and palace actively in the process of decision making.

Hostilities in the Shanghai area ceased on March 3.[35] Until that time Kido and leading palace figures were constantly concerned with the course of events and with possible courses of action, including palace involvement. Ultimately, and fortunately, the Prime Minister was able to settle the issue without calling on the emperor. The degree of activity at the palace, however, indicated that active involvement was a distinct possibility if the Prime Minister were not able to bring hostilities to an end on the basis of his own political resources.

Just how close the palace came to involvement is indicated by the following events. On Sunday, February 21, Kido was at the golf course when a caddie ran up to him with a message from the Privy Seal: Makino wanted Kido back in Tokyo immediately. When Kido arrived at Makino's official residence at 4:30 p.m., Makino informed him that there was fear of war should reinforcements be sent to the

34. Ibid.
35. Sadako N. Ogata, p. 143.

Shanghai area. Since "advisory" procedures might be necessary, such as holding a conference of the Elder Statesman and Senior Retainers, Makino had decided to consult with Prince Saionji at the latter's villa in Okitsu. In preparation for his visit Makino had met with the emperor for instructions: the emperor had told him to obtain Saionji's views on troop reinforcements and other related issues.[36]

But, Makino continued, the Prime Minister had audienced with the emperor on the twentieth and assured him twice that reinforcements would not be sent to Shanghai for the time being. Makino therefore had decided to cancel his trip to see Saionji. Then, on the morning of the twenty-first, the Imperial Household Minister and the Grand Chamberlain visited Makino and told him that it might indeed be necessary to send reinforcements, depending on the course of the hostilities. Since the need would arise suddenly there would be no time to consult Saionji. Therefore, they argued, it would be desirable to know beforehand what Saionji's views were. As a result of his conversation with the Imperial Household Minister and the Grand Chamberlain, Makino had once again changed his mind and decided to see Saionji the following day, February 22. Kido therefore called Harada to make the necessary arrangements. Makino evidently visited Saionji on the twenty-second, but Kido makes no mention of what happened.[37]

Unfortunately, Kido does not note how the Shanghai crisis was ultimately resolved as far as the palace was concerned. He merely states that he met with the Privy Seal several times between February 22 and March 2, that he reported on the Shanghai Incident to Finance Minister Takahashi on February 27, and that the Prime Minister audienced with the emperor on March 2 about the resignation of the Governor General of Korea.[38] Since the Prime Minister proved capable of resolving the Shanghai crisis, however, no extraordinary involvement by the emperor and the palace occurred. But such involvement could have occurred at the Prime

36. Kido Kōichi, 1:141.
37. Ibid., pp. 141–42.
38. Ibid., pp. 142–46.

Minister's initiative and with the acquiescence of leading palace officials, most notably the Privy Seal.

Palace leadership was highly flexible and responsive to political events largely because of its efficient and wide-ranging network of contacts with the outside political, financial, and military worlds. As one of the links in this communication system, Kido acquired, through his secretarial associations, information that was placed at the disposal of one of these key palace officials: the Privy Seal. However informal the matrix of communication appeared, it efficiently embraced every sector bearing on the determination of public policy and extended in Kido's case via the Privy Seal to the emperor himself. As the Shanghai crisis illustrates, it was because of this network that the key palace officials were able to determine whether or not the emperor and extraordinary political advisory bodies should be activated to cope with a political emergency.

Kido's associations with palace officials other than the Privy Seal were of a more limited nature. Of the fifty-three persons whom Kido met four times or more, for example, only six were palace officials. Kido met with the Privy Seal forty-one times, the Imperial Household Minister eight times, the Vice Minister eight times, the Grand Chamberlain five times, the Deputy Grand Chamberlain six times, and the Deputy Grand Master of the Ceremonies five times.[39] Since the Deputy Grand Chamberlain, Marquis Hirohata Tadataka, had been in office only from September and his contacts with Kido were exclusively at Eleven Club meetings, he may be discounted as a "palace official," at least in 1932. Hirohata's predecessor as Deputy Grand Chamberlain, Kawai Yahachi, met Kido only twice during 1932. Excluding the Deputy Grand Chamberlain, then, Kido met with only five palace officials four or more times each. The number of meetings with these five totaled sixty-seven, of which twenty-six took place at offices, nineteen at official residences, and six at official conferences. Seven were involved with reports. "Official" contacts with the five palace officials therefore totaled fifty-eight of the sixty-seven (86.6 percent). Kido's mode of communication with palace of-

---

39. Kido also mentions, without comment or naming those present, ten meetings with the Imperial Household Ministry Counselors throughout 1932.

ficials was the precise reverse of that with the four outside public officials whom he met ten times or more: 93.5 percent of his meetings with these outside officials were informal.

It is clear from Kido's pattern of association that aristocratic ingroup, government officials (the outside), and palace officials (the inside) were distinct groups performing distinct functions in the matrix of palace politics. Social relations among members of the aristocratic ingroup facilitated information gathering and sharing when one or more of the ingroup held public office—in government or court. When Kido became Chief Secretary to the Privy Seal, a social network that belonged to him by virtue of birth and schooling allowed him to perform an important liaison function. The aristocratic ingroup became a vehicle for political integration between court and government.

Kido's official role as Chief Secretary to the Privy Seal was that of liaison between the Privy Seal and the outside world. Although a large part of the information gathered by Kido from outside officials via the aristocratic ingroup may have short-circuited at the Privy Seal's office, the Privy Seal was able to pass on to other leading palace officials and the emperor such information as he saw fit. Kido's role as Chief Secretary was fulfilled by informal contact with government officials and official contact with palace officials. The former involved obtaining information, the latter involved reporting and using it.

Japan's prewar aristocracy has frequently been called the bulwark of the throne. As Kido's associations indicate, his ingroup of the aristocracy was deeply involved in the politics of palace participation in the affairs of state. The informal contact Kido, Konoe, Harada, Okabe, and other members of Kido's ingroup maintained with a great number of public officials and social leaders illustrates concretely how this "bulwark" function was fulfilled in the 1930s.

A quasi-public class, the aristocracy comprised over 950 families by 1930. As we saw in chapter 3, some aristocrats and scions of aristocrats found haven in court offices. But some of those offices, like Kido's, were politically significant and not mere refuges from political involvement. The degree of political interaction among aristocrats and between aristocrats and nontitled government and court officials depended, moreover, on the offices they held in court and government as well as on their political aspirations. To normal social interactions within the aristocracy were added political relations that varied in intensity (frequency) and that were official, informal, or various combinations of both depending on the political roles its members played at any given time. Although Harada, for example, was a member of Kido's aristocratic ingroup, his association with Kido, in both its frequency and its informal modes of communication, was a direct reflection of the role of secretary that both Harada and Kido played in 1932. The second person Kido met most frequently, Viscount Okabe Nagakage, was also a member of Kido's Eleven Club ingroup. A politically ambitious member of the House of Peers, Okabe eventually became Minister of Education under Tōjō in 1943. Okabe was also Kido's predecessor as Chief Secretary to the Privy Seal. Konoe, like Okabe, was also a member of Kido's ingroup, politically ambitious, and deeply involved in Kido's political career and activities. Konoe was the third most prominent person in Kido's 1932 pattern of association. In contrast with the informal modes of communication between Kido and these three ingroup aristocrats, Kido's association with Privy Seal Makino, the fourth person he met most frequently in 1932, was almost completely official. A much older man, and completely outside Kido's normal set of aristocratic associations, Count Makino might never have met Kido except under the most fortuitous and casual circumstances had not Kido been his Chief Secretary or held another post that figured in the Privy Seal's role as a negotiator. Both the frequency of association and the mode of communication between Marquis Kido and Count Makino were completely dependent on the offices the two held; neither was dependent on the fact that Kido and Makino were members of the aristocracy.

Since membership in the aristocracy was given, and public office as well as political aspirations were variable, it follows logically that Kido's association with members of even his own ingroup, while maintained at a basic level of social interaction, would vary according to the offices and ambitions they held. Frequency of association and mode of communication between Kido and public officials, whether aristocrats or not, would also vary according to offices held. In other words, Kido's associations with political persons—however closely tied together by "class," "group," "age," "education," or even "policy preferences"—were almost entirely situational. They depended on offices mutually held and the roles those offices demanded. This was certainly true of Kido's associations as a secretary in 1932. It was also true of Kido as a bureaucrat in 1936.

THE BUREAUCRAT

From August 1933 to October 1937 Kido was Director of Peerage Affairs in the Imperial Household Ministry, a position that made him one of the six palace officers of direct imperial appointee rank.[40] As discussed in chapters 3 and 4, the Imperial Household Ministry was the primary bureaucratic structure for managing the Emperor-in-Court. The ministry exercised the emperor's prerogatives over his own affairs and the affairs of court, including management of the aristocracy. During 1936 Kido remained a Counselor to the Household Ministry as well. He was also concurrently Chief Secretary to the Privy Seal until June 13, 1936. Despite his overlapping functions, his role as a bureaucrat in one of the institutions of imperial prerogative is clear from his pattern of association for the year as a whole.

In 1936 Kido recorded meetings with 391 persons, 94 more than in 1932 (an increase of 31.6 percent). He met those 391 persons a total of 1,444 times, 417 more meetings than he had had in 1932 (an increase of 40.6 percent). His concurrent offices and the diversity of functions entailed by those offices increased his associates and associations markedly.

As table 13 reveals, the increases in Kido's associations were incurred almost exclusively in the "official" category. In 1932 Kido's informal meetings outnumbered his official by 873 to 154 (85 percent to 15 percent). In 1936, however, informal dominated official by 877 to 567 (61 percent to 39 percent). While Kido's informal meetings

40. The other regular direct imperial appointees at this time were: Privy Seal, Household Minister, Grand Chamberlain, Chief Aide, and Grand Master of the Ceremonies (*Shokuin Roku*, 1931, pp. 1–4, 92–93). For a description of the Office of Peerage Affairs, see above, p. 71.

TABLE 13. KIDO KŌICHI'S ASSOCIATIONS IN 1936: FREQUENCY AND MODE OF COMMUNICATION

Mode of Communication	Total[a] (1)		Ten or More[b] (2)		Nine or Less[c] (3)	
	No.	%	No.	%	No.	%
OFFICIAL						
Office	365	25.3	156	20.4	209	30.8
Official residence	71	4.9	54	7.0	17	2.5
Official conference	69	4.8	38	5.0	31	4.6
Imperial lecture	2	0.1	0	0	2	0.3
Kido's reports	20	1.4	17	2.2	3	0.4
Reports to Kido	40	2.8	33	4.3	7	1.0
Official subtotal	567	39.3%	298	38.9%	269	39.7%
INFORMAL						
Home	147	10.2	57	7.4	90	13.3
Informal meeting	35	2.4	14	1.8	21	3.1
Meals	205	14.2	114	14.9	91	13.4
Banquets	60	4.2	24	3.1	36	5.3
Eleven Club	55	3.8	43	5.6	12	1.8
Golf	220	15.2	155	20.2	65	9.6
Social and miscellaneous	155	10.7	61	8.0	94	13.9
Informal subtotal	877	60.7%	468	61.1%	409	60.3%
Total	1,444	100%	766	100%	678	100%

SOURCE: Kido Kōichi, 1: 454–532.

[a] Based on a total of 1,444 meetings with 391 persons Kido records having met in 1936. Average: 3.7 meetings per person.

[b] Based on 766 meetings (53.0% of the total) with the 37 persons Kido met 10 times or more. Average: 20.7 meetings per person.

[c] Based on 678 meetings (47.0% of the total) with the 354 persons Kido met 9 times or less. Average: 1.9 meetings per person.

NOTE: The notes to table 11 apply equally to table 13.

remained constant in number between 1932 and 1936, his official meetings jumped from 154 to 567, an increase of 268.2 percent over 1932. That Kido's role as a bureaucrat in 1936 entailed a marked increase in official modes of communication is also clear from the replacement of "meals" as the single most important mode of communication in 1932 (30.6 percent) by "office" in 1936 (25.3 percent).

As a bureaucrat—an official responsible for managing a specific jurisdiction within a component of imperial prerogative—Kido would be expected to have more contact with colleagues in that jurisdiction. Moreover, such associations would normally be official, since the work of administration was office work and policy coordination involving fellow administrators—that is, bureaucrats. If the role of secretary involved liaison and information gathering in an informal setting, that of bureaucrat involved administration in an official setting. The fact that Kido's secretary and bureaucrat roles overlapped for half of 1936, and the fact that his specific duties as a bureaucrat involved the aristocracy and consequent socializing at various functions, help explain why informal modes of communication continued to be dominant in 1936.

An examination of the thirty-seven persons Kido met ten times or more in 1936 (table 14) substantiates these expectations. Since Kido met twice as many persons ten or more times in 1936 as compared to 1932, his overlapping functions produced a wider set of frequent associates and decreased the average number of times he met them from 27.8 times per person in 1932 to 20.7 in 1936. Kido's bureaucratic role in 1936 also produced a new group of associates frequently met. As table 14 reveals, ten of the thirty-seven persons Kido met ten times or more in 1936 had not met Kido even once in 1932; five of the thirty-seven met Kido only once in 1932. Kido met but ten of the thirty-seven ten times or more in both 1932 and 1936. Six of those ten persons were members of the Eleven Club, two were members of Kido's immediate family, one was an aristocratic intimate outside the Eleven Club, and the last was the retired Privy Seal, Count Makino Nobuaki. Kido met these ten persons 375 times in 1932, accounting for 75 percent of his meetings with persons he met ten times or more that year. In 1936 he met these ten 244 times,

TABLE 14. PERSONS IN CONTACT WITH KIDO KŌICHI TEN OR MORE TIMES, 1936

(37 PERSONS)

Persons	Position	Number of Meetings		Dominant Mode of Communication, 1936	
		1936	*1932*	*Mode*	*Number*
BARON Harada Kumao	Sec'y to Prince Saionji	73	135	Meals	26 (35.6%)
Yuasa Kurahei	Imperial House-	*15*	0		
Matsudaira Tsuneo	hold Minister[a]	54		Office	28 (51.9%)
		39	0		
VISCOUNT Saitō Makoto	Privy Seal[a]	*11*	1		
		46		Office	28 (60.9%)
Yuasa Kurahei		*35*	0		
MARQUIS Matsudaira Yasumasa	Member, House of Peers; Sec'y to the Privy Seal	43	6	Meals	23 (53.5%)
MARQUIS Inoue Saburō	Member, House of Peers	41	13	Golf	31 (75.6%)
COUNT Mizoguchi Naosuke	Member, House of Peers; retired Lt. Gen.; businessman	36	3	Golf	34 (94.4%)
PRINCE Konoe Fumimaro	Pres., House of Peers	34	57	Meals	11 (32.4%)
BARON Itō Bunkichi	Pres., Nippon Mining Co., etc.; Member, House of Peers	34	8	Golf	33 (97.1%)
MARQUIS Hirohata Tadataka	Deputy Grand Chamberlain; Member, House of Peers	31	6	Office	15 (48.4%)
BARON Shirane Matsusuke	Vice Minister, Household Ministry (May 1936)	28	1	Office	13 (46.4%)
VISCOUNT Okabe Nagakage	Member, House of Peers	26	67	Meals or Eleven Club	Each 8 (Each 30.8%)
Iwanami Takenobu	Section Chief, Bureau of Peerage Affairs, Household Ministry	24	1	Office	9 (37.5%)

TABLE 14.—*Continued*

Persons	Position	Number of Meetings		Dominant Mode of Communication, 1936	
		1936	*1932*	*Mode*	*Number*
PRINCE Kitashirakawa and Family	Imperial family	17	1	Social	9 (52.9%)
Wada Koroku	Kido's brother	17	18	Golf	11 (64.7%)
VISCOUNT Matsudaira Keimin	Grand Master of the Ceremonies, Household Ministry	16	5	Office	4 (25.0%)
EMPEROR Hirohito	Emperor	16	2	Official residence	10 (62.5%)
COUNT Kodama Hideo	Kido's brother-in-law; bureaucrat	15	4	Home	7 (46.7%)
PRINCE Takamatsu Nobuhito	Imperial family (emperor's brother)	14	2	Official residence	7 (50.0%)
Matsumoto Kannosuke	Official attached to Prince Higashikuni	14	0	Office	11 (78.6%)
VISCOUNT Inoue Katsuzumi	Member, House of Peers; Naval officer	13	1	Golf	11 (84.6%)
PRINCE Asaka and Family	Imperial family	13	4	Official residence	5 (38.5%)
PRINCE Chichibu Yasuhito	Imperial family (emperor's brother)	12	5	Official residence	8 (66.7%)
Takahashi Toshio	Section Chief, Bureau of Peerage Affairs, Household Ministry	12	0	Office	5 (41.7%)
Naitō Saburō	Police official, Home Ministry	12	0	Office	8 (66.7%)
MARQUIS Sasaki Yukitada	Member, House of Peers	11	11	Eleven Club	8 (72.7%)
Kido Takazumi	Kido's son	11	10	Social	7 (63.6%)
VISCOUNT Oda Nobutsune	Member, House of Peers	11	13	Eleven Club	7 (63.6%)
PRINCE Saionji Kimmochi	Last of the Elder Statesmen	11	3	Office	7 (63.6%)

TABLE 14.—*Continued*

Persons	Position	Number of Meetings		Dominant Mode of Communication, 1936	
		1936	*1932*	*Mode*	*Number*
COUNT Ōtani Son'yu	Member, House of Peers	11	0	Golf	10 (90.9%)
Tokinori Hisashi	Brother-in-law; Army officer	10	0	Social	5 (50.0%)
COUNT Makino Nobuaki	Former Privy Seal	10	41	Home	4 (40.0%)
Arita Hachirō	Foreign Minister (April 1936)	10	6	Official residence	4 (40.0%)
VISCOUNT Uramatsu Tomoaki	Member, House of Peers	10	10	Eleven Club	8 (80.0%)
Oguma Shin'ichirō and family	Son of wealthy businessman Oguma Koichirō (?)	10	0	Home	6 (60.0%)
Naruse (Tatsu?)	Kido's son-in-law (?); Managing Director, Nippon Life Assurance Co. (?)	10	0	Golf	10 (100.0%)
PRINCE Higashikuni and family	Imperial family	10	3	Official residence	4 (40.0%)
Total		766	437		

ᵃ Kido met Privy Seal Saitō and his family 11 times. He met Yuasa Kurahei a total of 50 times: 15 times when Yuasa was Household Minister, 35 times after Yuasa had succeeded Saitō as Privy Seal. He met Matsudaira Tsuneo, who succeeded Yuasa as Household Minister, 39 times. Three persons, therefore, held two leading palace posts as a result of personnel shifts following the assassination of Privy Seal Saitō on February 26, 1936. By persons the count is Yuasa 50, Matsudaira 39, Saitō 11. By office the count is Household Minister 54, Privy Seal 46. Because of the importance of office, both person and office tabulations are included in table 14 for these three persons.

31.9 percent of his meetings with those in the ten or more frequency group. As measured by frequency of association, these ten persons were collectively more important to Kido in 1932 than they were in 1936.

Kido met only one palace offical (his direct superior, the Privy Seal) ten times or more in 1932, accounting for a mere 8.2 percent of Kido's meetings in that frequency group. In 1936, however, he met ten palace officials ten times or more, and these accounted for 35.0 percent of his meetings with those in the ten or more frequency group. As measured by frequency of association, palace officials, whose dominant modes of communication with Kido were official, were collectively the most important group in Kido's 1936 pattern of association. By way of contrast, Kido's aristocratic ingroup in the Eleven Club, whose dominant modes of communication with Kido were almost completely informal, had accounted for 68.2 percent of his meetings with those he met ten times or more in 1932 and were the core of his associations during that year. In 1936, however, the eight members of the Eleven Club who met Kido ten times or more accounted for only 31.2 percent of Kido's meetings in that frequency group.

Kido's meetings with two key palace officials, the Privy Seal and the Household Minister, numbered one hundred during 1936—13.1 percent of Kido's meetings with those he met ten times or more and 6.9 percent of his total meetings that year. Kido met with the Privy Seal and Imperial Household Minister less than half that number of times in 1932, and forty-one of the forty-nine times he met with both in 1932 were meetings with the Privy Seal, his official superior. In 1936, however, Kido met with the Privy Seal forty-six times and the Imperial Household Minister fifty-four times. Before his resignation as Chief Secretary to the Privy Seal on June 13 Kido met with the Privy Seal thirty-seven times, after his resignation only nine times. Kido's association with the Privy Seal was thus a function of office and not a social or status relationship. Since Kido was Director of Peerage Affairs throughout 1936, contact with his direct superior in this capacity, the Imperial Household Minister, should have remained constant, regardless of Kido's resignation as Chief Secretary. This was indeed the case. From January 1 to June 13

Kido met with the Imperial Household Minister thirty times; from June 14 to December 31 he met with him twenty-four times. The higher number of meetings in the January 1–June 13 period was caused by palace activity during the aftermath of the February 26 coup, when the Imperial Household Minister and Kido, along with the other leading palace personages, were closeted in the palace for over ten consecutive days.

Meetings with both these palace officials were primarily "official." Fifty-six of the one hundred meetings took place at offices, six at official residences, nine at official meetings, and seven involved reports, for a total of 78 (78 percent). Three persons held the two posts of Privy Seal and Imperial Household Minister during 1936 as the result of Privy Seal Saitō's assassination on February 26. Of the one hundred meetings, six were social calls of condolence and other calls on Saitō's family after February 26, inflating the "informal" figure. Such calls were of course expected of Kido under the circumstances but would not have occurred had Kido not been Saitō's Chief Secretary. Further substantiating the official nature of Kido's relationship with all three is the fact that during 1932 he met only one of them, the then Prime Minister Saitō, and him only once, at an official imperial banquet for Ministers of State.

The same pattern of official contact dependent upon official palace positions holds true for the remaining seven palace officials Kido met ten times or more during 1936, but with variation in the case of three. Four of the seven were strictly palace officials. Iwanami Takenobu and Takahashi Toshio were section chiefs directly under Kido in the Bureau of Peerage Affairs. Of the thirty-six times Kido met with both, thirty (83.3 percent) were official. Matsumoto Kannosuke, an official attached (*bettō*) to Prince Higashikuni, was also connected to Kido by virtue of office. Kido, as Director of Peerage Affairs, was involved in the appointment of persons to the entourage of members of the imperial family and other official duties regarding imperial family members. All of the fourteen times he met with Matsumoto were official. Vice Minister of the Imperial Household Ministry Baron Shirane Matsusuke met Kido a total of twenty-eight times, of which twenty-one (75 percent) were official. Both he and Kido were equally involved in matters of ministry administration.

Kido's associations with these four arose exclusively from their palace offices. Kido met them a total of seventy-eight times; sixty-five (83.3 percent) took place in an official setting. In 1932 Kido met only two of the four and those two but once each, emphasizing once again the direct correlation between offices held and frequency of association.

The last three palace officials Kido met ten times or more were Marquis Matsudaira Yasumasa, Marquis Hirohata Tadataka, and Viscount Matsudaira Keimin. Their patterns of association with Kido varied considerably from those of the other seven palace officials. Two, Marquis Matsudaira and Marquis Hirohata, were members of the Eleven Club; Viscount Matsudaira was Marquis Matsudaira's uncle. Kido met these three only seventeen times in 1932; in 1936, however, he met them a total of ninety times. Marquis Matsudaira first entered the palace bureaucracy in 1936 as Kido's successor as Chief Secretary to the Privy Seal. Marquis Hirohata first entered the palace in late 1932 as Deputy Grand Chamberlain. Viscount Matsudaira had held a court office in 1932 that was of no relevance to Kido's secretarial role. Although all three were ingroup aristocrats, therefore, the relation between the 1936 palace offices of all three and Kido's palace offices in 1936 provides the most reasonable explanation for the changes in frequency of association between 1932 and 1936 and for the modes of communication with Kido during 1936.

Matsudaira Yasumasa was the only palace official whose modes of communication with Kido in 1936 were overwhelmingly informal: 88.5 percent of their meetings took place in an informal setting and the dominant mode of communication between them was meals (53.5 percent). During the five and a half months of 1936 before he succeeded Kido as Chief Secretary to the Privy Seal, Matsudaira met Kido seventeen times, or 3.1 times a month. During the remainder of 1936 he and Kido met twenty-six times, or 4.0 times per month. The nature of Matsudaira's new office and the fact that Kido was his predecessor in that office largely explain the mode of communication between them as well as the increased frequency of association. The role of secretary, as we have just seen, called for the gathering of political information at meals and in other informal settings conducive to an "open exchange of views"—a relaxed environment in which the participants could talk together as "persons," not formal officeholders. If Matsudaira pursued the same secretarial role as had Kido, which he apparently did, the only person with whom he would meet on an overwhelmingly official basis would be his official superior, the Privy Seal. Second, Kido's and Matsudaira's palace offices in 1936 had very little to do with one another, even though they were in the same component of imperial prerogative. There was no reason for them to meet officially, and given their ingroup association in the Eleven Club it is not surprising that informal modes of communication prevailed between them.

More importantly, however, Kido was Matsudaira's predecessor in office and probably recommended Matsudaira to succeed him. Predecessor and successor were bound by ties of courtesy, obligation, and self-interest—ties which were informal, not official. Kido, for example, maintained regular contact with his own predecessor as Chief Secretary to the Privy Seal, Viscount Okabe Nagakage, who was also a member of the Eleven Club ingroup. In 1932, well over a year after Kido had succeeded Okabe, Kido met Okabe sixty-seven times: 97.0 percent of their meetings were informal and the dominant mode of communication was meals (41.8 percent). The pattern of association between Kido and his predecessor was thus repeated between Kido and his successor. Ingroup association between Kido and Matsudaira was therefore expanded because of two factors: (1) Matsudaira's new secretarial role, and (2) predecessor-successor relations.

Kido's mode of communication with Hirohata Tadataka, also a member of the Eleven Club, was the complete reverse of that with Matsudaira Yasumasa: 87.1 percent of Kido's meetings with Hirohata in 1936 occurred at official places. Hirohata had become Deputy Grand Chamberlain in September 1932 after twenty years in the Ministry of Communications. From February 26, 1936 until November of that year Hirohata was virtually Grand Chamberlain while Grand Chamberlain Suzuki was recovering from wounds inflicted by the February 26 insurgents. Throughout most of 1936, therefore, Hirohata performed the role of one of the six direct imperial appointees at court. Had Kido not been one of those six officials and had Hirohata not been Grand Chamberlain pro tempore it is quite likely that a very different pattern of association would have prevailed. As it was, Kido's role as a leading palace bureaucrat and Hirohata's role as chief attendant to the emperor in 1936 transformed an informal and infrequent ingroup association into an official and frequent palace association.

The last of the ten palace officals was Viscount Matsudaira Keimin, who had been Grand Master of the Ceremonies since August 1934. Like Kido, he was one of the six palace officials of direct imperial appointee rank. Palace ceremonies, whether Shinto rites or diplomatic functions involving foreign notables, obviously concerned members of the imperial families and the aristocracy whose affairs were managed by Kido. This may account for the increase in association between the two, from five meetings in 1932 to sixteen in 1936. Only seven of their meetings in 1936 were official, however. A relative of one of Kido's aristocratic intimates and a palace official of equal rank whose duties involved Kido's official functions, Matsudaira Keimin belongs in the ambiguous category of social-official associate. Both office and social station serve to explain his place in Kido's 1936 pattern of association.

Kido's meetings with these ten palace officials may thus be classified as official-superior (three), official-inferior (four), and official-ingroup (three). The frequency of association with all ten depended primarily on palace offices held, not social relationships. These ten accounted for 180 of the 298 official meetings with persons Kido saw ten or more times in 1936. Judging by Kido's experience as a palace official, therefore, communication between a bureaucrat and those in the same bureaucratic organization was predominantly official rather than informal. Reinforcing this conclusion is the fact that the dominant mode of communication with these ten palace officials was office in all cases but one, Marquis Matsudaira Yasumasa. His exception to the rule of bureaucratic association may be explained simply by the mode of operation called for by the role of Chief Secretary to the Privy Seal: informal contact between the Chief Secretary and his predecessor, as well as with government officials and officials at court not related to him by official duties. This was well documented by Kido's informal communication with his predecessor, Viscount Okabe Nagakage, and Kido's overwhelmingly informal contact with government officials in 1932.

If palace officials were a new type cluster in Kido's 1936 pattern of association, so also were members of the imperial family. In 1932 Kido met with the emperor and members of the imperial families a total of 21 times; in 1936 his association with them increased to 114. Kido had met no member of the imperial family ten times or more in 1932; in 1936 he met six ten times or more. Because Kido's office in 1936 gave him duties with regard to the imperial families as well as the aristocracy, such associations followed as a matter of office.

Sixteen of the thirty-seven persons Kido met ten times or more in 1936 were palace officials or imperial family members. They accounted for 45.7 percent of his associations in that frequency category. Since he had met none of these sixteen persons ten times or more in 1932, Kido's role as a palace bureaucrat clearly brought him a new set of associates based on his new office.

Of these sixteen persons eleven were titled aristocrats. As in 1932, aristocratic associations dominated Kido's political network. But as these eleven aristocrats illustrate, Kido's aristocratic colleagues in 1936 were a diverse group and largely new faces. Twenty-five of the thirty-seven Kido met ten times or more in 1936 were titled, and these twenty-five accounted for 71.4 percent of Kido's meetings with those in the ten or more frequency category. In addition to the eleven who were palace officials and members of the imperial family, five, accounting for 17.6 percent of Kido's meetings with those he met ten times or more, were golfing cronies. With the possible exception of Marquis Inoue Saburō, none of these five appears to have figured in Kido' political role during 1936. One of the remaining nine aristocrats was Kido's brother-in-law, Count Kodama Hideo. Kido gives no indication that Kodama, a prominent bureaucrat of ministerial rank, was influential either in Kido's career or in the performance of Kido's political functions. The eighteenth aristocrat was Count Makino Nobuaki, Kido's former superior. Despite Makino's retirement from the office of Privy Seal and from public life in 1935, Kido kept in touch with him apparently as a matter of courtesy. Because Makino was no longer Privy Seal, however, the number of meetings between the two decreased from forty-one in 1932 to ten in

1936. Moreover, only two of the ten meetings in 1936 took place under official circumstances. Since their official relationship no longer prevailed, therefore, frequency of association decreased markedly and the mode of communication was reversed from official to informal. Prince Saionji, the nineteenth aristocrat, met Kido ten times during 1936, most meetings taking place in the aftermath of the February 26 coup attempt. After his resignation as Chief Secretary to the Privy Seal in June 1936, however, Kido met Prince Saionji only once during the remainder of 1936, and that was a courtesy call concerned with his resignation. Kido's meetings with Saionji, few though they were during his career as Chief Secretary, were therefore a function of Kido's secretarial role in the process of advising the throne.

The remaining six aristocrats were members of the Eleven Club. These six, plus the two Eleven Club members who were palace officers, accounted for 31.2 percent of Kido's associations with those he met ten times or more. In 1932 the corresponding percentage (68.2 percent) was more than double. Meetings with all Eleven Club members cited by Kido decreased from 367 in 1932 (35.7 percent of Kido's total meetings in 1932) to 261 in 1936 (18.1 percent of Kido's total meetings in 1936). Meetings at Eleven Club sessions also declined, from 71 in 1932 to 55 in 1936. The role of Kido's aristocratic ingroup diminished markedly, therefore, when Kido's role changed from secretary to bureaucrat. After June 1936 Kido was no longer required to use his aristocratic circuit for gathering political information, since he was no longer Chief Secretary to the Privy Seal. Most affected was Kido's association with Prince Saionji's political secretary, Baron Harada Kumao. Although Harada was still the central figure in Kido's network of association in 1936, their meetings decreased from 135 in 1932 to 73 in 1936. After June 1936 Kido's role as bureaucrat did not require the secretary-to-secretary liaison that was so important in 1932. Harada met Kido an average of 7.3 times a month prior to Kido's resignation in 1936; during the remainder of 1936 they met 5.1 times a month. Because Harada was still a secretary, as well as a member of Kido's aristocratic ingroup, and because Kido was an important palace bureaucrat, however, meetings between the two remained at a high level.

Although Kido maintained his center of gravity in ingroup

aristocratic associations, therefore, (1) these decreased or changed in frequency of association according to offices held, (2) Kido's role as a bureaucrat brought him new and wider aristocratic associations than in 1932, and (3) palace officials became Kido's most important set of associates, replacing the aristocratic ingroup.

Paralleling these changes, there was a decrease in Kido's contact with "outside" government officials. Kido's four main links to the outside political world in 1932 are not found among the thirty-seven persons Kido met ten times or more in 1936. In 1932 Kido met Colonel Suzuki thirteen times, party politican Inukai twelve times, Foreign Ministry bureaucrat Tani eleven times, and police chief Fujinuma ten times. The displacement of these four persons may be explained rather easily. First, Kido was no longer a secretary after June 1936 and did not need the same types of political contacts thereafter. Second, these four persons no longer held the offices they had had in 1932, offices which had made them politically relevant to Kido in performing his secretarial role.

Fujinuma, for example, was not Chief of Metropolitan Police in 1936. His successor was Ishida Kaoru, whom Kido met six times during 1936. Kido was also in frequent contact with police chief Naitō Saburō (twelve times).[41] Kido's contact with the Foreign Ministry was maintained via Arita Hachirō, Vice Minister of Foreign Affairs and the Foreign Minister (April 1936), whom he met ten times during 1936. Given the concern of the Imperial Household Ministry with palace security and the palace's deep concern with foreign policy directions, Kido's associations with the police and the Foreign Ministry, though not intense, were not out of the ordinary. Most notable, however, is Kido's lack of sustained contact with autonomous representatives of the military. The two military officers Kido met ten times or more were Tokinori Hisashi, Kido's brother-in-law, and Inoue Katsuzumi, a golfing crony. Their

---

41. Meetings with these two police officials thus totaled eighteen. Interestingly, fourteen of these meetings took place after Kido had resigned as Chief Secretary to the Privy Seal. Since the security of the imperial family and the aristocracy was one of the prime concerns of all leading palace bureaucrats, it is not extraordinary that Kido should have maintained frequent contact with the Home Ministry police, especially the Tokyo Metropolitan Police. The February 26 coup might also have made palace officials far more security-conscious than they had been.

234 of PALACE POLITICS

TABLE 15.   TYPES OF PERSONS KIDO MET TEN TIMES OR MORE, 1936 AND 1932

	1936			1932		
	Persons	*No. of Meetings*	*% of Total*[b]	*Persons*	*No. of Meetings*	*% of Total*[c]
Titled aristocrats (including imperial personages)	25	547	71.4	11	410	82.0
Palace officials	10	268	35.0	1	41	8.2
Eleven Club members	8	239	31.2	8	341	68.2
Imperial family	6	82	10.7	0	0	0
Business leaders	3	80	10.4	1	16	3.2
Kido's family and in-laws	5	63	8.2	2	28	5.6
Government officials	3	37	4.8	2	22	4.4
Military officials	2	23	3.0	1	13	2.6
Party officials	0	0	0	1	12	2.4
Total[a]	62	1,339		27	883	

[a] The persons add up to more than 37 in 1936 and 18 in 1932, and the number of meetings to more than 766 in 1936 and 500 in 1932, because the categories used are not mutually exclusive. For example, all Eleven Club members were titled aristocrats and some were palace officials. Kodama Hideo was a titled aristocrat, a government official, and a member of Kido's family.

[b] Based on a total of 766 meetings.

[c] Based on a total of 500 meetings.

association with Kido was based on family and aristocratic ties and involved nonpolitical activities. The absence of someone like Colonel Suzuki from Kido's group of frequent associates is therefore symbolic of the drop in Kido's contact with the military during 1936.

Table 15 lists the types of persons Kido met ten times or more in 1932 and 1936 and their frequency of association with Kido in each year. In 1932 Kido's associations with four autonomous representatives from the "outside" (government, military, and party) totaled 9.4 percent of his meetings with those in the ten or more frequency category. In 1936, however, only two such autonomous representatives are to be found in this frequency category, accounting for a mere 2.9 percent of Kido's associations with those he met ten times or more. As Kido's role changed from secretary to bureaucrat, therefore, the role of autonomous contacts with the outside world of politics decreased. Table 15 also summarizes the major shifts in all categories of persons Kido met, emphasizing once again the primacy of official associations with palace colleagues in 1936, when Kido was primarily a bureaucrat, and the parallel decrease in association with ingroup aristocrats of the Eleven Club.

These changes in Kido's pattern of association were paralleled by a marked change in dominant modes of communication, as table 16 reveals. In discharging his role as secretary in 1932, Kido's dominant mode of communication with those he met ten times or more was overwhelmingly informal: 94.4 percent of those he met ten times or more were linked to Kido primarily by informal modes of communication. The only exception was his association with his palace superior, Privy Seal Makino. In 1936, however, only 54.1 percent of those he met ten times or more were linked primarily by informal modes of communication. Moreover, the informal

TABLE 16. DOMINANT MODES OF COMMUNICATION WITH PERSONS MET TEN TIMES OR MORE, 1936 AND 1932

Dominant Mode	Number of Persons in 1936		Number of Persons in 1932	
Office	11		0	
Official residence	6		1	
"Official" subtotal	17	(45.9%)	1	(5.6%)
Meals	4		9	
Informal meetings	0		1	
Golf	7		2	
Home	3		0	
Eleven Club	3		4	
Social and miscellaneous	3		1	
"Informal" subtotal	20	(54.1%)	17	(94.4%)
Total	37	(100%)	18	(100%)

NOTE: In cases where a tie occurred in the dominant modes of communication for a given person, the first figure in tables 12 and 14 is used for that person, arbitrarily.

percentage for 1936 is greatly inflated because of the inclusion of some eleven persons whose dominant mode of communication was informal but who had little or nothing to do with Kido's 1936 political roles: family members and golfing cronies. The number of politically relevant types in 1936 was twenty-six of the thirty-seven persons Kido met ten times or more; in 1932, fifteen of eighteen persons. In both years the dominant mode of communication with politically irrelevant persons was informal. Official modes of communication dominated in the case of seventeen of the twenty-six (65.4 percent) politically relevant persons in 1936; in 1932, however, official modes of communication dominated in the case of only one of fifteen (6.7 percent).

In 1936 Kido's secretarial role was supplemented and then replaced by a bureaucratic role. The change in political roles altered his pattern of association significantly, primarily from informal meetings with members of his aristocratic ingroup and outside political persons to official meetings with fellow officials in the palace. Kido's aristocratic ingroup remained the fixed base of his political operations from 1932 through 1936 but decreased in importance. The Eleven Club, the Sixth Day Club, and other regular meetings such as the Tuesday Luncheon Club continued to function as before and Kido's attendance remained fairly constant. During 1936 the Eleven Club met eight times, there was at least one meeting of the Sixth Day Club that Kido attended, and he was present at six Tuesday Luncheon Club sessions. On the other hand, his association with public officials in the government and the military decreased in 1936, and those officials he did see in 1936 varied greatly from those he met in 1932. All these variations can be accounted for by changes in offices between 1932 and 1936: the changes in Kido's associates, frequencies of association, and modes of communication between 1932 and 1936 were largely dependent on changes in Kido's palace role and the offices held by the persons Kido met.

Finally, the total number of Kido's associations and associates increased greatly between 1932 and 1936. These increases can be accounted for by (1) new associates acquired by new offices, as just indicated, (2) Kido's overlapping roles in 1936, and (3) associational accretions normal to any politically active person as he moves up the political ladder. We have noted, for example, that Kido maintained frequent contact with Count Makino Nobuaki during 1936, well after Makino had retired as Privy Seal. Kido also kept in regular contact with his predecessor as Chief Secretary to the Privy Seal during 1936, almost six years after Kido had replaced him. Kido even maintained contact, though infrequent, with his former colleagues in the Ministry of Commerce and Industry. Throughout his political career, therefore, Kido acquired a constantly expanding range and number of associations as the result of changes in his public offices and his attendant political advancement. With his appointment as Lord Keeper of the Privy Seal in 1940, Kido's pace of associational activity became breathtaking.

KIDO'S APPOINTMENT AS LORD KEEPER
OF THE PRIVY SEAL

Kido resigned from his post as Director of Peerage Affairs to become Minister of Education in Prince Konoe's first Cabinet on October 22, 1937. For the next two years he tasted the flavor of Cabinet politics, first as Education Minister and Welfare Minster under Konoe and then as Home Minister under Prime Minister Hiranuma Kiichirō. Given his long-standing association with Prince Konoe, his entry into Konoe's Cabinet was "in the nature of things." Since Konoe remained as Minister without Portfolio in the Hiranuma Cabinet, which succeeded his, it is not at all surprising that Kido remained in the Hiranuma Cabinet as well. When Kido was appointed Lord Keeper of the Privy Seal on June 1, 1940, therefore, he brought to that office ministerial experience, as had all his predecessors with the exception of Tokudaiji Sanenori and Fushimi Sadanaru.

Kido's appointment as Privy Seal was, of course, far more important than his appointment as Chief Secretary to the Privy Seal ten years earlier. In 1940 he was to become the emperor's chief adviser on Cabinet changes—and remain in that capacity for over five years. Consequently, his appointment brought to bear imperial advisers, leading political figures, palace officers, and their respective secretaries.

Involved in Kido's selection were (1) Baron Harada Kumao, Prince Saionji's political secretary, who claims to have suggested Kido to (2) Prince Saionji, last of the Elder Statesmen, who at ninety years of age strained to keep from advising the throne on any issue; (3) Chief Secretary to the Privy Seal Matsudaira Yasumasa, playing a liaison-catalyst role for (4) Privy Seal Yuasa Kurahei, dying of emphysema, who in cooperation with (5) the Imperial Household Minister, Matsudaira Tsuneo, and with the approval of (6) the Prime Minister, Yonai Mitsumasa, formally recommended Kido as Privy Seal. Leading imperial advisers, such as (7) Senior Retainer Wakatsuki Reijirō, (8) Senior Retainer Okada Keisuke, and (9) Senior Retainer and President of the Privy Council, Prince Konoe Fumimaro were involved, as were advocates of specific candidates, such as (10) Izawa Takio. Even (11) Kido was consulted as to a proper successor to Yuasa, not imagining that he himself would be chosen. Last, (12) the emperor sanctioned Kido's appointment, having queried his principal palace officers as to the most suitable person to be his chief adviser-in-attendance. The caution and secrecy with which all these participants went about selecting the new Privy Seal, so characteristic of prewar Japan's privatized decision making in general, are illustrated in the course of initiation, consultation, negotiation, and recommendation that led to Kido's appointment.

On the evening of May 3, 1940 Harada Kumao visited Kido: Privy Seal Yuasa Kurahei was ill and, since there was no immediate prospect of his recovery, the problem of replacing him would arise sooner or later.[42] Commenting after the war on this meeting with Harada, Kido notes: "At this time I didn't even dream that I would be nominated as his successor, and it appears that this was not at all in Harada's mind either."[43] Then, on May 8, the Chief Secretary to the Privy Seal, Matsudaira Yasumasa, visited Kido and Harada. When Matsudaira stated that the Privy Seal's illness would probably make it necessary to replace him, Harada said that Prince Saionji wished to have Kido succeed Yuasa. Dumbfounded, Kido bluntly

42. Kido Kōichi, 2:783; Kido Nikki Kenkyū Kai, p. 120.
43. Kido Nikki Kenkyū Kai, p. 120.

asked Harada if this were in fact Prince Saionji's idea or his own. Harada replied that he had merely informed Saionji that Privy Seal Yuasa would soon have to be replaced: Saionji had then suggested Kido.[44]

> I was completely stunned. I had noticed before that Saionji was gracious enough to bestow his trust and his affection on me; I could not but be moved that he would bestow such faith as this, however. But having served the Lord Keeper of the Privy Seal as his Chief Secretary, and knowing intimately how trying the Privy Seal's work is, I stated my view that Prince Konoe should be Privy Seal, and for President of the Privy Council Baron Hiranuma would be appropriate.[45]

On May 29, Chief Secretary Matsudaira visited Kido again and asked Kido what his thoughts were on a successor to Yuasa. Kido once again recommended Konoe; if Konoe would not accept then Baron Hiranuma was the only alternative.[46] When Harada visited Kido on May 31, however, he intimated that Kido would be recommended to succeed Yuasa. Kido resisted strongly:

> Not only do I have no confidence in dealing with this important position; I also feel an obligation regarding the establishment of the new party, which I discussed with Prince Konoe and Count Arima this past twenty-sixth, to help Prince Konoe and make the new party a great success. On that I am in real difficulty.[47]

Finally, on June 1, Imperial Household Minister Matsudaira Tsuneo called Kido: he wanted Kido to meet him at his official residence. When Kido appeared at 10:30 a.m., Matsudaira mentioned having Kido appointed Privy Seal. Once again Kido declined: he was too junior and simply not suitable for such a position. The Imperial Household Minister replied that Prince Konoe, Privy Seal Yuasa, Prime Minister Yonai, and other "top leaders" were united in recommending him. For Kido to refuse, thinking only of his personal convenience, would not do. Kido was unable, however, to understand why Konoe of all people had recommended him, given

44. Ibid.; Kido Kōichi, 2:783.
45. Kido Nikki Kenkyū Kai, p. 120. A terse verification of Kido's disclaimer is also found in the diary (Kido Kōichi, 2:783).
46. Kido Kōichi, 2:787–88; Kido Nikki Kenkyū Kai, p. 122.
47. Kido Nikki Kenkyū Kai, p. 122. The party referred to is the Imperial Rule Assistance Association designed by Konoe and others to replace the political parties.

their conversation of the twenty-sixth. Kido therefore asked Matsudaira to wait until he had asked Konoe what Konoe really had in mind for him.[48]

Kido called on Konoe immediately. Konoe explained his position as follows:

> What I had most hoped for was for you to work with me in establishing the new party, and I feel the same way now as well. Since the view supporting you for Privy Seal was the united view of the top leaders, starting with the Elder Statesman [Prince Saionji], it would not do for me alone to oppose. And the position of Privy Seal is also extremely important; in paving the way for the new party I shall organize presently, your being in the position of Privy Seal will be helpful in many ways. Therefore, I also came around to endorsing [your appointment]. Since that's the way it is, I would like very much for you to accept, though it be a burden to you.[49]

When Konoe put it this way, Kido felt he could not decline simply on the basis of his personal desires. He made up his mind to accept and telephoned the Imperial Household Minister to that effect.

At the time Kido did not think to ask who the other "top leaders" were. While he was in Sugamo Prison at the end of the war, however, he had occasion to read the biography of Izawa Takio and found that at Izawa's behest both Privy Seal Yuasa and Senior Retainer Wakatsuki Reijirō had come to Kido's support.[50] However, Prince Konoe, at that time President of the Privy Council, was once again the most instrumental person in Kido's appointment to high office. Konoe shifted to Kido's support when the weight of pro-Kido views among other top leaders became unanimous. And it was only after Kido had cleared his nomination with Konoe that Kido consented to become Privy Seal. Since Kido was one of Konoe's confidants and deeply involved in Konoe's political aspirations and plans, Kido as Privy Seal would continue to be "helpful in many ways."

Although Kido claims that Harada was not thinking of Kido to succeed Privy Seal Yuasa when they met on May 3, Harada had

---

48. Ibid.; Kido Kōichi, 2:788.
49. Kido Nikki Kenkyū Kai, p. 122.
50. Ibid., p. 123.

brought up the issue of Yuasa's ill health with Prince Saionji as early as April 17. Harada told Prince Saionji:

I think Kido would be all right as the Privy Seal's successor, but suddenly to put Kido in office now would have too strong an impact. So for now how about making Kido Imperial Household Minister and, should the case arise, transfer him from Imperial Household Minister to Privy Seal?

To which Saionji replied: "I think that's a fine idea, really good, but I don't want you to say a word that I was strongly in favor, or that I broached the subject."[51] Apparently, Kido was under consideration three weeks before he himself knew about it.[52]

Since it was his role to report a feasible consensus in the form of a reply to the throne, Prince Saionji remained aloof until all the barometers of opinion had been read. As late as May 27, for instance, Saionji told Harada to tell people that he was merely "listening."[53] But it seemed that he was beyond even reporting a consensus. On May 29, the emperor evidently told the Imperial Household Minister to have Harada ask Saionji's opinion on Yuasa's successor. The Imperial Household Minister spoke with Harada on the thirtieth and told him to see Saionji at Okitsu immediately. When Harada saw Saionji on the thirty-first, Saionji refused to respond to the emperor's questions on grounds of old age and distance from recent political developments. Saionji finally suggested "someone like Ichiki [Kitokurō] or Okada [Keisuke]," his fellow constitutional monarchists, but he remained silent when Harada asked him for permission to relay this to the emperor.[54] Harada reported to Saionji that evening that Kido had ultimately

51. Harada Kumao, 8:224–25. The precedent for such an appointment procedure had been set by Makino Nobuaki, Household Minister from 1921 to 1925 and then Privy Seal from 1925 to 1935. The practice was continued by Yuasa Kurahei, Household Minister from 1933 to 1936 and Privy Seal from 1936 to 1940.

52. Althouth Harada records a conversation with Kido after his April 17 meeting with Prince Saionji, Kido notes no meetings with Harada between April 11 and May 2. Since Harada's record is an oral statement recorded by another person at ten-day intervals, Kido's daily diary, written by himself, would appear more reliable on specific details such as dates and meetings. Harada also dictated long passages that were mere hearsay, frequently embellishing his accounts with his own commentary.

53. Harada Kumao, 8:250.

54. Ibid., pp. 251–53.

been recommended to the throne by the Imperial Household Minister. Saionji was very pleased:

> In fact, as you have just said, if the predecessor first recommends a successor, then the State Minister who is to countersign—that is, the Imperial Household Minister—agrees to this and His Majesty gives his sanction, nothing could be better. I am completely satisfied.[55]

Saionji's attempt to keep out may be explained in two mutually supporting ways. First, as Elder Statesman he was to express a consensus, not dictate a choice. This involved selecting a "suitable" person, one who would satisfy various representatives of opinion- and policy-making groups and meet certain criteria of political style and viewpoint. Second, Prince Saionji was genuinely disenchanted with his role as Elder Statesman and for the past several years had tried in vain to "retire" from this advisory position to the throne. When Saionji approved the selection of Kido he was in effect ratifying an official process for selecting top political leaders: the predecessor recommends, those Ministers of State who countersign the appointment agree, and the emperor sanctions. This leaves Saionji out completely, as well as others not directly involved by law in the appointing process, and makes appointment to office largely an intramural process within the given bureaucratic structure.

By 1940 Harada's role as secretary to the last of the Elder Statesmen appears to have been more that of advocate and initiator than pure liaison. It seems in fact that Kido was put into Saionji's head by Harada, and not suggested by Saionji himself, as Kido suspected on May 8. Saionji's refusal even at the twelfth hour to recommend a successor to the Privy Seal allowed Harada—and the other concerned public officials—to go ahead with Kido's appointment. After his conversation with the Imperial Household Minister on May 30, Harada commented:

> For some time before I had had various thoughts concerning a successor, and, since I had had to listen to various views, I had spoken to Konoe and also heard the views of Matsudaira [Imperial Household Minister], Admiral Okada, and others. When it came to a decision, then, it amounted to saying: "Kido is the safest. With Kido, since he knows quite

55. Ibid., p. 254.

a bit about palace matters and is also conversant with recent political conditions, well, Kido will be fine." When at that point I checked with the Prime Minister and heard his thoughts, he said: "I have no objection to Kido."[56]

As Prince Saionji's secretary, Harada appears to have done Saionji's job of negotiating a consensus in 1940. Since the ritual of "asking the Elder Statesman at Okitsu" was preserved to the very last, Harada was permitted to perform Saionji's role. The ultimate decision was made and reported by the Imperial Household Minister, in consultation with Privy Seal Yuasa, and evidently midwifed by Harada.

As Saionji's better half in 1940, Harada was very concerned that the process of consensus taking and consensus resolution be thorough but highly contained. On May 17 Harada claims to have met the Prime Minister and told him to give careful consideration to a possible successor to Privy Seal Yuasa:

> Since ultimately both the Imperial Household Minister and you are to make direct decisions on this upcoming problem, the Imperial Household Minister might possibly make some recommendations directly to His Majesty. And if that happens the case will be closed—so watch that side of things carefully.[57]

One of the imperatives to secrecy in Harada's mind was a premature recommendation to the emperor of Yuasa's successor, closing the selection process. Imperial sanction was the final act of the consensus resolution process, and a clear recommendation to the throne invariably elicited imperial sanction.[58] Harada wanted the process of consensus taking to run its full course to avoid a rash decision on the new Privy Seal.

The Chief Secretary to the Privy Seal, Matsudaira Yasumasa, appears to have acted as an impartial informant and liaison in Kido's appointment. Neither Kido nor Harada records any preferences given by the Chief Secretary as to Yuasa's successor. The Chief

56. Ibid., p. 252.
57. Ibid., pp. 245–46.
58. Under certain circumstances, however, leaders declined or were prevented from taking office even after imperial appointment. Konoe declined the imperial command to form a Cabinet in 1936. As we saw in the conclusion to chap. 4, General Ugaki was prevented from forming his Cabinet in 1937 when the Army refused to appoint an Army Minister.

Secretary did, however, press for a decision by informing the principals regularly of Yuasa's health and urging immediate consideration of a successor. The Chief Secretary was also concerned that the issue be kept contained and secret, even among the principals. On May 4, for example, he talked with Harada:

> This is top secret, but the Privy Seal's condition is really not very good. He himself finally said: "I cannot possibly go on." And he talked to the Imperial Household Minister about this as well. Well, he is thinking of some way to regain his health and intends to resign soon. Don't talk about this with Konoe or Kido just now.[59]

On May 6 or 7, the Chief Secretary again spoke with Harada and told him that Privy Seal Yuasa had suggested as his successor Wakatsuki Reijirō, Ugaki Kazunari,[60] or Kido. He then asked Harada to speak to no one until he had heard from the Imperial Household Minister and not to speak with the Imperial Household Minister himself.[61] The Chief Secretary to the Privy Seal was therefore instrumental in keeping the decison-making circuit closed, at the same time that he kept Harada informed. He also attempted to preserve the decision-making primacy of the two chief palace figures concerned: the Privy Seal and the Imperial Household Minister. Despite Harada's liaison ambulations and his recommendations, the final decision was apparently made by these two palace officials.

The emperor appears to have played an active role in Kido's appointment. On hearsay, Harada quoted the emperor as saying to the Imperial Household Minister on May 29:

> Wakatsuki, for example, is also a candidate [for Privy Seal], but there is the fact of the London Treaty problem, and the fact that he was president of the Minseitō for many years; the mood of the opposition party will never relent. Won't that prove a bar? And Konoe is good, but flocks of various kinds of people are a bit too close [to him], and further, in the future, it will be necessary in fact for him to be in charge of the party; I

---

59. Harada Kumao, 8:237.
60. Ugaki Kazunari was at this time a retired general turned bureaucrat-politician. Born in 1868, Ugaki was Minister of the Army under three Prime Ministers, including Wakatsuki Reijirō, between 1924 and 1927, and again from 1929 to 1931. During his career he had managed to alienate himself from a number of military leaders and consequently lost his chance to become Prime Minister in the 1930s.
61. Harada Kumao, 8:239.

would like, therefore, to avoid making him Privy Seal now. Hiranuma seems to keep secrets, but Okitsu [i.e. Prince Saionji] just simply will not support him. Kido I think is good, but he is a bit young and to extinguish his future political career would be sad—but who?[62]

The emperor added, "Among these, who does Saionji think is good? Are there others besides these?"[63] Evidently the emperor did express opinions about the selection of the official who would serve as his closest and most important link with the government. First, he couched suggestions as questions. Second, the criteria he applied were (1) lack of opposition from influential quarters of Japanese political society, (2) seniority and experience, and (3) low involvement in a given political policy or political stance. Wakatsuki and Hiranuma had opposition, Kido was too young, and Konoe too involved. The emperor did not mention a desirable political policy as a criterion for any candidate. In fact, there is no discussion by either Harada or Kido of any policy criteria in the selection of the Privy Seal—pro Anglo-American, pro civilian, for example—or of concrete programs a candidate would advise the throne to adopt. The implication in the entire nominating and appointing process was that the Privy Seal was to be an impartial adviser, untainted by involvement in any specific policy or program. Third, the emperor's participation left wide latitude to those responsible for advising the throne on a new Privy Seal; he did not really declare for a specific person. The most that can be said is that the emperor very mildly intimated that Kido was the least objectionable.

Kido's appointment as Privy Seal, in contrast to his appointment to the post of Chief Secretary to the Privy Seal ten years earlier, thus brought to bear the top echelon of consensus takers and consensus makers: Senior Retainers, Prince Saionji, palace officials, the Prime Minister, the emperor. And Kido was not the only candidate proposed for that important office. The resolution process was one of elimination, and Kido was the "safest," as Harada suggested. Kido's own behavior during the appointment process was similar to that ten

---

62. Ibid., pp. 251–52. Since appointment to the office of Privy Seal, with the one exception of Katsura in 1912, always terminated a successful career on the "outside", Kido's appointment would in effect "extinguish his future political career."

63. Ibid., p. 252.

years earlier, when he was appointed as Chief Secretary. First, as in 1930, Kido was not a candidate by his own request: he was placed in office by others. Whereas he was neither excited nor displeased about his 1930 appointment, he appears to have been genuinely opposed to becoming Privy Seal in 1940. His refusal to accept the post in 1940 went far beyond the self-effacing courtesies of Japanese propriety: he had other plans, he was too young, and he did not want an office that was both a demanding pressure point in the political process and dangerous to life and limb. He was literally pressed into service. According to Harada, Kido was recommended to the throne (May 31) even before he had accepted (June 1).[64]

Second, there were no formal job interviews. Not even the emperor interviewed Kido prior to his appointment. And when Kido met the Imperial Household Minister on June 1 it was to be pressed into service, not to be interviewed on policies and programs. Kido was never asked what he "stood for." Finally, only a very small number of persons had a say in Kido's appointment as Privy Seal. He was reported to the throne by the Imperial Household Minister and sanctioned by the emperor, after consultations with a small group of "top leaders" from the government. No formal body passed on Kido's appointment, which was a matter for the emperor and his individual advisers exclusively.

THE NEGOTIATOR

Just how demanding the office of Privy Seal was for Kido may be readily appreciated from table 17. Although Kido recorded having met 384 persons in 1941, 7 less than in 1936, he saw those 384 persons 1,920 times, a 33.0 percent increase in meetings over 1936 and an 87.0 percent increase over 1932. Moreover, those Kido met ten times or more in 1941 averaged 32.5 meetings per person. In 1932 the comparable figure was 27.8 (table 11); in 1936, 20.7 (table 13). As Privy Seal, Kido was a far busier person than he had ever been before in his palace career.

64. Ibid., pp. 253–54.

TABLE 17. KIDO KŌICHI'S ASSOCIATIONS IN 1941: FREQUENCY AND MODE OF COMMUNICATION

Mode of Communication[d]	Total[a] (1)		Ten or More[b] (2)		Nine or Less[c] (3)	
	No.	%	No.	%	No.	%
OFFICIAL						
Office	791	41.2	625	56.6	166	20.4
Official residence	439	22.9	182	16.5	257	31.5
Official conference	31	1.6	10	0.9	21	2.6
Imperial lecture	5	0.3	0	0	5	0.6
Kido's reports	14	0.7	12	1.1	2	0.2
Reports to Kido	60	3.1	51	4.6	9	1.1
Imperial report[e]	7	0.4	2	0.2	5	0.6
Official subtotal	1,347	70.2%	882	79.8%	465	57.1%
INFORMAL						
Home	263	13.7	101	9.1	162	19.9
Informal meetings	14	0.7	4	0.4	10	1.2
Meals	102	5.3	45	4.1	57	7.0
Banquets	34	1.8	17	1.5	17	2.1
Eleven Club	46	2.4	4	0.4	42	5.2
Golf	5	0.3	3	0.3	2	0.2
Tour[f]	12	0.6	12	1.1	0	0
Social and miscellaneous	97	5.1	37	3.3	60	7.4
Informal subtotal	573	29.8%	223	20.2%	350	42.9%
Total	1,920	100%	1,105	100%	815	100%

SOURCE: Kido Kōichi, 2: 847–937.

[a] Based on a total of 1,920 meetings with 384 persons Kido records having met in 1941. Average: 5.0 meetings per person.

[b] Based on 1,105 meetings (57.6% of the total) with the 34 persons Kido met 10 times or more. Average: 32.5 meetings per person.

[c] Based on 815 meetings (42.4% of the total) with the 350 persons Kido met 9 times or less. Average: 2.3 meetings per person.

[d] In 1941 Kido was not as careful to distinguish place of meeting as he had been in 1932 and 1936. When he reports visitors to his residence it is almost always impossible to tell whether he means his official residence or his home. This was not a problem in 1932 and 1936 because in those years Kido was not an official of high enough rank to warrant an official residence. I have therefore tabulated as *Official residence* meetings

The increase in Kido's activity was directly related to official duties. For the first time in the three years examined, official modes of communication predominated over informal. In 1941, 70.2 percent of Kido's meetings took place in an official setting. As a secretary in 1932, official modes of communication accounted for only 15.0 percent of Kido's meetings (table 11); as a bureaucrat in 1936, 39.3 percent (table 13). In 1932 "office" accounted for a mere 7.6 percent of Kido's total meetings (table 11). Office became important to Kido in discharging his administrative duties as Director of Peerage Affairs in 1936, accounting for 25.3 percent of his meetings that year (table 13). Office became even more important when Kido took his post "at the emperor's side" as chief political adviser; 41.2 percent of Kido's total meetings in 1941 occurred at offices, primarily his own office in the palace. The next most important mode of communication was official residence, accounting for 22.9 percent. These two modes of communication, therefore, accounted for almost two-thirds of Kido's total meetings in 1941. In short, the palace was the primary place where Kido performed his negotiator role as the emperor's chief consensus taker and consensus maker in politics.

Despite the great increase in his total associations in 1941, moreover, Kido's informal modes of communication declined absolutely in comparison to 1932 and 1936—from 873 meetings in 1932 (table 11) and 877 in 1936 (table 13) to 573 meetings in 1941. Certain informal modes of communication declined drastically. Meals, so important to Kido's secretarial role in 1932, accounted for only 102 meetings and a mere 5.3 percent of Kido's total meetings in 1941. In 1932, 314 of Kido's meetings occurred at meals, accounting for 30.6 percent of his total meetings that year (table 11). The press and nature of Kido's official duties during 1941 also decreased

---

on weekdays and as *Home* meetings on weekends, as far as visitors coming to Kido's residence were concerned. The *Official residence* figure may be inflated by as much as 10 percent.

  e The category *Imperial report* indicates reports to the throne that Kido attended. These were substantially different from the more general imperial lectures, in that they were policy position reports.

  f *Tour* refers to imperial outings, mainly to the imperial villa at Hayama, on which Kido accompanied the emperor or empress.

  NOTE: The notes to table 11 apply equally to table 17.

activities that were purely social or recreational. "Golf" and "social and miscellaneous" accounted for 102 meetings and 5.3 percent of Kido's total meetings in 1941. In 1932 the comparable figures were 196 and 19.1 percent (table 11); in 1936, 375 and 26.0 percent (table 13). Finally, each of the modes of informal communication that was significant in terms of frequency during 1941—home, meals, social and miscellaneous, Eleven Club, and banquets—was more important in the nine or less frequency group than in the ten or more group. In other words, the less a person met Kido during 1941 the more likely their meeting would take place under informal circumstances.

Conversely, frequency of association in 1941, in contrast to 1932 and 1936, was directly correlated with official modes of communication. The more a person met Kido the more likely their meetings were to occur at official places to accomplish official functions. Over 79 percent of Kido's meetings with those he met ten times or more in 1941 were official in mode of communication, but only 57 percent of his meetings with those in the nine times or less group took place in an official setting. Variation between the two frequency groups was 22.7 percent. In 1932 official modes of communication with those in the two frequency groups varied by only 2.3 percent, and in the opposite direction. In 1936 the variation was an insignificant 0.8 percent. As a secretary in 1932 and a bureaucrat in 1936, moveover, office meetings took place more often with those in the nine or less frequency group than with those in the ten or more group: 8.9 percent in the nine or less group as compared to 6.2 percent in the ten or more group during 1932 (table 11) and 30.8 percent as compared to 20.4 percent during 1936 (table 13). In 1941, however, 56.6 percent of Kido's meetings with those he met ten times or more occurred at offices, while only 20.4 percent of his meetings with those in the nine or less group took place in that setting. Thus, as Kido's official position and role in the palace bureaucracy changed in nature and increased in political weight, (1) associations increased in frequency, (2) those associations increasingly took place under official circumstances, and (3) frequency of association ultimately became positively correlated with official modes of communication, especially "office."

"Official residence" as an official mode of communication does, however, pose difficulties. In 1941 Kido had an official residence, as he had not had in 1932 and 1936. Access by visitors to Kido's official residence was very much like access to his home and involved communication that was both social and official. Second, as pointed out in note d to table 17, it was frequently impossible to distinguish visits to Kido's official residence from those to his home. Under such circumstances, were visits to Kido's official residence "informal" or "official"? Did they involve political duties or nonpolitical activities? Perhaps it would have been more logical to combine the "official residence" and "home" categories and classify both as informal modes of communication, since both "offical residence" and "home" meetings increased markedly over 1932 and 1936, combining to account for 36.6 percent (702 meetings) of Kido's total meetings in 1941. In 1932 "official residence" accounted for only 27 meetings and "home" for 144, combining for 171 meetings and only 16.7 percent of Kido's total meetings that year (table 11). In 1936 "official residence" and "home" numbered 71 and 147 respectively, combining for 218 meetings and only 15.1 percent of Kido's total meetings that year (table 13).

There are, however, several reasons for attempting to distinguish the two and for making "official residence" an official mode of communication. First, not all official residence visits were visits to Kido. At least 77 of the 439 official residence meetings, for example, were visits by Kido to the palaces of the emperor and members of the imperial families. Second, many of the visits to Kido's residence were, in fact, official visits while others were made in the performance of political duties—especially those by the Chief Cabinet Secretary, police officials, and Kido's own Chief Secretary. Third, even if "official residence" involved a mix of official and informal modes of communication, it is useful to attempt to separate "official residence" from "home" for purposes of comparing Kido's modes of communication as negotiatior with those as secretary in 1932 and as bureaucrat in 1936. Fourth, the great increase in visits to both Kido's official residence and his home suggests that Kido was a focal point around which political forces congregated, officially and informally. With the exception of the emperor and members of the imperial families, political leaders almost invariably went to see Privy Seal Kido, not vice versa. It is important to discover as accurately as possible what kinds of access various sorts of people had to the emperor's chief negotiator in politics.

Who, then, were the persons who congregated most frequently around Kido during 1941? Table 18 lists the thirty-four persons Kido met ten times or more in 1941, their positions, frequency of association with Kido for 1932 and 1936 as well as 1941, and the dominant mode of communication with each during 1941. As in 1932 and 1936, Kido's new political role involved him with new sets of people politically significant to that role. Of the thirty-four persons, Kido reports having had no contact with thirteen in either 1932 or 1936. He met but twelve in all three years, and only four persons ten times or more in all three years. Two of these four were members of Kido's family and politically irrelevant. Quite clearly, therefore, Kido acquired a new set of associations in his office as Lord Keeper of the Privy Seal.

Second, only nine of the thirty-four in the ten or more frequency group, or 26.5 percent, were titled aristocrats, including the emperor and members of the imperial families. These nine aristocrats accounted for 47.9 percent of Kido's meetings in that frequency group. In 1932, however, 61.1 percent of those whom Kido met ten times or more were titled, accounting for 82.0 percent of Kido's meetings in that frequency group. In 1936 the percentages were 67.6 percent and 71.4 percent respectively. Aristocrats were no longer the core of Kido's associations as they had been when he was a secretary and a bureaucrat. In 1941, moreover, the role of Kido's Eleven Club ingroup declined drastically. As table 19 indicates, only three of the thirteen Eleven Club aristocrats met Kido ten times or more in 1941; eight had done so in 1932 and 1936. These three accounted for a mere 12.3 percent of Kido's meetings with those in the ten or more frequency group during 1941. In 1932 Eleven Club members had accounted for 68.2 percent of his meetings in that frequency group; in 1936, 31.2 percent. With the exception of Prince Konoe, Prime Minister throughout most of 1941, and Marquis Matsudaira Yasumasa, Kido's Chief Secretary, members of the Eleven Club were almost invisible in Kido's 1941 pattern of association.

TABLE 18. PERSONS IN CONTACT WITH KIDO KŌICHI TEN OR
MORE TIMES, 1941

(34 PERSONS)

Person	Position	Total Number of Meetings			Dominant Mode of Communication, 1941	
		1941	1936	1932	Mode	Number
EMPEROR Hirohito	Emperor	313	16	2	Office	272 (86.9%)
PRINCE Konoe Fumimaro	Prime Minister	93	34	57	Office	52 (55.9%)
GENERAL Hasunuma Shigeru	Chief Aide-de-Camp	82	0	0	Office	73 (89.0%)
Matsuoka Yōsuke	Foreign Minister	55	0	1	Office	34 (61.8%)
Matsudaira Tsuneo	Imperial Household Minister	45	39	0	Office	29 (64.4%)
GENERAL Tōjō Hideki	Army Minister, Prime Minister	44	0	0	Office	38 (86.4%)
MARQUIS Matsudaira Yasumasa	Chief Sec'y to the Privy Seal	33	43	6	Official residence	7 (21.2%)
ADMIRAL Hyakutake Saburō	Grand Chamberlain	32	1	0	Office	27 (84.4%)
Yamazaki Iwao	Superintendent General of Metropolitan Police	27	0	0	Office	12 (44.4%)
MARQUIS Komatsu and family	Future in-laws	23	1	0	Official residence	8 (34.8%)
Wada Koroku	Brother	21	17	18	Home	11 (52.4%)
Hirose Hisatada	Director of the Cabinet Legislation Bureau; House of Peers	21	0	0	Official residence	13 (61.9%)
ADMIRAL Toyoda Teijirō	Minister of Commerce and Industry; Foreign Minister	20	0	1	Office	12 (60.0%)

TABLE 18—*Continued*

Person	Position	Total Number of Meetings			Dominant Mode of Communication, 1941	
		1941	*1936*	*1932*	*Mode*	*Number*
GENERAL Suzuki Teiichi	Director of the Cabinet Planning Board	20	3	13	Office *or* Official residence	Each (Each 7 35.0%)
COUNT Kanroji Osanaga	Deputy Grand Chamberlain	19	1	1	Office	14 (73.7%)
Korematsu Jun'ichi	Businessman; bureaucratic "sec'y"	18	0	0	Official residence	10 (55.6%)
Hashimoto Seikichi	Director of the Police Bureau, Home Ministry	17	1	0	Official residence	9 (52.9%)
Hara Yoshimichi	Pres. of the Privy Council	16	0	0	Office	10 (62.5%)
Yamashita Kamesaburō	Shipping magnate	16	0	0	Official residence	9 (56.3%)
Matsui Seikun (Kūka)	Right-wing ideologist	15	1	0	Official residence	12 (80.0%)
BARON Itō Bunkichi	Businessman; Member, House of Peers	15	34	8	Home	10 (66.7%)
Higuchi Chikao	Son-in-law	15	0	0	Home	5 (33.3%)
Kido Takahiko	Son	15	7	0	Social	10 (66.7%)
Kido Takazumi	Son	14	11	10	Social	5 (35.7%)
Okada Fumihide	Ex-Home Ministry, Welfare Ministry bureaucrat	13	0	0	Official residence *or* Home	Each (Each 5 38.5%)
GENERAL Abe Nobuyuki	Senior Retainer	13	0	0	Home	4 (30.8%)
Watanabe Yoshio	Newspaperman; consultant to the Cabinet's Information Bureau	12	0	0	Official residence	9 (75.0%)
Tōgō Shigenori	Foreign Minister	12	0	0	Office	9 (75.0%)
PRINCE Takamatsu	Emperor's brother	12	14	2	Official residence	10 (83.3%)
Tomita Kenji	Chief Cabinet Sec'y	12	0	0	Official residence	6 (50.0%)

TABLE 18—*Continued*

		Total Number of Meetings			Dominant Mode of Communication, 1941	
Person	*Position*	*1941*	*1936*	*1932*	*Mode*	*Number*
Shimozono Sakichi	Newspaperman; Makino Nobuaki's "confidant"	11	4	0	Office	6 (54.5%)
EMPRESS Nagako	Empress	11	6	1	Official residence	9 (81.8%)
BARON Harada Kumao	Ex-sec'y to the late Prince Saionji	10	73	135	Official residence	5 (50.0%)
Ogura Masatsune	Minister of State; Finance Minister	10	1	2	Office	4 (40.0%)
Total		1,105	307	257		

The remarkable drop in Kido's aristocratic associations in 1941, both in terms of persons and frequency of association, was largely the result of his negotiator role as Privy Seal, an office that made him the emperor's chief link with the government. The leading government officials—as indeed the leading court officers—during the 1930s were not for the most part titled aristocrats but persons of achievement in the real polity who might eventually achieve titles for their contributions to the state and society.[65] It was these government and court officers who were Kido's key associates in his role as adviser to the throne.

This is clearly demonstrated by a situational categorization of the thirty-four persons Kido met ten times or more and the frequency with which Kido met persons in each category. Three of the thirty-four were members of the imperial family, including the emperor.

65. This was the case, for example, with Ichiki Kitokurō and Suzuki Kantarō, who were created barons after long careers in government and service at the side of the emperor in one of the four leading palace offices.

TABLE 19. KIDO'S ASSOCIATION WITH ELEVEN CLUB MEMBERS

Person	1932 Total Meetings	1932 Eleven Club	1936 Total Meetings	1936 Eleven Club	1941 Total Meetings	1941 Eleven Club
Harada Kumao	135	7	73	4	10	1
Okabe Nagakage	67	8	26	8	8	7
Konoe Fumimaro	57	0	34	1	93	2
Sakai Tadamasa	24	3	6	3	4	4
Kuroki Sanji	24	8	8	7	7	6
Oda Nobutsune	13	8	11	7	6	6
Sasaki Yukitada	11	8	11	8	4	4
Uramatsu Tomoaki	10	9	10	8	7	7
Sōma Taketani	8	6	4	0	—	—
Matsudaira Yasumasa	6	4	43	6	33	1
Hirohata Tadataka	6	6	31	1	7	2
Arima Yoriyasu	4	2	4	2	2	1
Yanagisawa Yasutsugu	2	2	0	0	5	5
Total	367	71	261	55	186	46

Nine were government officials of Cabinet rank (direct imperial appointee),[66] and five were government officials below that rank. Court officers who were direct imperial appointees numbered three, those below that rank, two. Five were in-laws or members of Kido's family who were irrelevant to Kido politically. Three were businessmen and three ideologists and/or mass media representatives.[67] Only one was linked to Kido primarily as a member of the Eleven Club in 1941; Harada Kumao held no office that would explain his place in Kido's associations that year other than his membership in Kido's ingroup. Prince Saionji had died in late 1940 and with his death had gone Harada's importance as a secretary in the political system. The

66. These nine include General Abe Nobuyuki, who was a Senior Retainer and "officially" involved with Kido in the selection of new Prime Ministers. Abe's eldest son was married to Kido's eldest daughter.

67. One of the three, Watanabe Yoshio, was a newspaperman who had become a consultant to the government's Information Bureau of the Cabinet Secretariat. He later became secretary to Kido's brother-in-law, Minister of State Kodama Hideo.

number of Kido's meetings with persons in each category and the percentage of meetings according to each category are as follows:

Emperor and imperial family (3 persons)	336	(30.4%)
Government officials of Cabinet rank (9 persons)	283	(25.6%)
Government officials below Cabinet rank (5 persons)	90	(8.1%)
Court officials of direct imperial appointee rank (3 persons)	159	(14.4%)
Court officials below direct imperial appointee rank (2 persons)	52	(4.7%)
In-laws and family members (5 persons)	88	(8.0%)
Businessmen (3 persons)	49	(4.4%)
Ideologists and mass media representatives (3 persons)	38	(3.4%)
Eleven Club members (1 person)	10	(0.9%)
Total	1,105	(100%)

The emperor and imperial family, government officials of Cabinet rank, and court officials of direct imperial appointee rank impressively dominated Kido's associations in 1941, accounting for 70.4 percent of his associations with those he met ten times or more and 40.5 percent of his total associations that year.

Modes of communication between Kido and persons in these various situational categories also varied significantly. Table 18 indicates that "office" was the dominant mode of communication with one of the three imperial family members (the emperor), with eight of the nine government officials of Cabinet rank, with only one of the five government officials below Cabinet rank, with all three court officials of direct imperial appointee rank, with one of the two court officials below that rank, and with only one of the twelve persons in the remaining four categories. Office, therefore, was the overwhelmingly dominant mode of communication with the emperor, government officials of Cabinet rank, and court officials of direct imperial appointee rank—political persons with whom Privy Seal Kido would normally be expected to associate, frequently and officially, in the performance of his political duties.

Table 20 gives a detailed presentation of modes of communication according to situational categories. From these figures it is readily apparent that the higher the person's office in government or court

TABLE 20. KIDO KŌICHI'S MODES OF COMMUNICATION WITH THOSE HE MET TEN TIMES OR MORE IN 1941, BY SITUATIONAL CATEGORY

Mode of Communication	Situational Category							
	Emperor and Imperial Family		Government Officials					
			Cabinet Rank		Below Cabinet Rank		Total	
	(1)		(2)		(3)		(4)	
OFFICIAL	No.	%	No.	%	No.	%	No.	%
Office	273	81.3	166	58.7	26	28.9	192	51.5
Official residence	33	9.8	24	8.5	41	45.6	65	17.4
Official conference	1	0.3	8	2.8	0	0	8	2.1
Imperial lecture	0	0	0	0	0	0	0	0
Kido's reports	1	0.3	10	3.5	0	0	10	2.7
Reports to Kido	0	0	36	12.7	2	2.2	38	10.2
Imperial report	0	0	2	0.7	0	0	2	0.5
Official subtotal	308	91.7%	246	86.9%	69	76.7%	315	84.5%
INFORMAL								
Home	0	0	14	4.9	21	23.3	35	9.4
Informal meetings	0	0	1	0.4	0	0	1	0.3
Meals	8	2.4	15	5.3	0	0	15	4.0
Banquets	8	2.4	3	1.1	0	0	3	0.8
Eleven Club	0	0	2	0.7	0	0	2	0.5
Golf	0	0	0	0	0	0	0	0
Tour	12	3.6	0	0	0	0	0	0
Social and miscellaneous	0	0	2	0.7	0	0	2	0.5
Informal subtotal	28	8.3%	37	13.1%	21	23.3%	58	15.5%
Total	336	100%	283	100%	90	100%	373	100%

TABLE 20.—*Continued*

Situational

Court Officials

OFFICIAL	Direct Imperial Appointee Rank (5) No.	Direct Imperial Appointee Rank (5) %	Below Direct Imperial Appointee Rank (6) No.	Below Direct Imperial Appointee Rank (6) %	Total (7) No.	Total (7) %
Office	129	81.1	18	34.6	147	69.7
Official residence	9	5.7	8	15.4	17	8.1
Official conference	1	0.6	0	0	1	0.5
Imperial lecture	0	0	0	0	0	0
Kido's reports	1	0.6	0	0	1	0.5
Reports to Kido	6	3.8	7	13.5	13	6.2
Imperial report	0	0	0	0	0	0
Official subtotal	146	91.8%	33	63.5%	179	84.8%
INFORMAL						
Home	3	1.9	6	11.5	9	4.3
Informal meetings	1	0.6	2	3.8	3	1.4
Meals	4	2.5	4	7.7	8	3.8
Banquets	1	0.6	1	1.9	2	0.9
Eleven Club	0	0	1	1.9	1	0.5
Golf	1	0.6	0	0	1	0.5
Tour	0	0	0	0	0	0
Social and miscellaneous	3	1.9	5	9.6	8	3.8
Informal subtotal	13	8.2%	19	36.5%	32	15.2%
Total	159	100%	52	100%	211	100%

Category

	In-laws and Family Members (8)		Businessmen (9)		*Others* Ideologists and Mass Media Representatives (10)		Eleven Club (11)		Total (12)	
	No.	%	No.	%	No.	%	No.	%	No.	%
	2	2.3	3	6.1	8	21.1	0	0	13	7.0
	15	17.0	21	42.9	26	68.4	5	50.0	67	36.2
	0	0	0	0	0	0	0	0	0	0
	0	0	0	0	0	0	0	0	0	0
	0	0	0	0	0	0	0	0	0	0
	0	0	0	0	0	0	0	0	0	0
	0	0	0	0	0	0	0	0	0	0
	17	19.3%	24	49.0%	34	89.5%	5	50.0%	80	43.2%
	29	33.0	21	42.9	4	10.5	3	30.0	57	30.8
	0	0	0	0	0	0	0	0	0	0
	11	12.5	2	4.1	0	0	1	10.0	14	7.6
	3	3.4	1	2.0	0	0	0	0	4	2.2
	0	0	0	0	0	0	1	10.0	1	0.5
	1	1.1	1	2.0	0	0	0	0	2	1.1
	0	0	0	0	0	0	0	0	0	0
	27	30.7	0	0	0	0	0	0	27	14.6
	71	80.7%	25	51.0%	4	10.5%	5	50.0%	105	56.8%
	88	100%	49	100%	38	100%	10	100%	185	100%

the more likely it was that his meetings with Kido would occur at an office. For example, 58.7 percent of Kido's meetings with Cabinet ranking government officials (column 2) took place at offices, almost invariably Kido's palace office. On the other hand, Kido's office meetings with government officials below Cabinet rank (column 3) accounted for only 28.9 percent of his meetings with those officials. For persons in the second echelon of government and below, Kido was most accessible at his official residence (45.6 percent) and his home (23.3 percent). The same applies to court officials: 81.1 percent of Kido's meetings with court officials of direct imperial appointee rank (column 5) took place at offices; only 34.6 percent of his meetings with the two court officials below that rank (column 6) occurred at offices. Kido's meetings at his official residence and home with these two (column 6) accounted for 15.4 percent and 11.5 percent respectively. Since both worked with Kido at the palace, their meetings with him at palace offices were naturally higher in percentage than those of government officials of comparable rank. In short, government officers of Cabinet rank had direct access to the throne. They could see Kido at his palace office with great ease. Those of lesser rank and without such access saw him when and as they could—normally before Kido went to his palace office or after he had returned.

Second, Kido did very little socializing with either government or court officials. "Social and miscellaneous" meetings with government officials Kido met ten times or more (column 4) amounted to a mere 0.5 percent of their meetings; with court officials (column 7), only 3.8 percent. Kido had no golfing engagements with government officials and only one with court officials. Even home meetings accounted for but 9.4 percent of his meetings with government officials (column 4) and only 4.3 percent of his meetings with court officials (column 7). There was almost no correlation between Kido's official and informal associations as measured by modes of communication.

By way of contrast, Kido's meetings with persons in the remaining four categories (column 12) were more informal (56.8 percent) than official (43.2 percent). Only 7.0 percent were office meetings, while 14.6 percent were social and miscellaneous. Since official residence accounted for 36.2 percent and home for 30.8 percent of Kido's meetings with these persons (column 12), however, access to his official residence and to his home was relatively open to all his associates—government and court officials, businessmen, ideologists, and mass media representatives. Even Kido's family members and in-laws met Kido at his official residence 17.0 percent of the times they met (column 8).

Why did these associates, frequencies of association, and modes of communication prevail during 1941? The politics of place and station in prewar Japan made the palace the centripetal point around which political leaders gathered to seek imperial sanction for their policies; the emperor was the final ratifier of all national policies. It was the Privy Seal's official duty to render "advice and assistance" in regular attendance on the emperor as Emperor-in-State, as ultimate ratifier of political decisions. If the Privy Seal were fulfilling his negotiator role in politics, therefore, the top government leaders would be in constant communication with Kido and Kido would be in constant communication with the emperor. During 1941 Kido met with the emperor a total of 313 times; 272 were audiences at palace offices or the emperor's villa ("office"), 14 were meetings at the emperor's palace residence ("official residence"), 1 was an "official conference," 8 were "meals," 8 "banquets," and 10 were "tours"—accompanying the emperor to and from a place, such as the imperial villa at Hayama.[68] If Harada Kumao was the cornerstone of secretary Kido's associations in 1932, the emperor was the key person in negotiator Kido's pattern of association in 1941. Fully 16.3 percent of Kido's total meetings in 1941 were with the emperor. It is also evident that Kido's association with the emperor was overwhelmingly an official relationship: 272 (86.9 percent) of Kido's 313 meetings were audiences on matters of na-

68. The fourteen meetings tabulated as "official residence" were social calls on the emperor—New Year's Greetings, Birthday Felicitations, and Imperial Gifts. I have not tabulated Kido's presence at "imperial reports" or "imperial lectures" as meetings between Kido and the emperor: both totaled twelve. Nor have formal banquets at the palace been counted when persons attending were not listed by Kido: there were at least nine such occasions. Kido also took part in eighteen other untabulated palace ceremonies. Association with the emperor was if anything greater in 1941 than shown in table 18.

tional policy and personnel. The official description of the Privy Seal's office and Kido's pattern of association with the emperor were therefore in close agreement during 1941.

Kido records more meticulously the time of each audience than the content or subject of his discussion with the emperor. Most of his audiences, which lasted from approximately ten minutes to one hour and fifteen minutes, were merely recorded as "audienced from such and such a time to such and such a time." Occasionally the subject was noted. Those audiences noted in detail, however, illustrate the nature of the emperor's ratifier role and reveal the communication routes between the emperor and the government. Kido's audiences also reveal how important the Privy Seal was as the emperor's confidant on all policy matters, military as well as civil—if the two can be distinguished during 1941.

In audience between 2:45 and 3:15 on January 23, for example, the emperor told Kido that he had delayed replying to both Chiefs of Staff until he had spoken with the Foreign Minister about plans for Southeast Asia. Kido replied that he would speak with the Foreign Minister. The Chief Aide-de-Camp came to Kido's office to discuss the matter at 3:20. At 5:00 Kido talked with Foreign Minister Matsuoka, before Matsuoka audienced. Kido then audienced again from 6:30 to 6:40. The emperor told Kido that both Chiefs of Staff would be summoned the following morning and ordered to reach agreement with the government before establishing what would amount to an ultimatum for Thailand. After Kido returned home he informed the Chief Aide of the emperor's desires.[69] The emperor, in consultation with the Privy Seal, had decided on a course of action that would unite government and military, but without dictating the content of the policy concerned.

On November 30 the emperor told Kido that, according to what Prince Takamatsu had reported to him that morning, the Navy appeared to have its hands full and to want to avoid war with the United States. When he asked Kido what he thought about the situation, Kido replied that the emperor must be fully convinced before assenting to such a momentous decision as war with the United

69. Kido Kōichi, 2:851.

States. The emperor should summon the Navy Minister and the Chief of the Navy General Staff immediately, as well as speak with the Prime Minister. After the Prime Minister audienced at 3:30 p.m., the Navy Minister and the Chief of the Navy General Staff were duly summoned. At 6:35 p.m. Kido audienced once again: the emperor told him that both Navy leaders had appeared fully confident in their replies to his questions. Kido was consequently ordered to tell the Prime Minister to proceed as planned, which he did immediately.[70] Kido therefore advised the emperor on courses of action to bring unity to national policy. Rather than dictating a policy or program, however, both the emperor and his Privy Seal sought assurance that the appropriate government and military leaders were fully confident and united in *their* national policy.

The emperor's role was to keep the consensus-making process honest. By questioning leaders in audience and by exerting pressure via his palace advisers he assured himself that any policy he ratified had been thoroughly discussed and represented a genuine consensus among the policy makers. But he was kept from active and direct participation in the consensus-making process by formalities and precedents governing his relations with government leaders, individually and collectively. For example, it was not the practice for military and government leaders to appear before the emperor until policies had been carefully worked out and agreed to among them. Kido notes that a "new precedent" was set when the Chief of the Navy General Staff, the Chief of the Army General Staff, and Prime Minister Konoe audienced together on February 1. Previously, Kido continues, important decisions of the Liaison Conference (the top government-military policy council at that time) were reported in Imperial Conference, and less important ones were reported separately by members of the government or the military.[71] Prior to Prime Minister Konoe's unusual February 1 audience, the only group presentation to the throne was the rather inflexible Imperial Conference, which made no provision for free exchanges of opinion: an Imperial Conference was the final formality in ratifying a top-level consensus on crucial national policies. On August 11, for example,

70. Ibid., p. 928.
71. Ibid., p. 853.

the emperor informed Kido that "however formal previous Imperial Conferences had been," he desired to question the participants of the next Imperial Conference (September 6) until he was sufficiently satisfied that a united policy had been achieved.[72] Kido, however, would not allow the emperor such a participant role.[73] The emperor could thus bring pressure to bear only in individual audience and mediate between the military and government only via the Privy Seal and other palace leaders, such as the Chief Aide-de-Camp.

Since the Privy Seal assisted the emperor in this critical, if indirect, unifying function, it is not surprising that the emperor kept Kido informed on military policies and plans. Frequently the emperor confided what had been told him in audience by the Chiefs of Staff as well as by the military Ministers of State and exchanged views with Kido on military plans and activities. On January 18, for example, the emperor told Kido in detail what Army Chief of Staff Sugiyama had told him about the Army's plans to bring the "China Incident" under control. Again, on January 20, the emperor talked about the military's "long-term guideline for military operations against China," this time as reported by the Army Minister. The emperor's sentiments on military trends were also shared with Kido. On March 13 the emperor expressed to Kido his worries about the "subjective tendencies of the Army." When the emperor objected to the Prime Minister's plans to set an age limit on Supreme War Councillors he asked Kido about transmitting his objections to the Army Minister via the Chief Aide; Kido approved.[74]

Although Kido advised the emperor on courses of action and received information from the emperor with regard to military activities and plans, he was never the emperor's direct link with the High Command. Privy Seal Kido had only five meetings with the two Chiefs of Staff in 1941. Those five meetings took place at the palace and at the initiative of the Chiefs of Staff. The only significant contact between Kido and extra-palace military leaders was with the Army and Navy Ministers. During 1941 Kido met the Army Minister twenty times, the Navy Minister seven. Because the Army

72. Ibid., p. 901.
73. Ibid., p. 905.
74. Ibid., pp. 849, 850, 862, 919.

and Navy Ministers were members of the Cabinet—and legally concerned with military administration as opposed to military operations—they were involved in the government as well as the military side of Japanese politics. Consequently, Kido had access to them and they to him by virtue of their offficial roles. The High Command audienced directly with the emperor, almost never stopping to talk with the Privy Seal. When the Army or Navy Minister audienced, however, he would frequently speak with Kido. With the exception of the Prime Minister and the Foreign Minister, Kido's contact with the Army and Navy Ministers was as frequent as that with other Cabinet ministers, or more so.

The emperor's direct liaison with the High Command was his Chief Aide-de-Camp, Hasunuma Shigeru. It was the Chief Aide's liaison on behalf of the emperor that brought him and Privy Seal Kido together. As one of the palace's four leading officials, the Chief Aide performed for the military the same role that the Privy Seal performed for the government. Since the emperor capped the military and the government, both the Chief Aide and the Privy Seal were key offices in the institutional arrangement for the final reconciliation and ratification of military-government demands. And since the emperor was not a free participant in the negotiating process, coordination fell largely to the Chief Aide and the Privy Seal.

Only when Kido became Privy Seal, therefore, did he have significant communication with the Chief Aide. As table 18 indicates, the Chief Aide was the third person most frequently met by Kido during 1941 and the most frequently met court official. Kido met the Chief Aide eighty-two times that year. In 1932, however, Kido met with the Chief Aide but twice; in 1936, only eight times.

Privy Seal Kido's relation with the Chief Aide was first one of information sharing and second one of relay. The Chief Aide was Kido's most important military source of information on Army policies and reports to the throne by the High Command. On January 25, for example, the Chief Aide came to Kido's office to inform him of what the Chief of Staff had reported to the throne concerning the Indochina question. On February 1 the Chief Aide once again came to Kido's office, this time to report in detail on the "outline of policy measures for Indochina and Thailand" should Thai-

land accept Japanese intervention. The Chief Aide also passed on to
Kido reports from other Aides-de-Camp as well as from military at-
tachés stationed abroad. On June 11 Kido received via the Chief
Aide a report on Russo-German relations prepared by a military at-
taché in the Soviet Union. The Chief Aide also functioned as a
barometer of military opinion and future plans. He came to Kido's
office on June 3 to tell him that it might soon be necessary to hold a
Liaison Conference "in order to clarify attitudes on the policy of
pushing south."[75] Through the Chief Aide, therefore, Kido was kept
regularly informed on military plans, policies, and prospects. Since
89 percent of Kido's meetings with the Chief Aide took place at
palace offices (table 18), information sharing between them was
perceived by both to be an official duty.

   Although Kido maintained a mutual consultation relationship
with the Chief Aide, Kido was the main beneficiary of the information sharing aspect of their association. Almost invariably the
Chief Aide came to Kido's office, indicating further that both
perceived the Privy Seal to be entitled to military information affecting national policies. Kido did discuss the emperor's thoughts on
the military and on military policies, however. When the emperor
told Kido in March about the "subjective tendencies of the Army"
Kido promptly relayed this to the Chief Aide. Again, after
audiencing on March 4 Kido told the Chief Aide what the emperor
thought of General Hata Shunroku's plans for the South Seas area.[76]
Kido does not state that he reported information received from the
Chief Aide to the emperor. Evidently, he used such information as a
basis for advising the emperor on large national issues involving both
the military and the government.

   Finally, Kido was occasionally used by the emperor to transmit
his wishes to the High Command via the Chief Aide. As already
noted, Kido transmitted the emperor's wishes to the Chief Aide after
Kido had audienced late on January 23. The emperor also had the
Chief Aide keep in touch with the Privy Seal on military reports. On
July 30 the Chief Aide came to see Kido, on orders from the emperor, to talk about that evening's report by the Chief of the Navy

   75. Ibid., pp. 852, 853, 881, 878–79.
   76. Ibid., pp. 862, 860.

General Staff.[77] Given the information sharing, mutual discussion, and liaison among the emperor, Privy Seal, and Chief Aide, the palace appears to have been a major bridge between top military and government leaders. The emperor was the keystone in the arch. On either side of him were the Privy Seal and Chief Aide, spans to the government and the military respectively. These two negotiatiors kept each other constantly informed of policies advocated and actions taken by leaders of the institutions of imperial prerogative, most of whom had direct access to the throne: Cabinet members on one side and the High Command on the other.

If Privy Seal Kido's relation to the military side of Japanese politics was primarily intra-palace and indirect, his relation to the civil side was also intra-palace but direct and considerably more intense. Including the Army and Navy Ministers, Kido met with Cabinet ministers 304 times. His associations with Cabinet ministers also surpassed his meetings with the other three palace officials of direct imperial appointee rank, 304 to 159. From these statistics it is clear that the Privy Seal's official duties on behalf of the emperor were primarily channeled toward the government.

After the emperor, Kido was most frequently in communication with Prince Konoe Fumimaro. Prime Minister until October 18, Konoe met with Kido a total of ninety-three times in 1941. While Konoe was Prime Minister he met with Kido eighty-four times; after his resignation the two met only nine times. As Prime Minister, Konoe saw Kido an average of 8.8 times a month; after he resigned, he saw him only 3.6 times a month during the remainder of 1941. As Army Minister, Tōjō Hideki met Kido twenty times from January 1 to October 18, or 1.9 times a month. After he became Prime Minister, however, Tōjō met Kido twenty-four times, or 9.6 times a month, during the remainder of 1941. Kido thus met with the Prime Minister 108 times during 1941, making the Prime Minister the most important political person, after the emperor, to Kido's role as Privy Seal. The dominant mode of communication with both Konoe and Tōjō throughout 1941, moreover, was office: 55.9 percent of Kido's meetings with Konoe and 86.4 percent of his

---

77. Ibid., p. 895.

meetings with Tōjō were held in offices (table 18), almost always Kido's palace office. Association between the Privy Seal and the Prime Minister was therefore an official relation dependent on offices held, not the persons as persons. The key palace adviser was constantly in touch with the key government leader.

The second most frequently contacted member of the government in 1941 was the Foreign Minister, seventy-eight meetings.[78] Like Kido's mode of communication with the Prime Minister, his association with the Foreign Minister was overwhelmingly official. Kido met the Foreign Minister at the Privy Seal's office or at the palace fifty-three times (67.9 percent) and received seventeen (21.8 percent) reports from him. Kido reported only twice to the Foreign Minister, indicating that the Privy Seal was officially entitled to receive government information. During 1941 the Prime Minister also reported more often to Kido than the reverse, sixteen reports to eight. The common practice for both the Prime Minister and the Foreign Minister was to visit Kido at the palace before or after their audiences with the emperor. It was a rare occasion for Kido to visit a government official; government officials, including the Prime Minister, came to the Privy Seal—not the reverse.

Kido's frequency of communication with the Foreign Minister indicates the emperor's—and palace leadership's—abiding concern with problems of foreign policy, not unnatural in the year that Japan began the greatest war in her history. The following example illustrates both the emperor's concern and the Privy Seal's role as the emperor's direct liaison with the government. On Saturday, June 21, Kido had a lengthy dinner meeting with Prime Minister Konoe and Home Minister Hiranuma about the question of "Cabinet responsibility" should war break out between the Soviet Union and Germany: Kido strongly urged Konoe not to resign because there was no issue of Cabinet responsibility involved on this occasion.[79]

78. There were three Foreign Ministers in 1941: Matsuoka Yōsuke (to July 18), Toyoda Teijirō (July 18–October 18), and Tōgō Shigenori (October 18 on). Kido met these three a total of eighty-seven times in 1941; seventy-eight of these meetings occurred with the three as Foreign Ministers.

79. When the issue of "Cabinet responsibility" arose the portent was ominous—a Cabinet resignation was impending. In this instance a war between Germany and the USSR would bring up Japan's obligations under the Tripartite Pact. Since Japan also had, as of April 13, 1941, a neutrality pact with the USSR, Konoe felt he had to take the responsibility for such an impasse—that is, to resign (Kido Kōichi, 2:883; Yanaga, p. 592).

The following day at 2 p.m. General Suzuki Teiichi, President of the Cabinet Planning Board, telephoned Kido to inform him that war had indeed broken out. Then, at shortly after 4 p.m., Foreign Minister Matsuoka called Kido for an audience with the emperor to report on the outbreak of the Russo-German war. Kido had Chamberlain Tokugawa check with the emperor for a convenient time and Matsuoka's audience was arranged for 5:30 p.m. Kido then requested an audience for himself, *before* Foreign Minister Matsuoka audienced, to report on his talk with Konoe and Hiranuma the previous evening.[80]

Kido gives the gist of his report to the emperor as follows:

It appears that the views of the Foreign Minister are not entirely at one with those of the Prime Minister regarding the attitude and policy our country should take in the event of war between Germany and the Soviet Union. And the disposition our country makes on this issue will importantly affect the course of the nation's destiny. Therefore, when the Foreign Minister audiences today I would hope that you would in effect tell him, regardless of what interpretations on this policy he might give you, that he should discuss the matter thoroughly with the Prime Minister, given the extreme gravity of this event, asking him if he had completed his discussions with the Prime Minister on this. I would ask that you indicate your inner thoughts on the primacy of the Prime Minister, if you will forgive my presumption.[81]

Matsuoka then audienced, after which the emperor summoned Kido. The emperor was extremely anxious about Japan's strength and about the unity of the High Command and the government, given that Matsuoka's policy would result in simultaneous military advances in both the south (Indochina) and the north (Soviet Union). Kido therefore telephoned Konoe and Hiranuma. Having spoken with Hiranuma, Kido finally reached Konoe at 9 p.m. and told him about Matsuoka's audience. At 12:30 a.m. Konoe called Kido back to report that he had spoken with Matsuoka and that what Matsuoka had said in audience was not a plan for immediate action but a long-range estimate of alternatives. Kido later reported this to the emperor. The Chief Aide came to Kido's office shortly after Kido

80. Kido Kōichi, 2 : 883–84.
81. Ibid., p. 884.

had audienced to talk about the outbreak of the Russo-German war and its implications.[82]

Matsuoka's differences with the Prime Minister over foreign policy cost him the Foreign Minister's portfolio and nearly brought down the Cabinet in July. In June he disagreed with the Prime Minister on Japan's obligations to assist Germany; in July he argued a get-tough policy toward the United States, a stance at great variance with the Prime Minister's emphasis on negotiation.[83] The above example does, however, illustrate the Privy Seal's advisory function, both to the throne and to the Prime Minister. In this instance, Privy Seal Kido advised the emperor to uphold the Prime Minister's position as *primus inter pares* in the Cabinet. Whereas Kido records no intervention on behalf of or against the High Command, he felt perfectly free to act as the Prime Minister's spokesman to stifle disunity *within the government.*

The Privy Seal also advised the Prime Minister on the problem of Cabinet responsibility—the issue or issues involving resignation—as well as general policies. Although the Prime Minister had direct access to the throne, he consulted the Privy Seal before reporting such drastic action as a Cabinet resignation. In the above instance Kido claimed credit for forestalling a Cabinet resignation on the outbreak of the Russo-German war. As Privy Seal Kido's close friend since childhood, Prime Minister Konoe quite possibly relied on Kido as a consultant more readily than he would have another Privy Seal. For whatever reason, Konoe frequently unburdened himself to Kido. After Konoe had audienced on October 9, for example, he talked at length with Kido about the prospects for an agreement with the United States. Kido spelled out in great detail why the September 6 Imperial Conference decision setting an October deadline on negotiations with the United States could and should be reexamined.[84] Kido's frequency of communication with Konoe's successor as Prime Minister, General Tōjō Hideki, however, indicates that such a consultative relationship was built into the office of Privy Seal. The Privy Seal was one of the key consultants for the Prime Minister, as

82. Ibid.
83. Ibid., pp. 890–92.
84. Ibid., p. 912.

well as a key adviser to the emperor, judging from frequency of communication and official behavior.

Whereas Kido did not report a single instance of his relaying imperial summons to members of the High Command in 1941, he did perform such a liaison function with government leaders. For example, on January 22 Kido telephoned Foreign Minister Matsuoka and told him to report to the emperor immediately should it be decided to place a time limit for Indochina to respond to Japan's demands. On February 28 Kido called Matsuoka after the emperor had questioned him on foreign policy toward Thailand and Indochina. Kido also relayed between emperor and Prime Minister. On April 21 and June 4 Kido relayed information from the Prime Minister to the emperor. After the emperor had checked with the Navy Minister and the Chief of the Navy General Staff on November 30 he ordered Kido to tell the Prime Minister to proceed according to plan.[85]

Kido's direct relations with members of the government allowed him to give the throne authoritative advice on matters initiated and developed by the government. On February 18, as well as the June 22 instance cited above, the Privy Seal cautioned the emperor on a substantive policy issue. When Kido audienced on February 18 he suggested that the emperor have the government examine carefully the impact Foreign Minister Matsuoka's trip to Europe would have on Japan's relations with England and the United States.[86] The Privy Seal and the emperor were deeply involved in evaluating policy trends and alternatives to war. On November 19 Kido spelled out the possible alternatives to war and agreed with the emperor that the Senior Retainers should be consulted if a decision for war appeared likely.[87]

As in the case of military reports to the throne, the emperor kept his Privy Seal informed and consulted with him about the reports of ranking government officials. On February 5, for example, the emperor discussed Ambassador Honda's report to the throne.[88] It

85. Ibid., pp. 851, 858, 870, 879, 928.
86. Ibid., p. 857.
87. Ibid., pp. 923–24.
88. Ibid., p. 854. Honda Kumatarō was ambassador to the Republic of China from 1940 to 1942.

should be noted that Kido was almost never present at the audiences of either High Command or government personnel. Kido attended only seven reports to the throne: six by ambassadors and the Foreign Minister and one by the Prime Minister. Kido did not nor was he apparently entitled to attend reports to the throne by the military; he was seldom present when government officials reported.

Kido operated between the emperor and the government and the military, directly or indirectly, on an almost exclusively verbal basis—and quite frequently on hearsay. Very few documents passed through Kido's hands. The verbal transactions among emperor, Prime Minister, Chief Aide, and others were recorded privately in Kido's diary and possibly in diaries kept by other members of the network. The only formal written record Kido mentions is that of the Senior Retainers' conference on October 17, when Kido's recommendation that Tōjō succeed Konoe as Prime Minister was agreed to.[89] If such verbal transactions allowed flexibility, they also permitted each individual in the communication network to interpret momentous policy issues as he saw fit, with no appeal to the written record. Such a practice could, and did, give rise to many "misunderstandings" among government and military leaders, as we have seen in previous episodes involving palace leaders (see above, pp. 145–50, 154–55).

From Kido's pattern of associations as Privy Seal in 1941 it is abundantly clear that the palace was extremely important as a negotiating institution in the formation of prewar national policies. Privy Seal Kido was the emperor's direct adviser on government affairs and indirect adviser on military affairs, as the emperor attempted to bridge the gap between government and military demands, to assure some semblance of unity in government and military policies. Palace activity in this respect was intense, with Kido in almost daily contact with the emperor Saturdays and Sundays as well as weekdays, and regardless of the hour of day—especially during such crises as the outbreak of war between Germany and the Soviet Union, Konoe's resignation, and the decision for war against the United States.

89. Ibid., p. 919.

Given the high degree of palace activity in politics, it is not surprising that leading palace officials were in frequent contact with Kido. The key court officer for Privy Seal Kido, as we have seen, was the Chief Aide-de-Camp. As discussed in detail above, the only sustained "official" way for Kido to communicate with the High Command and to obtain information about the "trends of the times" within the military components of imperial prerogative was indirectly via the Chief Aide. Including the Chief Aide, five of the thirty-four persons Kido met ten times or more in 1941 were high court officials. These five accounted for 19.1 percent of Kido's meetings with those in the ten or more frequency group. Although neither the Grand Chamberlain nor the Household Minister was deeply involved in the negotiation process, they met Kido thirty-two and forty-five times respectively during 1941. Both were kept informed and were consulted by Kido on general policy trends. The fact that Privy Seal Kido had frequent meetings with the Grand Chamberlain, in marked contrast to 1932 and 1936, suggests that the Grand Chamberlain was of some significance in palace politics. On February 28, for example, Kido visited the Grand Chamberlain's office to speak with him about the emperor's "mental state" and other matters. On October 4 the Grand Chamberlain came to Kido's office to talk about Japan's relations with the United States. Occasionally Kido discussed political matters with the Imperial Household Minister as well. On November 4, for example, the Household Minister came to Kido's office to discuss prospects for the success of Japan's policy toward the United States.[90]

The last two court officers Kido met ten times or more during 1941 were his Chief Secretary, Matsudaira Yasumasa, and one of the two Deputy Grand Chamberlains, Kanroji Osanaga. The frequency and mode of communication between Privy Seal Kido and his Chief Secretary require no elaboration, given our discussion of Kido's role as Chief Secretary in 1932 and 1936. Kanroji, a life-long member of the Imperial Household's inner side, apparently took it upon himself to keep in touch with the Privy Seal. Since the Grand Chamberlain had been a career Navy officer it is quite possible that

90. Ibid., pp. 859, 911, 921.

Kanroji felt himself best qualified to look after matters affecting the Emperor-in-Chambers.

Kido's associations with his palace colleagues suggest that all four of the top palace officers were mutually responsible for coordinating the imperial institution's role in the prewar Japanese polity. The Privy Seal was the emperor's chief negotiator with the government, the Chief Aide his chief negotiator with the military—particularly the military's operational command. Although the Privy Seal was the more important of the two, given his duty of advising the throne on Cabinet formations, both he and the Chief Aide advised the emperor on how best to coordinate state policies. The frequency of communication between the two, the nature of that communication, the frequency and nature of Kido's association with Cabinet ministers, and Kido's behavior toward the emperor support the conclusion that the palace was in fact fulfilling its central role in the process of top-level policy negotiation and imperial ratification in prewar Japanese politics. The prominence of the Chief Aide in Kido's 1941 network of association also suggests that the Privy Seal and the Chief Aide were the key palace officers for managing the Emperor-in-State. The Household Minister and the Grand Chamberlain, on the other hand, were the two key palace officers for managing the Emperor-in-Court. Most of Privy Seal Kido's meetings with the Household Minister and Grand Chamberlain were concerned with court administration, imperial family matters, palace personnel, imperial outings, banquets, and arrangements for audiences. The two palace officers responsible for the Emperor-in-Court coordinated their actions with the two palace officers primarily responsible for the Emperor-in-State. Given the ambiguous distinction between the Emperor-in-Court and the Emperor-in-State that emerged in actual practice and the role flexibility of palace offices, all four palace leaders were involved, in varying degrees of intensity, with the central process of political negotiation that led to imperial ratification.

KIDO KŌICHI AS AN "OFFICIAL" IN PREWAR
JAPANESE POLITICS

Kido's behavior in three different offices within one institution of imperial prerogative, the Imperial Household Ministry, has demonstrated three situational roles within the prewar Japanese political system. Because all three roles were the result of Kido's offices within a bureaucratic structure, they may be subsumed under the "Official" category of political personality developed by Maruyama Masao. Maruyama describes three types of political personality that "serve to formulate not only the fascist period but the entire political world of Imperial Japan": "the Portable Shrine, the Official, and the Outlaw (or *rōnin*)."[91]

> The Shrine represents authority; the Official, power; the Outlaw, violence. From the point of view of their position in the national hierarchy and of their legal power, the Shrine ranks highest and the Outlaw lowest. The system, however, is so constituted that movement starts from the Outlaw and gradually works upwards. The Shrine is often a mere robot who affects other people by 'doing nothing' (*wu wei*).
>
> The force that 'holds aloft' the Shrine and that wields the real power is the Official (civilian or military). His rule over the powerless people is based on the legitimacy that descends from the Shrine. He in his turn is being prodded from behind by the Outlaw.[92]

These three personality types are to be found not only in the nation at large but also within the specific organizations that constitute the national polity:

> If we examine the internal structure of the established political parties, for example, we find that the president of the party is the Shrine, the chairman and the secretary-general hold actual power as Officials, and the pressure groups contain the Outlaws. In the total political structure

91. Maruyama Masao, *Thought and Behaviour*, pp. 130, 128.
92. Ibid., pp. 128–29.

members of the rightist organizations occupy the position of Outlaws; but within each organization we again find the tripartite hierarchy, . . .[93]

Each of Maruyama's three personality types is based on the behavior of politically active persons within the national polity and politically relevant organizations. Excluded are the "powerless people" at the base of society who did what they were told by the political system but were otherwise politically inert.

In table 21 I have attempted to summarize the positions, personalities and kinds of influence that pertain to each of Maruyama's political types. Ultimately, the Official was the most powerful because he was in a legal position to manipulate the Shrine in the national polity, his specific political organization, or both. The Outlaw, the political activist at the base of society or any given political organization who is "content if he can storm about irresponsibly at the bottom of the hierarchy, uttering great yells of delight and dumbfounding the rest of the community,"[94] could only influence political outcomes by pressuring the Official, the sole political type able to manipulate the Shrine and thereby produce authoritative decisions.

TABLE 21.   MARUYAMA'S TYPOLOGY OF POLITICAL PERSONALITY

	Outlaw	*Official*	*Shrine*
Behavior	VIOLENT in word and deed; sensationalist, adventurist, and irresponsible	CIRCUMSPECT in word and deed; evades responsibility, submits to actions taken by others as *faits accomplis*	ROBOT in word and deed; sanctions whatever is submitted by Officials
Position (National Polity)	Bottom	Middle or upper	Top
Position (Organization)	Activist member	Officer	President
Personality	Abnormal	Normal	Normal
Nature of Influence	Pressure	Power	Authority

SOURCE: Maruyama Masao, *Thought and Behaviour*, pp. 84–134.

93. Ibid., p. 130.
94. Ibid., p. 129.

Maruyama's typology is widely used to explain the alleged derangement in Japanese government during the decade prior to Pearl Harbor. There are, however, serious logical and empirical difficulties with his typology—difficulties characteristic of the macrosocietal analyses offered by many Japanese scholars to explain political behavior in this period. Maruyama's typology, moreover, is so highly generalized that it obscures the political roles and behavior that made the Japanese government effective. By examining the political behavior of Kido Kōichi, his associates, and other political actors in relation to Maruyama's typology we may perhaps show what those roles and patterns of behavior were.

The first problem is to correlate position (office, rank, status) and personality—the age-old problem of the degree to which the office determines the man or vice versa. Maruyama argues strongly for a positional explanation of behavior. A political actor could not be at the base of society and be a Shrine or Official in the national polity, nor could he be an Outlaw at the top of the national polity. Similarly, a lowly member of a political organization could not be a Shrine or Official within that organization, nor could its president be an Outlaw in the organization. Not only does position correlate with behavior, but a person will and must change his behavior when he changes position. "If an Outlaw gets ahead in the world, he may develop into a petty bureaucrat and become more 'moderate'; if he advances still further, he may even in the end find himself being carried on people's shoulders as a Shrine. . . : unless the Outlaw can transform himself so that he becomes like an Official or a Shrine, he has no hope of attaining high rank."[95]

However,

> The same man may behave as an Outlaw to those above him, but regard those below with the eyes of an Official. Another man may be held aloft as a Shrine by the lower elements, while he serves those above as a loyal, circumspect Official.[96]

If this is the case, position does not explain behavior or typologize political personality in any meaningful sense. One Official might

95. Ibid.
96. Ibid.

manipulate his superior as a Shrine, another Official of exactly the same rank and position might serve "those above as a loyal, circumspect Official," while yet another Official of the same rank and position "may behave as an Outlaw to those above him." Under such circumstances, three exactly equal positions produced three different types of behavior toward the same persons. These same three Officials might also be Officials or Shrines toward the same persons below them. It might appear that Maruyama's typology at least rules out Outlaw behavior by a superior toward an inferior or Shrine behavior by an inferior toward a superior. But he also argues that "these three types do not, of course, represent fixed categories. Frequently two or *three* of them will be blended in a single individual."[97] If this is so the behavior and personality of a political actor cannot be explained or typed by reference to any position he might hold.

The difficulties in Maruyama's positional explanation of political behavior are further illustrated by the following hypothetical case, which approximates the situation and behavior of the young officer insurgents involved in the February 26 Incident of 1936. Army Lieutenant A was an Official toward his troops and a circumspect Official toward his superior, Major B. He was a dedicated young officer who had no dealings with Outlaw societies or any other political organizations outside the Army; he obeyed orders to the letter and without question. Army Lieutenant C, of the same rank and position, was an Outlaw toward his superior, the same Major B. Like Lieutenant A, Lieutenant C was an Official toward his men. Unlike Lieutenant A, however, Lieutenant C was an Official in Outlaw society Y and an Outlaw in Outlaw society Z. The behavior of Lieutenant A was consistently Official to both inferiors and superiors; the behavior of Lieutenant C was a blend of types but, given his constant involvement in rightist activities and assassination plots, almost completely Outlaw in the national polity. Yet both Lieutenant A and Lieutenant C were of precisely the same "position" in the national hierarchy of Officials. Suppose, then, that Major B ordered Lieutenant A to station troops around the Prime

97. Ibid., my emphasis.

Minister's residence and to distribute rightist propaganda proclaiming the "restoration of the emperor to direct imperial rule." Major B, an Outlaw Official in collusion with (or "prodded from behind" by?) Outlaw Official Lieutenant C, then planned to have Lieutenant C and other collaborators assassinate the Prime Minister and other "evil advisers close to the throne." Lieutenant A dutifully stationed his troops and passed around handbills. Lieutenant C and his friends "dutifully" assassinated the Prime Minister. Lieutenant A's behavior became Outlaw *because* he was an obedient Official: he was an Outlaw in spite of himself.

More important is the fact that Major B and Lieutenant C were effective Outlaws precisely because they were Officials. They had officers and men to command as well as weapons available for use in carrying out their Outlaw projects. An official could not only be an Outlaw in the national polity but also be, in fact, a "better" Outlaw because he was an Official. This was evidently true of some Officials much higher than our hypothetical Major B and Lieutenants A and C. Maruyama points out, for example, that as the secretary-general of the Seiyūkai, Mori Kaku's "role in the party was that of supreme Official; but as far as political function and behaviour were concerned he was closer to an Outlaw."[98] Having been secretary-general of one of Japan's greatest political parties from 1929 to 1931, Mori then served as Chief Cabinet Secretary from 1931 to 1932, certainly a high Official position in Maruyama's national hierarchy. It is reasonable to surmise that only his death in 1932 prevented Mori from becoming a higher Official—and quite possibly even more of an Outlaw.

It is therefore conceivable that when an Outlaw got ahead in the world and attained increasingly higher Official positions he became more Outlaw, not "more 'moderate.'" Matsuoka Yōsuke, Foreign Minister from July 1940 to July 1941, is a revealing example. Maruyama notes that Matsuoka was one of the "borderline cases" among "some of the genuine psychopaths" who appeared in the Tokyo war crimes trials after World War II.[99] Although Matsuoka

98. Ibid., p. 130.
99. Ibid., p. 91. At the war's end Matsuoka became completely demented and died before his trial was completed.

served briefly in the lower house of the Imperial Diet, he was a career diplomat who had received his secondary and college education in the United States. In career and position he should have epitomized the Official ideal. On the contrary, however, Matsuoka epitomized Outlaw mentality and behavior. Matsuoka's rashness, profuse and contradictory pronouncements, and irresponsible policy proposals left his Official colleagues astonished, even those in the military. At a Liaison Conference meeting in May 1941, for example, Matsuoka spoke of the possibilities of going to war with Germany, Great Britain, the United States, and the Soviet Union— at the same time or one after the other—and of the necessity in this regard to "make up our minds now" on Japan's policy in Southeast Asia. "With a bluntness unusual in Japan even in jest, Navy Minister Oikawa turned to his colleagues and observed, 'The foreign minister is crazy, isn't he?' "[100] Matsuoka's Outlaw personality found its fullest expression when he reached one of the highest positions in the national hierarchy, that of Foreign Minister.

The cases of both Mori and Matsuoka suggest that rather than progressing in timidity and circumspection as they rose in Official positions, Outlaws gained increasing opportunity to give vent to their Outlaw personalities and to have greater Outlaw impact on political outcomes. Mori and Matsuoka did not evolve from Outlaws to petty Officials and then Shrines in the national polity, but from Outlaws to bigger Outlaws as they ascended the ladders of Official success. In the case of Mastuoka it is even conceivable that he evolved from a discreet lower ranking Official in the Foreign Ministry into an Outlaw Foreign Minister.

A second difficulty with Maruyama's typology is the relation between positions in one or more concrete political organizations and national polity position. I have attempted to diagram Maruyama's national polity and three of its component organizations in figure 2. The national polity was a hierarchy of political types, with Shrines at the top and Outlaws at the bottom. But the national polity was

---

100. Butow, *Tojo*, p. 208. We have seen that Matsuoka's willful recklessness in 1941 was of constant concern not only to the Prime Minister but also to Privy Seal Kido and the emperor. Butow's study of Tōjō is punctuated with examples of Matsuoka's Outlaw behavior in high Official places, including his whirlwind replacement of "weak-kneed" Foreign Ministry diplomats.

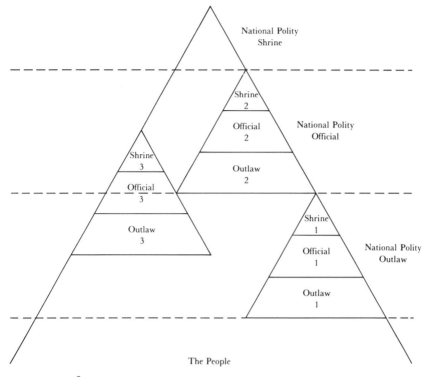

FIGURE 2. POSITIONAL ARRANGEMENT OF SHRINES, OFFICIALS, AND OUTLAWS IN MARUYAMA'S TYPOLOGY

also made up of concrete organizational hierarchies—rightist societies, political parties, the bureaucratic components of imperial prerogative. What, then, is the relation between one's intraorganizational position and his national polity position? Maruyama is clear that all members of a rightist society were Outlaws in the national polity, regardless of whether they were Shrines or Officials within the society. As figure 2 illustrates, a rightist society might be depicted as a pyramid composed of Shrine 1, Official 1, and Outlaw 1 in the Outlaw category of the national polity. It was not the position or behavior of an individual within the society that positioned him in the national polity, but the behavior of his *organization*.

On the other hand, a bureaucratic component of imperial prerogative might be depicted as a pyramid in the national polity composed of Shrine 2, Official 2, and Outlaw 2. Although Maruyama does not position bureaucracies in the national polity, all members of a government bureaucracy must necessarily fall in the Official category if legal-hierarchical "power" in the national polity has any meaning. But because a given Official might be more Outlaw than Official in his national polity behavior, regardless of his bureaucratic position, there is once again no meaningful correlation between intraorganizational position and national polity position. An Official might be a Shrine, Official, or Outlaw in his bureaucratic organization and an Outlaw, Official, or even Shrine in his national polity behavior. In contrast to Outlaw organizations, moreover, it was not the behavior of the organization that typed or explained the behavior of persons belonging to an Official organization but the behavior of those persons despite the position of their organization in the national polity and regardless of their intraorganizational positions. The Army's behavior in China; the rationalization of that behavior by many senior officers; the Outlaw activities of radical young officers in the assassinations and assassination plots that culminated in the February 26 Incident; and the rationalization of some or most of such activities by certain senior officers, as in the case of Colonel Imamura's defense of the October plotters (see chapter 3), all suggest, that the behavior of Army officers at certain times and in certain situations made that Official organization in national polity position an Outlaw organization in national polity behavior.

The problems posed by an Official organization are somewhat similar to those that apply to the "established" political parties. Maruyama does not position political parties in the national polity, although he asserts that any given political party was composed of his tripartite hierarchy. Because its leaders were frequently government officials, a political party could not be placed exclusively at the bottom of Japanese society and therefore was not completely Outlaw in position. Neither was it a formal institution of government and therefore completely Official in position. Depending on the behavior of its members at any given time, a political party might be positioned in various places in the national political hierarchy. A political party might be more Outlaw in behavior when out of power, more Official or even Shrine when in power. For example, members of a party out of power did on occasion engage in violence, inflammatory propaganda and irresponsible attacks against Cabinets formed by another political party, by bureaucrats, or by a combination of both. The pyramid in figure 2 composed of Shrine 3, Official 3, and Outlaw 3 is an attempt to position a party of mixed behavior: one that was out of power, whose president had at least once been a high Official in the government, some of whose officers had at one time served as government Officials, and whose "pressure group" members were Outlaws both within the party and within the national polity. But once again, the organizational positions of party members within the party do not correlate with national polity positions in any consistent manner. And the behavior of party members in the national polity varied sometimes with the political situation of the party as an organization, sometimes with the "personality" composition of the party regardless of the party's political situation.

Organizational membership poses further problems for national polity position and behavior. A political actor in prewar Japan was not generally a member of only one political organization but held multiple memberships and positions. Baron Hiranuma Kiichirō provides an example. A career official in the Justice Ministry, he became a Privy Councillor in 1924 after having served as Minister of Justice. In 1924 he organized the National Foundation Society (*Kokuhon Sha*) of which he became president. "Although by and large the society was a stronghold of traditional conservatism, it also had an extremist element."[101] Hiranuma was also an "adviser" to the National Founding Association (*Kenkoku Kai*), a rightist society organized in 1926 by one of the more violent Outlaw types, Akao Bin. Here we have a very high government Official who was logically prodding himself from behind in the national polity as the Shrine (or Official) of Outlaw political organizations.

The behavioral relation between organizational offices and national polity types becomes enormously entangled when a given political actor holds different offices or memberships in three or more political organizations. For example, take the not implausible case of a (1) party secretary-general who was an inexperienced bureaucrat but served as (2) Home Minister in a Cabinet of which his party

101. Maruyama Masao, *Thought and Behaviour*, p. 316.

president was Prime Minister. He was also (3) honorary chairman of a rightist society as well as (4) director of a business firm. As party secretary-general and Home Minister he was an Official with at least two potential Shrines to manipulate: the Prime Minister-party president and the emperor. As an inexperienced Home Minister, however, he was most likely a Shrine to the Officials who ran the ministry. As the honorary chairman of a rightist society he was organizationally a Shrine but nationally an Outlaw. As the director of a business he was an Official within the company but as a "pressure group" member of his political party he was an Outlaw within the party, and possibly the national polity. Not only did he serve as two types in the national polity simultaneously; he was also two types, Outlaw and Official, simultaneously within the party and toward the same persons—including himself.

A third difficulty involves relations among the three political types: initiative, lines of influence, manipulation. Accepting Professor Maruyama's description of type behavior for the moment, let us first examine the internal cohesion of each type as a class of political actors. All members of rightist societies, for example, were Outlaws. Maruyama points out, however, that

> . . . , a united front never emerged from the right-wing movement in spite of fairly advantageous conditions. Unity was constantly intoned, but as soon as they had joined together, they split apart and exchanged abuse. Since they were associations centered on a paternal boss, they could only be small-scale; each struggled to elevate its own deity.[102]

The Outlaw class of political types was therefore internally fragmented.

Fragmentation was even more characteristic of Officials. As we saw in chapter 4, competition to declare the Imperial Will among Officials in the pluralized institutions of imperial prerogative was intense by 1930. Professor Maruyama notes that one result of the political structure created under the Meiji Constitution was that "modern Japan was . . . burdened with its 'original sin': the pluralism of political power." There were "confrontations within the

102. Ibid., p. 79.

military bureaucracy" and "the horizontal splits among Japan's wartime leaders" "were for ever being atomized."[103]

> Thus we find a series of confrontations on progressively lower levels: among the leaders, civilian versus military officials; among the military, Army versus Navy; within the Army, War Ministry versus General Staff; within the War Ministry, Military Affairs Bureau versus Military Service Bureau; and so forth. In the same category is the notorious hostility between officials in the Cabinet Planning Board, the Manchoukuo Government, and the Home Ministry.[104]

The competition among Officials and among Outlaws suggests the possibility that one set of Outlaws might have been used by one or more sets of Officials to pressure another set or sets of Officials, that the relation between Outlaws and Officials was not pressure by the former as a group on the latter as a group but manipulation—overt or covert, explicit or tacit—of certain Outlaws by certain Officials against other Officials.

Maruyama argues that "suppressing fascism from below, . . . fascism from above made rapid progress." Seventeen leaders of the 1936 coup attempt were executed: "The fate of Kita, Nishida, and the young officers of the February Incident is justly expressed in the Chinese proverb, 'when the cunning hares have been killed, the hunting dogs go into the cooking pot.' "[105] Who were the cunning hares? Surely, the "moderate" Officials currently or formerly in the bureaucratic institutions of imperial prerogative who were the targets of the February Incident: Prime Minister Okada Keisuke, Grand Chamberlain Suzuki Kantarō, Privy Seal Saitō Makoto, former Prime. Minister Takahashi Korekiyo, former Privy Seal Makino Nobuaki. Who were the hunting dogs? The Outlaws who led the coup attempt or were related to it by behavior and ideological persuasion. But most important, who put the hunting dogs into the cooking pot? And who brought on fascism from above? The only real possibility is a set or sets of Officials—a group or groups of the "new bureaucrats" and military renovationists—who demanded the right

103. Ibid., pp. 127, 123–24.
104. Ibid., p. 124.
105. Ibid., p. 67.

to declare the Imperial Will in politics and to restore "national unity" in the place of pluralist warfare among the institutions of imperial prerogative.

General Mazaki Jinzaburō's behavior at the time of the February 26 Incident in 1936 suggests such collusion among Outlaws and Officials against other Officials—or at least an attempt to capitalize on extremist Outlaw action in order to control the government. A leader of the Army's Imperial Way Faction, General Mazaki had been forced to resign as Inspector General of Military Education in 1935 by Control Faction officers of the Army. The February 26 insurgents were proponents of the Imperial Way Faction who looked to Mazaki and other generals of that faction for leadership. Mazaki was in full-dress uniform at 8 a.m. on February 26, only a few hours after the coup had broken out. Decked out in his formal finery, he met the insurgent officers at the Army Ministry and was greeted like a "victorious general come back from the war." He then went to see Prince-of-the-Blood Fushimi, Chief of the Navy General Staff, and told him that there was no other recourse but to look to an imperial rescript for a "Shōwa Restoration" and to anticipate its being carried out by the formation of a "strong Cabinet." After his talk with Fushimi, he went to the palace, still in formal uniform; it is not unlikely that he expected to be called upon to form such a Cabinet then and there. Investigation by the military police (kempeitai) revealed that he had been deeply involved with the young officers who plotted and executed the coup attempt.[106]

Mazaki was not appointed Prime Minister but placed in the Reserves, and the Imperial Way Faction lost much of its previous power in both the Army and the government. The Officials who manipulated or hoped to use Outlaw pressures lost. The most severe losses were suffered by the "moderate" Officials—the targets of the coup: their power was severely curtailed from 1936 until 1945. The winners were the Army's Control Faction Officials and their colleagues in the Navy and the civil bureaucracy: they capitalized on

---

106. Nezu Masashi, pp. 156–57. "Shōwa Restoration" (Shōwa Ishin) was a term in vogue among rightists during the 1930s. In direct imitation of "Meiji Restoration," it meant that the emperor must be "restored" to his rightful place at the center of politics—usually by the elimination of "evil advisers next to the throne" and the "reconstruction" of the state under "direct imperial rule." It is my guess, not Nezu's, that Mazaki expected to be made Prime Minister.

the successful use of Outlaw violence by the Imperial Way Faction against moderate Officials, and on the mistakes of the Imperial Way Faction's Officials in the way they did so, to consolidate bureaucratic "fascism from above."

Of course, the very presence of Outlaws and Outlaw terrorism critically affected the outcome of political struggles within the Official class. Assassination and the threat of assassination became important political means, utilized with or without skill and with or without success, of exerting pressure "from below." In terms of mentality and behavior, the Outlaws of the 1930s were very little different from the loyalist assassins and protagonists of the Meiji Restoration. Both were zealous nationalists; both demonstrated their "pure hearts" by wielding the "shining sword" against those in high places. Several Outlaws of the 1850s and 1860s, however, rose to the peak of the Meiji polity to become "statesmen of original merit"; the Outlaws of 1936 were put "into the cooking pot." The Outlaws of the 1850s and 1860s were instruments of pressure that contributed to the Meiji Restoration; several of them then contributed to Japan's remarkable and successful emergence as a great power. The Outlaws of the unsuccessful Shōwa Restoration were instruments of pressure used to consolidate a bureaucratic monolith in government and then discarded.[107]

Despite Outlaw violence during the 1930s there was no "restoration." Outlaw violence actually strengthened Official control over the state. And even the unprecedented defeat of 1945 and the unprecedented stationing of occupation forces on Japanese soil did not break the control of the Officials. One is led to suspect that Officials were powerful rather than timid, that it was they who made the Japanese government a Government. One is also led to the conclusion that meaningful functional roles within the Official class prevented the Japanese polity from disintegrating under the most severe domestic and international pressures. Our examination of

---

107. On violent loyalist activity preceding the Restoration see Marius B. Jansen, *Sakamoto Ryōma and the Meiji Restoration* (Princeton: Princeton University Press, 1961). It is unfortunate that Maruyama does not compare the behavior of his Outlaw with that of the Restoration loyalist. Although the Outlaws of the 1930s might well be called "pseudo-loyalists," given the changed nature of Japanese society and politics, their behavior was very similar to the violent, emotional, and "irrational" behavior of many of their "loyalist" precursors.

Kido Kōichi's behavior in three different palace offices has revealed at least three such roles: the secretary, the bureaucrat, and the nego-tiator. Kido's behavior revealed that these roles were not unique to him, either as a distinctive personality type or as a highly statused member of the aristocracy, but were inherent in the offices he held. Moreover, Kido's associations in each role demonstrated not only that other political actors performed similar roles but also that still others performed different roles: those of ratifier (the emperor), policy advocate (officials such as Hiranuma Kiichirō and Matsuoka Yōsuke, who headed various factions and coalitions), and instrument of pressure (right-wing radicals). These roles, which involved various patterns of behavior within the Official class of political ac-tors, made Japan a powerful polity in both its policy successes and policy failures.

Maruyama, however, cites Kido only to illustrate the weak and evasive Official in "the massive 'system of irresponsibilities' that constituted Japan's fascist rule."[108] Both Kido and Konoe are singled out to exemplify the relationship between Outlaws and Officials:

> Note, for instance, the peculiar relations between Prince Konoe and Mr. Inoue Nisshō, or again those that connected Marquis Kido to men like Mr. Hashimoto Tetsuma of the Purple Cloud Pavilion and Mr. Matsui Kūka. When Mr. Takuya Dempu of the Politics and Learning Society, who went in for blackmailing Senior Retainers, was arrested in conne-xion with a certain major incident in the Palace, Marquis Kido wrote in his diary that he felt as if 'a grain of rice sticking to the sole of my foot' had been removed (3 March 1933). This neatly illustrates what members of the ruling class felt about the lower-ranking Outlaws and suggests the relationship between them.[109]

How salient in fact were Outlaws in Kido's life as an Official? What influence did they have?

I have compiled a list of forty-nine Outlaws or possible Outlaws including (1) those cited specifically by Maruyama as Outlaws, and (2) those who were or might have been Outlaws, given the manner in which they appear in Kido's diary. In this latter category are those who invited themselves to Kido's home or official residence at strange hours to "talk" (for example, Ōkawabara Nittō)—usually

108. Maruyama Masao, *Thought and Behaviour*, p. 128.
109. Ibid., pp. 129–30. The date of Kido's diary entry is March 2, not March 3.

TABLE 22. KIDO KŌICHI'S OUTLAW ASSOCIATES

	Number of Meetings		
Name	1932	1936	1941
Hasama Shigeru	0	0	2
Hashimoto Tetsuma	0	0	1
Inoue Nisshō	0	0	3
Kiriyama Masashi	2	0	0
Matsui Kūka (Seikun)	0	1	15
Ōkawabara Nittō	2	1	0
"Shigeki"	0	0	5
Suridate Kazuo	0	6	9
Yasuoka Masaatsu	1	0	0
Yoshida Masuzō	0	0	9
Total	5	8	44

about imminent crises and the need for drastic political solutions, those who held no positions of note and therefore do not appear in Japanese biographical dictionaries and were not otherwise identifiable (for example Suridate Kazuo), and those who were prominent right-wing propagandists but not listed as Outlaws by Maruyama (for example, Yoshida Masuzō). Some of the persons whom I have listed as Outlaws, therefore, may or may not have been Outlaws.

Of the forty-nine Outlaws or possible Outlaws, only ten met Kido in one or more of the three years in which his associations have been analyzed. These ten and the number of times they met Kido in each year are listed in table 22. It should be readily apparent that in terms of frequency of association Outlaws were of singular obscurity, accounting for 0.5 percent of Kido's associations in 1932, 0.6 percent in 1936, and 2.3 percent in 1941. If frequency of association is any measure of influence, Outlaw influence on Kido was infinitesimal.

In only one of the three years examined did an Outlaw appear with any degree of prominence. In 1941 Matsui Kūka met Kido fifteen times. Matsui, whom Harada Kumao called a "political parasite" (seijigoro),[110] emerges in Kido's diary for the first time in

110. Harada Kumao, 3:229, 244.

March 1935, when he came to Kido's office to "talk about the political situation" and "urge the necessity for the establishment of a Konoe Cabinet."[111] Kido met Matsui a total of ten times in 1935. Most of these meetings involved "reports" by Matsui on trends within the military and "exchanges of views" on the political situation, during which Matsui often talked about "political crises." In July, for example, he came to Kido's office to report on the "critical nature of the present situation"; he also said that he "hoped for the resignation of the Privy Seal."[112] Along with making such recommendations Matsui reported on his own activities and those of others. On August 12, 1935 he called Kido to tell him that the Chief of the Military Affairs Bureau, Nagata Tetsuzan, had been critically wounded by a disgruntled Army officer—forty-five minutes after the attack on Nagata had occurred. Kido called the Privy Seal immediately and reported the assassination.[113] In this instance Kido received accurate and useful information from Outlaw Matsui that was of importance in discharging his role as Chief Secretary to the Privy Seal. Other Outlaws performed a similar function. Inoue Nisshō, for example, visited Kido at his official residence in 1941 to report on his meeting with Konoe and to tell Kido about his own future plans.[114] Matsui and other Outlaws like Inoue evidently delighted in acting as information brokers to Kido and other high political leaders. Although Kido records only one meeting with Matsui in 1936, the two were in frequent communication from 1937 on. In his relation to Kido, Matsui was a self-appointed secretary who kept Kido informed, willy-nilly, and at the same time attempted to prod Kido and other Officials "from behind" with extremist and irresponsible proposals.

Given the infrequency with which Kido met Outlaws and the quasi-secretarial role that they often played in their meetings with him, how is their influence to be determined? There are two possibilities. First, the concrete demands of the Outlaws were translated into some form of positive accommodating action by Official Kido.

111. Kido Kōichi, 1 : 393.
112. Ibid., p. 421.
113. Ibid., pp. 423–24.
114. Ibid., 2 : 861.

Kido indicates no instance of responding to Outlaw pressure in this manner during the three years I have examined. On the contrary, he even opposed Outlaw suggestions directly. When Matsui urged the resignation of the Privy Seal in July 1935, for example, Kido told him to "rethink" the matter since his opinion "rested on facts that were all but entirely mistaken."[115] Inoue Nisshō came to see Kido in January 1941 and informed him that the political situation was tense and that there was danger of a terrorist incident. If such an incident were to occur, continued Inoue, there was no one but the venerable Tōyama Mitsuru to bring the situation under control.[116] Although Kido did not counter Inoue's recommendation, the possibility of a Cabinet under Tōyama, the octogenarian doyen of Outlaws, was patently absurd even in the frenzied nationalism of the months preceding war with the United States. There was no need for Kido to respond to such a recommendation; on the other hand, he was alerted to the possibility of a terrorist incident.

The second possible form of influence over Kido is a negative one. Kido might have refrained from a course of action under Outlaw pressure. Again, he gives no instance in his diary during the three years examined of altering his course of action as the result of his Outlaw associations.

Takuya Dempu provides us with a better example of Outlaw "pressure" not only on Official Kido but also on the political system in general. Takuya was one of the classic Outlaws—the *Lumpenpolitiker* who stormed about irresponsibly at the base of society threatening those in high places by word and deed. Kido reports no meetings with Takuya, who appears in Kido's diary only as the subject of police reports and the cause of anxiety to palace officials. Takuya makes his debut in Kido's diary in September 1931. He had published a newspaper article "as usual attacking the Privy Seal" but which on this occasion was "particularly fierce," "tending to incite assassination." Kido spoke with two Household Ministry secretaries about the Takuya attack and they agreed that since the situation was such that "it was less and less possible to rely on those in the Tokyo Metropolitan Police Office," measures had to be taken to deal with

115. Ibid., 1:421.
116. Ibid., 2:849.

this problem first. Kido discussed the matter with the Vice Minister of the Imperial Household Ministry, who concurred.[117]

Takuya kept up his attacks until March 1933, when he was finally arrested. Informed of Takuya's arrest by the police, Kido made the diary entry cited by Maruyama above. A full quotation of that entry reveals why Takuya was an irritant to Kido: "[His] was an existence like a grain of rice sticking to the sole of [my] foot; but I feel much better now that ugly rumors have come to an end because he has been taken into custody."[118] As the Privy Seal's Chief Secretary, Kido was naturally and rightly concerned with actions, like Takuya's, that threatened the life of his official superior. The only "influence" Outlaw Takuya had, therefore, was to prod Kido and other palace Officials to have the police arrest him.

That an atmosphere of intimidation and violence surrounded those "close to the throne" during the 1930s is indisputable. What to do about such Outlaw activity, however, was squarely in the hands of the Officials. If a set of threatened Officials lacked the means to control Outlaw activities, they would be forced to rely on those Officials who did. This was precisely the case with Outlaw Takuya's threats and the difficulties encountered by palace Officials in having police Officials arrest him. The instruments of coercion were in the hands of the military services and the Home Ministry. During the 1930s one or the other had to be persuaded to control Outlaw activity.[119]

For Kido, therefore, Outlaws were (1) self-appointed "secretaries" who were useful to him, however irresponsible their policy views (Matsui Kūka); (2) tangential nuisances who treated Kido to mystical political talk (Ōkawabara Nittō); or (3) threats to the lives

117. Ibid., 1:102.
118. Ibid., p. 223. Takuya was again on the loose shortly after his arrest and publishing the same kind of attacks. In March 1936, in the aftermath of the February 26 Incident, he was once again arrested; thereafter he ceased to threaten Kido and other palace officials.
119. It is Professor Oka Yoshitake's opinion that the "go-stop" incident of 1933, which has been discussed in the introduction to chap. 4, ended any possibility that the Home Ministry's police could be used to check the Army, at least directly (interview, April 20, 1972). By extension, it might be argued that the police were ineffective against those Outlaws who enjoyed Army protection. Although the Imperial Household Ministry had a Bureau of Imperial Guards, its units were infected by Outlaw thought and behavior, as we saw in the conclusion to chap. 3. As challenges to peace and security in the nation at large, moreover, Outlaw activities were not under the Guards' jurisdiction but that of the police.

of palace Officials and to palace security who prompted palace Officials to take action against them (Takuya Dempu). The Outlaws just mentioned were all classic Outlaw types—irresponsible zealots outside Kido's organization, the Imperial Household Ministry, who attempted to pressure him from "outside" and "below." Since Maruyama's Outlaw could also exist within a given Official's organization, Kido may have been subject to pressure by the lowest members of the Household Ministry as well. But in no instance during the three years analyzed did Kido report any such pressure. He simply did not meet with the lowest ranking personnel of the palace. Neither from within the Imperial Household Ministry nor from the outside did Outlaw pressure figure prominently in Kido's behavior. In fact, the more Outlaw their behavior, the less likely Outlaws were to meet Kido and the more likely the were to be the subjects of efforts by Kido and other Officials to have them arrested. Kido never met Takuya Dempu, for example, nor did he record having met two of the most radical Outlaws, Kita Ikki and Nishida Zei, during the period covered by his diary.

That Kido should have had forty-four meetings with Outlaw types in 1941, however, demonstrates that his Outlaw associations did increase when he became Lord Keeper of the Privy Seal. Bathing in imperial light, he attracted moths. Maruyama has suggested that gaining proximity to the emperor was a motivational factor in the behavior of political actors in prewar Japan. For Outlaws, association with someone close to the emperor may have given them a vicarious sense of proximity, and therefore of importance. Whatever their motivation, Outlaws were known for their bravado. Barging in on Privy Seal Kido was as much an act of swagger as it was purposeful action to persuade. When Outlaws met Kido in 1941, in contrast to the period prior to Kido's becoming Privy Seal, they did so exclusively at his official residence or home, where they could catch him at odd hours. Thirty-one of Kido's forty-four meetings with Outlaws in 1941, for example, took place at his official residence and the remainder at his home. The Privy Seal's office was apparently off limits to Outlaws. That Kido should have had any dealings with Outlaws may speak more for the resourceful effrontery of the Outlaw than the timidity of the Official.

Finally, many Officials were in essential agreement with military expansion abroad, Japanism, and statism, as advocated by Outlaws. Although contemptuous of the Outlaw life style and opposed to their methods of political pressure, Officials like Kido may have been in sympathy with some or all of their views. If such were the case, it is not logical to assert that such Officials yielded to Outlaw pressure out of timidity: yielding to someone with whom one is already in agreement is a dubious measure of influence.

It has been shown, both here and in the previous chapter, that those Officials who were policy advocates, as opposed to those who were neutral bureaucrats, either manipulated or condoned Outlaws in order to dominate the Japanese polity, or that they struggled at the risk of life and limb to control Outlaw activity and to counter the political demands made by Outlaws and sympathetic Officials. In neither case can such Official behavior be called "timid," "power-dwarfed," or "weak."

Kido's most important associates in 1932, 1936, and 1941 were not Outlaws. As Chief Secretary to the Privy Seal in 1932, his primary Official associates were four officers of bureau-chief level in four distinct institutions of imperial prerogative outside the palace and one official in the palace. These five, however, accounted for only 17.4 percent of Kido's meetings with those he met ten times or more that year. Kido's relations with the four government Officials, moreover, involved information gathering and sharing, not "influence." Nor did Kido manipulate his palace superior, the Privy Seal, as a Shrine. Kido's relation to the Privy Seal, as we have seen, involved liaison, reporting, and consultative functions. Kido's behavior was "loyal" and "circumspect" but not timid, weak, or fawning. Kido and the Privy Seal frequently consulted and shared information as equals on matters of grave importance, but it was always at the initiative of the Privy Seal that Kido's advice was used in rendering advice to the throne.

Kido's chief associates in 1932 were eight hereditary aristocrats in the House of Peers who were also members of Kido's Eleven Club. These eight accounted for 68.2 percent of his meetings with those in the ten or more frequency group. None held office in Kido's component of imperial prerogative, the Imperial Household

Ministry, during 1932. Only one of the eight—Kido's predecessor as Chief Secretary to the Privy Seal—had been a palace Official. Four of the eight held or had held government offices; four apparently had no government experience outside the House of Peers. These eight associates were a diverse group of persons whose base of operations was the House of Peers.

But what position did the House of Peers occupy in the national polity? In what category or categories did its members belong? Was it an organization composed of the tripartite hierarchy? The position of the House of Peers, given the status and achievements of its members, was unquestionably high. But some of its members, such as the princes-of-the-blood, could be nothing but Shrines in the national polity, regardless of their membership in the House. Others, like some of the scholars, businessmen, and aristocrats, had never held government office but were neither Outlaw nor Shrine in behavior. Yet others had had long and distinguished careers in the bureaucratic components of imperial prerogative. In its membership, therefore, the House of Peers was a mixture of persons of high status or high achievement in practically every valued activity in the Japanese polity. Finally, these men of diverse backgrounds and social status were organized into loosely knit clubs, subsets, and even political parties. The House of Peers was an association of associations and individuals, not an organizational hierarchy. In short, the House of Peers did not fit the tripartite organizational model, and its members, by station and behavior, did not fit any consistent personality typology.

Although association among members of the House of Peers was not of any particularly consistent pattern, Kido's association with his eight aristocratic associates in the House of Peers during 1932 illustrates one pattern of association pertinent to a significant group of Peers. None of the eight was related to Kido as a Shrine, Official, Outlaw, or combination of such behavioral characteristics. Their associations with Kido and with each other were based on the egalitarian comfort of mutual membership in an elite status group and enhanced by mutual involvement in one another's political aspirations and careers (for example, Konoe and Kido) and by the kinds of roles they played in the political system at any given time (for example, Secretary Harada and Secretary Kido, Prime Minister

Konoe and Privy Seal Kido). Influence among all these aristocrats was mutual. We saw, for example, that Konoe was of key importance in influencing Kido to become Chief Secretary to the Privy Seal in 1930 and Privy Seal in 1940. On the other hand, Konoe frequently consulted Kido and relied on Kido's judgment, as on the issue of Konoe's resigning when Germany and the Soviet Union went to war in June 1941. Although there may have been mutual influence between Secretary Harada and Secretary Kido in 1932, their association was not one of "influence" but of liaison, information gathering, and information sharing in fulfillment of their secretarial roles. In fact, information gathering and sharing were the key political functions performed by Kido and all members of the Eleven Club during 1932.

Such functions were extremely important in building cross-institutional coalitions of policy advocates in the institutions of imperial prerogative. We saw, for example, that Kido's aristocratic associates in the House of Peers, both Eleven Club members and nonmembers, brought together "new bureaucrats" in the civil ministries, such as Tani Masayuki of the Foreign Ministry, and those in the military services, such as Suzuki Teiichi, during 1932.[120] Both Tani and Suzuki became Ministers of State, in 1942 and 1941 respectively.

In 1936, when Kido was Director of Peerage Affairs, a notable shift in his Official associations occurred. His chief associates that year were ten Officials in the palace, who accounted for 35.0 percent of his meetings with those in the ten or more frequency category. Meetings with two purely Official representatives from other institutional components of imperial prerogative raised his meetings with Officials to 37.8 percent of his meetings with those he met ten times

---

120. For a penetrating and enlightening discussion of the "new bureaucrats," see Robert M. Spaulding, Jr., "The Bureaucracy as a Political Force, 1920–45,"in *Dilemmas of Growth in Prewar Japan*, ed. James W. Morley (Princeton: Princeton University Press, 1971), pp. 33–80, and his "Japan's 'New Bureaucrats,' 1932–45," in *Crisis Politics in Prewar Japan: Institutional and Ideological Problems of the 1930s*, ed. George M. Wilson (Tokyo: Sophia University, 1970), pp. 51–78. In the latter essay (page 52), Spaulding gives the following characteristics of the new bureaucrats: "a pragmatic nationalism emphasizing the economic role of the state, a willingness to collaborate with like-minded men in other ministries and in the military services, and a desire to change the existing order from within by non-revolutionary means." Obviously, Kido and his aristocratic associates were involved in facilitating the process of collaboration among such like-minded policy advocates.

or more. An Eleven Club aristocrat, secretary Harada, accounted for 9.5 percent and six Shrines—the emperor and five members of the imperial families—accounted for 10.7 percent. The remaining persons in the ten or more frequency group were other aristocratic associates (including Prince Saionji), golfing partners, and members of Kido's family. If frequency and nature of association are any measures of influence, Official types and certain aristocratic associates, such as Secretary Harada, were most influential in Kido's behavior as a bureaucrat in 1936, just as Eleven Club aristocrats were most important in Kido's behavior as a secretary in 1932.

When Kido became Privy Seal another marked transformation in his patterns of association occurred. Associations with the supreme Shrines in the Japanese polity, primarily the emperor, increased to 30.4 percent of Kido's meetings with those he met ten times or more. Kido's meetings with government Officials whom he met ten times or more in 1941 increased to 33.8 percent, his meetings with palace officials decreasing to 19.1 percent. In 1941, therefore, Kido's associations with both Officials and Shrines increased markedly over 1936, as they had in 1936 in comparison to 1932. The Officials Kido met in the ten or more frequency category also changed markedly in comparison to 1936.

It is difficult to ascertain which Officials, quasi-Official aristocrats, and Shrines were foremost in influencing Kido's behavior, given the marked shifts in associates and frequencies of association both within and among types in 1932, 1936, and 1941. Prince Konoe is the only person Kido met thirty times or more in all three years examined. However, not only did frequency of association between them vary in accordance with the offices they held, but it is extremely difficult to determine who influenced whom in terms of policy preferences. Kido and Konoe were deeply involved in each other's political careers, and they exercised mutual influence on each other in making up their minds about policy objectives, political strategies, and political tactics.

It is unquestionable that as Kido grew in bureaucratic stature he gained greater access to the highest Shrines in the Japanese polity: the emperor, imperial princes, and other members of the imperial families. As a secretary in 1932, Kido met no one in the imperial family category ten times or more. As a court bureaucrat in 1936, 10.7 percent of Kido's meetings with those he met ten times or more were with the emperor and imperial families; as negotiator to the throne in 1941, 30.4 percent. According to Maruyama's typology, therefore, it became increasingly possible for Official Kido to "hold aloft" the supreme Shrines in Japanese politics, manipulating them against the "powerless people" or those below Kido in his organizational hierarchy. Let us examine the relation between Officials and Shrines, focusing on Kido's behavior during 1941, when he was in the best position to "hold aloft" the emperor. As Privy Seal, Kido was the Official closest to the throne, the emperor's most frequently consulted adviser, and he controlled the imperial seal and the seal of state which stamped all decisions as authoritative.

The emperor's position at the pinnacle of the national hierarchy made him the ultimate Shrine in the Japanese polity, and the supreme ratifier of all decisions. No government proposal to the emperor was an authoritative decision of state without the emperor's approval. Did such approval automatically make the ratifier a Shrine? Maruyama's discussion of the Shrine personality is very ambiguous, suggesting both that ratification itself makes the ratifier a Shrine and that manipulation by others in the course of the ratification process makes the ratifier a Shrine—or both do. But there is a very important distinction between ratification as authority and ratification as manipulation. Whether the ratifier was the rubber stamp for proposals made by others, whether he modified such proposals, or whether he initiated the proposals that he himself ratified are questions of great significance in analyzing the decision-making process. But these questions do not touch on the legal fact that the final decision was authoritative—assuming, of course, that the ratifier was the established and accepted institution for ratification in the political system for such decisions and that "manipulation" of the ratifier, when and if it occurred, was not illegal. Because all proposals stamped with the imperial seal and seal of state were authoritative decisions of state, that fact alone does not make the emperor a Shrine. In order to show Shrine behavior on the part of the emperor it must be demonstrated that the emperor "automatically" sanctioned proposals placed before him—regardless of his agreement or disagreement.

Kido's relationship with the emperor throughout 1941 indicates a meticulous observance of the Privy Seal's role as negotiator to the throne. At no time in 1941 did Kido use imperial rescripts to bombard institutional opponents, as Ozaki Yukio accused Prime Minister Katsura of doing in 1913. The very fact that Kido met with the emperor at least 313 times during 1941 suggests, moreover, that the emperor was no mere robot, dumbly manipulated by Kido or even by other high Officials such as the Prime Minister and Chiefs of Staff. Were the emperor merely a rubber stamp Kido could have affixed the imperial seal and seal of state to decisions he and his colleagues had agreed to without bothering to engage in constant communication and consultation with the emperor. Privy Seal Kido was not, however, a policy advocate but a compromise negotiator, and the emperor played an important part in that negotiator role. Privy Seal Kido's duty, as he evidently perceived it, was to see that the emperor was presented consistent and unified policies and decisions for ratification. When such consistency and unity were lacking, however, the emperor and his palace advisers had considerable room for initiative and maneuvering. We have seen, for example, that both Kido and the emperor were active in bringing unity to the Cabinet when Foreign Minister Matsuoka's proposals and actions in 1941 went counter to Prime Minister Konoe's policy of negotiation with the United States. We also saw that the emperor exercised initiative that same year in seeing that the Navy was "fully confident" of its position toward the United States.

The first of the emperor's initiatives was exercised in keeping himself informed at all stages of the policy-making process, particularly in regard to foreign policy. On April 28, 1941, for example, Kido was at home with a cold when his Chief Secretary came to see him. The emperor had asked the Deputy Grand Chamberlain two questions: how was he to ask questions about foreign policy issues and so forth, when, as today, the Prime Minister, the Foreign Minister, and the Privy Seal were all confined at home by illness, and what had happened recently in Japan's relations with the

United States. Kido replied on both of these points and had the Chief Secretary report to the throne on his behalf.[121] The emperor exercised considerable initiative in pressuring his leading Officials for information, and, as in the example just cited, was successful in doing so even under unfavorable circumstances. Obviously, the emperor's ability to acquire information not only from his Privy Seal but also from his other leading Officials was a necessary precondition for exercising whatever influence he might have had over policy directions prior to his ratification of any given policy.

But the emperor did not simply keep himself informed; he also pressured his Officials in regard to the correctness and consistency of their policies. On the evening of July 30, 1941, for example, the Chief of the Navy General Staff reported to the throne on Navy policies. The following morning the emperor informed Kido in detail about the report and the replies given by the Chief of Staff in response to the emperor's questions. The Chief of Staff, Admiral Nagano Osami, wished to avoid war if it were at all possible, as had the preceding Chief of the Navy General Staff, Prince-of-the-Blood Fushimi. According to Admiral Nagano, it appeared that a negotiated settlement with the United States would be impossible unless Japan withdrew from the Tripartite Pact. If, however, there were no settlement with the United States and Japan should thereby lose her source of oil, her oil reserves would last only two years. If war did break out, the reserves would be consumed in a year and a half and there would be no alternative but to find new supplies. In response, the emperor told Admiral Nagano that if Admiral Nagano believed that Japan could win in the event of war, then he himself believed Japan could win: but would it not be difficult to achieve as great a victory against the United States fleet as Japan's victory in the Battle of the Japan Sea against the Imperial Russian fleet in 1905? Admiral Nagano replied that such a victory was well nigh impossible.[122]

The emperor, after telling Kido of Admiral Nagano's report and replies, said that such a war of desperation would be truly perilous. Responding to the emperor's concern, Kido replied that Admiral Nagano's views were too simplistic. The Tripartite Pact was not a bar

121. Kido Kōichi, 2 : 871.
122. Ibid., p. 895.

in reaching a negotiated settlement with the United States. In fact, because the United States respected international treaties so highly, he thought it very doubtful that U.S. confidence in Japan would be deepened if Japan abrogated the pact; on the contrary, Japan might incur the contempt of the United States by doing so. There were still various other avenues open to Japan in negotiating with the United States and these had to be exploited constructively and with tenacity. Kido told the emperor that he would press Prime Minister Konoe in particular on this.[123]

After his audience, Kido's diary records the following events for the remainder of July 31:

> *Noon.* talked with Navy Minister Oikawa; chatted about the views Chief of Staff Nagano had reported to the throne.
> *1:00.* the Chief Aide came to the office; chatted about the same matter.
> *1:30.* Count Kanroji came to the office; I was relieved to hear that a reply arrived from Marquis Komatsu which stated his desire that the marriage arrangements between Takazumi and Miss Nobuko go forward.
> *2:20.* Prince Konoe came to the office; conversed after [his] audience with the emperor.
> *From 3:40 to 4:05.* audienced with the emperor.
> *7:00.* Terasaki, Chief of the America Bureau, came to my residence; received a telegram.[124]

Thereafter Kido was in constant contact with Prime Minister Konoe about the posibilities of negotiation with the United States, occasionally noting in great detail his recommendations to Konoe (August 2, 1941) and Konoe's proposals and recommendations, which on one occasion (August 5) involved a lengthy written memorandum delivered to Kido by messenger.[125] It is clear, therefore, that (1) the emperor was actively concerned about the possibility of war with the United States and expressed his doubts about the Navy's capabilities, should war break out, to both the Navy and the Privy Seal, (2) Privy Seal Kido and the emperor consulted each other about what should be done, and (3) the Privy Seal acted on problems

---

123. Ibid., p. 896.
124. Ibid.
125. Ibid., pp. 896–98.

raised by the emperor, usually exercising his own judgment as to the best or most feasible way of dealing with them.

Even when presented with a unified policy, moreover, the emperor occasionally pressed his views if he disagreed. During the Imperial Conference of September 6, 1941, for example, the emperor offered an unprecedented criticism of his highest Officials in their assembled presence by reading one of the Emperor Meiji's poems. The poem, which questioned the violence in the world when all desired peace, was recited at the end of the conference which formalized a unanimous decision, reached by the government at that time, to go to war with the United States if negotiations had not succeeded by late October.[126] The emperor's recitation was unquestionably counter to the Imperial Conference's decision and a rebuke specifically to the Navy General Staff.

In short, the Emperor-in-Chambers was by no means a robot manipulated dumbly by his Officials—an inactive Shrine who "affects people by 'doing nothing.'" The emperor expressed his preferences and concerns to those Officials who appeared before him in his palace sanctuary. Although the actions taken by the Officials did not always support the emperor's views, those views did provoke responses by the relevant Officials—especially the Privy Seal. As Emperor-in-Public, however, the emperor was used as a Shrine to keep the "powerless people" in line; however active the emperor was with his Officials "privately" as Emperor-in-Chambers, he was displayed in public in such a manner as to elicit obedience to state policies. The emperor's appearances as public Emperor-in-State were high ceremony, rigidly formal. His name was used to justify all laws and ordinances; he was theoretically the fount of government authority and therefore of popular obedience. In this he was indeed the "property" of the Officials. But the manipulative relationship between Shrine and Official is simply not borne out by Kido's behavior. Kido and the emperor influenced each other mutually in arriving at what the emperor should or should not ratify and should or should not do even as Emperor-in-Chambers. And Kido did not record any attempts to use the emperor's name to pressure his Official

126. Ibid., pp. 907–08.

colleagues without the emperor's knowledge and consent. Finally, the Privy Seal was by no means the only Official who audienced with the emperor. The emperor was in constant communication with all four palace leaders, the Prime Minister, the Ministers of State, the Chiefs and Deputy Chiefs of the General Staffs. If these Officials disagreed among themselves in the presence of the emperor, as they occasionally did by giving contradictory reports and replies to the throne, the emperor might have been in a position of making choices, not in one of being manipulated. When a policy was ratified by the emperor it was invariably the Imperial Will, and therefore authoritative. But whose policy was it? That exclusively of the Officials? That of Officials prodded from behind by Outlaws? That of Officials with the agreement of the Shrine? That of the Shrine with the agreement of the Officials? Which Officials and why?

Although the emperor was the highest Shrine, moreover, he was not the sole Shrine at the top of the national polity. His three brothers and the male members of the imperial families were also Shrines. Prince-of-the-Blood Admiral Fushimi was Chief of the Navy General Staff from February 1932 to April 1941. Prince-of-the-Blood General Kanin was Chief of the Army General Staff from December 1931 to October 1940.[127] Just as was the case with Maruyama's Outlaws and Officials, therefore, the Shrines may have been a fragmented class of political actors. Manipulation, when and if it occurred, might have been manipulation of one Shrine by the Officials in his organization against other Shrines and their organizations.

Prince Fushimi, for example, took a hard-line stance against the London Naval Treaty in 1930; as an admiral on the Supreme War Council he caused considerable trouble to protreaty partisans throughout the negotiation and ratification process. It is even alleged that he was called down for his actions by Grand Chamberlain Suzuki.[128] Fushimi's appointment as Chief of the Navy General Staff in 1932 was questioned by Prince Saionji and other "moderate" leaders because of Fushimi's behavior during 1930. When Prince Kanin had been proposed as Chief of the Army General Staff in

127. Tōyama and Adachi, pp. 95–96, 92–93.
128. Okada Keisuke, pp. 48–49; Harada Kumao, 1 : 32–35, 118–20.

1931, moreover, Saionji had argued that it was unwise for an institution of government to "shoulder" an imperial prince. No imperial prince should be in such a "position of responsibility." The same was applied to Prince Fushimi's appointment as Chief of the Navy General Staff in 1932.[129]

Prince Fushimi continued to cause trouble as Chief of the Navy General Staff. In 1934 he supported a "lecture" to the throne by the former Deputy Chief of the Navy General Staff, despite the emperor's clear disapproval. Although such a lecture was a matter of courtesy to the recently resigned Deputy Chief, the emperor feared that he would use the opportunity not to lecture but to voice the Navy's opposition to the status quo established by the London Naval Treaty. Once the emperor "heard" such a policy, then antitreaty partisans would argue that it was "national policy" to abrogate the treaty.[130] On July 12, 1934 Prince Fushimi audienced with the emperor in his capacity as a member of the imperial family. After expressing the Navy's views on arms reduction, he handed the emperor a letter which demanded parity in naval armaments and added that if parity were not achieved "the Navy could not be controlled." The emperor had the letter returned to Fushimi without comment. Even Chief Aide Honjō thought it highly improper for a prince-of-the-blood, audiencing as a member of the imperial family, to use that means of access to proffer his partisan views on military and foreign policies. After Fushimi's audience, moreover, the Navy Minister evidently pressed the Prime Minister to accept the parity proposal because it had already been reported to the throne.[131] Here was a clear case of "using" an imperial family member, with his obvious consent, to counter an established policy supported by the emperor. The Navy Officials who wrote the parity letter "used" Fushimi's imperial status to gain access to the emperor, and then used the audience to argue that their policy was national policy because it had been "reported to the throne." Shrine was "used" against Shrine.

The emperor's brothers were also of constant concern, especially

129. Harada Kumao, 2:197–99. Harada's account leads one to believe that Prince Fushimi's appointment was initiated and pushed through by antitreaty forces in the Navy.
130. Honjō Shigeru, pp. 180–81.
131. Ibid., pp. 191–92.

his first brother, Prince Chichibu, who was deeply involved with rightist fanatics, both military and civilian. A friend of Nishida Zei (one of the purer Outlaw types), Chichibu began associating with radical officers as early as 1927. Chichibu was also actively involved with renovationist bureaucrats and their sympathizers in other institutions of imperial prerogative, including Prince Konoe:

> In September 1932 Prince Konoe recommended Prince Chichibu for the post of lord keeper of the privy seal, a position which would have given him great power over the emperor. But this was vetoed by Prince Saionji. Instead the prince was assigned to the General Staff. . . .
> Prince Chichibu was not only an imperial prince. Until Prince Akihito's birth in December 1933, he was also the apparent heir to the throne and would have become emperor had Hirohito died or abdicated for reasons of health. . . . It is significant that, in the early 1930s, critical remarks began to be made against the emperor by such army men as General Mazaki, court princes such as Higashikuni and other dignitaries such as Prince Konoe.
> The rebels [of 1936] themselves, in spite of their reverance for the imperial institution, would have shed few tears if Hirohito had abdicated in favor of his brother or his minor son with his brother as regent.[132]

Chief Aide Honjō Shigeru records in his diary on September 7, 1933 that on one day in late 1931 or early 1932 Prince Chichibu had a fierce argument with the emperor. Chichibu told the emperor that direct rule by the emperor was necessary and in that event suspension of the constitution would be unavoidable. Later the em-

---

132. Ben-Ami Shillony, "The February 26 Affair: Politics of a Military Insurrection" in *Crisis Politics in Prewar Japan*, pp. 36–37. Shillony's essay, the most incisive dissection of the February 26 Incident to appear in English, shows not only that Prince Chichibu supported the rebels but also that other members of the imperial family, such as Prince Higashikuni and Prince Asaka, were in sympathy with the plot. Support by General Mazaki, who was informed by the rebels of their plans one month before the insurrection occurred, and other Army leaders is also abundantly clear: "The extensive political connections of the February 1936 rebels indicate that the Affair was of a much more serious character than is usually assumed. It was serious not because extremist junior officers imposed their views on a spineless establishment, but because powerful elements of the establishment had decided to extend their support to a group of fanatic idealists in the lower echelons of the military.

The February 1936 rebellion was not a mere mutiny, although it was later so described by those whose interest was in depicting it as such. . . . If it was an insurrection, then it was the insurrection of a whole segment of the Japanese military, from top to bottom, against another segment wielding power through the General Staff" (Ibid., p. 49). In short, the February 26 coup attempt was an extensive plot that came very close to success. The emperor's clear and steady opposition to the rebellion was one of the major causes for its suppression (Ibid., pp. 39, 42–43).

peror told the Grand Chamberlain that he could not possibly agree to anything that would tarnish the virtue of his ancestors: he ruled in accordance with the constitution and it was impossible for him to destroy something created by the Emperor Meiji, which suspension of the constitution would surely amount to.[133]

Prince Chichibu continued to be a problem even during 1941, when renovationists controlled the government and traditionalist Kido was at the emperor's side as Privy Seal. The problem was how to keep Chichibu from meddling in politics, and those who had to solve it were the emperor and the leading palace officials. On September 16 Privy Seal Kido audienced with Prince Takamatsu, the emperor's second brother, to talk about a diplomatic settlement with the United States. In the course of their discussion, Prince Takamatsu suggested that Prince Chichibu be kept informed of Imperial Conference decisions and other matters of national policy and that Kido arrange reports for that purpose. Kido replied that if Prince Chichibu were in good health, such reporting would occur as a matter of course; he also promised that he would seek advice on Prince Takamatsu's suggestion.[134] The next day Kido audienced with the emperor and they talked about Takamatsu's proposal. The emperor argued that it would be premature to discuss national policies with Chichibu; Chichibu's recovery might be impaired. On September 19 Kido talked with Deputy Grand Chamberlains Kanroji and Hirohata about Takamatsu's stance, and on September 20 he discussed the same matter with the Imperial Household Minister and the Director of Peerage Affairs. Then, on September 22, Kido talked about Chichibu's recent state of health with Prince Chichibu's aide (*bettō*) and audienced again with the emperor.[135] Finally, on September 26, Kido called on Takamatsu to report on the proposal. Kido told Takamatsu that in the judgment of the emperor, the Imperial Household Minister, and the attending physician, it was not yet time for Chichibu to be brought into consultations on important state policies.[136] Kido and his palace colleagues had suc-

133. Honjō Shigeru, p. 163.
134. Kido Kōichi, 2:907.
135. Ibid., p. 908.
136. Ibid., p. 909.

ceeded in isolating Prince Chichibu from the political process in 1941.

As this and the previous examples have illustrated, imperial princes were highly statused personages on the periphery of the palace negotiation process who constantly threatened the palace's delicate machinery for resolving political conflict. If such persons were Shrines, dumbly manipulated as robots in the political system, they were manipulated against one another, and especially against the emperor. In other words, they were Shrines in multiple institutions of imperial prerogative who intensified, rather than mitigated, the competition among institutions, factions, and coalitions to declare the Imperial Will in politics. It was the divisiveness among Shrines, dumbly manipulated or not, rather than their type of behavior in the national polity as a whole, that was important in the political process. Imperial princes posed serious problems to the unity of state policies and were a constant challenge to the negotiating skill of the palace leaders, who had either to unite them around the emperor and his Officials or to negotiate them out of the political process altogether. Kido was largely successful in such negotiation, and primarily at the second strategy, not only in 1941 but throughout his tenure as Privy Seal from 1940 to 1945.

In none of the years we have analyzed, however, were Shrines, much less Outlaws, the most important group of political personalities in Kido's pattern of associations. As table 23 reveals, Officials and quasi-Officials (aristocrats with limited or no experience in court and government who were members of the House of Peers) were of key importance in all three years. Table 23 attempts to classify Kido's Official associates as officeholders, former officeholders, and other kinds of Officials, such as members of the House of Peers, in order to illustrate the diversity of Officials Kido met ten times or more and the changes in Kido's associations within the Official class as his palace role changed from secretary to bureaucrat to negotiator. It is readily apparent that as Kido rose in the Official hierarchy his associations with officeholders of higher, equal, and lower rank increased: from 27.4 percent in 1932 to 41.2 percent in 1936 to 50.5 percent in 1941. Association with former officials who were members of the House of Peers and with members of the

TABLE 23.   KIDO KŌICHI'S ASSOCIATES IN 1932, 1936, AND 1941:
TYPE AND FREQUENCY OF ASSOCIATION FOR THOSE MET TEN
TIMES OR MORE

	1932		1936		1941	
Type	No. of Meetings	%	No. of Meetings	%	No. of Meetings	%
Shrines	0	0%	82	10.7%	336	30.4%
Emperor	0	0	16	2.1	313	28.3
Other imperial family	0	0	66	8.6	23	2.1
Officials	456	91.2%	636	83.0%	650	58.8%
Officials of equal or higher rank who held office in court or government during all or part of the year	137	27.4	141	18.4	429	38.8
Officials of lower rank who held office in court or government during all or part of the year	0	0	175	22.8	129	11.7
Former officials who were members of the House of Peers	202	40.4	200	26.1	10	0.9
Other former officials	0	0	20	2.6	44	4.0
Members of the House of Peers with no court or government experience	117	23.4	100	13.1	38	3.4
Outlaws	0	0%	0	0%	15	1.4%
Others (family, etc.)	44	8.8%	48	6.3%	104	9.4%
Total	500	100%	766	100%	1,105	100%

House of Peers with no court or government experience decreased
accordingly: from 63.8 percent in 1932 to 39.2 percent in 1936 to a
mere 4.3 percent in 1941. As Kido became a higher Official,
therefore, his associations with Officials increased and those with
quasi-Officials decreased.

The predominance of Officials in Kido's patterns of association, the increase in contact with officeholding Officials as Kido advanced in Official rank, and the diversity of contact within the Official category can be explained by the nature of Kido's offices and official duties. As a palace Official, Kido associated with persons with whom he was supposed to associate by virtue of his and their offices. Such associations are simply not explained by reference to Maruyama's typology of political personality. Since Official associations were primary to Kido's political life, moreover, it is a misrepresentation to suggest that his interactions with Outlaws and Shrines were of primary importance in his political behavior. Even when Kido was closest to the throne and in constant communication with the emperor-Shrine, associations with Officials dominated his behavior with those political personalities outside that category.

Kido brought to each of his three offices and the roles they entailed his own political style, skills, ingroup associations, personal aspirations, and policy preferences. These elements, interacting with Kido's offices and official duties, generated patterns of behavior that were far more complex and functional to the political process than Maruyama's typology of political personality-behavior reveals. Kido's behavior illustrated three roles that were critical to the prewar governing process: secretary, bureaucrat, and negotiator. His associations reveal that others performed similar roles, while yet other political actors functioned as policy advocates, instruments of pressure, and ratifiers. It is time to conclude by incorporating these roles, and the matrix of association that linked them together, into a working model of decision making in prewar Japan.

CHAPTER SIX

PALACE AND POLITICS IN
PREWAR JAPAN: AN INTERPRETATION

THE LATE E. E. SCHATTSCHNEIDER has written:

> *Democratic government is the greatest single instrument for the socialization of conflict in the American community.* . . . Government in a democracy is a great engine for expanding the scale of conflict.[1]

A democratic society is a free society, and "a free society maximizes the contagion of conflict; it invites intervention and gives a high priority to the participation of the public in conflict."[2] Underlying the democratic socialization of conflict are a host of critically supportive values: the desirability of open competition, free involvement, and free inquiry in politics; the right of all citizens to vote for the candidates of their choice; a belief in the election of public officials, in legislative enactment of laws by accountable representatives, in individual equality before the laws. Democratic society thrives on individual initiative, open competition among individuals and groups, and publicity. But democratic government also seeks to rule effectively by bringing the maximum number of citizens into the marketplace of politics. Since all in theory have the right to participate, for example, all in theory are bound by the decisions of "their" demo-

---

1. E. E. Schattschneider, *The Semi-Sovereign People: A Realist's View of Democracy in America* (New York: Holt, Rinehart and Winston, 1967), p. 13. His emphasis.
2. Ibid., p. 5.

311

cratic government. By "socializing conflict," it might be argued, a democratic government hopes to resolve conflict and thereby govern effectively. One is therefore tempted to modify Schattschneider's maxim to read:

> Because democratic government is the greatest single instrument for the socialization of conflict in the American community, it governs effectively.

Ideally, democracy embraces values and procedures that make desirable and possible the orderly expansion of orderly conflict; ideally, socialization of conflict in a democracy is a means of resolving conflict peaceably and therefore an effective strategy of governing.

Socialization of conflict, however, is but one strategy of governing. At the other pole of strategy is the privatization of conflict. "A look at political literature shows that there has indeed been *a long-standing struggle between the conflicting tendencies toward the privatization and socialization of conflict.*"[3] Being the opposite of socialization, privatization of conflict limits the number of participants in a given conflict, discourages "outsiders" from entering the conflict, keeps issues from public scrutiny, and utilizes the "principle of unanimity of decision" among those few resolving the conflict.[4] If democracy in the United States has relied primarily on strategies of socialization, prewar Japanese government relied equally on strategies of privatization. Prewar Japanese politics involved the inverse of Schattschneider's maxim on democratic government in America and might be phrased as follows:

> The imperial government was the greatest single instrument for the privatization of conflict in the prewar Japanese community. Government in prewar Japan was a great structure for contracting the scale of open conflict.

Prewar Japanese society attempted to minimize the contagion of conflict; it discouraged intervention and gave a low priority to the participation of the public in conflict. Underlying the privatization of conflict in prewar Japanese politics were a host of critically supportive values: the undesirability of open competition, free involvement, and free inquiry in politics; the duty of all enfranchised subjects to vote for those

3. Ibid., p. 7. His emphasis.
4. Ibid., pp. 8–9.

who would loyally serve the Imperial Will; a belief in the imperial appointment of public officials, in the imperial sanction of all laws consented to by a dutiful assembly of elected subjects of the empire, in individual obedience to acts of government. Imperial Japanese society thrived on disguised initiative, hidden competition among individuals and groups, and rumor. The imperial government hoped to rule effectively by bringing a minimum number of subjects into the imperial corridors of politics. By privatizing conflict the imperial government hoped to resolve conflict and thereby govern effectively.

Just as socialization of conflict is both a strategy and an ideal in American democracy, so privatization of conflict in prewar Japanese politics was both a strategy and an ideal. In chapter 2 we saw that the ideal underlying the Meiji Constitution was that of imperial prerogative. The strategy was to bring the decision-making process into the corridors of the 275-acre palace in which the emperor's prerogatives were castled, sealed off by walls and moats and guarded by the gatekeepers of the Imperial Will. The separation of court and government, palace autonomy, and the fusion of rites and court were devices to enhance the transcendental immutability of imperial prerogative, to make the palace an inviolable sanctuary for the resolution of political conflict, and thus to make conflict among political leaders invisible. Decisions were to appear "inevitable," "in the nature of things," "a matter of course." Public harmony was the mark of good government and good governors. We have seen, for example, that Motoda Eifu criticized Itō Hirobumi in the 1880s for being unable to control "public sentiment"; the presence of public conflict and criticism meant that Itō had fallen short of ideal statesmanship. Public harmony was to be attained, in part, by the quietude and unity of governmental leaders as they carried the Imperial Will forth unanimously from the palace for public display. It was also to be attained in the Imperial Diet by the public expression of unity between emperor and subjects, government and people. Ideally, the Imperial Diet was not to be a forum for open competition among the people over political office and public policy. The Imperial Diet was to be a harmonious assembly of imperial subjects to assist the emperor and the government in achieving unanimity and harmony.

To state that harmony and unanimity were the ideals of Japanese politics does not, of course, mean that conflict was in fact lacking. Prewar Japanese politics, from the Restoration of 1868 to 1945, was rife with personal and factional strife. Assassination and assassination plots were common occurrences, not just aberrations of the 1930s: oligarch Ōkubo Toshimichi was assassinated in 1878, Itō Hirobumi in 1909 (in Harbin by a Korean), Prime Minister Hara Kei in 1921, Prime Minister Inukai Tsuyoshi in 1932, Privy Seal Saitō Makoto in 1936. By the late 1920s, moreover, rivalry among and within the institutions of imperial prerogative was the hallmark of Japanese politics. Nor did prewar Japan lack public disturbances and political movements. It was to create harmony and consensus that ideals and strategies of privatization were employed: techniques of privatization were adopted to cope with conflict, however successfully, because conflict was endemic to Japanese politics, however disguised.

What were the issues that agitated Japanese politics and how did the palace relate to political conflict? Speaking of British politics during the reign of George III, Richard Pares states that political issues

> were necessarily and even rightly concerned with the composition and the behaviour of the executive.
>
> The Government existed, in those days, not in order to legislate but in order to govern: to maintain order, to wage war and, above all, to conduct foreign affairs. These things made up, in those times, nine tenths of government; and most of the controversies which divided politicians and parties concerned foreign affairs, or those questions about the distribution of the national effort in war-time, which were connected with foreign affairs. The most prominent single issue was what one might call the 'German question.'—. . .
>
> When this controversy slept—as it often did—there was nothing to think about, in the middle eighteenth century, but the control and composition of the executive government itself. Indeed, when there is nothing to do but to govern, no other subject is worth thinking about.[5]

Whether Pares is accurate regarding British politics in the late eighteenth century I am simply not qualified to judge; but his statement applies neatly to Japanese politics throughout the period 1868 to 1945 if one modifies the specifics of the issues and takes ac-

5. Richard Pares, *King George III and the Politicians* (London: Oxford University Press, 1967), pp. 4–5.

count of differences in political styles. The issues facing Japan throughout that period primarily involved foreign policy and the composition of the Cabinet, including who was to be Prime Minister. Of course, plans for industrialization and economic development, concerns not salient in late eighteenth-century English politics, greatly affected Japan's choices and alternatives on both sets of issues.

Issues of diplomacy, of war and peace, were ever present as Japan struggled to gain and maintain Great Power status, to "stand tall in the world": the unequal treaties (1855–94), Japanese domination first in Korea (1873–1910) and then in East Asia (1910–45), alliances with the Great Powers to preserve Japan's primacy in East Asia—first with England in 1902 and then with the Axis in 1940, war with China in 1894 and again in 1937, war with Imperial Russia in 1904, war against Germany in 1914, war against the United States and the Allies in 1941. The composition of the Japanese executive was of equal importance in national politics. At first, leading government positions were subject to competition among a small number of oligarchs. After 1900, however, the battle over cabinet posts and the Prime Ministership was increasingly waged among the plural institutions of imperial prerogative—the Imperial Diet, the military, the civil bureaucracies. Each of these institutions, creatures of Japanese political modernization, sought to maximize its voice and ultimately to declare, alone or in concert with allies, the Imperial Will in politics. Between 1885 and 1945 there were no less than forty-three Cabinets, or one every 1.4 years. However privatized, the competition over "the composition and the behaviour of the executive" was fierce.

Prewar Japanese government did, in fact, exist "not in order to legislate but in order to govern." And the power to govern was lodged firmly in the Japanese executive. The power to appoint the Prime Minister and Cabinet ministers was an imperial prerogative (*Constitution of the Great Empire of Japan,* Article 10), as was the power to declare war, make peace, and conclude treaties (Article 13). As such, both the composition of the prewar Japanese executive and the conduct of foreign affairs were subject to privatized conflict resolution ultimately ratified by the emperor. The Prime Minister and

Ministers of State were not officially appointed until they had been formally invested by the ceremony of direct imperial appointment at the palace; the formation of a new Cabinet always dated from the day of that ceremony. A declaration of war could only be legitimate if it emanated from the palace and carried the imperial seal and great seal of state, both in the custody of the Lord Keeper of the Privy Seal. The decisions leading to war against Imperial Russia in 1904 and against the United States in 1941 were ultimately made by no more than fifteen persons convened in Imperial Conference at the palace. Both appointments of the Prime Minister and declarations of war were expressed as the unanimous consensus of the emperor's close advisors, including the top executive leaders. Neither was subject to a vote in the Imperial Diet.

At no time during the prewar period did the Japanese executive—the officials and advisers to the throne entitled to "render advice and assistance" to the emperor—surrender the right to initiate the appointment of the leading officials of state, both military and civilian, or the right to conduct foreign policy. Those forces and influences in Japanese society who wished to make policy had no other recourse but to capture positions in the Japanese executive that would allow them to render advice and assistance to the throne and thereby take part in the declaration of the Imperial Will. At no time during the prewar period did the palace surrender the right to ratify the consensus reached by the Japanese executive. Responsibility for ratifying the national consensus in prewar Japanese politics was lodged in the palace, not in an open legislative forum or in socialized election procedures. The palace was the apex of the privatized decision-making structure in Japanese politics, ideally and strategically.

This somewhat exaggerated statement of the privatization of conflict in prewar Japanese politics and the relation of the palace to the privatization process is not intended by any means to obscure the immense changes in Japanese society and in the composition of its political forces that occurred during the prewar period. It does, however, point to the centrality of norms and strategies of privatization and the centrality of the palace throughout the prewar period, regardless of the emergence of new political forces, changes in policies, and the pluralization of government institutions. In other words, those forces wishing to gain a voice in or to dominate Japanese politics, whatever their organization and policies, had to consider the imperial referent in decision making. The radical left, notably the Communist Party of Japan, was forced to deny the imperial referent and consequently the entire structure and operation of prewar Japanese government. The radical right, most notably the fascists led by Kita Ikki and others, felt obliged, on the contrary, to claim a monopoly over the Imperial Will and to declare itself sole interpreter.

More important, however, were the institutions and persons actually responsible for conducting the affairs of government. In the late Meiji period, 1885 to 1912, an oligarchy of some ten men comprised the inner circle for advising the emperor on the composition of the government and on foreign policy. These men were the creators of modern political institutions, not their creatures. The spirit of personal competition that prevailed among them was not paralyzed or aggravated by institutional competition. Although Yamagata Aritomo had been the guiding force behind the creation of a modern army, his dedication to that enterprise did not prevent him from cooperating with Itō Hirobumi, the oligarch primarily responsible for creating the constitution and nurturing the civil institutions of government. The appointment of Matsukata Masayoshi as Prime Minister in 1892 was made, as we have seen, at the recommendation of four oligarchs, including both Yamagata and Itō. Itō and Yamagata were also in complete accord on going to war with Russia in 1904.[6] When war broke out between Japan and Russia, therefore, the government was unified: "neither the problem of State Affairs and Supreme Command nor opposition between the Cabinet and

6. On the events leading to the decision for war against Imperial Russia, see Gaimu Shō, ed., *Nihon Gaikō Monjo* (Tokyo: Gaimushō Zōhan, 1958), ser. 47, vol. 37, no. 1, pp. 92–93; *Gensui Kōshaku Ōyama Iwao*, pp. 629–634; and Yamamoto Eisuke, *Yamamoto Gombei* (Tokyo: Jiji Tsūshin Sha, 1958), pp. 134–41. Although I cannot locate the source for the anecdote, Yamagata is alleged to have thrown his arms around Itō at the end of the Imperial Conference of February 4, 1904, when the decision for war was finalized, and said to Itō that he sympathized profoundly with Itō's plight: if Japan lost Yamagata would die a glorious death in battle; Itō, however, would have to reconstruct Japan from the wreckage and humiliation of defeat.

Senior Retainers over jurisdiction existed."[7] The government and the military, the Cabinet and the Elder Statesmen, were united under the leadership of a truly independent coterie of oligarchs. As "politicians of original merit" (*genkun seijika*), Itō, Yamagata and the other few members of the Restoration leadership believed it their privilege to answer the emperor's inquiries concerning the selection of the Prime Minister and the determination of basic state policies, especially in matters of war and peace.[8]

After 1912, however, the oligarchic unity surrounding the throne gradually gave way to institutional competition to declare the Imperial Will in Japanese politics. The institutions created by the oligarchs between 1868 and 1890 gradually produced their own leaders. The feedback of institutional elites created the politics of special pleading by leaders who were products of exclusive standardized achievement routes maintained by each bureaucratic component of government. Such leaders competed among themselves for the right to declare the Imperial Will, frequently on behalf of their institutional constituencies. All institutions of government, moreover, had their justification in imperial prerogative. The military claimed its right to declare the Imperial Will on the basis of the emperor's prerogative of supreme command over the armed forces. By the 1930s, the concept of "national defense," based on the prerogative of supreme command, became the rationalization for the military's massive intervention in politics. Quarrels between the military and the Foreign Ministry frequently degenerated into jurisdictional disputes over the imperial prerogative of supreme command and the imperial prerogative to conduct foreign policy, especially in regard to Japan's China policy. There were jurisdictional disputes between the "emperor's police" of the Home Ministry and the "emperor's soldiers" of the Army.

Although not a bureaucratic institution, the Imperial Diet also claimed its primacy in the institutional foray over the Imperial Will on the basis of imperial prerogative—the emperor's legislative prerogative. During the 1920s, for example, the slogan "normal course of

7. Iwabuchi Tatsuo, "Kido Naifu no Sekinin," *Shinsei (Nova Vita)*, October 1, 1945, p. 11.

8. Inada Masatsugu, p. 25.

constitutional government" was an assertion by the Imperial Diet of its primacy in declaring the Imperial Will. This did not necessarily mean that either or both the House of Peers and House of Representatives should elect the Prime Minister and his Cabinet; it did mean that the palace should appoint as Prime Minister the leader of the majority or major political party, preferably in the lower house—the House of Representatives. Whether or not the palace appointed such a Prime Minister, however, was up to the judgment of those "close to the throne," most notably, in the 1920s and 1930s, Prince Saionji, the ex-Prime Ministers, and the Privy Seal.

The appointment of the Prime Minister was simply a prerogative of the throne. Like the appointment of the Prime Minister, all institutional claims on the Imperial Will had to be ratified in the palace; it was there that political decisions ultimately became the Imperial Will. The components of imperial prerogative—the Imperial Diet, the Army and Navy, the Foreign Ministry, the Home Ministry— exerted policy and personnel pressures, but the palace took the barometer readings and measured the vectors of pressure. During the 1930s the pressure of the military component of the imperial prerogative could not be ignored. The barometer readings taken by the palace after 1932 increasingly pointed to a high pressure area moving toward national mobilization for war, national defense predicated on military domination of Asia, and Cabinets amenable to the military's policies.

Those close to the throne, however, never permitted the military complete dominion. Institutional balances were still maintained in the composition of the Cabinet, though the military representatives carried the most weight. Even at the height of the Pacific War, the military failed to capture dominion at the side of the emperor: at least two of the four leading palace officers were moderate or "circumspect" representatives from the "outside" bureaucracy. It was precisely because of the palace's barometer reading and ratification functions that all channels to all components of imperial prerogative had to be kept open. If the Cabinet was to reflect the "trends of the times" in its composition and policies, the palace, because of its ratification function, had to have the means and skills required to measure those trends. Thus, as Prince Saionji argued, the Imperial

Household Ministry itself had to be kept "in line with the times" by appropriate leaders from the "outside"; otherwise, it would lose its "*raison d'etre*."

We may, then, conclude with Maruyama that governmental operations in prewar Japan did not embody " 'political process,' namely, *public* competition among diverse social groups for the control of a State apparatus that in itself is regarded as neutral."[9] Japan's process of privatized decision making fell far short of any Western model of democracy, as Maruyama rightly claims. But if politics in prewar Japan was not a public process, are we then justified in arguing, as Maruyama does, that "a more irrational arrangement prevailed in which decisions depended on fortuitous human relations, psychological coercion by the Elder Statesmen and other 'officials close to the Throne,' shifts in the relative strength of cliques, deals among wire-pullers and bosses, assignation-house politics, and so forth"?[10]

Speaking of Chōshū domain between 1840 and 1868, Albert Craig has elaborated the mechanism of policy change and power transfer in a feudal government:

> A change from one clique to the other could be effected by switching about a small number of men. Members of the opposing bureaucratic clique might still be in the government, but, once removed from the key positions, their function would be purely administrative. Also, . . . not all of the officials in the han [domain] government belonged to the two cliques. There remained a strong uncommitted center of gravity made up of neutralist officials.
>
> Because of this neutral middle group and the small number of key positions, a small change was at times sufficient to transfer power from one clique to the other. The daimyo [lord of the domain] and the Elders [advisory council of leading retainers] were in the position to make this change. Yet, throughout the Bakumatsu period [ca. 1840–67], the daimyo and Elders of Chōshū were incompetent. . . . However, in spite of their ineptitude, the daimyo and the Elders remained the ultimate source of power within the han; rule by either clique was rule in the name of the daimyo and with the approval of most of the Elders.
>
> This combination of weakness and authority accounts for the frequent change from one clique to the other. Since the daimyo and the Elders were

9. Maruyama Masao, *Thought and Behaviour,* pp. 229–30. His emphasis.
10. Ibid., p. 232.

weak they were easily swayed by "public opinion." When . . . the dominant feeling in the han was one of the need for reform, they would put the reformists in power. When a reaction arose against the reform, . . . they reverted to the moderate. . . .

But in spite of their personal shortcomings, the daimyo and Elders could not be completely dominated by either clique in power, because socially and politically their positions were so far above those of the bureaucratic cliques. . . . The power to appoint officials, . . . remained in the hands of the daimyo who, it seems, was influenced mainly by the "public opinion" of the collectivity of Elders and some of his highest-ranking retainers. These in turn were sensitive to a much wider compass of opinion that probably included their own retainers, merchants, samurai bureaucrats, and others.[11]

Although the Chōshū model cannot be applied in its feudal purity to the entirety of the prewar Japanese political process, it is remarkably relevant to the role of the palace from 1868 to 1945. The emperor, of course, held a far more prominent position as head of the entire Japanese nation than did the daimyo of Chōshū, one of over two hundred domains that made up the feudal polity of Tokugawa Japan. The emperor's position was also far more complex in its composition than that of a feudal lord, however powerful. In his transcendental role as emperor were fused his traditional role as high priest to the Japanese people, the role of feudal lord acquired when the shogun returned his powers to the emperor in 1867, and the role of constitutional monarch acquired in 1889 when the emperor obtained monarchical prerogatives in a constitutional legal order. Yet the emperor did perform the same ratification function in Japanese politics from 1868 to 1945 that the daimyo of Chōshū performed from 1840 to 1867.

In performing his role the emperor was assisted by advisers, "those close to the throne," much as the daimyo of Chōshū was assisted by the Elders. Again, while there are differences in the nature of those advisers, their function was remarkably similar. The Elders of Chōshū were the highest feudal retainers in the entourage of the daimyo, holding their positions by right of birth. Almost all those close to the throne between 1868 and 1945, however, held their

11. Albert M. Craig, *Chōshū in the Meiji Restoration* (Cambridge, Mass.: Harvard University Press, 1961), pp. 114–15.

positions as a result of "achievement"—success in bureaucratic leadership outside the palace. This was true, as we have noted, of the four leading palace officials whose primary role, as a collectivity, was to guard the emperor's ratification function and to act as catalysts in the process of reaching the consensus on which the Imperial Will in Japanese politics was based.

Like the daimyo of Chōshu, the emperor was also "influenced mainly by the 'public opinion' of the collectivity" of his advisers, who, like the Elders of Chōshū, approved of their lord's actions before those actions were taken. By the 1930s the function of advising the throne on political appointments as basic as the appointment of the Prime Minister and on policy decisions as basic as international treaties was performed by the Elder Statesman (Prince Saionji), the Senior Retainers (ex-Prime Ministers), the President of the Privy Council, and the Privy Seal. These were the primary negotiators in the process of imperial ratification. Although they may have had policy preferences in their roles as negotiators, they were not primarily political activists or policy advocates: they did not lead active political groups, public or private, once they attained the role of adviser to the throne. Their primary responsibility was to assist the emperor in reaching the Imperial Will in politics. If they held policy preferences, as most of them apparently did, they attempted to have those preferences realized as the Imperial Will if it were possible to do so. During 1930, for example, Prince Saionji was firmly convinced that Japan must continue to court the United States and Great Britain by ratifying the London Naval Treaty; he allied with Prime Minister Hamaguchi Osachi and other leaders against the Navy General Staff. But Saionji and the rest of those close to the throne (including the four leading palace officials) would not persist in policies that in their judgment would endanger the transcendental role of the emperor.[12]

This meant essentially that the negotiators would advise the emperor to appoint as Prime Minister that person most able to "cope with the situation" or to ratify that policy most "in line with the times" at any given moment. In so doing they were influenced by

12. Harada Kumao, vol. 1, passim.

their estimate of "public opinion" as well as by their personnel and policy preferences. The emperor's advisers, like the Elders of Chōshū, were "sensitive to a much wider compass of opinion." Such "public opinion" was not public in the commonly understood sense of that term. It was not measured by public opinion polls, elections, or other public testing devices. Nor was it made public in the press, radio, or other means of public communication. By public opinion was meant the views of persons who counted, not the public at large. By the 1930s those who counted were the bureaucratic policy advocates who directed the plural institutions of government. What counted was the weight assigned by the negotiators to any one or combination of such policy advocates and the importance attached, once again by the negotiators, to any one or combination of the components of imperial prerogative—Imperial Diet, Foreign Ministry, Army, Navy.

The information gathered about the policy advocates and their components of imperial prerogative was acquired through an elaborate network of privatized communication and was destined not for the public but for the negotiators, to assist them in producing the unanimous Imperial Will for public display. The hub of the communication process among the negotiators was the sanctuary of the palace itself, at least when they or their representatives met to reach a consensus. We have seen, for example, that Privy Seal Kido's central base of operations as a negotiator in 1941 was unquestionably the palace. For Saionji, as Elder Statesman, the palace served only as the formal place to report the consensus. Other negotiators, including the palace leaders, went to see Saionji at his villa at Okitsu if the need arose. More often they relied on Saionji's secretary, Baron Harada Kumao. The breathtaking pace of activity maintained by Harada and Kido, when Kido served as Chief Secretary to the Privy Seal, illustrates the key role played in the communication process by the secretary, who gathered information on policy preferences and opinion trends within the components of imperial prerogative at informal meetings, homes, restaurants, and clubs. The information so gathered was destined primarily for the negotiators in their capacities as advisers to the throne, not for the public. Both Harada and Kido, for example, were annoyed when newspaper reporters asked questions, as they frequently did, about such rumors as the imminence of a Cabinet resignation. According to their own records, Kido and Harada held the press in contempt and counted it a matter of pride to remain tight-lipped with reporters— or better yet, to put off their questions skillfully. Newspaper reporters were "outsiders."

Policy initiatives, however, did not reside primarily with the negotiator or the secretary, but with the policy advocate. "Policy," as used here, does not refer to those decisions that could be made and implemented by one component of government essentially without reference to the others. Ordinarily, for example, the emperor's trips to the imperial villa at Hayama were decided upon and arranged by the Imperial Household Minister and court officials, without much more than formal notification to the government. Rather, by "policy" is meant decisions that required negotiation among the components of imperial prerogative and subsequent imperial ratification: the appointment of the Prime Minister and his Cabinet, foreign policy, the national budget, economic planning.

The imperial government of Japan in the 1930s was far greater in scope of operations and far more complex than the administration of Chōshū in the 1840s. For example, clique rivalries in Chōshū apparently did not have the added complexity of institutional rivalry that characterized Japanese government in the 1920s and 1930s. Yet policy was initiated, as in Chōshū, by "bureaucratic cliques" of policy advocates and their followings in the imperial government. Though not as unified as the Chōshū bureaucratic cliques, bureaucratic opinion centers during the 1920s and 1930s held the initiative in advocating the policies with which the negotiators and secretaries dealt. And like the policy process in Choshū, policy changes could be realized by "switching about a small number of men," however difficult the process of switching might have been. Finally, there appears to have been a vast neutral center of bureaucrats in the imperial government, much as there had been in the administration in Chōshū: persons who merely administered the affairs of court and government.

One side of the competition to declare the Imperial Will in politics during the 1920s and 1930s was strictly institutional: the Foreign

Ministry versus the Army on jurisdiction over China policy, the Army versus the Navy over budget allocations for national defense and strategic priorities, the Home Ministry versus the Army over police jurisdiction. A second side was intrainstitutional, involving factionalism over personnel promotions and institutional priorities, such as that found in the Army between the Imperial Way Faction and the Control Faction, among others.[13] Factionalism at the micro-institutional level, paradoxically, allowed macro-opinion centers to form on the interinstitutional level. A policy group within one institutional component of imperial prerogative sought allies within others. The pro-German faction within the Foreign Ministry, for example, found support in the Justice Ministry and the Army. The pro–Anglo-American side of the Foreign Ministry found allies in the Navy and Finance Ministry. The primary role of the negotiators and the secretaries was to discover and sustain suitable interinstitutional opinion groupings that would declare the Imperial Will in politics effectively.

During the 1920s and 1930s, two basic bureaucratic opinion centers might be identified: the constitutionalists and the renovationists. The former group of policy advocates favored (1) nonintervention by the military in "politics"; (2) if not party Cabinets, at least party Prime Ministers; (3) international alliance with the United States and Great Britain; and (4) preservation of the emperor as a constitutional monarch. The renovationists favored (1) national mobilization and military preparedness, largely at military initiative; (2) "transcendental" Cabinets free from political party influence and representation; (3) international alliance with the Axis powers; and (4) an absolutist or mystical theory of "direct imperial rule" with the emperor as "god manifest." Both groups were essentially bureaucratic. Several constitutionalist leaders, such as Hamaguchi Osachi, had also, however, served in the House of Representatives for many years. Even some of the renovationists, such as Matsuoka Yōsuke, had served in that House. And both the constitutionalists and the renovationists were concerned with increasing Japan's international reputation and prestige. The dif-

13. On the complexity of Army factionalism, see James B. Crowley, "Japanese Army Factionalism in the 1930's," *Journal of Asian Studies* 31, no. 3. (May 1962): 309–26.

ferences between the two opinion centers involved the means to reach that end: the constitutionalists sought to win power and prestige internationally by cooperating with the United States and Great Britain; the renovationists looked to Germany and its allies as the wave of the future. Finally, both groups were "anti-Communist," but again they differed on how best to deal with the Soviet Union while agreeing generally on the suppression of Communists at home.[14]

The constitutionalists, whose policies gained preeminence in government with the appointment of Hara Kei as Prime Minister in 1918, had their counterpart negotiator group in the palace: the constitutional monarchists. As discussed in chapter 4, the constitutional monarchists were led by Prince Saionji Kimmochi as Elder Statesman and by Count Makino Nobuaki, Baron Ichiki Kitokurō, Baron Suzuki Kantarō, and Viscount Saitō Makoto as leading palace officials from 1921 to 1936. After 1936, when a conservative bureaucrat, Baron Hiranuma Kiichirō, replaced negotiator and constitutional monarchist Ichiki as President of the Privy Council, the renovationists gained preeminence in national policy making. The negotiators who responded favorably to renovationist initiatives were the traditionalists, led outside the palace by Prince Konoe Fumimaro and inside the palace after 1940 by Marquis Kido Kōichi.

Whatever their policy preferences and associations, however, both the constitutional monarchists and the traditionalists were primarily responsible for maintaining the transcendence of the throne. The role of negotiator did not permit the latitude of policy initiative and

14. The constitutionalist and renovationist groups have been discussed briefly in chaps. 4 and 5. My discussion of these policy-advocating coalitions and of factional operations within the institutions of imperial prerogative has dealt in generalizations that help to illuminate the role of the palace in the prewar political process; in fact, of course, policy-advocating coalitions and factional operations were far more complex than I have indicated. Itō Takashi's analysis of factions, groups and coalitions during the 1930 London Naval Treaty controversy, for example, shows that opinion groups were both fragmented and complex. He places groups and leaders on a graph having Progressive-Restorationist and Gradualist-Renovationist axes that gives a far more accurate representation of opinion configurations than my constitutionalist-renovationalist dichotomy (Itō Takashi, "Conflicts and Coalitions," esp. pp. 174–75). My dichotomy, however, is useful in analyzing the role of the palace in politics, as opposed to the total political process, because it points to the basic conflict over the specific role of the imperial institution that characterized Japan's political leadership not only in the 1930s but also during the entire period from 1889 to 1945.

policy advocation allowed to the bureaucrat as an institutional spokesman. Although Prince Saionji, for example, favored the constitutionalist position against the military, he would not allow the emperor to take any action that would visibly involve the throne in decision making. In 1934, Privy Seal Makino and Grand Chamberlain Suzuki urged that the emperor call an Imperial Conference in order to restrain the military. Saionji vetoed the proposal: if events developed contrary to the Imperial Conference decision, the imperial virtue would be tarnished by a "wrong" decision that formally involved the emperor. When even the emperor hoped that an Imperial Conference in 1937 might be useful in checking extremism, thereby helping to restore peace with China, Saionji again vetoed the proposal: a decision reached in the presence of the emperor in formal conference might miscarry.[15]

Saionji applied the same policy of imperial transcendence in selecting those who were to serve in positions of palace leadership. Kido Kōichi, for example, relates that Saionji opposed Konoe Fumimaro's appointment as Imperial Household Minister in 1932: Konoe had too many friends in too many quarters and would, given his weaknesses, find it difficult to resist their solicitations and "admonitions."[16] Whatever his policy and personnel preferences, therefore, Saionji attempted to keep the emperor from direct and visible involvement in political decision making and to prevent those who would so involve him from acquiring positions of palace leadership. Saionji constantly warned even against the emperor's being too greatly concerned with politics during the 1930s: if the emperor became identified as the direct proponent of a given policy he might eventually suffer the same fate that befell the German Kaiser and the monarchy in Germany following World War I.[17]

Although they placed a different emphasis on different opinion aggregates, the traditionalists were equally concerned with the emperor's transcendence. Konoe Fumimaro and Kido Kōichi, as we have seen, had greater rapport with the renovationists than did Saionji and the constitutional monarchists. Kido, however, was fully

15. Inada Masatsugu, pp. 38–41.
16. Kido Kōichi, 1 : 208.
17. Kimura Ki, *Saionji Kimmochi* (Tokyo: Jiji Tsūshin Sha, 1958), p. iii.

aware that utmost discretion was required in regard to the emperor's political involvement. In 1939, when he was Home Minister in Konoe's first Cabinet, Kido is reported to have said:

> Basically, His Majesty is a scientist; he is a pacifist as well as extremely liberal. Consequently, if we do not get some change in His Majesty's way of thinking in the future, an extraordinary gulf is possible between His Majesty and the right-wing. If this comes about, what happened to the Emperor Kōmei, whose close advisers were completely changed by the shogunate, might happen here. In order to entice the Army along while appearing to be dragged along by the Army, therefore, the emperor must take a posture that shows a little more understanding of the Army.[18]

Whether Kido believed that the military should make policy and whether he sympathized with right-wing opinion are not the issues here. Strategically, Kido was concerned that the emperor's antimilitary views would endanger the transcendence of the throne if widely known to the public. He was less concerned that the emperor was, as Emperor-in-Chambers, antimilitary than that the emperor, as Emperor-in-Public, might *appear* to be antimilitary. Given the "nature of the times," the Emperor-in-Public simply could not afford to appear, in Kido's judgment, antimilitary.

Like Saionji, Privy Seal Kido also attempted to keep the throne from direct involvement in the decision-making process. Kido was opposed, for example, to the appointment of an imperial prince as Prime Minister in October 1941. If peace were likely, which it was not, an imperial prince would be acceptable. It was another thing for an imperial prince, as Prime Minister, to lead Japan into war with the United States. If the war ended in disaster, the imperial institution would be jeopardized.

> The reasoning behind Kido's objection to an imperial prince being nominated premier [Prime Minister] was unquestionably sound. As lord privy seal, he bore a heavy responsibility for overseeing the continued maintenance of an imperial institution unblemished in any way. It was against that duty that every proposal affecting the throne was weighed.[19]

When the emperor told Kido in August 1941 that he wished to

18. Inada Masatsugu, p. 65. Emperor Kōmei (1821–67, reigned 1846–67) was the father of the Emperor Meiji.
19. Butow, *Tojo,* p. 288.

conduct the questioning directly at the scheduled September 6 Imperial Conference, Kido restrained him: the President of the Privy Council, Hara Yoshimichi, would do the questioning for the emperor; it would be suitable for the emperor only to issue a warning at the end of the discussion, given the gravity of the decision to be reached.[20]

The position of both these groups of negotiators from 1921 to 1945 was far more complicated and unstable than that enjoyed by the Elders of Chōshū in 1840. Neither the constitutional monarchists nor the traditionalists held their positions by right of birth. The emperor's advisers, the functional equivalent of the Elders of Chōshū, were more vulnerable to attack by "public opinion" because they were appointed rather than hereditary officials. They were not much higher in social and political status than those who challenged them on defining the Imperial Will. Those policy advocates who wished to declare the Imperial Will, in other words, could and did challenge the negotiators, who were responsible for defining the Imperial Will for ratification by the emperor.

Second, the negotiators of the Imperial Will had not only to cope with greater institutional complexity than prevailed in Chōshu; they also had to deal with a much wider scope of public opinion. The Imperial Diet, however inadequate as a democratic forum for the socialization of conflict, was nonetheless a public place for the public expression of criticism, thus serving to expand the scope of conflict. More importantly, public opinion had become increasingly socialized by an active press, by social groups whose views were largely dependent on what was reported in the press, and by a voracious news-consuming public. Even though "privatized public opinion"—the views of policy advocates and bureaucrats in the institutions of imperial prerogative—remained the basic sources for negotiator decisions, by 1930 the negotiators and their secretaries were forced to consider socialized public opinion in reaching their decisions—public attitudes and group demands reported by the press and other mass

20. Inada Masatsugu, pp. 74–75; Kido Kōichi, 2:901–05; *Taiheiyō Sensō e no Michi*, ed. Nihon Kokusai Seiji Gakkai, Taiheiyō Sensō Genin Kenkyū Bu, 7 vols. (Tokyo: Asahi Shimbun Sha, 1963), 7:254–55. A deadline on the negotiations with the United States was under consideration at this conference. If negotiations were not successfully concluded by that date, war with the United States would be "inevitable."

media. However much Kido and Harada disliked dealing with the press, for example, they were visited by reporters whenever a crisis or rumor of crisis arose.

Moreover, socialized public opinion was manipulated by the policy advocates to exert pressure on the negotiators; Army and Navy leaders did not hesitate to feed rumors to the press or to spread propaganda leaflets during the London Naval Treaty discussions and during the campaign against Minobe's organ theory. We have seen, for example, that the attack on Minobe's doctrines was a public attack in the Diet and in the press, as well as an attack by the renovationists in the privatized corridors of conflict resolution, against the constitutionalists and constitutional monarchists. One purpose of the attack on Minobe was to dislodge negotiator Ichiki Kitokurō from the Presidency of the Privy Council. A constitutional monarchist, Ichiki had been given his post by Saionji and the constitutional monarchists in an unprecedented move to block renovationist Hiranuma's elevation from the Vice-Presidency to the Presidency in 1934. In 1936 the renovationists, aided by socialized public opinion, were successful in removing Ichiki from the Presidency of the Privy Council, as they had been in 1933 in removing him as Imperial Household Minister.

In order to dampen the extremism of renovationist policies and to preserve the transcendence of the imperial institution, the constitutional monarchists were forced to bring the traditionalists into the palace and into positions of primacy in the negotiation process. The transition had begun as early as 1930, when Kido Kōichi was made Chief Secretary to the Privy Seal. It was completed in 1940 when Kido was appointed Privy Seal, by that time the most important negotiator role in the process of defining the Imperial Will. The constitutional monarchists were forced to acknowledge the fact, after assassinations and assassination plots from 1930 to 1936, that they were simply not able to "cope with the situation" any longer. They were no longer able to negotiate a united national policy. More seriously, they would be unable to maintain the transcendence of the throne if they persisted in their policies. The point of no return was reached on February 26, 1936, when a bloody coup was directed against them. The Privy Seal was murdered. The Grand Chamberlain was seriously wounded. Though former Privy Seal Makino escaped the assassins, as did Prince Saionji, the coup was clearly a frontal attack on the constitutional monarchists as negotiators of the Imperial Will. For the first time in Japan's modern history, a leading palace official had been assassinated and another seriously wounded. Had the constitutional monarchists not retreated the emperor himself might have been placed in jeopardy.

By retreating into the background, the constitutional monarchists also preserved a political system based on values and strategies of privatized conflict resolution, a system rooted in the concrete practices of Japanese feudal decision making but operating in the context of laws and structures adapted from Western systems of constitutional monarchy. In that system policy decisions were ratified by the emperor; they were not reached by an open collision of views in public forums. The highest political leaders were appointed by the emperor, and such appointments were not subject to public elections or review by publicly elected bodies. When elections and representative forums played a role in policy and personnel decisions they did so only as one of the variables—and usually an unimportant one—taken into consideration by those responsible to the throne for negotiating the consensus on which imperial ratification was based. The system fell far short of any Western model of democracy, as Maruyama claims. Values and strategies of socialized conflict resolution were all but absent in the political process.

However undemocratic in terms of socialized processes for resolving conflict, the prewar Japanese government was nonetheless a very effective government. Capping Japan's system of privatized conflict resolution, the palace was a delicate and responsive mechanism for negotiating the Imperial Will in politics—for finalizing authoritative decisions of state. My examination of Kido Kōichi's palace career has indicated that three political roles were essential to the operation of that mechanism: the negotiator, the bureaucrat, the secretary. All three roles were to be found not only in actual political operations but also in the official descriptions of government and court offices. Two of the roles, those of negotiator and secretary, were to be found in the extra-constitutional system for advising the throne on Cabinet appointments and basic foreign policy decisions. Kido's associations also indicated that in addition to neutral administrative bureaucrats there were bureaucratic policy advocates who headed opinion coalitions and factions within the institutions of imperial prerogative. Negotiators, in evaluating the "trends of the times" and advising on who would be able to "cope with the situation," concerned themselves with the merits and strengths of these policy advocates and their coalitions. The "unanimous" consensus resulting from negotiator efforts was ratified by the emperor, the supreme ratifier in the Japanese polity. Instruments of pressure—the "traditional" privatized means of pressure, such as assassination and the threat of assassination, clique building and positioning "behind the scenes," and face-to-face persuasion hidden from public view, as well as "modern" socialized means of pressure, such as the mass media, elections, mass protests, and appeals to the public—were utilized by policy advocates in convincing negotiators of the validity and power of their positions. Secretaries were vital communication links among political leaders, especially among negotiators and policy advocates, and they provided much of the critical information on which negotiators based their judgments.

Kido Kōichi's behavior and associations in the 1930s suggest that Japanese officials performed their roles with remarkable sensitivity to the differentiations involved and to the rules of the game of privatized decision making. There was nothing fortuitous about the political behavior of persons filling such roles; but there was considerable difficulty, given the nature of the system, in finding out just what persons were doing when they were doing it. The negotiator withdrew political conflict from public scrutiny, hoping to contract the scope of conflict and thereby resolve the issues involved. The seeds of political conflict originated primarily within the closed components of imperial prerogative. These components were either bureaucratic or were run largely by bureaucratic policy advocates, who aggregated policy demands within the corridors of power and formed cross-institutional coalitions "behind the scenes." Policy advocates pressured negotiators and opposing policy advocates by manipulating various instruments of pressure. Policy initiative, policy advocating, and conflict resolution were basically privatized processes, despite the growth of modern institutions, such as the Diet and the mass media, for socializing conflict. The most important political information on which political figures acted was acquired by private means. The secretaries to political leaders operated on an almost exclusively verbal basis. Their function in the political system was much like the "vassal telegraph" which was so critical to decision making in the Tokugawa Shogunate.[21] Secretaries, like loyal vassals, literally informed the entire structure of prewar Japanese politics.

The highly flexible nature of such roles, the sensitivity and skill of the actors performing them, and the commitment of those actors to norms and styles of privatized decision making produced a highly integrated and responsive governing process. However distasteful the resulting decisions might appear to present-day Japanese critics of the prewar political system, all decisions of national importance had to be reached by negotiation and compromise. However wrong the decisions might ultimately have been, the privatized process of conflict resolution ensured that time would be taken in arriving at the Imperial Will. As a result, the palace acted as a brake on extremism throughout its prewar existence. Just as that institution prevented Japan from becoming a purely fascist state in the 1930s, so it allowed Japan in 1945 to reach its decision to surrender before the nation was annihilated. The premise of prewar government in Japan was imperial prerogative. And it was the palace that provided the all-important negotiation and ratification mechanism at the apex of the political process which allowed the government to govern, however changed the complexion of political forces, however varied the policy demands made on the political system in the course of Japan's political modernization.

---

21. The term "vassal telegraph" is Conrad Totman's (*Politics in the Tokugawa Bakufu: 1600–1843* [Cambridge, Mass.: Harvard University Press, 1967], p. 202). For an analysis of the role of liege vassals and clique politics in the Tokugawa polity, see especially chap. 9.

BIBLIOGRAPHY

Administrative Management Agency. *Chart of Japan's Central Government Organization: 1960.* Translated by the Japanese Politics Economy Research Institute. Tokyo: Japanese Politics Economy Research Institute, n.d.

Akita, George. *Foundations of Constitutional Government in Japan, 1868-1900.* Cambridge, Mass.: Harvard University Press, 1967.

Baba Tsunego. *Gendai Jimbutsu Hyōron.* Tokyo: Chūō Kōron Sha, 1930.

Bagehot, Walter. *The English Constitution.* London: Kegan Paul, Trench, Trübner, 1904.

Beasley, W. G. "Councillors of Samurai Origin in the Early Meiji Government, 1868-1869." *Bulletin of the School of Oriental and African Studies, University of London* 20 (1957): 89-103.

Bōjō Toshinaga. *Kyūchū Gojū Nen.* Tokyo: Meitoku Shuppan Sha, 1969.

Borton, Hugh. *Japan's Modern Century.* New York: Ronald Press, 1955.

Butow, Robert J. C. *Japan's Decision to Surrender.* Stanford: Stanford University Press, 1954.

—— *Tojo and the Coming of the War.* Princeton: Princeton University Press, 1961.

Coox, Alvin D. "Year of the Tiger." *Orient/West* 9, no. 4 (July–August 1964).

Craig, Albert M. *Chōshū in the Meiji Restoration.* Cambridge, Mass.: Harvard University Press, 1961.

Crowley, James B. "Japanese Army Factionalism in the 1930s." *Journal of Asian Studies* 31 no. 3 (May 1962): 309-26.

—— *Japan's Quest for Autonomy: National Security and Foreign Policy, 1930-1938.* Princeton: Princeton University Press, 1966.

Dai Jimmei Jiten. Edited by Shimonaka Yusaburō. 10 vols. Tokyo: Heibon Sha, 1937-41.

335

Elton, G. R. *The Tudor Revolution in Government: Administrative Changes in the Reign of Henry VIII*. Cambridge: Cambridge University Press, 1953.

Fujita Hisanori. *Jijūchō no Kaisō*. Tokyo: Kōdan Sha, 1961.

Fujiwara Hirotatsu. *Kanryō: Nihon no Seiji o Ugokasu Mono*. Tokyo: Kōdan Sha, 1964.

Fukumoto Kunio. *Kanryō*. Tokyo: Kōbundō, 1959.

Gaimu Shō, ed. *Nihon Gaikō Monjo*. Tokyo: Gaimu Shō Zōhan, 1958. Ser. 47, vol. 37, no. 1.

Gendai Kazoku Fuyō. Tokyo: Nihon Shiseki Kyōkai, 1929, 1931.

Gendai no Keifu. Tokyo: Chūnichi Shimbun Shuppan Kyoku, 1965.

Gensui Kōshaku Ōyama Iwao. Tokyo: Ōyama Gensui Den Kankō Kai, 1935.

Gikai Seido Shichijū Nen Shi (Kizokuin-Sangiin Giin Meikan). Edited by Shūgiin-Sangiin. Tokyo: Ōkura Shō Insatsu Kyoku, 1960.

Gikai Seido Shichijū Nen Shi (Shūgiin Giin Meikan). Edited by Shūgiin-Sangiin. Tokyo: Ōkura Shō Insatsu Kyoku, 1962.

Goseitoku Fukyū Kai. *Meiji-Taishō-Kinjō Santei Seitoku Roku*. Edited by Watanabe Ikujirō. Tokyo: Handoku Kai, 1933.

Hackett, Roger F. *Yamagata Aritomo in the Rise of Modern Japan, 1838-1922*. Cambridge, Mass.: Harvard University Press, 1971.

Hakushaku Chinda Sutemi Den. Edited by Kikuchi Takenori. Tokyo: Kyōmeikaku, 1938.

Hakushaku Hirata Tōsuke Den. Tokyo: Hirata-haku Denki Jimusho, 1927.

Hakushaku Yamamoto Gombei Den. Edited by the Ko-Hakushaku Yamamoto Kaigun Taishō Denki Hensan Kai. 2 vols. Tokyo: Yamamoto Kiyoshi, 1938. Vol. 1.

Hara Kei Nikki. 9 vols. Tokyo: Tōkyō Kengen Sha, 1950. Vol. 2.

Hara Kei Nikki. Edited by Hara Keiichirō. 5 vols. Tokyo: Fukumura Shuppan Kabushiki Kaisha, 1965. Vols. 3, 5.

Harada Kumao. *Saionji-kō to Seikyoku*. 9 vols. Tokyo: Iwanami Shoten, 1950-56.

Harootunian, H. D., and Bernard Silberman, eds. *Modern Japanese Leadership*. Tucson: University of Arizona Press, 1966.

Hattori Shisō. *Zettai Shugi Ron (Zōho)*. Tokyo: Tōdai Kyōdō Kumiai Shuppan Bu, 1949.

Hibino Yukata. *Nippon Shindo Ron, or the National Ideals of the Japanese People*. Translated by A. P. McKenzie. Cambridge: Cambridge University Press, 1928.

Hijikata-haku. 2d ed. Tokyo: Tōyō Insatsu Kyoku, 1914.

Hirano Yoshitarō. "Meiji Ishin ni okeru Seiji-teki Shihai Keitai." *Nihon Shihon Shugi Hattatsu Shi Kōza*. Vol. 1. Tokyo: Iwanami Shoten, 1932-33.

Hiranuma Kiichirō. *Hiranuma Kiichirō Kaiko Roku*. Tokyo: Hiranuma Kiichirō Kaiko Roku Hensan Iinkai, 1955.

Holtom, Daniel Clarence. *National Faith of Japan: A Study in Modern Shintō*. London: Kegan Paul, 1938.

Honjō Shigeru. *Honjō Nikki*. Tokyo: Hara Shobō, 1967.

Hōrei Zensho. Tokyo: Ōkura Shō Insatsu Kyoku, 1869—.

Huntington, Samuel P. "The Political Modernization of Traditional Monarchies." *Daedalus* 95, no. 3 (Summer 1966): 763–88.

Ienaga Saburō et al. *Kindai Nihon Shisō Shi Kōza*. 8 vols. Tokyo: Chikuma Shobō, 1959. Vol. 1, "Rekishi-teki Gaikan."

Ihara Yoriaki. *Kōshitsu Jiten*. Tokyo: Fuzambō, 1938.

Ijiri Tsunekichi. *Rekidai Kenkan Roku*. Tokyo: Chōyōkai, 1925.

Ike Nobutaka. *Japan's Decision for War: Records of the 1941 Policy Conferences*. Stanford: Stanford University Press, 1967.

Imamura Hitoshi. *Kōzoku to Kashikan*. Tokyo: Jiyū Ajia Sha, 1960.

Imperial Household Ministry Documents (IHMD) supplied by the Imperial Household Agency, unpublished, some handwritten:
"Ekken Hyō."
"Gyōkō Hyō" (1933).
"Kyū Kōshitsu Zaisan no Hyōka" (1946).
"Kyūtei to Kyū Kōzoku."
Roster of Chief Aides-de-Camp and Aides-de-Camp, 1925–1945 (1965, untitled).
Roster of Leading Palace Officials, 1869–1963 (1964, untitled).
"Ryōbo Su Ichiran Hyō."
"Shōchoku Roku" (1917—).
"Sho Sankō Hyō."
"Shu Ekken Hyō."

Inaba Masao. "Nihon no Sensō Shidō: Sono Kikō to Jissai (1)." *Kokubō* 10, no. 7 (March 1962): 72–86.

—— "Nihon no Sensō Shidō; Sono Kikō to Jissai (2)." *Kokubō* 10, no. 8 (April 1962): 81–101.

Inada Masatsugu. "Taiheiyō Sensō Boppatsu to Tennō Genrō oyobi Jūshin no Chii." In *Taiheiyō Sensō Genin Ron*, edited by the Nihon Gaikō Gakkai. Tokyo: Shimbun Gekkan Sha, 1953.

Inoue Kiyoshi. *Tennō Sei*. Tokyo: Tōkyō Daigaku Shuppan Kai, 1953.

Irie Saburō. *Tennō no Shokutaku*. Tokyo: Kyōdō Shuppan Sha, 1954.

Irie Sukemasa. *Jijū to Paipu*. Tokyo: Mainichi Shimbun Sha, 1957.

—— *Tennō-sama no Kanreki*. Tokyo: Asahi Shimbun Sha, 1962.

Ishida Takeshi. *Sengo Nihon no Seiji Taisei*. Tokyo: Mirai Sha, 1961.

Ishiwatari Sōtarō. Tokyo: Ishiwatari Sōtarō Denki Hensan Kai, 1954.

Itō Hirobumi. *Commentaries on the Constitution of the Empire of Japan*. Translated by Itō Miyoji. 3d ed. Tokyo: Chū-ō Daigaku, 1931.

Ito Takashi. "Conflicts and Coalitions in Japan, 1930: Political Groups

[and] the London Naval Disarmament Conference." In *The Study of Coalition Behavior: Theoretical Perspectives and Cases from Four Continents*, edited by Sven Groennings, E. W. Kelley, and Michael Leiserson. New York: Holt, Rinehart and Winston, 1970.

Iwabuchi Tatsuo. "Kido Naifu no Sekinin," *Shinsei (Nova Vita)*, (October 1, 1945): 9–12.

Izu Kimio. *Tennō Sei no Rekishi*. Tokyo: Tampa Shorin, 1947.

Jansen, Marius B. *Sakamoto Ryōma and the Meiji Restoration*. Princeton: Princeton University Press, 1961.

Kai, Miwa, and Phillip B. Yampolsky. *Political Chronology of Japan, 1885–1957*. New York: East Asian Institute of Columbia University, 1957.

Kaigo Tokiomi. "Motoda Eifu." *Nippon Kyōku Sentesu Sōsho*. Vol. 19. Tokyo: Bukyō Shoin, 1942.

Kakehi Katsuhiko. *Dai Nippon Teikoku Kempō no Kompon Gi*. Tokyo: Iwanami Shoten, 1936.

—— "Shinto—The Way of Gods: Introduction to Its Teachings." *Kannagara: Kōgaku Kai Zasshi* 5, no. 7 (August 1, 1932): 1–10.

Kamiyama Shigeo. *Shin Tennō Ron*. Tokyo: Shin Kagaku Sha, 1953.

—— *Tennō Sei ni kansuru Riron-teki Sho Mondai*. Tokyo: Ashi Shuppan Shin Sha, 1956.

Kampō. Tokyo: Naikaku Insatsu Kyoku, 1885—.

Kanroji Osanaga. *Sebiro no Tennō*. Tokyo: Tōzai Bummei Sha, 1957.

Kawai Kazuo. "The Divinity of the Japanese Emperor: Political and Psychological Problems." *Political Science* (Wellington, N.Z.) 10, no. 2 (September 1958): 3–14.

—— *Japan's American Interlude*. Chicago: University of Chicago Press, 1960.

Kido Kōichi. *Kido Kōichi Nikki*. 2 vols. Tokyo: Tōkyō Daigaku Shuppan Kai, 1966.

Kido Nikki Kenkyū Kai. *Kido Kōichi Kankei Monjo*. Tokyo: Tōkyō Daigaku Shuppan Kai, 1966.

Kimura Ki. *Meiji Tennō*. Tokyo: Shibundō, 1956.

—— *Saionji Kimmochi*. Tokyo: Jiji Tsūshin Sha, 1958.

Kokuritsu Kokkai Toshokan. *Kempō Shiryō Tenji Kai Mokuroku*. Tokyo: 1957.

Kokutai no Hongi: Cardinal Principles of the National Entity of Japan. Edited by Robert King Hall. Translated by John Owen Gauntlett. Cambridge, Mass.: Harvard University Press, 1949.

Kominterun: Nihon no Jōsei to Nihon Kyōsan Tō no Nimmu ni kansuru Hōshin Sho (32-nen Tēze). [Tokyo]: Nihon Kyōsan Tō Shuppan Kyoku, [1950].

Kunai Chō Chōkan Kambō Hisho Ka. *Kunai Chō Shokuin Roku*. Tokyo: 1962.

Kunai Shō, ed. *Genkō Kunai Shō Hōki Shū*. 2 vols. Tokyo: Dai Nippon Hōrei Shuppan Kabushiki Kaisha, 1927.

Kunai Shō Shokuin Roku. Tokyo: Kunai Daijin Kambō, 1921–43.

Kurihara Kōta. *Ningen Meiji Tennō*. Tokyo: Surugadai Shobō, 1953.

Kuroda Hisata. *Tennō Ke no Zaisan*. Tokyo: Sanichi Shinsho, 1966.

Kyūtei Kishadan. *Kunai Chō*. Tokyo: Hōbun Sha, 1957.

Linebarger, Paul M. A., Ardath W. Burks, and Djang Chu. *Far Eastern Governments and Politics: China and Japan*. 2d ed., rev. Princeton: D. Van Nostrand Company, 1956.

Maruyama Masao. *Nihon no Shisō*. 8th ed. Tokyo: Iwanami Shinsho, 1964.

—— *Thought and Behaviour in Modern Japanese Politics*. Edited by Ivan Morris. London: Oxford University Press, 1963.

Matsudaira Tsuneo Tsuisō Roku. Edited by the Tokyo PR Tsūshin Sha. Tokyo: Matsudaira Tsuneo-shi Tsuioku Kai, 1961.

Matsushita Keiichi. *Sengo Minshushugi no Tembō*. Tokyo: Nihon Hyōron Sha, 1965.

Matsushita Yoshio. *Meiji Gunsei Shi Ron*. 2 vols. Tokyo: Yūhikaku, 1956. Vol. 2.

Maxon, Yale Candee. *Control of Japanese Foreign Policy: A Study of Civil-Military Rivalry, 1930–1945*. Berkeley and Los Angeles: University of California Press, 1957.

Miller, Frank O. *Minobe Tatsukichi: Interpreter of Constitutionalism in Japan*. Berkeley and Los Angeles: University of California Press, 1965.

Minobe Tatsukichi. *Kempō Kōwa*. 1st ed., rev. Tokyo: Yūhikaku, 1918.

—— "Waga Kokutai to Kokka Gainen." *Shinsei* (December 1945): 17–19.

Miyazawa Toshiyoshi. *Kempō*. 4th ed., rev. Tokyo: Yūhikaku, 1953.

—— "Kokumin Shuken to Tennō Sei to ni tsuite no Oboegaki: Odaka Kyōju no Riron o Megutte." *Kokka Gakkai Zasshi* 62, no. 6 (June 1948): 1–34.

—— "Kōshitsu Hō." In *Shin Hōgaku Zenshū*, edited by Suehiro Gentarō. Tokyo: Nihon Hyōron Sha, 1940. Vol. 2, pt. 2.

Naikaku Kiroku Ka. *Genkō Hōrei Shūran*. Tokyo: Teikoku Chihō Gyōsei Gakkai, 1920, 1923, 1942.

Najita, Tetsuo. *Hara Kei in the Politics of Compromise, 1905–1915*. Cambridge, Mass.: Harvard University Press. 1967.

Nakano Tomio. *The Ordinance Power of the Japanese Emperor*. Baltimore: John Hopkins University Press, 1923.

Nakase Jūichi. *Kindai ni okeru Tennō Kan*. Tokyo: Sanichi Shobō, 1963.

Nezu Masashi. *Tennō Shōwa Ki*. 2 vols. Tokyo: Shiseidō, 1961. Vol. 1, "Dai Nippon Teikoku no Hōkai."

Nihon Jimbutsu Shi Taikei. 7 vols. 3d ed. Tokyo: Asakura Shoten, 1963. Vol.7.

Nihon Kindai Shi Kenkyū Kai. *Tennō Sei ni kansuru Sho Mondai*. Tokyo: Kawade Shobō, 1954.

Ninagawa Arata. *Meiji Tennō*. Tokyo: Sanichi Shobō, 1956.

—— *Tennō: Dare ga Nihon Minzoku no Shujin Dearu ka?* Tokyo: Kōbun Sha, 1952.

Odaka Tomoo. *Kokumin Shuken to Tennō Sei*. Tokyo: Kokuritsu Shoin, 1947.

Ogata, Sadako N. *Defiance in Manchuria: The Making of Japanese Foreign Policy, 1931-1932*. Berkeley and Los Angeles: University of California Press, 1964.

Ogawa Kaneo. *Kyūtei*. Tokyo: Nihon Shuppan Kyōdō Kabushiki Kaisha, 1951.

Okada Keisuke. *Okada Keisuke Kaikoroku*. Tokyo: Mainichi Shimbun Sha, 1950.

Okada Keisuke. Tokyo: Okada Taishō Kiroku Hensan Kai, 1956.

Okazaki Saburō and Tsuchiya Takao. *Nihon Shihon Shugi Hattatsu Shi Gaisetsu*. Tokyo: Yūhikaku, 1937.

Okubo Genji. *Problems of the Emperor System in Postwar Japan*. Tokyo: The Japan Institute of Pacific Studies, 1948.

Pares, Richard. *King George III and the Politicians*. London: Oxford University Press, 1967.

Pittau, Joseph. *Political Thought in Early Meiji Japan: 1868-1889*. Cambridge, Mass.: Harvard University Press, 1967.

Sakamaki Yoshio. *Kōshitsu Seido Gairon*. N.p., n.d.

—— *Kōshitsu Seido Kōwa*. Tokyo: Iwanami Shoten, 1934.

Sakisaka Itsurō. *Nihon Shihon Shugi no Sho Mondai*. Tokyo: Shiseidō, 1958.

Sawamoto Kenzō, ed. *Hakushaku Tanaka Seisan*. Tokyo: Tanaka-haku Denki Kankō Kai, 1929.

Scalapino, Robert A. *Democracy and the Party Movement in Prewar Japan: The Failure of the First Attempt*. Berkeley and Los Angeles: University of California Press, 1962.

Schattschneider, E. E. *The Semi-Sovereign People: A Realist's View of Democracy in America*. New York: Holt, Rinehart and Winston, 1967.

Shiga Yoshio. *Kokka Ron*. Tokyo: Nauka Sha, 1949.

Shillony, Ben-Ami. "The February 26 Affair: Politics of a Military Insurrection." In *Crisis Politics in Prewar Japan: Institutional and Ideological Problems of the 1930s*, edited by George M. Wilson. Tokyo: Sophia University, 1970.

Shimozono Sakichi. *Makino Nobuaki-haku*. Tokyo: Jimbunkaku, 1940.

Shishaku Saitō Makoto Den. 3 vols. Tokyo: Zaidan Hōjin Saitō Shishaku Kinen Kai, 1941. Vol. 3.

Shively, Donald H. "Motoda Eifu: Confucian Lecturer to the Meiji Emperor." In *Confucianism in Action*, edited by David S. Nivison and Arthur F. Wright. Stanford: Stanford University Press, 1959.

Shokuin Roku. Tokyo: Ōkura Shō Insatsu Kyoku, 1886—.

Shumpo Kōtsui Shōkai. *Itō Hirobumi Den*. 3 vols. Tokyo: Shumpo Kōtsui Shōkai, 1940. Vol. 2.

Sōrifu. *Kanchō Benran*. 20 vols. Tokyo: Ōkura Shō Insatsu Kyoku, 1958. Vol. 2, "Sōrifu II."

Spaulding, Robert M., Jr. "The Bureaucracy as a Political Force, 1920–45." In *Dilemmas of Growth in Prewar Japan*, edited by James W. Morley. Princeton: Princeton University Press, 1971.

—— "Japan's 'New Bureaucrats,' 1932–45." In *Crisis Politics in Prewar Japan: Institutional and Ideological Problems of the 1930s*, edited by George M. Wilson. Tokyo: Sophia University, 1970.

Suzuki Hajime, ed. *Suzuki Kantarō Jiden*. Tokyo: Jiji Tsūshin Sha, 1968.

Suzuki Kantarō.' *Suzuki Kantarō Jiden*. Edited by Suzuki Hajime. Tokyo: Ōgikukai, 1949.

Suzuki Kantarō Den. Tokyo: Suzuki Kantarō Denki Hensan Iinkai, 1960.

Suzuki Takeshi. *Shūsenji Saishō Suzuki Kantarō-ō: Jūsan Kaiki ni Omou*. Tokyo: Jimbutsu Jidai Sha, 1960.

Suzuki Yasuzō. *Meiji Kempō to Shin Kempō*. Tokyo: Sekai Shoin, 1947.

Taiheiyō Sensō e no Michi. Edited by the Nihon Kokusai Seiji Gakkai, Taiheiyō Sensō Genin Kenkyū Bu. 7 vols. Tokyo: Asahi Shimbun Sha, 1963. Vol. 7

Takanishi Kōshi. *Shiseki Kaidai (Denki Hen)*. Tokyo: Meiji Shoin, 1935.

Tanaka Sōgorō. *Kindai Nihon Kanryō Shi*. Tokyo: Tōyō Keizai Shimpō Sha Shuppan Bu, 1941.

—— *Tennō no Kenkyū*. Tokyo: Kawade Shobō, 1951.

Tiedemann, Arthur. "The Hamaguchi Cabinet, First Phase, July 1929– February 1930: A Study in Japanese Parliamentary Government." Ph.D. dissertation, Columbia University, 1959.

Toda Shintarō. "Kigyō Shihon to Tennō Sei." *Shinsei* (March 1946): 9–12.

Tokutomi Iichirō. *Kōshaku Katsura Tarō Den*. 2 vols. Tokyo: Ko-Katsura Kōshaku Kinen Jigyō Kai, 1917. Vol. 2

—— *Kōshaku Matsukata Masayoshi Den*. 2 vols. Tokyo: Kōshaku Matsukata Masayoshi Denki Hakkō Jo, 1935. Vol. 2

—— *Kōshaku Yamagata Aritomo Den*. 3 vols. Tokyo: Yamagata Aritomo-kō Kinen Jigyō Kai, 1933. Vol. 2.

Tomita Kōjirō. *Tanaka Seisan-haku*. Tokyo: Seisan Shoin, 1917.

Totman, Conrad D. *Politics in the Tokugawa Bakufu: 1600–1843*. Cambridge, Mass.: Harvard University Press, 1967.

Tōyama Shigeki. *Meiji Ishin Shi*. "Iwanami Zensho," vol. 128, 17th ed. Tokyo: Iwanami Shoten, 1962.

Tōyama Shigeki and Adachi Yoshiko. *Kindai Nihon Seiji Shi Hikkei.* Tokyo: Iwanami Shoten, 1961.

Tsuda Shigemaro. *Meiji Seijō to Shin Takayuki.* Tokyo: Jishōkai, 1928.

Tsuji Kiyoaki. *Nihon Kanryō Sei no Kenkyū.* Tokyo: Kōbundō, 1952.

Tsuneishi, Warren M. "The Japanese Emperor: A Study in Constitutional and Political Change." Ph.D. dissertation, Yale University, 1960.

Tsushima Tadayuki. *Nihon ni okeru Marukusu Shugi: Futatsu no Henkō ni taisuru Tōsō.* Tokyo: Sangen Sha, 1949.

Uesugi Shinkichi. *Kokutai Kempō oyobi Kensei.* Tokyo: Yūhikaku, 1917.

Umeda Toshihiko. *Nihon Shūkyō Seido Shi.* Kyoto: Hyakkaen, 1962.

Watanabe Ikujirō. *Meiji Tennō.* 2 vols. Tokyo: Meiji Tennō Shōtoku Kai, 1958.

—— *Meiji Tennō to Hohitsu no Hitobito.* Tokyo: Chigura Shobō, 1938.

Webb, Herschel F. *The Japanese Imperial Institution in the Tokugawa Period.* New York: Columbia University Press, 1968.

Yamakawa Hitoshi. *Yamakawa Hitoshi Jiden: Aru Bonjin no Kiroku.* Edited by Yamakawa Kikue and Sakisaka Itsurō. Tokyo: Iwanami Shoten, 1962.

Yamamoto Eisuke. *Yamamoto Gombei.* Tokyo: Jiji Tsūshin Sha, 1958.

Yamazaki Tanshō. *Tennō Sei no Kenkyū.* Tokyo: Teikoku Chihō Gyōsei Gakkai, 1959.

Yanaga, Chitoshi. *Japan since Perry.* New York: McGraw-Hill Book Company, 1949.

Yanagihara Byakuren. "Yanagihara Ichii Tsubone no Kainin," *Bungei Shunjū* (Tokushū) no. 10 (October 1956): 40–46.

Young, James Sterling. *The Washington Community, 1800–1828.* New York: Columbia University Press, 1966.

INDEX

Abe Nobuyuki, 160; as Army politician, 161; as Prime Minister, 117, 161

Absolutism, 3–4

Access to the throne: Prince Fushimi Hiroyasu's abuse of, 304; role of the Grand Chamberlain, 147–48, 149, 154–55

Aides-de-Camp: and the aristocracy, 85–86; autonomy of, 81–86; and the Chamberlains, 81, 84, 86, 157; composition of, 82–83; creation of Office of, 81*n*, 157; duties and functions of, 81–82, 157; and the Imperial Household Ministry, 60; and institutional pluralism at court, 86; as members of the inner side of the Imperial Household Ministry, 63; *see also* Chief Aide-de-Camp

Anami Korechika, 85

Araki Sadao: as Army politician, 161; and the Army's Imperial Way Faction, 161; and Chief Aide Honjō Shigeru, 161*n*; and the *gōsutoppu* incident (1933), 100–1

Aristocracy: abolished, 2; and the Aides-de-Camp, 85–86; as bulwark of the throne, 2, 74, 218–19; and the Chamberlains, 74–75; composition of, 71, 73–74, 218; fiscal rewards to, 74; identification with imperial Shinto rites, 72–73; and the Imperial Household Ministry, 24, 70–75, 91; importance to Kido Kōichi as Chief Secretary to the Privy Seal, 203–12, 218–19; importance to Kido Kōichi as Di-

rector of Peerage Affairs, 220, 231–33; importance to Kido Kōichi as Privy Seal, 251, 254; and palace leadership, 116

Arita Hachirō, 233

Army: balance with the Navy at court, 141–42; and the Chang Tso-lin affair, 144, 149, 150, 160; and the Chief Aide-de-Camp, 142–43, 158–68, 170, 182–84; Control Faction of (q.v.); and the February 26 Incident, 164–67, 282; and the Hamaguchi Cabinet, 103; Imperial Way Faction of (q.v.); and the Imperial Will, 95, 101, 142; and military representation at the emperor's side, 60, 81–84, 90, 141–42, 160–61, 182–84, 185–86; and the October Incident, 92–95; as an "Outlaw" organization, 282; participation in politics, 162–63; rivalry with the Home Ministry, 100–1, 292*n*, 318; and Saionji's second Cabinet, 104, 140; "subjective tendencies" of, 264, 266; and Tanaka Giichi, 144, 187–88; and the Tōjō Cabinet, 103; and Ugaki Kazunari, 188–89; *see also* Aides-de-Camp; Imperial prerogative (of supreme command)

Board of Chamberlains, *see* Chamberlains (Board of)

British politics under George III: and prewar Japanese politics, 314–16

Bureaucracy: and Japanese political

Bureaucracy (*Cont.*)
modernization, 10; as an organization in the national polity, 281–82; primacy in politics of, 3–4, 10, 91, 106, 195; *see also* "Bureaucrat"; Japanese (bureaucratic) fascism; "Policy advocate"; Renovationists
"Bureaucrat": Kido Kōichi as, 194–95, 220–37, 275–309; as a political role, 9, 194–95, 222, 288, 324

Cabinet (informal), 17–18, 18*n*; as the direct advisory group to the emperor, 22
Cabinet: as a coalition of institutional elites, 102–5; composition of, 315–16; creation of the Cabinet system, 24, 175; inner Cabinet, 186–87; and the palace, 105; "responsibility," 268, 268*n*; role of, 102; and Sanjō Sanetomi, 175–76; "transcendental" Cabinets, 98, 131, 137–38, 325; *see also* Hamaguchi Osachi; House of Representatives; Okada Keisuke; Political parties; Saionji Kimmochi; Tōjō Hideki
Ceremonies, Board of the: and the Chamberlains, 78; evolution of, 30–31; and foreign dignitaries, 64
Ceremonies, Office of the, 30
Chamberlains, 74–79; and the Aides-de-Camp, 81, 84, 86; and the aristocracy, 74–75; Board of, 76, 78–79, 169; and the Imperial Guards, 94; and the inner side of the Imperial Household Ministry, 63; *see also* Grand Chamberlain
Chang Tso-lin: murder of, 144, 160
Chang Tso-lin affair, 144–45, 148–51; and the Army (q.v.); and the emperor, 144–45, 146–47; and Tanaka Giichi, 144, 188
Chichibu Yasuhito (Prince-of-the-Blood): political involvement of, 304–7
Chief Aide-de-Camp, 81*n*; abolition of the office of, 2; autonomy of, 142, 182; career backgrounds of, 142, 158–59; China experience of, 158–59, 161; duties and role of, 81–82, 105–6, 157, 265, 267; as General Staff informant (spy), 156–57, 159, 161*n*, 170; and the Grand Chamberlain, 142–43, 153, 155, 157, 169, 170; and Hara Kei, 159; Hasunuma Shigeru

as, 159, 262, 265–67, 269–70; Honjō Shigeru as, 160–70, 304, 305; and the Imperial Household Minister, 169–70; and the London Naval Treaty, 153–55; as a "negotiator," 170, 274; as Privy Councillors, 159; and the Privy Seal, 165–70; and Privy Seal Kido Kōichi, 262, 265–67, 269–70; Saionji Kimmochi's lack of control over, 189
Chinda Sutemi (Grand Chamberlain), 141
Chōshū (domain): as a decision-making model for the prewar Japanese political process, 320–23, 324, 329; and the Imperial Household Minister, 123–24; and the Meiji oligarchs, 102*n*, 123; and the Meiji Restoration, 122–23
Civil Government (*Dajōkan*), 17; and the Government of Rites (*Jingikan*), 28–30, 32
Clique, *see* Faction
Club(s), *see* Eleven Club; Sixth Day Club; Tuesday Luncheon Club
Confucianism: and the role of the emperor, 26, 33; and Shinto rites, 33
Consensus, *see* Emperor; "Negotiator"; Palace; Palace leadership; Traditionalists
Constitutionalists: as "policy advocates," 325–26, 326*n*
Constitutional monarchists: control of the palace, 107, 111–12, 181, 189; and the February 26 Incident, 330–31; and the Grand Chamberlain, 141–43; and the Imperial Household Minister, 129–32; and imperial transcendence, 326–27; influence on the emperor, 168; and the London Naval Treaty, 150, 156; and Minobe's theory of constitutional monarchy, 111–12; as "negotiator(s)" (q.v.); political partisanship of, 111–13, 141–42, 150, 156; and the traditionalists, 112–13, 190, 326–29, 330; *see also* Ichiki Kitokurō; Makino Nobuaki; Saionji Kimmochi; Suzuki Kantarō
Constitutional monarchy, *see* Constitutional monarchists; Emperor; Minobe Tatsukichi
Control Faction (Army), 99; and the February 26 Incident, 286–87; and intrainstitutional factionalism, 325
Court, *see* Emperor-in-Court; Imperial

Household Minister; Imperial Household Ministry; Palace; Palace leadership

Court finances, 64–70; and the aristocracy, 74; and palace autonomy, 65, 67–68, 69; political uses of, 70, 127–28, 128n; and the role of the emperor as social paragon, 127; see also Imperial House Economic Council

Court Nobles: importance of Sanjō Sanetomi as, 175; and the Restoration Government, 18

Decision making, see Privatized decision making; Socialized decision making

Diet, see Imperial Diet

"Eastern ethics, Western techniques", 38–39, 72

Elder Statesmen (Genrō), 55, 318, 320; conference of, 215–16; Council of, 180; and the imperial prerogative of appointment, 106, 180–81; and the Imperial Will, 129, 187; and Kido Kōichi's appointment as Privy Seal, 238–39, 241–43, 245; last of the, 112, 181; as "negotiator(s)", 8, 105, 178, 322; and the Privy Seal, 172, 173, 177–78, 179, 180; see also Saionji Kimmochi

Eleven Club (Jūichikai), 209; centrality to Kido Kōichi's role as a "secretary," 205–6, 210–12, 296; formation and function of, 198; and Kido Kōichi as a "bureaucrat", 222, 226, 228, 229, 232–33, 235, 236; and Konoe Fumimaro, 198; members of, 205–6, 205n; and Privy Seal Kido Kōichi, 251, 255

Emperor: antimilitary views of, 328; and the appointment of Kido Kōichi as Privy Seal, 238, 244–45, 246; and the appointment of Suzuki Kantarō as Grand Chamberlain, 142, 143n; change in constitutional role (1947), 1–2; and the Chang Tso-lin affair (q.v.); and Chichibu Yasuhito (Prince-of-the-Blood), 305–7; and the Chief Aide-de-Camp, 265, 267; and Chief Aide Honjō Shigeru, 161–68, 170; and the consensus-making process, 263–64; and constitutional monarchy, 14–15, 38–39, 47, 321;

"cultivating the virtue" of, 19–21, 140; and the February 26 Incident, 164–67, 305n; and Fushimi Hiroyasu (Prince-of-the-Blood), 304; and Imperial Conferences, 263–64, 302, 327, 328–29; and the imperial line (ancestors), 6, 40–41, 42; and the Imperial Will, 6, 47, 52, 54–56, 303; and the London Naval Treaty, 153–54; and Minobe's theory of constitutional monarchy, 163–64, 168; and negotiations with the United States, 299–301; personal role in politics, 4–5, 6, 15, 47–49, 54–56, 262–64, 266–67, 268–69, 299–303; personality of, 11; and Privy Seal Kido Kōichi, 261–64, 266–67, 269–70, 271–72, 298–303; public criticism of, 26n, 56–57; as a "ratifier," 4–5, 6, 8, 11, 47, 55, 56, 195, 261–63, 298–303, 315, 321, 331; and the role of the feudal lord (daimyo), 321–23; and the Shanghai crisis (1932), 213–14, 216–17; and Shinto deities (rites), 27–28, 32, 47, 53; and shogunal powers, 6, 13–15, 37, 47, 321; as a "Shrine," 298–99, 302; as social paragon, 53–54, 64, 70, 127; and the Sun Goddess, 27; and Tanaka Giichi, 144–47; in the Tokugawa period, 14; and war with the United States, 262–63, 271, 300; see also Emperor-in-Chambers; Emperor-in-Court; Emperor-in-Public; Emperor-in-State; Imperial prerogative; Imperial Will; Meiji Emperor; Taishō Emperor

Emperor system (tennōsei), 3, 32, 175

Emperor-in-Chambers, 51–57; actions of emperor as, 302–3; and the Chamberlains, 75–79; and the Emperor-in-Public, 56, 328; and the October Incident (1931), 93–95

Emperor-in-Court, 51–54; and the Emperor-in-State, 56, 274; and the Imperial Household Minister, 105, 124, 127, 129; and the outer side of the Imperial Household Ministry, 64

Emperor-in-Public, 51–57, 302, 328

Emperor-in-State, 51, 55–57; and the Emperor-in-Court, 56, 274; and Japanese (bureaucratic) fascism, 190; and palace leadership, 106, 190

Faction (clique), 99, 139, 320–21, 324; *see also* Control Faction; Imperial Way Faction

Fascism, *see* Japanese (bureaucratic) fascism

Family state: Japan as, 57–58

February 26 Incident (1936), 188, 194; and the Army, 164–67, 282; causes change in palace leadership, 112; and Chichibu Yasuhito (Prince-of-the-Blood), 305n; and Chief Aide Honjō Shigeru, 161n, 164–68, 169; and collusion of "Officials" and "Outlaws," 285–87; and the emperor, 164–67, 305n; and Fushimi Hiroyasu (Prince-of-the-Blood), 286; impact on the constitutional monarchists, 142, 330–31; and Mazaki Jinzaburō (General, 160, 286; and the military establishment, 305n; and young insurgents, 278–79, 282, 285

Feudal government: and the prewar political process, 9, 320–23, 324, 333

Foreign Ministry: bureaucratic representation at court, 184–87; and the Imperial Household Minister, 119; and the imperial prerogative (of treaty making) (q.v.); and the Privy Seal, 172–73; *see also* Arita Hachirō; Matsuoka Yōsuke; Shidehara Kijūrō; Tani Masayuki

Fujinuma Shōhei, 209, 210, 211, 233

Fushimi Hiroyasu (Prince-of-the-Blood): abuse of access to the throne, 304; as Chief of the Navy General Staff, 84, 214, 286, 300, 303–4; and the February 26 Incident, 286; and the London Naval Treaty, 303, 304; as a "Shrine," 303–4

Fushimi Sadanaru (Prince-of-the-Blood): as Privy Seal, 177–78

Genrō, *see* Elder Statesmen

gōsutoppu incident (1933), 100–1, 292n

Grand Chamberlain: appointment of Suzuki Kantarō as, 141–43; career backgrounds of, 133–34; and the constitutional monarchists, 141–56, 169n; duties and role of, 105–6, 132–33, 147–48, 156; and the February 26 Incident, 330–31; and the Navy, 134, 142; Katsura Tarō as, 136–41; Suzuki Kantarō as, 143–56, 169–70; Tokudaiji Sanenori as, 134–36, 139; transition to bureaucratic leadership, 141

Hamaguchi Osachi: assassination of, 188; Cabinet of, 102–3; and the London Naval Treaty (q.v.)

Hara Kei: assassination of, 314; and Grand Chamberlain/Privy Seal Katsura Tarō, 137–40; on the political use of court finances, 128; and the preeminence of the constitutionalists, 326; views on palace leadership, 139–40

Hara Yoshimichi, 329

Harada Kumao: account of Prime Minister Tanaka Giichi's resignation, 145; career of, 206n; centrality to Kido Kōichi's role as a "secretary", 194, 206–9, 261, 323–24; and Kido Kōichi's appointment as Privy Seal, 238–39, 240–44; and Kido Kōichi as a "bureaucrat," 232, 297; and the London Naval Treaty, 154–55; and Privy Seal Kido Kōichi, 255; role in Cabinet changes, 207; *see also* Saionji Kimmochi

Hasunuma Shigeru, 84, 159; and Privy Seal Kido Kōichi, 262, 265–67, 269–70, 273, 274, 301

Hata Shunroku, 159

Hijikata Hisamoto, 122, 123n

Hiranuma Kiichirō: Cabinet of, 237; and "Cabinet responsibility", 268; as a government "Official," 283; and Foreign Minister Matsuoka Yōsuke, 269; as a "policy advocate," 288; as a possible Privy Seal, 239, 245; as President of the Privy Council, 239, 326, 330

Hirata Tōsuke: appointment as Privy Seal, 178; and Cabinet changes, 180; as Imperial Household Ministry Consultant, 178–79; and the Privy Council, 179–80; as Privy Seal, 179–80; son of, 85

Hirohata Tadataka, 205n, 217, 228, 229–30

Home Ministry: bureaucratic representation at court, 87–89, 91, 184–86; and the Imperial Household Minister, 120–21, 122, 125; and the Imperial Household Ministry (q.v.); and imperial prerogative, 98; rivalry with the Army, 100–1, 292n, 318

Honjō Shigeru: appointed to the Privy Council, 159; appointment as Chief Aide-de-Camp, 161n; and Chichibu Yasuhito (Prince-of-the-Blood), 305–6; as Chief

Aide-de-Camp, 83–84, 160–70, 304, 305; China experience, 159; conflicts with the emperor, 163–64; defends Army interests, 161, 162–68; and the February 26 Incident, 161n, 164–67; and Fushimi Hiroyasu (Prince-of-the-Blood), 304; and Grand Chamberlain Suzuki Kantarō, 169–70; and Ichiki Kitokurō, 165; and Imperial Household Minister Yuasa Kurahei, 169–70, interpretation of the national polity, 166; as a military "spy" at the palace, 156–57, 161n, 170

House of Peers: and the Eleven Club (Jūichikai), 198, 205, 294; and the Hamaguchi Cabinet, 103; and the House of Representatives, 99; and the Imperial Household Ministry, 89, 90–91, 119, 172, 184; and Japanese (bureaucratic) fascism, 205n; and Kido Kōichi (q.v.); and Konoe Fumimaro, 152, 190, 190n, 205n and Minobe Tatsukichi, 131; and palace leadership, 114–16; and to Tōjō Cabinet, 103; see also Imperial Diet; Imperial prerogative (of legislation)

House of Representatives: and the Hamaguchi Cabinet, 102–3, 151; and the Imperial Household Ministry, 89, 90–91; and the institutionalization of imperial prerogatives, 97–99; and the Kiyoura Cabinet, 104; Minobe Tatsukichi's theory on, 39, 131; and palace leadership, 113–15; and "party" Cabinets, 137–39, 187–88; and the Tōjō Cabinet, 103–4; and "transcendental" Cabinets, 137–39; see also Imperial Diet; Imperial prerogative (of legislation)

Ichiki Kitokurō: antipathy of court conservatives and rightists, 143n; career of, 130, 143n; and the conference of Senior Retainers, 181; as a constitutional monarchist, 112, 129–31, 326; as Imperial House Economic Adviser, 179; as Imperial Household Minister, 129–30, 142–43, 152, 181, 196–97, 199, 217; interviews Kido Kōichi, 196–97, 199; and Minobe Tatsukichi, 130–31; as possible Privy Seal, 241; as President of the Privy Council, 119–20, 131, 165, 326, 330; and Saionji

Kimmochi, 112, 143, 326; and Suzuki Kantarō's appointment as Grand Chamberlain, 142–43; theory of constitutional monarchy, 130

Idemitsu Mambei, 163

Imamura Hitoshi, 92–94, 282

Imperial Conference (Gozen Kaigi): and the emperor, 263–64, 302, 327, 328–29; of February 4, 1904, 317n; and Prime Minister Konoe Fumimaro, 270; role of, 263; of September 6, 1941, 264, 302, 328–29; and the wars with Russia (1904) and the United States (1941), 316, 317n

Imperial Diet: and the Imperial Household Ministry, 89, 90–91, 119, 172, 184; and the Imperial House Law, 42; and the Imperial Will, 318–19; and the institutionalization of imperial prerogatives, 5, 97–99; and the legitimacy of state policies, 91, 316; Minobe Tatsukichi's theory on, 39, 98, 131; and "party" Cabinets, 138–39; and public harmony, 313; see also House of Peers; House of Representatives; Imperial prerogative (of legislation)

Imperial estate (property), 65–66, 70, 125, 128; see also Imperial Lands (and Forests), Bureau of

Imperial Family Council, 42, 42n, 43, 46, 58

Imperial Guards: and the Chamberlains, 94; complaints against the Imperial Household Ministry, 93–94; duties of, 64; and "loyalty," 93; and "Outlaws," 292n

Imperial House Audit Bureau, 70

Imperial House Economic Council, 69, 178–79

Imperial Household Minister: career backgrounds of, 118–20; and the constitutional monarchists, 129–32; and court finances, 70, 125, 127–28; duties of, 120–22; Ichiki Kitokurō as, 129–30, 142–43, 152, 181, 196–97, 199, 217; interaction with the government, 120–22, 124–25, 128–29; Itō Hirobumi as, 24–25, 119; Makino Nobuaki as, 111, 120, 124n, 129; Makino Nobuaki's views on, 123–24; and the Meiji Emperor, 126–27; role of, 105–6; Tanaka Mitsuaki as, 122–29; transition to bureaucratic leadership, 129; see also Kido Kōichi; Saionji Kimmochi

Imperial Household Ministry: and the Aides-de-Camp, 81–86, 90; and the aristocracy, 70–75, 85–86, 91; and the Chamberlains, 75–79, 80; consolidation of, 58–60; creation of, 17; and the Home Ministry, 87–89, 91; and the Imperial Diet (q.v.); Imperial Guards' complaints against, 93–94; and institutional pluralism, 86–95; and the Ladies-in-Waiting, 79–81; and the management of the Emperor-in-Court as Emperor-in-Public, 54, 63–74; number of officials in, 61; "rectification" of, 92–95; and Shinto rites, 30–31; as symbol of modern bureaucratic government, 58; as a top-level bureaucratic structure, 60–63

Imperial Household Secretary: and the "cabinet," 17–18; Itō Hirobumi as, 23–24; Tokudaiji Sanenori as, 19

Imperial House Law (Kōshitsu Tempan): contents, 43; drafting of, 23, 25; interpretations of, 41–46; and the Privy Council, 42, 43, 46, 58

Imperial institution: dignified mystery of, 52–53; and modernization, 5–6, 53–54; and the modernizing oligarchs, 52–53, 80; and the national polity, 38–39, 38n; and the plural institutions of government, 95; popular loyalty to, 26–27, 32–33, 35, 39n, 47; and Shinto rites, 15, 27–28, 32, 53; and shogunal powers, 13, 14, 15, 37, 47; as state within a state, 58, 60; as a state writ small, 90; as symbol of the nation as people, 53, 95; in the Tokugawa period, 14; transcendence of, 6–7, 13–14, 26–27, 43, 47, 95n, 112–13, 190, 326–28, 330; see also Emperor; Emperor-in-Chambers; Emperor-in-Court, Emperor-in-Public; Emperor-in-State; Meiji Emperor; Palace; Palace leadership; Taishō Emperor

Imperial investments, 66–67; see also Court finances

Imperial Lands (and Forests), Bureau of, 65–66, 68, 70

Imperial line: and the Imperial House Law, 42; and sovereignty, 6, 40–41

Imperial prerogative, 1; of appointment, 15, 105, 113, 180–82, 181n, 187–89, 191,

207, 315–16, 319, 322–23; and Cabinet coalitions, 102–5; and the imperial line, 41; institutionalization of, 5, 57, 86, 97–105, 149–50, 184–87, 315, 323; of legislation, 5, 15, 39, 97–99, 100, 104, 318–19; and political leadership, 99–101; and political legitimacy, 6, 35–37, 39, 313, 333; and the role of the palace, 105, 187; and Shinto rites, 35–38; of supreme command, 5, 15, 37, 98–99, 101n, 142, 153, 186, 318; of treaty making (war, peace, diplomacy), 98, 150, 186, 315, 316, 318

Imperial princes: as "Shrines," 303–07; see also Chichibu Yasuhito; Fushimi Hiroyasu; Fushimi Sadanaru; Takamatsu Nobuhito

Imperial Rule Assistance Association, 190–91, 239n

Imperial tombs, 64

Imperial Way Faction (Army), 160–61; and the February 26 Incident, 286–87; and intrainstitutional factionalism, 325

Imperial Will: coordination of, 170; and decision making, 6; and the emperor's personal will, 6, 40–41, 47, 54–56; and the imperial ancestors, 6, 40–41, 47; institutional competition over, 5, 95, 100, 101, 105, 187, 284, 315, 318, 319; as the national interest, 160; and the "negotiator," 322, 329, 331; and popular mobilization, 52–53; and the privatization of conflict, 313, 316, 317; and the radical left, 317; and the radical right, 317; and the ratification process, 6, 55, 118, 303, 319, 329; and the role of the palace, 187, 191–92, 319, 331, 333

Inner Cabinet, 186–87

Inner shrine (kashikodokoro), 30, 71

Inoue Kaoru, 179, 180

Inoue Nisshō: and Konoe Fumimaro, 288; as an "Outlaw," 290–91

Inoue Saburō, 231; and Kido Kōichi's aristocratic network, 209–10; and the renovationist bureaucrats, 209n

Institutional pluralism, 284–86; and the court bureaucracy, 7, 86–92, 95; and palace leadership, 7–8, 57, 105, 111, 113, 184–87; see also Cabinet; Imperial institution; Imperial prerogative; Imperial Will; Palace

Instrument of Government (*Seitaishō*), 16

"Instrument of pressure," 95, 288; and the "negotiator," 330, 332; "Outlaws" as, 285–87, 288–94; and the "policy advocate," 330, 332; as a political role, 9

Inukai Takeru, 209, 210, 211, 233

Inukai Tsuyoshi; assassination of, 188, 314; as Prime Minister, 188, 210, 213–17

Irie Sukemasa, 76–77, 77n, 132

Itagaki Taisuke, 123

Itō Hirobumi: accused of violating the distinction between court and government, 22–25, 138; and the aristocracy, 71–72, 73–74; assassination of, 314; and court finances, 65, 178; criticized by Motoda Eifu, 25, 313; as Elder Statesman (oligarch), 317–18; and the Imperial House Economic Council, 178; as Imperial Household Minister, 24–26; 58, 65, 119; as Imperial Household Secretary, 23–24, 58; and the Imperial House Law, 41–42, 43–44; and the imperial institution, 38–39; and the *Jiho*, 21, 21n; and the Meiji Constitution, 35–36, 38–39; and the national polity, 35; as a "policy advocate," 175; as President of the Privy Council, 36, 119; as Prime Minister, 24–25, 119, 180; resignation as Imperial Household Minister, 25–26; and Sanjō Sanetomi, 23, 174–76; and Yamagata Aritomo, 23, 317, 317n

Itō Hirokuni, 75

Iwakura Tomomi: and court finances, 65, 128; and the *Jiho*, 21n; and the Ladies-in-Waiting, 80; and Motoda Eifu, 18; and the Rules and Regulations Bureau, 23n; and Saionji Kimmochi, 135

Izawa Takio: and Kido Kōichi's appointment as Privy Seal, 238, 240

Japanese (bureaucratic) fascism, 275; evolution of, 189; and the February 26 Incident, 285–87; and the House of Peers, 205n; and the Imperial Will, 317; and Konoe Fumimaro, 190–91; and the palace, 192, 333; and the traditionalists, 189–91

Japanese politics: and British politics under George III, 314–16

Jiho (Advisers-in-Attendance): abolition of, 22; and the assassination of Ōkubo Toshimichi, 20; competition with the "cabinet," 21–22; creation and duties of, 19; criticism of the Meiji Emperor, 20, 56–57; and Itō Hirobumi, 21; and the Ladies-in-Waiting, 80; Sasaki Takayuki as, 19–20, 21–22, 135; and Tokudaiji Sanenori, 19, 135

Kakehi Katsuhiko, 45

Kanroji Osanaga, 77, 79, 80, 111, 273–74, 301

Katō Kanji: as Chief of the Navy General Staff, 153–56, 169

Katsura Tarō: as Grand Chamberlain and Privy Seal, 111, 136–41, 184; and Imperial Household Minister Tanaka Mitsuaki, 124–25; Ozaki Yukio denounces, 138–39, 299; and Yamagata Aritomo, 111, 116, 130n, 136–37, 138–39

Kido Kōichi: and the Army and Navy Ministers, 264–65, 267, 301; associations as a "bureaucrat" compared with his associations as a "secretary," 220–26, 231–37; associations as a "negotiator" compared with his associations as a "bureaucrat" and as a "secretary," 246–54; as a "bureaucrat," 194–95, 220–37; as a "bureaucrat" with the emperor and imperial family, 231, 297, 298; as a "bureaucrat" with government officials, 233–34, 296; as a "bureaucrat" with palace officials, 195, 226–31, 296; categories of associates as Privy Seal, 254–59; and Chief Aide Hasunuma Shigeru, 262, 265–67, 269–70, 273, 274, 301; and Chief Secretary Matsudaira Yasumasa, 238–39, 243–44, 273, 299–300; as Chief Secretary to the Privy Seal, 8, 194, 199–220, 294–96, 330; and the Chiefs of Staff (High Command), 263–65, 271, 272, 300–1; diary of, 193–94, 193n, 201n; as Director of Peerage Affairs, 8, 194–95, 220–37, 296–97; and the Eleven Club (q.v.); family connections, 117; and the Foreign Minister, 268–70, 271; and the Grand

Kido Kōichi (*Cont.*)
Chamberlain, 217, 229–30, 273, 274; and
Harada Kumao (q.v.); and the House of
Peers, 203–5, 205n, 294–96, 307–8; and
Konoe Fumimaro (q.v.); as Minister in the
Konoe and Hiranuma Cabinets, 237, 328;
and the Ministers of State, 195, 256, 267;
and negotiations with the United States,
300–1; as a "negotiator" with the emperor
and imperial family, 195, 261–64, 266–67,
268–70, 271–72, 274, 299–303, 306–7,
309; as a "negotiator" with government
officials, 195, 256–60, 261, 264–65,
267–72, 297; as a "negotiator" with
palace officials, 195, 265–67, 273–74, 297;
and "Officials," 294–97, 307–9; and
Okabe Nagakage (q.v.); and "Outlaw"
Inoue Nisshō, 290–91; and "Outlaw"
Matsui Kūka, 289–90, 292; and
"Outlaw" Ōkawabara Nittō, 288, 291;
and "Outlaws," 288–94; and "Outlaw"
Takuya Dempu, 288, 291–93; and prewar
political roles, 8–9; and the Prime
Minister, 267–68, 270–71, 272, 301; and
Prince Chichibu Yasuhito, 198, 306–7;
and Prince Takamatsu Nobuhito, 306; as
Privy Seal, 8, 112–13, 181–82, 191, 195,
246–74, 293, 297, 298–303, 306–7, 326,
328–29, 330; and Privy Seal Makino
Nobuaki, 194, 196, 197, 198–99, 202,
207, 208, 212–17, 219, 226; and Privy
Seal Saitō Makoto, 226–27; and the renovationists (new bureaucrats), 191, 296,
296n, 326, 327; roles in palace politics,
8–9, 194–95, 287–88, 309, 331–33; and
Saionji Kimmochi, 207, 212, 232, 239,
241, 242; as a "secretary" with
government officials, 208–11, 294, 296; as
a "secretary" with palace officials,
212–18, 294; and the Shanghai crisis
(1932), 213–17; and "Shrines," 297–307;
and the Sixth Day Club, 212, 236; and
Suzuki Kantarō, 113; and the system for
advising the throne, 181; and Tōjō Hideki,
113, 267–68, 270, 272; as a traditionalist,
112–13, 191, 327–29, 330; and the
transcendental role of the emperor,
327–29; *see also* Aristocracy; Emperor;
Matsudaira Tsuneo

Kiyoura Keigo: Cabinet of, 104
Kodama Hideo, 117, 231
Komeda Torao: criticizes the Meiji Emperor,
20
Konoe Fumimaro: and Cabinet responsibility, 268, 268n, 270; and the House of
Peers, 152, 190, 190n, 205n; and the Imperial Rule Assistance Association,
190–91, 239, 240, 244; involvement with
Kido Kōichi's political career, 219, 297;
and Japanese (bureaucratic) fascism,
190–91; and Kido Kōichi's appointment as
Chief Secretary to the Privy Seal, 196–97,
198, 199, 296; and Kido Kōichi's appointment as Privy Seal, 238–40; and
Kido Kōichi's aristocratic network, 198,
210, 211; and the London Naval Treaty
(q.v.); as a "negotiator," 190n; and "Outlaws," 288; as a possible Privy Seal, 239,
244, 245; as Prime Minister, 190–91,
191n, 205n, 237, 263, 267–71, 272,
295–96, 301, 328; and Privy Seal Kido
Kōichi, 267–71, 272, 295–96, 301; and the
renovationists (new bureaucrats), 326–27;
and the traditionalists, 112, 326, 327,
vetoed as Imperial Household Minister by
Saionji Kimmochi, 327
Kuroda Kiyotaka, 24n, 176, 180
Kwantung Army, 159, 161

Ladies-in-Waiting, 60, 63; duties of, 79–80;
and the *Jiho*, 80; and the Restoration
leaders, 80–81
Liaison Conference, 186, 186n, 263
London Naval Treaty: and the Chief Aide-
de-Camp, 153–55; and Chief of the Navy
General Staff Katō Kanji, 153–54, 155,
156, 169; and the constitutional monarchists, 150, 156; and the emperor, 153–54;
and Grand Chamberlain Suzuki Kantarō,
143, 153–56, 169; and Imperial
Household Minister Ichiki Kitokurō, 152;
institutional forces involved in, 98,
150–51; issues at stake, 151; and Konoe
Fumimaro, 152, 190n; and Okada
Keisuke, 152, 154, 188; and Prime
Minister Hamaguchi Osachi, 151, 153,
188, 322; and the Privy Council (q.v.);
and Privy Seal Makino Nobuaki, 152–53;

and Saionji Kimmochi, 151–53, 187, 188, 322; and Saitō Makoto, 152, 188; and Shidehara Kijūrō, 152; and Wakatsuki Reijirō, 151–52
Lord Keeper of the Privy Seal, see Privy Seal

Makino Nobuaki: attacks against, 143n, 290, 291–92, 331; and "bureaucrat" Kido Kōichi, 222, 231–32; career background of, 143n; and constitutional monarchist control of the palace, 111–12, 326; as Imperial Household Minister, 111, 120, 124n, 129; interviews Kido Kōichi, 196–97, 202; and the London Naval Treaty, 152–53; as a "negotiator," 194; as Privy Seal, 120, 142–43, 143n, 146, 152–53, 171, 177, 194, 206, 212–18, 219, 290, 291–92, 294, 327; resignation as Privy Seal, 171; and Saionji Kimmochi, 143, 143n, 152–53; and the Shanghai crisis (1932), 213–17; and Suzuki Kantarō's appointment as Grand Chamberlain, 142–43; and Tanaka Giichi's "military diplomacy," 146; views on a successor to Imperial Household Minister Nakamura Yūjirō, 123–24
Matsudaira Keimin, 228, 230
Matsudaira Tsuneo: and "bureaucrat" Kido Kōichi, 225n, 226–27; as Imperial Household Minister, 132, 225n, 226–27, 238, 239–40, 241–42, 243, 246, 273, 274, 306; and Kido Kōichi's appointment as Privy Seal, 238, 239–40, 241–42, 243, 246
Matsudaira Yasumasa: and "bureaucrat" Kido Kōichi, 228–29; as Chief Secretary to the Privy Seal, 238–39, 243–44, 251, 273, 299–300; and the Eleven Club, 205n, 228, 229; and Kido Kōichi's appointment as Privy Seal, 238–39, 243–44
Matsui Iwane, 160–61
Matsui Kūka: as an "Outlaw," 289–90, 292
Matsukata Masayoshi: death of, 112, 116, 181; as Elder Statesman, 111, 178, 180; and the Imperial House Economic Council, 178; and imperial investments, 66–67; as Prime Minister, 124, 180, 317; as Privy Seal, 111, 124, 178; recommends Hirata Tōsuke as Privy Seal, 178
Matsuoka Yōsuke: as Foreign Minister, 262, 268n, 268–70, 271, 279–80, 299; as an "Outlaw" and "Official", 279–80; as a "policy advocate," 288; as a renovationist, 325
Mazaki Jinzaburō: and Chief Aide Honjō Shigeru, 161–62; China experience of, 161; and the February 26 Incident, 160, 286; and the Imperial Way Faction, 160
Meiji Constitution (Constitution of the Great Empire of Japan), 1, 5, 13, 14–15; drafting and ratification of, 23, 24, 25, 35–37, 36n; and the Imperial House Law, 15, 41–42, 43–46; and the Meiji Emperor, 46; and the Ministers of State, 40; and the pluralism of political power, 5, 284; and the Privy Council, 36, 58; schools of interpretation, 44–46, 45n; and Shinto rites, 15, 35–37, 38; and sovereignty of the imperial line (imperial ancestors), 40–41; see also Imperial prerogative
Meiji Emperor: and the aristocracy, 71; criticism of, 20, 26n, 56–57; freedom of movement, 47–49; and Grand Chamberlain Tokudaiji Sanenori, 135; and the Imperial House Law, 46; and Imperial Household Minister Tanaka Mitsuaki, 126–27; and inner court life, 77; and Itō Hirobumi's appointment as Imperial Household Secretary, 23–24; and Itō Hirobumi's resignation as Imperial Household Minister, 25–26; and the Jiho, 20–21; and the Meiji Constitution, 46; and the Meiji oligarchs 56–57, 176; personal views on politics, 24, 24n, 49, 57
Meiji oligarchs, 102; cohesiveness of, 56–57, 76, 317–18; contrast with leaders of the 1930s, 102, 102n; control over the palace, 107–111, 123–24, 184; and court finances, 65, 128–29; domain origins of, 102n, 123–24; and Grand Chamberlain Tokudaiji Sanenori, 135–36, 156, 174; and Imperial Household Minister Tanaka Mitsuaki, 122–24, 128–29; and the imperial institution, 80–81; and institutional pluralism, 317–18; and the Jiho, 21–22; and nation building, 47; and political legitimacy, 39; and Privy Seal Sanjō Sanetomi, 174–76; and the Russo-Japanese War (1904), 317, 317n

Ministers of State: and palace leadership, 114–15, 118, 133, 172; responsibility to the emperor, 40; *see also* Cabinet; Kido Kōichi

Minobe Tatsukichi: attacks against, 39*n*, 131, 163, 330; and the constitutional monarchists, 112; emperor supports his constitutional theory, 163–64, 168; and the House of Peers, 39*n*, 131; and Ichiki Kitokurō, 130–31; interpretation of the Imperial House Law, 43–44; interpretation of sovereignty, 39*n*, 45, 45*n*, 131; loyalty to the imperial institution, 39*n*; on the role of the emperor, 39, 39*n*, 45, 130–31; and the supremacy of the emperor's legislative prerogative, 39, 98; Suzuki Kantarō supports his constitutional theory, 143; theory of constitutional monarchy, 39, 130–31

Mori Kaku: as an "Outlaw" and "Official," 279, 280

Motoda Eifu: criticizes Itō Hirobumi, 25, 313; and direct imperial rule, 18–19, 22*n*, 25–26; and the emperor as Confucian paragon, 22, 33; and imperial transcendence, 26*n*, 26–27; and Itō Hirobumi's appointment as Imperial Household Secretary, 23; and Itō Hirobumi's resignation as Imperial Household Minister, 25–26; and Ōkubo Toshimichi, 18; petitions Iwakura Tomomi, 18

Nagano Osami: as Chief of the Navy General Staff, 263, 267, 300

Nagata Tetsuzan, 209*n*, 290

Nakamura Satoru: as Chief Aide-de-Camp, 158, 159

Nakamura Yūjirō: appointment to House of Peers, 184; as Imperial Household Minister, 111, 117, 124, 129, 184; as protégé of Yamagata Aritomo, 117, 129

Nara Takeji: as Chief Aide-de-Camp, 153, 155, 158, 159, 168

National polity (*kokutai*): defined, 38*n*; Chief Aide Honjō Shigeru's statement on, 166; and the February 26 Incident, 166; and the imperial institution, 38, 38*n*; Itō

Hirobumi's statement on, 35; and Maruyama Masao's typology of political personality (roles), 275–84, 295, 297–98; Minobe Tatsukichi's "transgression" of, 39*n*, 131; Motoda Eifu's concept of, 26–27; and Shinto rites, 34

Navy: bureaucratic representation at court, 134, 141–42, 185–86; and the Grand Chamberlain, 134, 141–42; *see also* Imperial prerogative (of supreme command); Navy General Staff

Navy General Staff: emperor rebukes, 302; and the London Naval Treaty, 150, 152, 153; *see also* Fushimi Hiroyasu; Imperial prerogative (of supreme command); Katō Kanji; Kido Kōichi; Nagano Osamu; Suzuki Kantarō

"Negotiator": the Chief Aide-de-Camp as, 274; Chief Aide Honjō Shigeru as, 170; the constitutional monarchists as, 326–331; the Elder Statesmen as (q.v.); the emperor's advisers as, 105; the feudal Elders as, 322–23; the Grand Chamberlain as, 147; Grand Chamberlain/Privy Seal Katsura Tarō as, 139–40; Imperial Household Minister Tanaka Mitsuaki as, 122–23; Konoe Fumimaro as, 190*n*; military officers as, 184; and the national consensus, 7–8, 9, 105; and the palace, 7–8, 105, 323; and the "policy advocate" (q.v.); as a political role, 9, 325; the Privy Seal as, 105–6, 171, 175, 176, 178, 179–80, 195, 274, 299; Privy Seal Hirata Tōsuke as, 179–80; Privy Seal Kido Kōichi as, 195, 246–74, 288, 299, 307, 309; Privy Seal Makino Nobuaki as, 194; and public opinion, 323, 329–30; Sanjō Sanetomi as, 174–76; and the "secretary," 323, 325, 332; the traditionalists as, 326–29; *see also* Imperial Will; Kido Kōichi; Palace (and the negotiating process); Saionji Kimmochi; "Trends of the times"

New bureaucrats, *see* Renovationists

October Incident (1931), 92–93, 94

"Official": defined, 275; disunity of, 284–85; Hiranuma Kiichirō as, 283; and Kido

Kōichi, 294–97, 307–9; manipulation of "Outlaws," 285–87, 294; Matsuoka Yōsuke as, 279–80; Mori Kaku as, 279, 280; power of, 275–76, 287; position of, 275–76, 277–84; roles within the "Official" class, 287–88

Okabe Nagakage: and the Eleven Club, 198, 205n, 219; and Kido Kōichi, 198, 219; as Kido Kōichi's predecessor as Chief Secretary to the Privy Seal, 196n, 198, 229, 230–31

Okada Keisuke: Cabinet of, 171; and Grand Chamberlain Suzuki Kantarō, 145, 154; and the February 26 Incident, 188; and Kido Kōichi's appointment as Privy Seal, 238; and the London Naval Treaty (q.v.); nominated as Prime Minister, 188; as a possible Privy Seal, 241; and Prime Minister Tanaka Giichi, 145

Ōkawabara Nittō: as an "Outlaw," 288, 291

Okazawa Kiyoshi: as Chief Aide-de-Camp, 158

Ōkubo Toshimichi: assassination of, 20, 314; and the *Jiho*, 20–21; and Motoda Eifu, 18

Oracle sovereignty, 40

"Outlaw": defined, 275–76; disunity of, 284; and the February 26 Incident, 285–86, 287; as an "instrument of pressure," 287; and Kido Kōichi, 288–94; and Konoe Fumimaro, 288; manipulation by "Officials", 285–87, 294; Matsuoka Yōsuke as, 279–80; and the Meiji loyalists, 287, 287n; Mori Kaku as, 279, 280; position of, 275–76, 277–84; and terrorism, 287

Ōyama Iwao: as Privy Seal, 173, 177–78

Ozaki Yukio, 138–39, 299

Palace: and Cabinet coalitions, 105, 315–16; and foreign policy, 315–16; and the Imperial Will, 187, 191–92, 319, 331, 333; and institutional pluralism, 92, 95, 97, 319–20; and the national consensus, 7–8; and the negotiating process, 7–8, 90, 273, 323, 331, 333; and the privatization of conflict, 9, 315–17; and the ratification process, 90, 91, 102, 106, 333; as a refuge for aristocrats, 75; as sanctuary of the emperor's personal will, 49, 55–57; *see also* Constitutional monarchists; Imperial prerogative (and the role of the palace); Meiji oligarchs; "Negotiator"; Privatized decision making; Traditionalists; "Trends of the times"

"Palace group," 150

Palace leadership: and the aristocracy, 116; bureaucratization of, 184–87; career background of, 113–16; changes in, 7–8, 107, 111, 112–13; and the constitutional monarchists (q.v.); and the coordination of the role of the imperial institution, 274; Hara Kei's views on, 139–40; and the House of Peers, 114–16; and the London Naval Treaty, 152–53; and the Meiji oligarchs (q.v.); and the Ministers of State (q.v.); and Minobe's theory of constitutional monarchy, 111–12, 131; and the national consensus, 7–8, 105; and the Privy Council (q.v.); and Saionji Kimmochi (q.v.); and the Shanghai crisis (1932), 213–17; and the Supreme War Councillors, 114–15; and the theory of legitimacy, 117–18; and the traditionalists (q.v.); *see also* Chief Aide-de-Camp; Emperor-in-State; Grand Chamberlain; Imperial Household Minister; "Negotiator"; Privy Seal; "Trends of the times"

Parties, *see* Political parties

"Party" Cabinets, *see* House of Representatives; Political parties

Peerage Affairs, Office of, 71; *see also* Kido Kōichi (as Director of Peerage Affairs)

Peers, House of, *see* House of Peers

Peers School, 72–73

Pluralism, *see* Institutional pluralism

"Policy advocate": and the "bureaucrat," 195; the constitutionalists as, 325–26; 326n; Itō Hirobumi as, 175; and Kido Kōichi, 9, 195, 288; manipulation of "Outlaws," 294; manipulation of socialized public opinion, 330; and the "negotiator," 323, 324, 326–27, 329, 332; as a political role, 9; and "privatized public opinion," 329; the renovationists as, 325–26, 326n; and the "secretary," 323, 332

Political elites, 99–101

Political parties: as organizations in the national polity, 282–83; and "party" Cabinets, 187–88, 325; and the Privy Seal, 244–45; and "transcendental" Cabinets, 137–39, 187–88

Politicization: of society, 149, 149n

Prerogative, see Imperial prerogative

Privatization of conflict: and bureaucratic decision making, 9; defined, 312; and the imperial government, 312; and the palace, 9, 315–17; and the socialization of conflict, 9, 312; as a strategy of governing, 312, 314; as a value system, 312–13; see also Privatized decision making; Socialization of conflict; Socialized decision making

Privatized decision making: effects on the political process, 148–50, 155; and the palace, 150, 155, 316, 331; political roles in, 8–9, 331–33; and socialized decision making, 148, 331

Privy Council: and the Chief Aides-de-Camp, 159; and the Imperial House Law, 42, 43, 46, 58; and the London Naval Treaty, 98, 151, 152–53, 154–55; and the Meiji Constitution, 36, 58; and palace leadership, 114–15, 118–19, 133, 159, 172, 184; and Privy Seal Fushimi Sadanaru, 177; and Privy Seal Hirata Tōsuke, 179–80; and the Supreme War Council, 158

Privy Seal: abolition of the office of, 2; attacked by "Outlaw" Takuya Dempu, 291–92; career backgrounds of, 172–73; creation of the office of, 174–75; duties of, 173–74; Fushimi Sadanaru as (q.v.); Hirata Tōsuke as (q.v.); Katsura Tarō as (q.v.); Kido Kōichi as (q.v.); Makino Nobuaki as (q.v.); murder of, 330–31; as a "negotiator" (q.v.); Ōyama Iwao as (q.v.); Sanjō Sanetomi as (q.v.); Tokudaiji Sanenori as (q.v.); transition to bureaucratic leadership, 177; Yuasa Kurahei as (q.v.)

"Public opinion": antioligarch leaders of, 47; defined as the views of bureaucratic "policy advocates," 323, 329; and the Elders of Chōshū domain, 321; and the emperor, 20, 26, 26n, 56–57; and the emperor's advisers, 322–23; and Grand Chamberlain/Privy Seal Katsura Tarō,

136, 138; and Grand Chamberlain Suzuki Kantarō, 147, 154; Itō Hirobumi's inability to control, 25–26, 313; and the Jiho, 20; and the "negotiator," 322–23, 329–30; "privatized," 329; and Privy Seal Sanjō Sanetomi, 176; "socialized," 330, 332

"Ratifier": defined as a political role, 9, 288; see also Emperor; Palace

Renovationists, 209n, 296; attack on the constitutionalists and constitutional monarchists, 330; defined, 296n, 325–26; and the February 26 Incident, 285–86; and Kido Kōichi, 191, 327; and Konoe Fumimaro, 190, 327; and the moderates, 190; as "policy advocates," 325–27, 326n; union with rightist societies, 189

Representatives, House of, see House of Representatives

Restoration settlement (1868–1889), 5, 15, 16, 49, 51, 95

Rightist societies, 284; disunity of, 284; and Hiranuma Kiichirō, 283; as "Outlaw" groups, 281; union with the renovationists, 189

Right-wing radicals: attack on moderate leaders, 188; and the Imperial Will, 317; as "instruments of pressure," 288; see also "Outlaw"

Rites, see Shinto rites

"Rites and rule are one" (saisei itchi), 27; and the Restoration government, 28–30

Rites, Government of (Jingikan), 28–30

Rites, Ministry of (Jingi Shō), 29–30

Rituals, Board of, 31

Saigō Takamori, 80, 194

Saionji Kimmochi (Prince): blocks Hiranuma Kiichirō's appointment as President of the Privy Council, 330; blocks Hiranuma Kiichirō's appointment as Privy Seal, 245; and the Chang Tso-lin affair (fall of the Tanaka Cabinet in 1929), 144, 146, 149, 188; and the Chief Aide-de-Camp, 189; as a constitutional monarchist, 112, 116, 189, 326–27; death of, 182, 191, 255; as Elder Statesman (Genrō), 112, 181, 242–43; as the emperor's highest adviser,

116, 187–90, 207; foreign policy views, 187; and Hara Kei, 128, 137, 138, 139; and Harada Kumao, 194, 206, 206n, 207, 208, 211, 212, 213, 232, 238–39, 240–43, 255; on Imperial Household Ministers from the "outside", 118, 120, 129, 191; and the Imperial Household Ministry, 118, 189, 319–20; on imperial princes in "positions of responsibility," 303–4; and Itō Hirobumi, 116, 116n and Iwakura Tomomi, 135; and Katsura Tarō, 116, 137, 138; and Kido Kōichi, 207, 212, 232; and Kido Kōichi's appointment as Privy Seal, 238–39, 240–43, 245; and Konoe Fumimaro, 152, 190n, 327; and the London Naval Treaty (q.v.); and Makino Nobuaki, 143n, 146, 216; as a "negotiator," 322–23; and the palace leadership of the constitutional monarchists, 112, 143, 181; and "party" Cabinets, 187, 188; political partisanship of, 150, 187–89, 322; as president of the Seiyūkai, 137; as Prime Minister, 116; and the renovationists (new bureaucrats), 327; and Sanjō Sanetomi, 135; second Cabinet of, 104, 138; and the Senior Retainers, 171, 181; and the system for advising the throne, 181; and Tokudaiji Sanenori, 116, 135; and the "trends of the times," 319–20; and the transcendental role of the emperor, 322, 326–27; and Yamagata Aritomo, 128, 137, 138

Saitō Makoto: assassination of, 165, 181, 188, 227, 314, 330; and the constitutional monarchists, 326; and the February 26 Incident, 165, 188, 330; and the London Naval Treaty (q.v.); and the Okada Cabinet, 171–72; as Prime Minister, 181, 184, 186–87; as Privy Seal, 171–72, 181, 184, 188, 227, 330; Saionji Kimmochi nominates as Prime Minister, 188

Sanjō Sanetomi: as Chancellor, 18, 21, 23, 174, 175; defense of Itō Hirobumi, 23; and Itō Hirobumi, 174–76; and the Jiho, 21; and the Ladies-in-Waiting, 80; as a "negotiator," 175–76, 195; as Privy Seal, 173–76, 195; and Saionji Kimmochi, 135

Sasaki Yukitada: as Jiho, 19–22, 135

Satsuma (domain): and the Imperial Household Minister, 123–24, 124n; and the Meiji oligarchs, 102n, 123; and the Meiji Restoration, 122–23

"Secretary," 288; as a political role, 9, 194, 323, 332, 333; see also Harada Kumao; Kido Kōichi

Sekiya Teisaburō: as Vice Minister of the Imperial Household Ministry, 92–94

Senior Retainers: as advisers to the emperor, 105, 106, 187, 271, 322; Army criticizes as "weak," 170; conference of, 215–16, 272; and Kido Kōichi's appointment as Privy Seal, 238, 240, 245; as "negotiators," 8, 105; and Saionji Kimmochi, 171, 181; Saitō Makoto as, 171; and the system for advising the throne, 181

Shanghai crisis (1932), 213–17

Shidehara Kijūrō, 152

Shinto rites: adapted to serve the new national government, 27–28; and the aristocracy, 72–73; and Confucian moral force, 33; and the emperor, 27–28, 34–35, 37; Itō Hirobumi's use of, 35–36; and the Meiji Constitution, 35–37, 45; and the national polity, 34; and the separation of church and state, 37–39; and Western religion, 36; see also Ceremonies, Board of the; Imperial prerogative; Rites, Government of; Rituals, Board of

"Shōwa Restoration," 286, 286n, 287

"Shrine" (Portable): defined, 275–76; emperor as, 298–99, 302; imperial princes as, 303–7; position and role of, 275–76, 277–84

Sixth Day Club, 212, 236

Socialization of conflict: and democracy, 9, 311–12; as a strategy of governing, 312; as a value system, 311–12, 313; see also Privatization of conflict; Socialized decision-making

Socialized decision making, 148, 331; see also Privatized decision making

Supreme War Council (Councillors), 158; and the London Naval Treaty, 98, 150–51, 152; and palace leadership, 114–15

Suzuki Kantarō: appointment as Grand Chamberlain, 141–43, 143n; and Chief Aide Honjō Shigeru, 169; and Chief of Staff Katō Kanji, 153–56; and the collapse

Suzuki Kantarō (*Cont.*)
  of the Tanaka Cabinet (1929), 143–50;
  and the constitutional monarchists, 112,
  141–43; and the February 26 Incident,
  229, 330–31; as Grand Chamberlain,
  132–33, 143–56, 169, 330–31; and the
  London Naval Treaty (q.v.); and Okada
  Keisuke, 154; perception of the Grand
  Chamberlain's role, 146–47; political
  views of, 143; as President of the Privy
  Council, 184; as Prime Minister, 85, 113;
  and Privy Seal Kido Kōichi, 113, 229
Suzuki Teiichi: and "bureaucrat" Kido
  Kōichi, 233, 234; and Privy Seal Kido
  Kōichi, 269; as a renovationist (new bureaucrat), 296; and Secretary Kido Kōichi,
  209–10, 211

Taishō Emperor: Ichiki Kitokurō's "disrespectful acts" toward, 143n; illness of,
  163; and Kanroji Osanaga, 77; Katsura
  Tarō's tutoring of, 140–41; mother of, 79
Takamatsu Nobuhito (Prince-of-the-Blood),
  262, 306
Takuya Dempu: as an "Outlaw", 288,
  291–93
Tanaka Giichi, 144–47, 149–50, 187–88
Tanaka Mitsuaki: career of, 122–23, 123n;
  as Imperial House Economic Adviser, 179;
  as Imperial Household Minister, 122–27,
  128–29, 168; and the Meiji Emperor,
  126–27; and Prime Minister Katsura
  Tarō, 124–25; as a Tosa loyalist, 123
Tani Masayuki: and "bureaucrat" Kido
  Kōichi, 233; as a renovationist (new bureaucrat), 296; and Secretary Kido Kōichi,
  209, 210, 211
Tōjō Hideki: as Army Minister, 267;
  Cabinet of, 103–4; as Prime Minister,
  113, 191, 267–68, 270, 272; and Privy
  Seal Kido Kōichi, 113, 267–68, 270, 272
Tokudaiji Sanenori: criticized by the *Jiho*,
  19, 135; family connections of, 116–17; as
  Grand Chamberlain/Privy Seal, 134–36,
  139, 156, 173, 174, 176; and the Meiji
  oligarchs, 135–36; and Saionji Kimmochi,
  116, 135
Tosa (domain): and the Meiji Restoration,
  122–23

Tōyama Mitsuru: as an "Outlaw," 291
Traditionalists: control of the palace, 107,
  112–13, 326, 330; and imperial
  transcendence, 326, 327; and Japanese fascism, 190–91; and the national consensus,
  112–13, 191; and the "trends of the
  times", 112–13, 190–92; *see also* Constitutional monarchists; Kido Kōichi; Konoe
  Fumimaro; "Negotiator"
"Transcendental" Cabinets, *see* Cabinet
"Trends of the times": and advising the
  throne, 11, 187; and decision making, 9;
  and the Foreign Ministry, 186; and the Imperial Household Ministry, 118, 129, 189,
  191; and the military, 273; and the "negotiator," 9, 332; and the palace, 105,
  191–92, 319–20; and palace leadership, 9,
  105; and the "policy advocate," 9; and the
  Privy Seal, 174; and Secretaries Harada
  and Kido, 208; *see also* Traditionalists
Tuesday Luncheon Club, 236

Uchiyama Kojirō: as Chief Aide-de-Camp,
  158, 160
Uesugi Shinkichi: constitutional theory of,
  44–45, 45n
Ugaki Kazunari: career of, 244n; as possible
  Privy Seal, 244; recommended as Prime
  Minister, 188–89
Union of court and government, 16–26
Usami Okiie: as Chief Aide-de-Camp, 159

Wakatsuki Reijirō: caretaker government of,
  188; and Kido Kōichi's appointment as
  Privy Seal, 238, 240; and the London
  Naval Treaty (q.v.); as possible Privy
  Seal, 244, 245

Yamagata Aritomo: and the Aides-de-Camp,
  81n; Cabinet of, 176; and the creation of a
  modern army, 317; domination over the
  court, 111; grandsons of, 75, 85; and
  Hirata Tōsuke, 178; and Ichiki Kitokurō,
  143n; and the Imperial House Economic
  Council, 178; and Imperial Household
  Minister Tanaka Mitsuaki, 126; and Itō
  Hirobumi (q.v.); and Katsura Tarō, 111,
  116, 130n, 136–37, 138–39; and the merit
  aristocracy, 73–74; as an oligarch, 180,

317; as a possible Imperial Household Secretary, 23; receives funds from the Imperial Household Ministry, 128; and "transcendental" Cabinets, 137

Yamamoto Tatsuo: and Home Ministry rivalry with the Army, 100

Yonai Mitsumasa: and Kido Kōichi's appointment as Privy Seal, 238, 239

Yoshida Shigeru, 77

Yuasa Kurahei: and Chief Aide Honjō Shigeru, 169–70; as Imperial Household Minister then Privy Seal, 120; as Imperial Household Minister, 181, 225n, 226–27; and Kido Kōichi's appointment as Privy Seal, 238, 239, 240, 243, 244; as Privy Seal, 169–70, 181, 225n, 226–27, 238, 239, 240, 243, 244

STUDIES OF THE EAST ASIAN INSTITUTE

The Ladder of Success in Imperial China, by Ping-ti Ho. New York: Columbia University Press, 1962.

The Chinese Inflation, 1937–1949, by Shun-hsin Chou. New York: Columbia University Press, 1963.

Reformer in Modern China: Chang Chien, 1853–1926, by Samuel Chu. New York: Columbia University Press, 1965.

Research in Japanese Sources: A Guide, by Herschel Webb with the assistance of Marleigh Ryan. New York: Columbia University Press, 1965.

Society and Education in Japan, by Herbert Passin. New York: Bureau of Publications, Teachers College, Columbia University, 1965.

Agricultural Production and Economic Development in Japan, 1873–1922, by James I. Nakamura. Princeton: Princeton University Press, 1966.

Japan's First Modern Novel: Ukigumo of Futabatei Shimei, by Marleigh Ryan. New York: Columbia University Press, 1967.

The Korean Communist Movement, 1918–1948, by Dae-Sook Suh. Princeton: Princeton University Press, 1967.

The First Vietnam Crisis, by Melvin Gurtov. New York: Columbia University Press, 1967.

Cadres, Bureaucracy, and Political Power in Communist China, by A. Doak Barnett. New York: Columbia University Press, 1967.

The Japanese Imperial Institution in the Tokugawa Period, by Herschel Webb. New York: Columbia University Press, 1968.

Higher Education and Business Recruitment in Japan, by Koya Azumi. New York: Teachers College Press, Columbia University, 1969.

The Communists and Chinese Peasant Rebellions: A Study in the Rewriting of Chinese History, by James P. Harrison, Jr. New York: Atheneum, 1969.

How the Conservatives Rule Japan, by Nathaniel B. Thayer. Princeton: Princeton University Press, 1969.

Aspects of Chinese Education, edited by C. T. Hu. New York: Teachers College Press, Columbia University, 1970.

Documents of Korean Communism, 1918–1948, by Dae-Sook Suh. Princeton: Princeton University Press, 1970.

Japanese Education: A Bibliography of Materials in the English Language, by Herbert Passin. New York: Teachers College Press, Columbia University, 1970.

Economic Development and the Labor Market in Japan, by Koji Taira. New York: Columbia University Press, 1970.

The Japanese Oligarchy and the Russo-Japanese War, by Shumpei Okamoto. NewYork: Columbia University Press, 1970.

Imperial Restoration in Medieval Japan, by H. Paul Varley. New York: Columbia University Press, 1971.

Japan's Postwar Defense Policy, 1947–1968, by Martin E. Weinstein. New York: Columbia University Press, 1971.

Election Campaigning Japanese Style, by Gerald L. Curtis. New York: Columbia University Press, 1971.

China and Russia: The "Great Game," by O. Edmund Clubb. New York:Columbia University Press, 1971.

Money and Monetary Policy in Communist China, by Katharine Huang Hsiao. New York: Columbia University Press, 1971.

The District Magistrate in Late Imperial China, by John R. Watt. New York: Columbia University Press, 1972.

Law and Policy in China's Foreign Relations: A Study of Attitudes and Practice, by James C. Hsiung. New York: Columbia University Press, 1972.

Pearl Habor as History: Japanese-American Relations, 1931–1941, edited by Dorothy Borg and Shumpei Okamoto, with the assistance of Dale K. A. Finlayson. New York: Columbia University Press, 1973.

Japanese Culture: A Short History, by H. Paul Varley. New York: Praeger, 1973.

Doctors in Politics: The Political Life of the Japan Medical Association, by William E. Steslicke. New York: Praeger, 1973.

Japan's Foreign Policy, 1868–1941: A Research Guide, edited by James William Morley. New York: Columbia University Press, 1974.

The Japan Teachers Union: A Radical Interest Group in Japanese Politics, by Donald Ray Thurston. Princeton: Princeton University Press, 1973.

Palace and Politics in Prewar Japan, by David Anson Titus. New York: Columbia University Press, 1974.

The Idea of China: Essays in Geographic Myth and Theory, by Andrew March. Devon, England: David and Charles, 1974.

Origins of the Cultural Revolution, by Roderick MacFarquhar. New York: Columbia University Press, Vol. 1, 1974.

Shiba Kōkan, by Calvin L. French. Tokyo: John Weatherhill, Inc., forthcoming.